The Nova Scotia
DUCK TOLLING RETRIEVER

TOLLER LOVE

There are days you just have so much love, You're unable to show
As you watch your Toller puppy And its face is all aglow.

All aglow with learning, Head cocked to see and hear,
Ears erect with wonder, Another mystery made clear.

Obeying on the stay and down, Coming to your call,
Standing still for brushing, Loving you through it all.

The first swim — oh, the splashing, But she got the stick, sure did!
The tears are in my proud old eyes, Stinging on my lids.

The pushing then for love and pats, The slurp under my chin,
The run from pond through snow or grass Keeps pup and me both slim.

The growing up to Toller tricks, The bow, the rush, the grin
I swear they all know when to sneeze, I love them so it's a sin.

They follow me around the house, I stop—flop on my feet!
They'll wear themselves so ragged Till I at last sit down to eat.

And Tollers really love to swim, They dive in water deep
Till all I see is a magic swirl, And up with a clam they leap.

Teaching Tollers obedience Is the easiest thing I do,
Also the most rewarding, They try so hard for you.

They want to please and love me, For I love and care for them.
I've raised a dozen Tollers, All different but each a gem.

How many breeds can *you* name, When you open their doors for play
And twelve dogs romp around you, Not one runs away?

Then open their doors and in they go, Tongues lolling from the run
I seldom have to scold one, my Toller work is fun.

This poem was penned by one of the Toller's staunch Maritime boosters,
Roberta MacKenzie, on the day she parted with
the last pup from the last Tollerbrook litter, in 1981.

BIS BISS CKC IKC NSDTRC-USA AKC CH Vesper Mariner Coupe De Vale JH AX AXJ WCI VCX, "Schooner, owned by Deb Gibbs.

The Nova Scotia DUCK TOLLING RETRIEVER

Updated 2014

ALISON STRANG AND GAIL MACMILLAN

The Nova Scotia Duck Tolling Retriever

Copyright © 1996, 2000, 2014 by Alison Strang and Gail MacMillan
All rights reserved.
No part of this book may be used or reproduced in any
manner whatsoever without written permission
from the publisher, except in the case of
brief quotations embodied in critical reviews.
For permission, write to:
Alpine Publications, Inc.
P.O. Box 7027
Loveland, Colorado 80537
U.S.A.

ISBN: 978-1-57779-157-7

Book design by Dianne J. Borneman, Shadow Canyon Graphics

Cover Photo by Frédéric Bergeron

Chapter opening illustration and other illustrations by Anne McIntyre

Printed in the United States of America

Contents

Foreword by James B. Spencer ix
Introduction xv
Acknowledgements xvii

Chapter 1:   History of the Breed 1
What Is Tolling? 1 • Probable Origins 2 • On To England 2 • The Toller in North America 3 • The Modern Era Begins 9 • H.A.P. Smith 10

Chapter 2:   Harbourlights Kennel 15

Chapter 3:   The Circle Widens 23
John and Mary Sproul, Sproul Kennel 23 • Keith and Roberta MacKenzie, Tollerbrook Kennel 25 • Jim Jeffery and Doug Coldwell, Jeffery Coldwell Kennel 26 • Vic and Heather Dunphy, Marangai Kennel 29 • Derek and Pam Dunn, Kare Kennel 29

Chapter 4:   The Western Connection 33
Chin-Peek 33 • Chin-Peek Offshoots 35 * Wileen Mann, Sundrummer Kennel 36 • Rena Cap, Jalna Kennel 37 • Alison and Roy Strang, Westerlea Kennel 39 • Arline and Duncan MacDonald, Ardunacres Kennel 42 • More Recent Western Breeders 43

Chapter 5:   Tollers Come to Upper Canada 49
Ken and Brenda Stephens, Jem Kennel 49 • Ann Penner, Liscot Kennel 50 • Terry McNamee, Rosewood Kennel 50 • Paula and Irvin Collier, Colliers' Kennel 51 • Lillian Greensides and Karen Wright, Kylador Kennel 51 • Colin and Jacquie Riley, Rideau Kennel 53 • Quebec: La Belle Province 53 • Susan and Paul Kish, Foxgrove Kennel 53 • Wilfrid and Dianne Drouin, Bernache Kennel 55

Chapter 6:   The Americans Come Calling 57
United States Registrations and the American Toller Club 58 • Neil and Sue Van Sloun, Sylvan Kennel 59 • Laura Grossman White, Cinnstar Kennel 60 • John Hamilton and Marile Waterstraat, Lennoxlove Kennel 62 • Kirk and Anne Norton, Cabot Trail Kennel 63 • Paul and Patty Beran, Sagewood Kennel 63 • Gretchen and George Botner, Tradewinds Kennel 65 • Nelson and Evelyn Williams, Lonetree Kennel 66 • Sue Dorscheid and Mike Elmergreen, Springvale Kennel 67 • Lee Ann and Joe Gleason, Cayuga Kennel 67

Chapter 7   Back to Europe 69
Denmark 69 • Sweden 71 • Finland 75 • Norway 79 • United Kingdom 80 • And the Rest 83 • Australia 84

Chapter 8   The Toller Personality 85
Toller Protectiveness 85 • Tollers and Children 86 • Travels with Cabot 87 • Toller Toughness 88 • A Brave Little Toller 90 • Sensitivity 91 • Fearlessness 91 • First Toller 93

Chapter 9   An In-Depth Look at the Standard 95
    Canadian Standard 95 • American Standard 109

Chapter 10   The Art of Tolling 111
    A Treasury of Tolling and Toller Tips 111

Chapter 11   Field Training the Toller 117
    How to Field Train Your Nova Scotia Duck Tolling Retriever by Susan Kish 118

Chapter 12   The Versatile Toller 131
    Obedience 131 • Hunt and Working Certificate Tests 133 • Master Hunters 134 • Agility 135
    Flyball 136 • Rally 137 • Dock Diving 137 • Tracking 138 • Other Activities 138 • Conformation
    138 • Canadian Best in Show 139 • Canadian Specialty Shows 141 • U.S. Specialty Shows 142 •
    AKC Bests in Show 143 • Europe 144 • Color Photo Section 145-152

Chapter 13   Toller Good Citizens 153
    Therapy Dogs 153 • Canine Good Citizens 155 • Service Dogs 157

Chapter 14   Showing Your Toller 159
    Show Training 159 • Make Showing Fun 163 • Grooming 163

Chapter 15   In Sickness and In Health 175
    General Care 175 • Common Health Problems in the Toller 177 • Hereditary Diseases
    in Tollers 181 • Genetic Testing for Breeding Stock 184

Chapter 16   The Art of Breeding 187
    Breeding Systems 188 • Selling Good Tollers 189 • Breeding the All-Round Toller 189 •
    What Breeders Say 192

Chapter 17   Diary of a Litter 197

Chapter 18   Picking the Right Puppy for the Job .213
    The Show-ring Star 213 • The Field Puppy 217 • The Obedience Hopeful 218 • The Ideal Pet 218
    Finding the Right Owner 218 • Buyer Education 219

Chapter 19   Toller Pedigrees 223

Appendix: Original Canadian Standard 241
Glossary of Titles 243
Bibliography 245
Suggested Reading 247
Clubs 249
About the Authors 251
Index 253

FOREWORD

by James B. Spencer
"Retrieve" Columnist, *Gun Dog Magazine*

At last, at last, a book that explains this intriguing, mysterious breed! Gail MacMillan and Alison Strang not only know Tollers, but each has a strong writing background, so the book is as enjoyable to read as it is authoritative and informative.

Seldom has a breed so needed or so deserved such a book. Seldom has a breed suffered so from misinformation about its niche in the canine world. Over the years I have read many fanciful explanations of duck tolling in magazine articles written by "inquiring mind" journalists *sans* backgrounds in either dogs or duck hunting. Although entertaining (sometimes hilarious) fiction, these pieces have reflected poorly on the breed, especially among knowledgeable waterfowlers. After (rightly) sloughing off such an article, they (wrongly) disregard the breed, too.

Even those few articles which have correctly explained tolling have often hurt the breed. How? By focusing totally on tolling to the exclusion of the breed's other talents. In so doing, they imply that the Toller has only one talent, only one dimension. Such articles portray duck tolling as a magical, mystical, legendary sport of another era, something no longer available, something to be lamented but not pursued. This is not entirely true, for some hunters today find waterfowling situations in which tolling is effective, sometimes in the most unlikely surroundings. Even so, tolling opportunities are quite limited on today's busy waterways. Human logic being what it is, most readers conclude, "I don't have a place for tolling ducks, *ergo* I shouldn't get a Nova Scotia Duck Tolling Retriever."

Wrong conclusion! The Toller is much more than a duck tolling machine. A Toller can handle all the straight retrieving chores associated with more traditional forms of waterfowling (decoy and blind, jump shooting, pass shooting, and so forth). What's more, these bouncy little rascals make excellent upland flushers. They quarter with more pizazz and flush with more gusto than any other retriever breed. Some Tollers have enough slash and dash to give confirmed spanielites a delightful case of the goosebumps.

But the Toller can do much more than retrieve waterfowl and hunt to the gun in the uplands. The breed excels in obedience trials, agility, therapy work, and on and on. Tollers enjoy learning, enjoy pleasing their owners, so will happily pick up whatever their owners care to teach them. They are wonderful family pets because of their small size, their happy outlook on life, and their desire to fit into the family.

In this book, Gail MacMillan and Alison Strang explain *all* of the breed's talents, not just tolling. Of course, they do cover tolling, too — completely and accurately, but without making it the breed's end-all and do-all. They even flesh out their discussion of tolling with the thoughts of the late Avery Nickerson, who was to tolling what Babe Ruth was to home runs.

In addition to everything anyone might want to know about the breed itself, Gail and Alison narrate the history of the breed from its probable origins to its present form. Here they do much more than list what dogs begot what dogs, a la Genesis. They give the human side of the breed's history, too. They tell about the people who developed and redeveloped the Toller, the people who have improved and maintained it through the years. They tell about the people who are currently breeding quality Tollers throughout the world. Gail and Alison have not limited the scope of this book to Canada, or even to North America. They have covered the Toller throughout the world, and in remarkable detail.

This book is a priceless resource for anyone interested in the breed. Serious breeders — and we should have no other kind — can use it to help develop and improve their breeding programs. Judges (conformation, obedience, and field) can use it to better understand the Tollers that come before them. Trainers and handlers (again conformation, obedience, and field) can use it to help them adapt their training programs and handling techniques to the particular spectrum of personalities found within this breed. Beginning Toller owners can study it to better appreciate and understand their dogs. Experienced Toller owners can enjoy reading and re-reading the things they already know (and love) about the breed, perhaps saying, "Yes, yes, that's just how Ginger was when she was alive. Gee, I remember the time she . . . ."

Every general purpose dog nut who has a special interest in retrievers will have to have a copy of this book in his/her library. I belong to this group, and feel that this book fills a big gap, a nagging gap, on my retriever bookshelf. This book is a milestone for the Nova Scotia Duck Tolling Retriever.

But it is more than a breed milestone. It is the Toller's *first* book milestone, the one from which all future written milestones will be marked out and measured. Magazine writers will use this book as their main source of information about the breed (and perhaps start getting things right). Future generations of breed book authors will make this volume their foundation, their source, their point of departure.

We all — breeders, owners, writers, and general purpose dog nuts — owe Gail MacMillan and Alison Strang a huge "Thank you. Well done!"

This book is dedicated to the memory of the late Avery and Erna Nickerson.

Avery is shown here with some of his Harbourlights dogs.

Oil-stick painting by Lyla Menagh of Dual BISS Ch Westerlea's Bonny Bluenose, a top-winning and top-producing bitch bred and owned by Alison Strang.

*AKC CKC BISS Ch Littleriver's Decoy Dancer UDX RE JH NA NAJ AXP AJP VC, shown winning BOB at Westminster in 2005. He was the first NSDTRC-USA National Specialty winner in 2004. Dancer won two US Nationals and one Canadian National. Owner/trainer Corinne Beckner, Honeyrun Kennel. Breeder Doug Coldwell.
Photo © Custom Dog Design.*

Tollers Do It All . . .

Right: *Tolling ducks. Wallace's Fancy MacMillan, owned by Ron and Gail MacMillan.*

2nd Row: *(both photos) Foxgrove's Piper Bergen, a trained Avalanche Rescue Dog belonging to Dan Berg in Colorado.*

3rd Row*: Agility winner Slyder, owned by Terry & Kim Simons.*

4th Row: *(left) Chive, owned by Dan Rode, learning Flyball. (center) Water retrieve by Sassy, owned Diane Loiseau and Sue Kish. (right) Torque, owned by Kathy Koebensky-Como, competing in Agility.*

Introduction

Writing this book was both a labor of love and a voyage of discovery. It was begun out of love and admiration for the unique little red dogs commonly called Tollers. Work on the book soon took the authors on a voyage back in time, back to the canals and dikes of mid-sixteenth-century Holland, to the expeditions of French colonizer and explorer Nicholas Denys, and to the early decoys of England. As research drew closer to home, it became apparent how the wonderful people of Nova Scotia were responsible for saving this remarkable breed from extinction.

Early in this project, Gail MacMillan and Alison Strang became partners in this book venture. Both were hopelessly enamored with Tollers and decided to join forces. The massive difficulties confronting the writing of a book by two people living on opposite sides of Canada did not deter them; their love for the little red dogs overrode such "petty" considerations. The combination in all other ways, however, was excellent. Alison, a major Toller breeder and promoter, as well as a novice judge, covered the present-day Toller. Gail, a writer, historian, and devoted Toller fan, traced the history, development, and Maritime connections of the breed. Although they talked many hours by telephone and exchanged massive letters, not once did they have the opportunity to meet face-to-face. Nevertheless, a trust and respect grew between them.

Then another remarkable woman came their way. While Gail was purchasing her own Tollers, she came in contact with Toller experts W. Avery and Erna Nickerson of Yarmouth, Nova Scotia. Sadly, by the time the book was underway, Avery had died. Erna, however, was most generous with her assistance. With forty years of Toller experience behind her, Erna strongly supported the goal of retaining the strong hunting instincts of her Tollers.

For Alison and Gail, this project has come full circle. In the process they have travelled, researched, interviewed, studied, consulted, observed, and drawn on their own personal experiences. They believe they have produced a book that will be of lasting value for the present as well as for succeeding generations of Toller fanciers.

Ch. Westerlea's Betsy Sunshine WCX JH CD, bred and owned by Alison Strang, as a 12 year old at the fun field event for Veterans held at the Calgary Toller Specialty in 2011. Photo by by Gabi Orru.

ACKNOWLEDGMENTS

It is not easy for two people to write a book together when they live on opposite coasts of such a vast country as Canada and are not *au fait* with the latest electronic marvels. It is, therefore, not surprising that each of us has different people to thank for their invaluable help, both in the production of this book and in the ways they have enriched our lives.

Gail MacMillan wishes to credit the following for very special assistance: Laura Bradley, who marshalled the resources of Yarmouth County Museum; Gretchen Botner, who supplied so much U.S. information; Eldon Pace, for his keen memory and fund of anecdotes; Anne Norton; Paul and Patty Beran; Terry McNamee; Nicholas Karas; Jeff Howard and Ray Henry; David Wood, who was so generous with the results of his research into Toller roots; Doug Coldwell; James B. Spencer; Pam and Derek Dunn; Ron Smith; and Linda Vienneau.

The documents of the late Colonel Cyril Colwell are lasting monuments to one man's determination to preserve the tolling dog. Sincere thanks are expressed by the authors to John Colwell and his mother for their trust and generosity in assisting with the preparation of this book.

Alison Strang is deeply indebted to the following for their help and support in her Toller life and for much-appreciated input on this manuscript: Susan Kish; Sandra McFarlane; Jim Jeffery; veterinarians Drs. W. A. Zwamborn, M. N. Bussanich, and Bruce Archibald; the All-Breed judges, who kindly reviewed the Breed Standard chapter and offered helpful advice; all those who so generously contributed their information, precious photographs, and artworks for this book, especially Anne McIntyre for her lovely line drawings; Gretchen Botner; Paul Kish, Lynn Vail, and Joanne Bauldic for their patient assistance to a computer dummy; and all the beloved dogs that have so enriched my life.

Both authors wish to thank their spouses, Roy Strang and Ron MacMillan. This book is as much our husbands' as ours, and we thank them both for their patience and support.

Acknowledgments to the Second Edition

Since the book was first published many newer breeders in North America, Europe and Australia are leaving their own marks on the ongoing development of the Nova Scotia Duck Tolling Retriever. The impossibility of listing them all is a source of deep regret. This revision is, of necessity, very limited, as all of the original photographs were reproduced for offset printing and returned to their owners. No digital photo files were available so the previous edition has been scanned, limiting the amount of changes.

Special thanks go to all those who provided new photographs for this edition. Credit must be given to BookMobile Printing Co. for their excellent work in scanning the first edition so that it could be reprinted. Thanks to Marile Waterstraat for her assistance with club information and helping obtain photographs of the U.S. Tollers. Thanks to Betty McKinney, Publisher, for collecting and editing the new photographs and captions. Alison would like especially to thank John Gordon for ongoing invaluable computer help.

Not forgotten are puppy buyers, many of whom became friends, who have accomplished so much with our dogs.

*Five generations of Tollers. Left to right: Bud – HIT GMH CH Foxgrove's This Bud's For You CDX US/Cdn WCX;
Sprite – Ch OTCH Foxgrove's Mischief Maker SH US/Cdn WCX (Bud's daughter);
Taffy – Ch MOTCH Foxgrove's Circle of Life SH, US/Cdn WCX, RE, AGNV, AGNJV (Sprite's daughter);
Sassy – HIT OTCH Foxgrove's Whirling Dervish MH, US/Cdn WCX, AGI, AGIJ (Taffy's daughter);
Charger – HIT OTCH Foxgrove's Guilty as Charged SH, WCX, AGI, AGIJ (Sassy's son).
Bud was owned by Sue Kish, who co-bred the other four. Sprite and Charger owned by Sue Kish and Fred Bergeron;
Sassy and Taffy owned by Sue Kish and Diane Loiseau. Photo by Fred Bergeron.*

1
History of the Breed

I never would have believed it if I hadn't seen it with my own eyes. Black ducks are without equal among waterfowl in intelligence and wariness, hence are the most difficult to decoy. But I had just witnessed a horde of more than 2,000 of them act as if they had been hypnotized. An entire raft of blacks, abandoning all caution, has swum more than 300 yards in a matter of minutes to within a few feet of our blind. We hadn't set out decoys or called the ducks or enticed them with grain. Our only bait was a frolicking, foxlike dog that retrieved a stick thrown from the blind as fast as his owner could toss it out. We were tolling.

Nicholas Karas's lively description in the widely read American sporting magazine *Field & Stream* of September 1966 was one of a series of articles that helped to introduce Canada's gift to the hunting world: the Nova Scotia Duck Tolling Retriever. Until this time, the Toller had been kept pretty well hidden in southwestern Nova Scotia, where it is still known as the Little River Duck Dog. These articles alerted the sporting world to a "new" breed, one that, years later, is rapidly gaining acceptance around the world.

Actually, the Toller is far from new and can probably trace its origins farther back than many of the better-known and more established breeds. Although it was first given purebred status only in 1945 by the Canadian Kennel Club (CKC), its ancestry may be traced back to Europe before the sixteenth century. There is even mention of small dogs being used in ancient Japan to lure birds toward a falcon, but a veil has been drawn over any possible connection with today's Toller.

WHAT IS TOLLING?

Before embarking on the historical journey that Tollers have made since those early days, an explanation of the term "tolling" is desirable. In a hunting context, the word means to entice, or lure, game. Indeed, Webster's dictionary contains an explicit definition of "toll" as follows: "To entice game (esp. wild ducks) to approach by arousing their curiosity, as by the antics of a trained dog."

The tolling dog runs, jumps, and plays along the shoreline in full view of a flock of ducks or geese. The dog occasionally disappears, then reappears, arousing the curiosity of the birds, which come swimming or flying in to investigate. They are thus lured within gunshot range, and the Toller is subsequently sent out to retrieve any downed birds.

PROBABLE ORIGINS

There are several plausible theories about the origins of today's Toller, and it is best to mention them all, letting each reader decide on a favorite.

The theory that reaches farthest back in history is that the Toller is a descendant of the Dutch *Kooikerhond*. Indeed, the very word "decoy" comes from the Dutch word for a cage, *de kooi*. *Kooikerhondjen* (dogs belonging to the *kooiker* or duck trapper) originally were small, spaniel-like dogs used by Dutch hunters to lure rafting ducks into a planned trap. Trained to move in and out of low reed fences constructed along the banks of the ubiquitous Flemish dikes, the *Kooiker* dog allowed the ducks only brief glimpses of himself. This teasing excited the birds' curiosity and, following the flashes of dog, they were enticed farther and farther up the dike into canals, until finally they found themselves in mesh-covered ditches.

Described as being red and white, the colors that seemed most attractive to ducks, the *Kooiker* dog had a long coat and profusely feathered tail. He stood about fifteen inches (38 cm) high at the shoulder, was easily trained, and could withstand prolonged periods of wet and cold.

"Is our Toller really the descendant of the Royal Dog of Holland?" asks David Wood of Springhill, Nova Scotia, who has spent more than twenty years researching the history of the Nova Scotia Duck Tolling Retriever. Wood believes that the Dutch theory of the breed's origins is probably the most valid. He states, "There are presently significant differences in the two breeds, but 230 years of divergent breeding could have easily brought about these changes." Wood's ideas are reinforced by a Dutch visitor to the kennels of 1970s breeder Wileen Mann. Upon seeing her Sundrummer Tollers, the visitor exclaimed, "Why, these are just like *Kooikerhondjen!*"

ON TO ENGLAND

From Holland, the tracks lead to England. In the mid seventeenth century, the Dutch method of capturing ducks was introduced into England by engineers from Holland, who were brought in to drain part of the huge fens or marshes of East Anglia. To make the waterfowl traps effective, the little dogs and the duck cages of Flanders (the old name for parts of Holland and Belgium) were needed. At this time, Flemish people were

Kooikerhondjen. Courtesy David Hancock.

no strangers to cross–Channel shopping, because there had long been a considerable wool trade between the sheep breeders of England and Flemish weavers.

David Hancock, in his book *Old Working Dogs*, suggests that what was known in seventeenth-century England as the "red decoy dog" is highly likely to be one of the ancestors of the Toller. Colonel Hancock believes that the "coy dog," as it was more often called, was also a precursor of the Tweed Water Spaniel, one of the breeds established as being in the background of the Golden Retriever. Given the British genius for animal improvement, it is quite likely that descendants of the original *Kooiker* invaders changed over the years, possibly being bred with native spaniel-type dogs. The resulting offspring could eventually have lost a lot of their original white to become more of a red dog with white markings, like today's Toller.

Sir Ralph Payne-Galloway, in *The Book of Duck Decoys* published in London in 1886, described an English duck decoy as a pond or small lake, either natural or man-made, with a uniform depth of two to three feet (0.6–0.9 m), surrounded by trees and shrubs. Radiating from the pond was a series of up to eight curving ditches, or pipes, covered by net hoops. (A number of pipes was necessary to allow the decoyman always to be downwind of his quarry.) Each of these pipes was approximately 180 feet (55 m) long, tapering from about 20 feet (6 m) at the mouth to no more than two feet (0.6 m) at the end. Because a silent approach was necessary to avoid spooking the ducks on the pond, the maze of footpaths around the pipes was muted with sawdust. Approximately twelve overlapping reed screens were placed along two-thirds of the length of the outer curve of the pipe. Each screen, twelve feet long by six feet high (3.6 x 1.8 m), was arranged so that the decoyman could move along the paths unseen by the ducks, yet all the while being able to see them through peepholes.

The small, fox-like "piper dog," the English equivalent of the Dutch decoy dog, followed the same path as his master, but his job was to be seen in flashes between the screens. The ducks, for reasons no one has been able to fathom exactly, were attracted by these glimpses of the dog and swam up the pipe, only to be trapped at the narrow end, unable to escape. Thus, large numbers of ducks were ready for market long before fowling-pieces became commonplace.

H. C. Folkhard, in his book *The Wildfowler* published in 1864, describes a piper dog in this manner:

The breed or pedigree of a piper is not altogether material, though apparently peculiar to itself. The nearer the dog resembles a fox in size, figure and colour, the better; and, indeed, a cross between a fox and a dog is the identical result required. Such animals make the very best pipers that can be had, inheriting as they do a share of that cunning so essentially valuable in a good piper. But in absence of such, it is best that the dog be a reddish brown or red-and-white colour. It must be full of vivacity, very active and the more playful the better, but perfectly mute. If the dog barks, every bird will quit the decoy-pipe and decline to follow him.

Folkhard also explains that these trainable little dogs had erroneously been called mongrels, and, while there were not many in Britain, they were "not uncommon" in France. Even though written in the nineteenth century, this is an important statement when attempting to trace Tollers toward North America, because writings of early French explorers and colonizers make reference to dogs that bear an uncanny resemblance to Folkhard's piper and today's Toller.

THE TOLLER IN NORTH AMERICA

Nicholas Denys, explorer and colonizer of Acadia (as present-day Nova Scotia and New Brunswick were known) between 1630 and 1670, describes what might have been the introduction of the piper or decoy dog into North America by the French. This is, to our knowledge, the earliest documented reference to tolling dogs being used as retrievers.

When the foxes see the game approaching, they run and jump; then they stop suddenly in one jump, and lie down upon their backs. The

TOLLING DUCKS UP A DECOY PIPE

"*Decoyman enticing wild ducks up the decoy pipe by the use of a dog.*" From The Book of Duck Decoys *by Sir Ralph Payne-Gallwey. Drawn by the author.*

Left: Plan of a decoy with eight pipes. From The Book of Duck Decoys *by Sir Ralph Payne-Gallwey. Right: Nacton Decoy, Suffolk, England, as it is presently. Courtesy John Norris, Decoyman, Nacton Decoy.*

wild goose or duck keeps constantly approaching. When these are near, the foxes do not move anything but the tail. Those birds are so silly that they come even wishing to peck at the foxes. The rogues take their time and do not fail to catch one, which pays for the trouble.

We train our dogs to do the same, and they also make the game come up. One places himself in ambush at some spot where the game cannot see him; when it is within good shot, it is fired upon, and four, five and six of them, and sometimes more are killed. At the same time, the dog leaps to the water, and is always sent farther and farther out; it brings them back, and then is sent to fetch them all one after another.

After Denys's writings, a veil fell over the lives of these Acadian Tollers for nearly 200 years. Did they, like their French masters, become fugitives as a result of the Expulsion of the Acadians in 1755? This massive removal of French (Acadian) settlers from what is now the Canadian Maritime provinces of New Brunswick, Nova Scotia, and Prince Edward Island by British troops occurred after the British conquest of that part of North America in the mid-eighteenth century. Fearful that the resident French farmers and fishermen might rise up against the minority English speakers within those colonies, the British set about deporting Acadians to such far-flung destinations as Louisiana and France.

Many Acadians, however, refused to be uprooted from a land that they had considered their home for more than 150 years, and, in an effort to escape the deportation order, they fled into the backwoods and marshes of the region. Escaping with their masters, were the little red dogs a remarkably well-kept secret of a people whose very lives became largely dependent upon their ability to catch enough game to survive? If so, the tolling dogs would have been invaluable to them during their years in hiding. No pen recorded the many years during which Acadians lived as fugitives, and therefore, no one can ever be certain that the tolling retriever dogs were not a closely guarded secret of these hardy, determined people. And, perhaps if the Tollers did indeed take refuge with the Acadians, they, like their masters, were forced farther and farther

A 1917 photo taken in the Comeau's Hill area of Yarmouth County, Nova Scotia of a dog named Tunny that Eddie Kinney captioned: "This is the father of the breed." Courtesy Colonel Cyril Colwell Family.

from the larger settlements and diminished in numbers. Maybe their final domain was reduced to that area of Acadia where their talents were most effective — the great saltwater marshes, lakes, and islands of southwestern Nova Scotia, now officially known as Yarmouth and Digby counties. Even today these areas are locally called "the French shore" because of the many Acadian descendants living there.

Erna Nickerson of Yarmouth, Nova Scotia, widow of legendary tolling master W. Avery Nickerson, says that whatever the truth about their origins, Tollers have been around the French villages as long as anyone can remember. She recalls, "In 1945 Avery visited a neighbor, Eddie Kinney, then in his eighties. Mr. Kinney remembered his father and grandfather keeping

Tollers for hunting. That would place them in the Yarmouth area in the early 1800s."

This would appear to undermine a much-repeated theory about Toller origins, one that has been given widespread recognition by its inclusion in several well-circulated articles and pamphlets about the breed. This story tells how Yarmouth duck hunter James Allen obtained a liver Flat-Coated Retriever from the captain of one of the many ships that visited the busy port of Yarmouth around 1870. Allen is alleged to have mated this dog to a brown spaniel and then introduced crosses with breeds such as Labradors, Irish Setters, and the little, yellow border-collie-like dogs found in the area to produce a strain of excellent tolling dogs. It is claimed that small spitz-type dogs were later introduced to reinforce playfulness. Speculations have also been made about infusions of Golden Retriever genes as late as the early 1960s.

Another much-quoted idea declares that Micmac Indians, knowing the ways of the red fox, developed their own system of tolling waterfowl. Stringing a fox skin with the tail extending upward between two blinds, the Indians moved the skin back and forth across an open beach. Some believe that early French fishermen saw this cunning demonstration and proceeded to develop a dog to do the job. It seems much more plausible, however, to believe that the Indians' plan simply reminded these early settlers of the piper dogs that they had known at home. Perhaps they then imported a few of these decoy dogs and later added retrieving to their dogs' accomplishments.

Other sources declare that tolling (or "toling" as the term was commonly spelled when it was derived from the Middle English "tollen," meaning to draw or entice) began in Maryland. J. S. Skinner, in his book *The Dog and the Sportsman*, published in 1845, states that this is where the practice began. Other authors, including Folkhard, go on to cite the year 1820 and Havre De Grace, Maryland, as its actual birthdate and place. Folkhard's description appears in Montagu Browne's *Practical Taxidermy*, published at the end of the nineteenth century.

In a book entitled *The Dogs of Great Britain, America and Other Countries*, published in 1879, John Henry Walsh describes the process as follows:

A photo sent to Colonel Colwell by Eddie Kinney of Comeau's Hill, Yarmouth County, Nova Scotia, captioned: "The Sheriff Smith of Digby Strain." Courtesy the Colwell Family.

The system pursued on the Chesapeake Bay and the North Carolina sounds, and known as "tolling," is the most successful (for duck hunting). A small dog, an ordinary poodle or one very much similar to that, white or brown in color and called the toler breed, is kept for the purpose. It is trained to run up and down the shore in the sight of the ducks, directed by the motion of its owner's hand. The curiosity of the ducks is excited and they approach the shore to discover the nature of the object which has attracted their attention. They raise their heads, look intently, and then start in a body for the shore.

It is interesting to note that the author states that the dog capers along the shore directed by hand signals from his master, not in the process of a retrieve. He goes on to assert that these dogs were not allowed to go into the water after the game but that retrievers known as Chesapeake Bay dogs were used for this purpose.

Many fanciers today believe that the Chesapeake Bay Retriever and the Brittany Spaniel are either ancestors of the Toller or that they all had some common forebears. This speculation is given credence by the uncanny likeness between very young Toller and Chesapeake puppies. The existence of tolling dogs around Chesapeake Bay suggests possible common ancestors and could be the source of much of the extraordinarily strong retrieving drive of today's Toller, which is unlikely to have come directly from piper dogs. There is also a strong resemblance between some

Gunner, owned by Judge Vincent J. Pottier (not to be confused with Gunner I or Gunner II). Gunner was born in 1928 and died in September 1944 at age sixteen. Courtesy Yarmouth County Museum Archives.

Toller heads and those of Brittany Spaniels. Yarmouth was a very busy seaport during much of the nineteenth century, and it is quite possible that Brittany or Brittany crosses came over on visiting French schooners. Brittany Spaniels, pointing dogs that also retrieve, are said to be descended partly from small French land spaniels, engravings of which look very much like engravings of old piper dogs. Hence, the circle comes round again.

There is one old theory that can be dismissed by the laws of genetics. A stubbornly surviving speculation that the Toller began as the result of a fox-dog mating is now known to be a genetic impossibility, because the dog belongs to the genus *Canis* while the fox is of the genus *Vulpes*. Many colorful tales repeated this theory, however, causing Colonel Cyril Colwell, the man directly responsible for official CKC recognition of the Toller in 1945, to undertake much research trying to ascertain if there was any truth in the assertion. Colonel Colwell concluded, "It is the opinion of the writer that there is no fox blood in our Nova Scotia Tolling Retriever dogs."

It is possible, however, to have a coyote-dog cross, because both belong to the same genus. Eric Collier's popular *Three Against the Wilderness*, published in 1959, contains this brief reference to the coyote as a toller:

Gunner at a sportsmen's show that took place in Boston. Judge Vincent J. Pottier took Gunner to promote the breed and Yarmouth. The booth was sponsored by the Yarmouth County Fish and Game Association. The Micmac Indian is Chief Francis, who was a local Yarmouth County guide. Courtesy Yarmouth County Museum Archives.

Colonel Cyril Colwell. Courtesy the Colwell Family.

We were skirting a small lake whose shoreline was fringed with a waving growth of foxtail grass. I was watching a brood of young ducks swimming parallel to the far shore. Suddenly the ducklings huddled together and in close formation moved in toward the shore and the foxtail grass. There they turned, swam parallel to the shore again for a few yards, then breaking formation two of them began moving toward dry land.

Then I saw something that might have been a clump of foxtail grass waving in the wind but wasn't. "Coyote," I announced. The bushy tail of the coyote was waving gently to and fro like a flag fluttering in the breeze, as coyote tails have been waving in the long grass at water's edge ever since there have been coyotes — and ducks foolish enough to fall for the trick.

Coyotes are found in the Maritime provinces. Although there has been no record of a coyote-dog cross being used for tolling, this anecdote is an interesting addition to tolling lore and to the tolling fox legend, which has been substantiated on many occasions.

THE MODERN ERA BEGINS

For nearly twenty years prior to his death in 1923, H. A. P. Smith was an assiduous promoter of the Toller, which he knew as the Little River Duck Dog. Known as one of the most flamboyant characters ever produced by Nova Scotia, Smith was high sheriff of Digby County, president of the Nova Scotia Guides' Association, an avid outdoorsman, and a writer for several major outdoor magazines. His considerable output contained several articles devoted to Tollers, the earliest of them in 1907.

Not only did Smith actively promote the Toller, he also worked tirelessly to develop better dogs. When Colonel Cyril Colwell became interested in the history of the Toller, he traced the origins of Smith's dogs to the Little River area near Yarmouth, and in particular to the Kinney family. In his 1944 reply to Colonel Colwell's letter of inquiry, Eddie Kinney affirmed that he had supplied Smith with his foundation stock and added: "I have a litter coming and they are nearly all spoken for. I get $10.00 at four weeks old." So much for 1944 prices and breeding practices.

COLONEL COLWELL AND THE CKC

In 1936, the secretary-treasurer of the CKC, J. D. Strachan, wrote for information on the Toller to the Member of Parliament for Yarmouth, the Honorable Vincent J. Pottier, who was also a contemporary Toller authority. Colonel Colwell, who was then working to improve his Toller strain, also became involved in the negotiations with the CKC and redoubled his efforts to prove his dogs to be at least three generations purebred. By 1945, he had established such a line and had written the first detailed Breed Standard, thus meeting registration requirements for CKC recognition. This was duly granted, largely because of the perseverance and enthusiasm of Colonel Colwell.

Colonel Colwell's interest in Tollers had begun in the early 1920s when, fascinated by his first contact with the bright little dog, he made up his mind to own one. With the acquisition of his first Toller in 1924 came the realization of the breed's rarity and the distinct possibility that it could disappear altogether. Two horrendous distemper epidemics in 1908 and 1912 almost wiped out the small Toller population, so the colonel set out to try to save the breed. John Colwell recalls his father's many expeditions to southwestern Nova Scotia in attempts to find suitable breeding stock for what he called his Nova Scotia Tolling Retriever kennel.

"I remember what seemed like 1,000 Tollers around our place when I was a child," John Colwell jokingly exaggerated. In fact, Colonel Colwell acknowledged having owned eighty-two Tollers over a thirty-year period, fifteen of which were the first to be registered with the CKC. He shipped puppies as far away as Australia in his efforts to promote what he felt to be a unique dog. He also became a dedicated and meticulous historian, stretching his research from the backroads of Yarmouth County as far as the kennels of Baroness van Hardenbroek in Holland, one of the then very few breeders of *Kooikerhondjen*, from which he believed his Tollers might be descended.

Colonel Colwell found that Toller breeding was not without its difficulties, declaring in 1952 that his registered stock was reduced to only two animals. "I have had almost one hundred of these dogs," he wrote, "and have studied the breed for thirty years. Owing to a problem in genetics, my own stock failed to reproduce, and that is why the registered dogs have petered out." This might explain why no Tollers were registered between 1945 and 1960, and why re-registration was initiated, not from Nova Scotia, but from Saskatchewan, one of Canada's Prairie provinces.

Colonel Colwell kept detailed records and labeled photographs of many Tollers. The result is a precisely documented manuscript on the Toller and his kennel, which he hoped to publish. Unfortunately, ill health prevented his doing this and he died in 1965, unable to witness the remarkable spread of the breed that he did so much to preserve. His records are now a prized possession of his son, who plans to turn them over eventually to the Nova Scotia Provincial Archives.

H.A.P. SMITH

Henry Albert Patterson Smith, a breeder and staunch promoter of the tolling dog between 1885 and 1920, also was a writer for several major outdoor magazines. Fortunately, some of the articles written by Smith still survive. The following, which first appeared around 1916, was reprinted in Ontario Out of Doors *in June 1983 both as a tribute to Smith and his work and as an example of one of the best stories ever written about the tolling dog. These excerpts appear courtesy of* Ontario Out of Doors *magazine.*

If you are a dog man, the first time you see a tolling dog your attention will be at once arrested. Therefore, let us suppose that you meet the writer with a pair of tollers at heel and after looking critically at them you remark, as hundreds have done before, "What kind of dogs are those? Chesapeake Bays or what?' When the explanation is complete, your questions will come thick and fast. But we will suppose you are a duck shooter and are also skeptical and want to be shown, and it is finally agreed that we repair to where we know Black Ducks congregate.

It is not yet daylight when we reach our blind on the edge of the sandy shore of the St. Mary's Bay. Our dog is curled up tight, his nose covered by his fox-like tail, and he is the only one of the three of us comfortably warm. But just listen to those Black Ducks as their trembling quack reaches us from out there in the bay. Buff hears them too and, quick as lightning, his ears prick as he raises his head. If you touch him now, you will feel him trembling with suppressed excitement.

And now the east begins to pale and objects become discernible. Presently, we see a black line on the glossy surface of the water, which slowly develops into a flock of twenty birds or more. The tide is almost up to our blind this morning, and everything seems to favor us. The ducks are now in plain sight. Some of them know the danger zone of this shore from years of constant gunning. About 200 yards away they flap their wings and preen their feathers as the rising sun begins to warm them.

Now I guess we will "show" the dog. Reaching into the back pocket of my hunting coat, I pull out a hard rubber ball. Buff has watched my every movement, watch the pupils of his eyes dilate as he sees the ball. Did you ever see such concentration as he watches that sphere of rubber, next to his master? You are thinking "what a shame to scare those ducks" and that perhaps they may come to shore later on as the tide begins to fall, and you can't help feeling certain that every duck will "jump" as soon as they see the dog. But wait, you watch the ducks and, whatever you do, don't shoot until I give the word. It is the ruination of a tolling dog to shoot over him while he is outside the blind. If you do so, the dog will soon want the first chance himself, and when the birds come close he will plunge in after them, without waiting for the gun.

I toss the ball and away goes Buff. Picking it up, he saunters back and drops it in my hand. Out again goes the ball. I watch your face. Through the "peek hole" in the seaweed you study the birds.

Every duck looks intently at the dog and as the ball falls in among some dead seaweed, causing him to use his nose to find it, his bushy tail works and wiggles above the beach grass. A dozen birds turn and swim for shore, their necks, a second ago stretched so long, now disappear as they fold them in, and with soft "meauip-duip-meauip" they swim towards us. Buff plays beautifully, returning with the ball even faster then he romps after it. Now, as the dog comes

H.A.P. SMITH
(continued)

towards us again, the hot scent of Black Ducks smites his nostrils and, stopping with upraised paw, he looks towards them. But a chirp brings him back to us. See him tremble as we push up the safeties of our guns, and here are the birds right against us, though not well bunched, being strung out across our front. They are only thirty-five yards or so away when Buff drops the ball into my open palm for the last time, and I whisper "Down."

See that old chap stretch his neck and swim up and down looking with the keenest of all eyes for the dog, and now up go all heads and turn slowly from us, the birds swim together with their heads turned sideways looking over their shoulders at the blind. I nod and two pairs of twelve-bore barrels poke out above the fringe of seaweed of the blind. As we raise to shoot, Buff peeks over the blind beside me with a whimper and stiffened sinews waiting the report. Both shots snap out as one and into the air seven terrified birds spring straight up, three of the number falling to our second barrels. There are two cripples.

Buff by this time has almost reached the nearest drifting victims. Watch him swim! No need to tell him to retrieve; dropping his bird on the sand, he plunges in again and again until the eighth and last duck is safely recovered.

Last winter I feared I had lost Buff. Shooting from this very blind, I wing-broke a Black Duck, and, giving chase, the dog swam after his bird right out to sea beyond my anxious sight. The tide had turned and I ran along the shore with frantic haste trying to locate a boat. At last I gave it up and sorrowfully returned to fetch my gun, left behind in the blind. My dog's few little imperfections were all forgotten, and every cross world spoken to it was regretted, but to my utter surprise and joy upon reaching the blind, there lay the game little dog with the duck beside him.

Cognizant though Smith was of the amazing abilities of Tollers at the time he wrote that article, he was quick to admit that the little dogs still had the power to surprise and delight him with hunting prowess that he had not previously witnessed. This story appeared in Field & Stream, *April 1918.*

Although I thought I knew all there was to learn concerning the ability of tolling dogs in assisting the gun to obtain a bag of ducks, purely by accident I discovered not only that Canada Geese would toll, but also that ducks will walk as well as swim to the dog.

Late last winter I was waiting in a blind for wild geese. As the flood tide came nearer over the immense mud flats, sixty Canada Geese could be seen feeding along its edge but, with the perverseness of geese, they swam by, disappearing behind the point to the left of my cove.

A big bunch of Black Ducks were noisily feeding out front and when the flood had reached to about seventy-five yards from my blind, they, too, decided the danger zone was reached. After waiting until the salt tide had come to within about forty-five yards of my blind, I decided to toll them in.

I ran my tolling dog out on the marsh behind me, and he played for some minutes before the birds noticed him. At last two or three old ducks woke up and stretched their necks, announcing to the others with loud quacks that something unusual was in sight on shore. In a second every duck was interested and soon the tip end of the flock "broke off" and swam for shore. Reaching the sand, three birds stepped onshore.

Just at this moment I happened to glance up the bay and, to my surprise, noticed four wild geese about 500 yards sway swimming toward me as fast as their pads would propel them. It flashed through my mind that they had seen the ducks coming onshore and thought it was safe for them also. Motioning for the dog to drop beside me in the blind, I waited for their approach. However, as soon as the dog was out of their sight, they began to swim away. Suddenly it dawned upon me that it was the dog they wanted. Picking up the "tolling stick," I tossed it out across the sand to the marsh. Like a flash the dog was after it. A glance through the peek-hole in the blind confirmed my guess. There came the four "honkers" as straight and as fast as they could swim for the dog, and now, with the fine inconsistency of human nature, I wished those Black Ducks were miles away! Here they were right between me and the geese. In a few seconds every duck was onshore, standing with extended necks looking at the dog. In all my former experience of tolling ducks I had never seen birds step out of the water upon the shore. These ducks not only stepped out, but began to waddle up towards me like a battalion of recruits on parade. So curious became some of the birds that they waddled up within fifteen feet of the blind, a few of them even walking around trying to peck into it, to see where the dog had disappeared. Every second I feared this inquisitive advance guard would discover me and take alarm.

Along came the geese and, reaching the shore, two of them stepped out. They were in line and not more than thirty-five yards away. The other two were just at the edge of the tide, watching for the dog. Rising up to shoot over the blind, I of course scared the ducks, the whole flock jumping together in a solid bunch. So thickly were they packed together I could not see through them to get a shot at the geese. Hesitating, while they spread out, I at last saw two big birds flying across my right front. THe first one fell with three No. two shots in his neck. My next shot accounted for his mate.

The dog retrieved both of them and, running up to me, waited for his caress, which is always due him after a successful toll.

ORIGINAL TOLLERS REGISTERED WITH CKC IN MAY 1945

Colonel. Courtesy the Colwell Family.

Brownie. Courtesy the Colwell Family.

Kip, son of Betty and Rusty. Kip was born April 1938 and was later owned by Colonel G. K. Partington. Courtesy the Colwell Family.

Rex, born April 1941. Courtesy the Colwell Family.

Rusty, owned by Colonel Colwell. This photo is dated October 28, 1936 and is captioned by Colonel Colwell: "Rusty has just tolled in a nice flock and is still wet from the retrieve." Courtesy the Colwell Family.

ORIGINAL TOLLERS REGISTERED WITH CKC IN MAY 1945

Left: Lassie (on the left) and Rocco (on the right). Courtesy the Colwell Family. Below: Blondie. Courtesy Colwell Family.

Pink (on the left) and Gyp II (on the right). Courtesy the Colwell Family.

Gyp III. Courtesy the Colwell Family.

Peggy, born July 25, 1936 and killed in 1941, losing the bloodlines of this strain. Courtesy the Colwell Family.

Stamp reproduced courtesy of Canada Post Corporation.

On August 26, 1988, Canada Post, the government agency responsible for Canada's postal services, unveiled an issue of four new stamps at the Yarmouth County Museum in Yarmouth, Nova Scotia. Each depicted a native Canadian dog breed, in honor of the centennial of the Canadian Kennel Club. The breeds were the Toller, the Newfoundland, the Canadian Eskimo Dog, and the Tahltan Bear Dog — the latter is, alas, now extinct. Naturally enough, the Yarmouth ceremony centered around the Toller. Among those present were Avery Nickerson and John Colwell, son of Colonel Cyril Colwell. Both Mr. Nickerson and Colonel Colwell had dedicated a good portion of their lives to the preservation and promotion of the Toller.

On August 30, Canada Post held an official unveiling of all four stamps, the creation of Ontario artist Mia Lane, at the special CKC Centennial Show, which took place in conjunction with the fifth World Congress of Kennel Clubs in Toronto, Ontario. Three of the breeds depicted were represented by live dogs, the Toller being Ch. Westerlea's Tru Ray Red Rebel WC CDX TT, which Ms. Lane has used as her model. The release was also accompanied by a full-color booklet depicting the four breeds, and they were also featured on special First-Day Cover envelopes. Appropriately, the Toller shown in the booklet was Avery Nickerson's Harbourlights Scotia Boy.

Because the World Congress attracted delegates from all of the world's kennel clubs, the stamp ceremony and the National Toller Specialty Show held during centennial week proved to be marvelous showcases for the Toller to a large number of very knowledgeable dog lovers. It may be no accident that Toller numbers have increased enormously since 1988.

This may have also boosted an idea that had been circulating among Toller fanciers concerning the Toller gaining official recognition as Canada's own dog. Although national recognition has not materialized, the fiftieth anniversary of CKC recognition of the Toller eventually became the occasion for the Nova Scotia House of Assembly to pass a bill declaring the Toller the official Provincial Dog of Nova Scotia. Allister Surette, Member for Argyle, championed the idea and introduced the bill into the House. Unanimous approval was given just before the Fiftieth Anniversary National Toller Specialty, held in Halifax, Nova Scotia, in August 1995.

2 Harbourlights Kennel

It was a ten-year-old boy's passion for hunting that led to the founding of Harbourlights, one of Nova Scotia's most famous Toller kennels. Avery Nickerson as a child was so keen on waterfowling that he often ran away to hunt the lakes and marshes of his native Yarmouth County. His father, who failed to possess Avery's passion for the sport, was frequently appalled at his son's determination, but in spite of his best efforts, he failed to quench his son's enthusiasm.

"At fourteen years of age, the little red school did not interest me at all," Avery wrote later. "The teacher very well knew when a shotgun blast was heard and my hand went up to be excused to visit the outside, that I had to see the action which was only a few hundred yards away."

Fortunately for the little red dogs that were to become such a part of Avery's life, Dick Crowell, a hunting guide and family friend, soon became Avery's mentor. At Argyle, Yarmouth County, Crowell set about teaching young Avery all he knew about waterfowling, tolling, and Tollers.

Born in 1925 in Yarmouth County, the southwestern promontory of Nova Scotia that juts boldly out into the sea, Avery Nickerson later followed the calling that must have appeared obvious to many of his fellow countrymen — he joined the navy. The time was World War II, not a time of great optimism and hope, but during one of his home leaves, Avery discovered a sudden attraction to the Yarmouth schoolhouse that he had once viewed with such limited interest. A small, blond schoolteacher named Erna had become an instructor there, and shortly afterward they were married in a military ceremony aboard the HMCS *Cornwallis*.

His choice of a bride was a wise decision. Over the years, Erna became not only his partner in marriage but also his staunch supporter in his efforts to preserve and improve the hunting instincts of his beloved Tollers.

After the war, Avery returned home to Erna and Yarmouth County to become a fisherman and later a fisheries protection officer. Through the years, however, his intense interest in the little red dogs never waned.

Avery had been given his first Toller — an eighteen-month-old, untrained pup named Chum — when he was a teenager. And although Chum was gone when Avery returned from the navy, the young man's dedication to the breed was burgeoning. Even though Avery and Erna also kept setters for a time, there were always Tollers in their lives. Slowly but surely the little red dogs became paramount with the couple.

"Avery found upland bird hunting easier with the Tollers," Erna explains. "They hunt at a

W. Avery Nickerson with his first registered bitch, Harbourlights Autumn Cinderella. Courtesy Erna Nickerson.

Goldie of Schubendorf, the original bitch of Eldon Pace's famous Schubendorf Kennel. Courtesy Eldon Pace.

Eldon Pace, an avid conservationist and supervisor of the Nova Scotia Wildlife Park Mr. Pace was the owner of Schubendorf Kennels in Schubenacadie. Courtesy Eldon Pace.

slower pace in these conditions; you don't have to run to keep up with them."

At first they kept a breeding pair primarily to provide puppies for their own use, but later they decided to expand the operation. In the early 1960s, Harbourlights Autumn Cinderella became their first registered bitch.

When Eldon Pace of Schubenacadie disbanded his noted Schubendorf Kennels, he brought his remaining breeding stock to Harbourlights to join with the Nickersons' Tollers. These dogs also were innate hunters, strong in the traits desired by serious sportsmen and versatile in purpose.

Tollers by this time were beginning to receive wider recognition for their excellent abilities in attracting and retrieving waterfowl and in being fine upland bird dogs. As Tollers began to come into their own as show dogs, Avery and Erna determinedly left the production of show dogs to others and bred for coloring and instinct. Pre-

Harbourlights Kennel, Yarmouth, Nova Scotia, Canada. Photo by Erna Nickerson.

ferring to sell pups only to people who would actually use them as hunting companions, they dedicated their kennel to preserving the unique traits for which the dogs originally had been intended. Their goal was to produce dogs that would live up to the frequently used description of a Toller by people who knew them well — "the finest hunting companions on four legs."

The Nickersons' painstaking efforts paid off. Dogs from Harbourlights Kennel became recognized as the Cadillacs of hunting Tollers, desired by sportsmen throughout North America and Europe for their superior skills. The most successful lines in Sweden and the United Kingdom were developed largely from Harbourlights stock.

And to each serious writer and each dedicated sportsman, Avery Nickerson repeatedly and carefully explained the true tolling process and the training procedures required to produce a good tolling dog. Determined to dispel the many inac-

*W. Avery and Erna Nickerson with Gatter.
Courtesy Janet Wagner.*

After initial CKC registration in 1945 no further registrations were forthcoming. Several outbreaks of distemper had done great damage to the small Toller population and it took a number of years to rebuild stock. Following the lead of Hettie Bidewell in Saskatchewan, the two major Toller breeders in Nova Scotia decided to follow suit. CKC judge Harvey Gratton went to Avery Nickerson's Harbourlights Kennel to evaluate his dogs and those of Eldon Pace for purebred status under Article 33, Section 6A of CKC rules. Mr. Gratton later supplied the photographs taken that day by Eldon Pace to Larry Levsen, founder and first editor of Toller Talk. *These historic photos were published in Vol.2, issue No. 2 of* Toller Talk, *April 1975.*

Avery Nickerson is shown with his dogs Gem of Green Meadows and Autumn's Cinderella. The other two dogs are Eldon Pace's Goldie of Schubendorf and Majour of Schubendorf. All of these dogs are found in early Toller pedigrees.

Harbourlights Dulch, bred by W. Avery and Erna Nickerson. Note the alert, courageous posture, and fine markings. Courtesy Erna Nickerson.

A very influential sire, Harbourlights Scotia Boy, bred and owned by Avery and Erna Nickerson.

*Below:
Harbourlights Highland Chance, bred by Avery and Erna Nickerson and owned by Gail and Ron MacMillan.*

curacies surrounding Tollers, their working methods, and their history, he told his dogs' story in a video produced shortly before his death. The film shows Nickerson surrounded by happy, alert, vivacious little dogs.

According to those who knew him, Avery Nickerson could be gruff, particularly if he suspected that a person did not have the good of his dogs at heart. He needed to be completely assured of a person's honest and sincere desire toward the preservation of Tollers as unique hunting companions. Once reassured, however, he became a remarkable wealth of precise information.

"He was enthralled with waterfowling," Erna recalls. "When he wasn't actually hunting, he was building boats or carving decoys or training dogs. Out of season, he often used the dogs to get close-up photos of ducks and geese with his camera at a pond near our house. In the fall, he would frequently spend an entire month up in Colchester County hunting with his dogs."

After Avery's death in April 1992, Erna continued the tradition at Harbourlights Kennel

Above, Left: Harbourlights' famous stud, Harbourlights Scotia Boy, bred and owned by W. Avery and Erna Nickerson. Courtesy Erna Nickerson.

Above: Harbourlights Big Splash, bred by W. Avery and Erna Nickerson.
Courtesy Erna Nickerson.

Left: Oldholbans Mary Mac of Decoymans, a Toller at the Nacton Decoy, Suffolk, England. She is a descendent of Harbourlights Nova Nipper and Harbourlights famous stud Scotia Boy.
Courtesy John Norris.

Harbourlights Lac a Pac Pal. Note the heavily feathered, foxlike tail. Bred by Erna and W. Avery Nickerson. Courtesy Erna Nickerson.

One of Harbourlights' best Tollers, Ali Gatter. Courtesy Erna Nickerson.

Gatter, one of Harbourlights' prized Tollers Courtesy Erna Nickerson.

The Nova Scotia Duck Tolling Retriever
By W. Avery Nickerson

Nova Scotia duck tollers have passed the test
They are easier to train than all the rest
A lifetime's been spent to breed to perfection
With brains, temperament, style and action
They are little known from east to west
But with many hunters, they're considered the best.

Professional trainers would lack a job
If every hunter owned a tolling dog
So, hunters, believe what some call a myth
A toller's for real, and many insist
That the dog of the future will resemble Reynard
No decoys to carry, no working that's hard
They originated here, in what era of time?
No one really knows but if salt makes brine
These dogs were exalted by more than a few
They depended on them for the old-fashioned stew
No history written in those days of yore
It's talked about, but remains completely obscure.

Some novice breeders continue to write
Of a mystery as thick as a fog bank at night
What for? I don't know and I don't really care
But thank heaven I know that we've had our share.

With a gun and toller, let's go take a look
Maybe you'll see something to write in your book
Don't worry about decoys, he'll do his thing
Whether tolling on water and times on the wing
There may be a hundred or a number most greater
Wait till they see that little dog "Gatter."

It is days like this that one gets a kick
Every time like shot he goes out for the stick
Yes, they see him, they're moving in for his foxy style
They're swimming fast, they're about half a mile
You can hear the commotion, excitement galore
Every bird on the water is headed toward shore.

Throw a stick once more, they're almost in reach.
Those blacks are in windrows right up to the beach
Stay the dog in the blind, they're getting in tight
Take a shot on water or put them in flight
Guns to the shoulder, now "Gatter" steady
He's watching the birds, he's excited but ready.

Now, Gatter, old boy, they're out there dead
He retrieves every one, and with a pat on the head
He would go on and on with never an end
His exuberance undaunted and I'll tell you, friends,
If I live to be a hundred, I'll never be capable
Of describing this dog as less than incredible.

3
The Circle Widens

Won over by the Toller's appeal, new breeders slowly began to enter the fancy. Names that occur repeatedly in local tales of the dogs at this time are Eddie Babine, Adolphe Fitzgerald, Dick Crowell, and, of course, Avery Nickerson and Eldon Pace.

JOHN AND MARY SPROUL
Sproul Kennel

In 1969, two newcomers arrived on the small Toller stage and soon became major players. John and Mary Sproul of Springhill, Nova Scotia, had heard of the dogs, and John thought that he would like to try hunting with one. From Avery Nickerson, they obtained a puppy that grew up to be Ch. Red Rock Star CD (Rocky), foundation sire for the Sproul line. Rocky's best-known son was Ch. Sandy MacGregor of Sproul (Greg), one of the breed's first big winners and a highly influential sire. Greg was leading sire of Toller champions for a number of years and only recently was overtaken as top sire of obedience title holders. He was a star in the show ring in his own right and was Top Show Toller for 1975.

When Rocky was about nine months old, Mary decided to attend a dog show in Amherst, Nova Scotia, as a spectator and was delighted to find two Tollers entered. She was persuaded to try her hand at showing, and over the next twenty-four years, Mary attended innumerable Maritime shows with various Tollers.

So many interested people asked for information about Rocky that Mary thought it would be a good idea to begin a breeding program herself. Avery Nickerson offered her a choice of bitches from his kennel, and she unerringly selected a little pup that went on to fame as Ch. Harbourlights Autumn Fancy, dam of many champions, including Sandy MacGregor. Mary also bought Fancy's brother, Ch. Danny Boy of Harbourlights, whose daughters, bred to Greg, produced numerous show winners and fine obedience workers. The first Sproul litter contained their first champion and the first Toller to finish her championship in three straight shows, Ch. Scarlet Gem of Sproul, whose daughter went on to become the first dual champion.

Thanks to dogs like MacGregor and Danny Boy, and an array of fine bitches, the Sproul Kennel boasts an impressive list of Breed Firsts. This includes the honor of having bred the first Toller to win an All-Breed Best in Show, Ch. Sproul's Highland Playboy (Mork), owned and shown by Jim and Linda Barnes of Regina, Saskatchewan. After twenty-five years of showing and breeding the accolade that long eluded

23

Mary Sproul. With future champions?

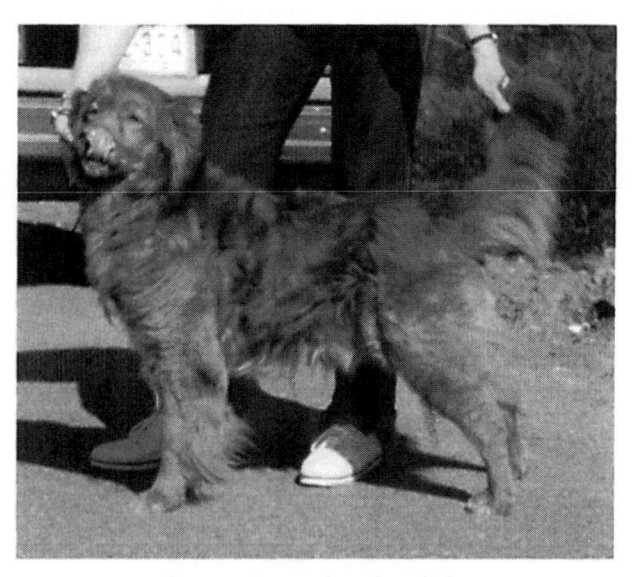

Ch. Danny Boy of Harbourlights, a very influential sire.

Ch. Red Rock Star CD, first Sproul Toller and founder of the Sproul line.

Above: Ch. Sandy MacGregor of Sproul, top winner and producer.

Left: Ch. (Can. Bda.) OTCh. Sproul's Angus MacBeth WC TT, owned and handled here by Anne Penner, and breeder Mary Sproul with Ch. Sproul's Mac-A-Doo.

John and Mary finally came their way in 1994, when their home-bred Ch. Sproul's Happy Higgins was awarded Best in Show by Tom Burke — the seventh time a Toller has placed so highly.

The Sprouls also bred three of the six Tollers that went all the way to Obedience Trial Champions. Two were Greg's daughters, OTCh. Gypsy Lady, owned and trained by David Wood of Nova Scotia, and Ch. OTCh. Sproul's Amber Gem, trained by owner Thelma Poikkimakki of New Brunswick to become the first Toller with a dual Ch. and OTCh. before her name.

Ann Penner of Ontario trained her Ch. (Can. Bda.) and OTCh. Sproul's Angus Macbeth WC TT (an older full brother to Mork) to his Obedience Trial Championship. Then he successfully passed a Working Certificate trial at age nine. Gus, one of only two Tollers to hold a championship in Bermuda, was also No. 1 Toller in the show ring for 1982.

Another MacGregor son is Ch. Sproul's Mac-A-Doo, winner of some eighty group placements at Maritime shows to establish a CKC record. Mac was Top Toller in 1979 and placed in the top three for six consecutive years. The first Toller ever to win a Best Puppy in Show, Mac was also an influential sire in the Maritimes.

One of the dogs closest to Mary's heart — Sproul's Apache Sundog (Sandy) — had no show record but played an important role in Mary's later breeding program. Sandy lost his left front leg in an accident, but he never let this stop him from doing everything that a good Toller can do. He swam, retrieved, jumped in the air to catch a ball or a frisbee, and loved everyone. Sandy died in 1994, but Mary has kept several of his young daughters.

The Sprouls took something of a sabbatical from showing during the 1980s to raise two granddaughters who became their responsibility. Now the girls are old enough to help Mary in the show ring, and no one was more excited than they were over Higgins' great win.

For many years, Sproul dogs led statistics in conformation and obedience, with forty-four champions and twenty-five obedience title holders recorded to the end of 1995. Since the early 1970s, the Sprouls have ranked alongside Avery and Erna Nickerson as the Maritimes' principal Toller breeders.

KEITH AND ROBERTA MACKENZIE
Tollerbrook Kennel

Keith MacKenzie was born in Lockeport on Nova Scotia's South Shore and grew up hearing tales about Little River Duck Dogs. The MacKenzies, who lived outside Fredericton, New Brunswick, bought their first Toller, Firefly Fawna, from Avery Nickerson in 1969. They ran their Tollerbrook Kennel on the Nickerson pattern, aiming for water-loving hunting dogs that were people-friendly. They also incorporated some of Dr. Nelson W. Stott's dogs into their line. Stott had acquired several Tollers from Eldon Pace in the mid-1960s and publicized them in the United States.

Roberta names Ch. Kim's Firefly Buck as the best dog that they ever owned. Buck, a great hunter with a lovable and energetic personality, also obtained his show championship and was No. 1 Toller for 1971. Ch. Keith's Firefly Brandy won several Best Puppy in Group awards in 1972.

The MacKenzies were active charter members of the Toller Club and acted in an advisory capacity on the 1980 revision of the Standard. However, as their daughters grew older, other activities intervened and they closed their kennel.

Kim's Firefly Buck, one of the founding fathers of Keith and Roberta MacKenzie's kennel in the early 1970s. Buck was bred by W. Avery and Erna Nickerson of Yarmouth, Nova Scotia. Courtesy Keith and Roberta MacKenzie.

One of Keith and Roberta MacKenzie's Tollers in action. Courtesy Keith and Roberta MacKenzie.

MacKenzie Gregory from Keith and Roberta MacKenzie's kennel. Courtesy Keith and Roberta MacKenzie.

Roberta was asked to judge Junior Handling at the 1991 Fredericton Toller Specialty, and this rekindled her interest. In 1993, the MacKenzies enlivened their household with a puppy obtained from Alec and Evelyn Hoyt's Yellowrose Kennel in Moncton, New Brunswick.

JIM JEFFERY AND DOUG COLDWELL
Jeffery Coldwell Kennel (later Little River)

Yarmouth born and bred, Jim Jeffery grew up hunting with Tollers, sometimes alongside Avery Nickerson, from whom Jim's father had bought the family's first Toller.

After graduating from university, Jim married Deanna Coldwell and returned to Yarmouth. Excited at the idea of Tollers being a true Canadian dog developed in his home county, Jim determined to promote the breed as Canada's national dog. His first male, obtained from Avery Nickerson in 1969, was Red (full brother to Tollerbrook foundation bitches), a fine hunter from the start. Jim fondly recalls Red struggling to drag in a black duck when he was only twelve weeks old.

As part of their strategy to help Tollers become better known, Jim and Deanna began showing Red, with Deanna handling, and made him Top Conformation Toller for 1970. Ch. Red Russel of Jeffery founded the Jeffery Coldwell Kennel when Jim went into partnership with Deanna's brother, Doug. Doug and Dawn Coldwell lived in an attractive farmhouse near Middleton, in Nova Scotia's Annapolis Valley. This became home to most of the kennel stock obtained from Chin-Peek and Schubendorf lines, as Jim and Deanna had moved to Ottawa and could keep only two or three dogs at their new home.

Red was Jim's pride and joy, so of course he also moved to Ottawa. They kept one bitch, Rapunzel of Jeffery Coldwell (Belle). Unbeknownst to Jim, Red "got at" Belle, and she whelped the one resulting puppy out in the garage in the body of an old car. A very surprised Jim found her there on a cold, snowy February morning in 1975, curled protectively around her baby. That single puppy turned out to be the kennel's biggest-winning star and leading stud dog, Ch. Crusader of Jeffery Coldwell CD (Bigs). The first Toller ever to win Group First, Bigs eventually sired nine champions, the most influential of which was BIS Ch. Westerlea's White Ensign (Tip).

Roy and Alison Strang went to Jim Jeffery in 1975 when they decided to investigate a Toller as

Ch. Red Russel of Jeffery, foundation sire for the Jeffery-Coldwell Little River dynasty.

Tollers wait on the shore for a retrieve. From front to rear, Ch. Florette Jeffery of Overton, Chin-Peek Wee Lady Susan, Ch. Red Russel of Jeffery, and Ch. Rusty Jeffery of Kemptville.

Icy waters of the Bay of Fundy do not deter this trio: Ch. Florette Jeffery of Overton, Ch. Red Russel of Jeffery (with stick), and Ch. Rusty Jeffery of Kemptville (rear).

a suitable dog for their youngest daughter. This led to the creation of the Westerlea dynasty. Oddly enough, Bigs was offered to the Strangs as a pup, but they stuck to their decision to begin with a female. Two years later, Ch. Shelburne of Jeffery Coldwell made the very long flight from Vancouver back to the kennel where she had begun life to be bred to the dog that the Strangs could have purchased in 1975. A lot hangs on such twists of fate.

Jim did a tremendous amount of promotional work for the Toller and was a prolific correspondent for the fledgling *Toller Talk* newsletter of the Nova Scotia Duck Tolling Retriever (NSDTR) Club of Canada, founded in 1974. He was among the first to suggest the formation of a national Toller club and wrote the first club constitution. Jim's articles were reproduced in the United States and Australia, as well as in several Canadian publications, and he maintained a wide correspondence with other Toller fanciers. He was active in pushing for a revision of the then-current Toller Standard, because his Yarmouth experience taught him that the first Standard did not accurately reflect the dog developed there.

In the late 1970s, the Jefferys moved to Elliott Lake in northern Ontario, and their two daughters began to grow up. Jim now felt that he was too remote from the scene of Toller action, so he gave up his half of the kennel to Doug Coldwell. Doug continues to operate Little River Kennel in the Annapolis Valley.

VIC AND HEATHER DUNPHY
Marangai Kennel

Large migrations of ducks arrive close to Fredericton, New Brunswick's capital, every November — mainly blacks from Labrador. Duck hunting is a chilly proposition for both hunter and dog. In the early 1980s, Vic Dunphy decided that a Toller would best fill his desire for a hunting dog, so he and his wife Heather went to Avery Nickerson. The Dunphys' acquisition, a son of Harbourlights Scotia Boy, grew up to be Ch. Harbourlights Joshua CDX TT (Josh), the first Harbourlights dog to have both a championship and the middle obedience degree. Josh, foundation sire for the Dunphys' Marangai Kennel, appeared in the list of Top Winning Obedience and Conformation Tollers for several years. Their original bitches came from the Sprouls.

In 1992, Vic was elected president of the NSDTR Club of Canada, and he has worked tirelessly to cement the club as a truly nationwide organization. He and Heather have run many classes in obedience, which, along with hunting, will always remain their chief interest.

DEREK AND PAM DUNN
Kare Kennel

Derek and Pam Dunn bought their first Toller, Windy of Jeffery Coldwell, as a family pet. Banner was nearly six years old when Brenda Stephens of Jem Kennel persuaded them to

Ch. Harbourlights Joshua CDX, a winner in both conformation and obedience for owners Vic Dunphy and Heather Connors-Dunphy, handled here by Mary Feeney. The judge is Marian Waite. Photo by Keseluk.

Kare Kennels' original Tollers (left to right): Ch. Rusty of Littleriver 2nd WC CD TT, Ch. Marangai Lady for Kare, Ch. Kare's Mistress of Littleriver WC CD TT, and Ch. Windy of Jeffery Coldwell II TT.

Ch. Kare's Atlantic Pryde CD, handled by owner/breeder Derek Dunn to one of her Group placements.

enter him in the Centennial Specialty in Toronto in 1988, where he gained the significant Winners Male award. This gave the Dunns a taste for the show ring, and they soon decided to breed Tollers. They acquired a bitch from both the Dunphys and the Sprouls, and they purchased a male from Little River Kennel. Their first litter arrived in 1989, not long before Derek, who serves with the Canadian Armed Forces, was posted to Nova Scotia. Derek and Pam established Kare Kennel in Eldon Pace's old stomping grounds, Shubenacadie, and have both Mr. Pace and Dr. Stott as neighbors.

The Dunns were instrumental in promoting hip and eye checking among Maritime breeders, and, along with fall hunting, they work their dogs in obedience and for field tests. Although Kare Kennel is still young, the name is becoming established through dogs such as Ch. Kare's Atlantic Pryde, winner of several Group placings and three Best Puppy in Group. Both Stud Dog and Brood Bitch trophies went to Kare dogs at the 1995 Toller Specialty in Halifax.

Newer Maritime kennels include those of Alec and Evelyn Hoyt of Moncton, New Brunswick (Yellowrose) and Roger and Mary Brooks of Halifax, Nova Scotia (Whitepoint).

Some of the older tolling men around Yarmouth would doubtless be amazed to learn that "their" dog is now spread across Canada and to various parts of the world. Perhaps, though, they would not be surprised, because no one knew better than they did the qualities of the dog they had developed.

A. McIntyre

A Norwegian Toller gallops over the hill in Norway.

4

The Western Connection

In the early 1950s, Tollers received a flurry of publicity, including a two-column story by Harold Shea in *Time* magazine. This news item featured brothers Fred and Paul Armstrong of Yarmouth, and how they hunted and tolled ducks with their little Tollers, Dusty and Tootsie. The major long-term effect of this publicity occurred when Hettie Bidewell of Moose Jaw, Saskatchewan, read a reworking of the Shea piece in the *Winnipeg Free Press*. Mrs. Bidewell, who already bred Pekingese, Rough Collies, and an occasional American Cocker Spaniel and Irish Setter, was immediately intrigued and wrote to Fred Armstrong for information.

CHIN-PEEK

Thus, Bidewell's Flip and Bidewell's Lady became the first Tollers to go west, making the long trip from Yarmouth to Moose Jaw by train. Flip somewhat resembled a small yellow Labrador, while Lady bore a strong likeness to a working Sheltie, with her big white collar, blaze, and full, thick coat. These two laid the foundation for Hettie Bidewell's line of Chin-Peek Tollers, which were the first to be registered with the Canadian Pedigree Livestock Association under an article allowing registration of dogs that were breeding true to type after several generations of carefully controlled matings.

Fifteen dogs were registered when the Toller received Canadian Kennel Club recognition in 1945. However, no further applications came in succeeding years until Hettie took the first steps to have her dogs reentered into official records. The late William Dawson, a well-known and highly respected All-Breed judge in both Canada and the United States, later vividly recalled countless trips made from his home in Prince Albert, Saskatchewan, to Moose Jaw to ensure that Hettie's Toller litters maintained type and were indeed purebred. Finally, the CKC gave its consent, and the first registered Nova Scotia Duck Tolling Retriever litter appeared in the 1959 Stud Book. The sire of this historic litter was Chin-Peek Golden Kim, who had been registered under Article 33, Section 6A of the Pedigree Livestock Act with the number 442960; the dam was Chin-Peek Trixie Girl, number 442957.

Hettie registered one litter in 1960 and another in 1961. Then, in 1962, the whole CKC Toller horizon widened when Nova Scotia breeder Eldon Pace contacted Hettie for information on correct CKC registration procedures. He and Avery Nickerson soon registered litters of their own after another All-Breed judge, Harvey Gratton had performed the same task as William Dawson.

Left: Chin-Peek Golden Belle, also one of the first of Hettie Bidewell's Tollers.

Below, Left: Hettie Bidewell with Ch. Chin-Peek Golden Taffie, Top Toller in Canada, 1964. Courtesy Terry McNamee, Rosewood Kennel.

Chin-Peek Trixie Girl, an early Toller at Hettie Bidewell's kennel.

Hettie Bidewell at a Toller picnic in Vancouver, British Columbia, 1986.

In the late 1960s, a kennel fire destroyed much of Hettie's painstakingly built-up stock. Undaunted, she obtained a male from Eldon Pace, Pat of Schubendorf, who was to play a key role in the renaissance of the Chin-Peek line. In exchange, Hettie sent a female, Chin-Peek Star's Lady, who was influential in the development of the Sproul line in Nova Scotia.

Chin-Peek dogs had several notable breed firsts, chief among them being the first Toller show champion, Ch. Chin-Peek Golden Taffie, in 1965, who was also Top Toller for 1964 and 1965. Another Chin-Peek bitch, Prom Gal, was Top Toller in 1962.

The Bidewell method was based largely on inbreeding, as were the programs of early Toller breeders "Down East." Hettie continued to inbreed her Tollers until the time she ceased breeding operations in the mid-1980s. Many dogs were small and of a light fawn or buff color, and they carried an overabundance of white, but many more were of good bone, correct size, type, and color. Hettie Bidewell will always bear a place of pride in Toller history for bringing the Toller to the west. In 1982, she was honored by the Canadian Kennel Club with a life membership, an accolade that she relished and richly deserved.

Although she relinquished her last Tollers in 1988, Hettie remained active in Grande Prairie, Alberta, and even enrolled at the local art college at the age of ninety!

CHIN-PEEK OFFSHOOTS

From the Chin-Peek line sprang the foundations for several later kennels, among them Alin-Decaro of Al and Inge Gray of Regina, Saskatchewan. Their chief place in Toller history comes from three littermates that were, respectively, winner of the first-ever National Specialty Show in 1979 and Top Obedience Dog in 1977, Ch. Todd of Alin Decaro CDX; Top Conformation Toller for 1976-77, Ch. Taddy of Alin Decaro; and Tundra of Alin Decaro CDX, Top in Obedience for 1974-75. Hasso of Alin Decaro sired these notable dogs, whose dam was Chin-Peek Misy Pipen.

The Grays passed their Tollers on to Larry Levsen, the founder and first editor of the Nova Scotia Duck Tolling Retriever Club of Canada's quarterly newsletter *Toller Talk*. Larry was one of the prime movers in starting the club, which was formed in June 1974, after he put out the first newsletter in January of that year telling fanciers about the planned club and asking for members. Within two short months there were forty charter members.

Among the fledgling club's most active members were Ron and Joanne Saxby of Regina, with Ron acting as the first club secretary. Ron and Joanne owned one of the first Group Placing bitches in the breed, Ch. Lady Saxby of Jeffery Coldwell, who was a regular winner at Saskatchewan shows. From Lady Saxby and Ch. Sandy MacGregor of Sproul, Ron and Joanne bred the Top Obedience Toller for 1980, Ch. Sayla's Banner MacGregor CDX.

Ken Armitage of Moose Jaw, Saskatchewan, was the first president of the new Toller club. When Ken and his wife Del returned from service overseas, they began a search for a suitable dog for two persistent children. That search led to Chin-Peek, where, as Hettie enthused about the "new Canadian breed," a cute Toller pup toddled over. It was love at first sight for the Armitages and the little pup that became Ch. Chin-Peek Majour Tyrol CD. Tyrol obtained his CD in three consecutive trials in 1971 and a qualifying score in Open in 1972, enough to earn him Top Obedience Toller for that year.

Young Randy Armitage trained Chin-Peek Fancy Red CD to three consecutive High in Trials. This achievement was recorded in Dogs in Canada and gave a big boost to Tollers, which were then just beginning to be noticed by the dog fancy at large.

Another Chin-Peek dog captured the attention of Prairie Obedience enthusiasts when she became the first Toller ever to earn an Obedience Trial championship. Barry Trites of Moose Jaw, Saskatchewan, had bought OTCh. Chin-Peek Lady Susan for his daughter in 1966. "I decided the dog I bought would have to be well mannered, so I got interested in training," Barry said during an interview a few years later. "Both of us were untrained when we went to our first class.

The first OTCh. Toller, Chin-Peek Lady Susan UD, with her son, Chin-Peek Chip Bar-Mar-Car CDX. Courtesy Barry Trites.

Ch. (Can. Bda.) Contriev Drummer Boy CD with handler James Campbell in Bermuda, 1978.

It took about ten months before she was trained, and she finished highest scoring dog in the class."

Lady Susan, Top Obedience Toller in 1968 and 1970, was bred to her sire, Pat of Schubendorf, to produce Barry's other Obedience dog, Chin-Peek Chip-Bar-Mar-Car CDX. Chip garnered the No. 1 place in Obedience for 1969.

Around 1970, the Toller finally spread from coast to coast. Norm and Louise Aitken of Abbotsford, British Columbia, acquired their first Tollers from Chin-Peek, but they could not have known that when they bred Chin-Peek Lady de-Laine to Chin-Peek Kitt's Pat, they were assuring their place in Toller history. A male from this breeding became the first Toller "star" in the show ring.

WILEEN MANN
Sundrummer Kennel

Wileen Mann came across Tollers by chance. While recuperating at her Vancouver home from an illness in 1971, she was intrigued by an article in the *Canadian Star Weekly*. A short hunt led her to the Aitkens. Good luck accompanied Wileen's first choice, as the pup grew up to become the immortal Ch. (Can. Bda.) Coltriev Drummer Boy CD, the first Toller to really draw the attention of the dog world. When Wileen began competing with Dummer, he was a skinny, leggy youngster that quickly impressed Obedience folks in British Columbia with his enthusiasm and learning ability. He achieved his CD at the age of only eleven months in three straight trials, and twice he placed second in his class.

Drummer, whelped in December 1972, began his Conformation wins with a Group fourth when he was fourteen months old. Wileen moved to Fort St. John in northeastern British Columbia and became involved with a growing family, and as a result, she put Drummer in the care of professional handler Jimmy Campbell. The pair had a string of notable Group placements in both Canada and Bermuda, including a first in Bermuda. Always a crowd pleaser, the little fellow won many hearts for Tollers in the 1970s, both in Canada and in Bermuda, where he was fondly recalled during later visits by other Toller fanciers.

In 1975, Wileen visited several major Nova Scotia kennels and returned to Fort St. John with two bitches and a dog from John and Mary Sproul, all of which were destined to leave a mark on the breed: Ch. Sproul's Highland Lassie (Cherry), Ch. Sproul's Highland Belle, and Ch. Sproul's Highland Commander (Willie). Cherry attracted the attention of a visiting writer with her retrieving drive and enthusiasm. The resulting article led British Columbia newcomer Alison Strang to purchase a Willie/Cherry puppy that grew up to be Ch. Sundrummer's Seawitch (Lucy). Together with her best partner, Ch. Westerlea's White Ensign, Lucy built the foundations for Westerlea Kennels.

Ch. Sundrummer's Seawitch, 1982. Photo by Hellard.

After the loss of Drummer at age fourteen, Wileen had no more dogs, but in 1991, she and her new husband Ron Cook bought a Toller as a pet to share their home in Arizona. Westerlea's Spirit of Sundrummer (numbering Drummer, Belle, and Lucy among his ancestors) is a living reminder of the Sundrummer line and brought the Sundrummer-Westerlea connection full circle.

RENA CAP
Jalna Kennel

As Hettie Bidewell gradually reduced her breeding operations, the Toller banner on the eastern Prairies was carried by Rena Cap at Jalna Kennel in Brandon, Manitoba. Rena, the only charter member of the Toller Club who still has a membership, bought her first Toller, Dodee de Lamar, in 1974 as an Obedience prospect. When Rena decided to breed Tollers in 1976, however, she approached Doug Coldwell in Nova Scotia. These negotiations resulted in the arrival of Ch. Contessa of Jeffery Coldwell, winner of a Best Puppy in Group. Tessa was already in whelp to Ch. Crusader of Jeffery Coldwell, and the resulting litter was the foundation of the Jalna line. One of these pups, Ch. Jalna's Eager Boots CDX, went to Terry McNamee, then living in Brandon, and became the foundation for Terry's Rosewood Kennel.

Alas, Tessa was lost in a disastrous kennel fire. After picking up the pieces, Rena Cap contacted John and Mary Sproul, who sent her the pups that became Ch. Sproul's Earl of Jalna CD (Teddy) and Ch. Sproul's Jennifer Jalna (Jenny). Both of these dogs had much influence on the Jalna line, as did Boots's brother, Ch. Jalna's Red Emperor, which, when bred to Jenny, produced a number of champions. Among these were Ch. Jalna's Firefox and Ch. Jalna's Brazen Brat, prominent names

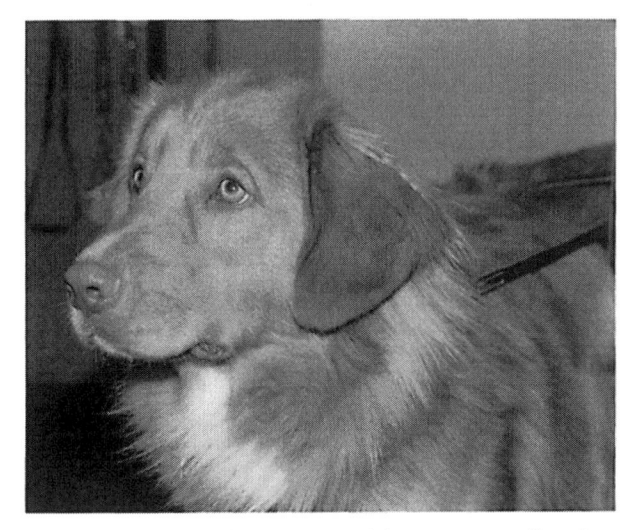

Ch. Sproul's Earl of Jalna CD (Teddy), an outstanding sire for Jalna Kennel.

A top winner, Ch. Jalna's Quest for Glory CDX, taking a break from competition.

Ch. Jalna's Our Only One CD, one of Rena Cap's big-winning dogs. The sire is Ch. Jalna's Red Emperor, and the dam is Sproul's Jennifer Jalna. Photo by Barry Freedman.

*Ch. Jalna's Delightful Dream, representing the newer Jalna generation, taking a four-point win with breeder Rena Cap in Edmonton, September 1993.
Photo by Mikron.*

in the pedigrees of many later Jalna winners. At the end of 1995, Jalna could claim twenty-seven recorded champions and thirteen Obedience titles.

The biggest-winning Jalna dog to date is Ch. Jalna's Quest for Glory CDX (Casey). Owned and handled by Sheila Paul of Vancouver, British Columbia, Casey achieved Top Toller in 1985, after being No. 2 for the two preceding years. Casey was sired by Teddy out of another from the first Jalna litter, Jalna's Elegance in Red. He was also the first dog to obtain a CDX Obedience title on the West Coast, as well as being foundation sire for the Ardunacres line.

Numerous Jalna dogs were sent as foundation for kennels in Sweden and Finland, and the Jalna influence is still strongly visible in a number of Scandinavian Tollers. Rena also sent the first Tollers to Holland.

ALISON AND ROY STRANG
Westerlea Kennel

The top-achieving Toller kennel at the end of 1995 is that of Alison and Roy Strang, whose Westerlea prefix is attached to the highest number of title holders in Conformation, Obedience, and Field tests.

In 1965, the Strangs moved from what is now Zimbabwe to Fredericton in New Brunswick. However, Roy's ecological studies of the barrens of southwestern Nova Scotia kept him in that part of the world for six months of each year. The family spent summers in Shelburne and Liverpool counties of Nova Scotia and soon came to hear reports of the Little River Duck Dogs, which were fairly common there. During that period, Alison was more interested in Newfoundlands, so it was not until 1975 that a Toller joined the family as a pet and potential show dog for the youngest Strang, Catriona. Ch. Shelburne of Jeffery Coldwell, Westerlea's foundation bitch, exerted much influence through her son, BIS BISS Ch. Westerlea's White Ensign. Tip was whelped in 1977 in Surrey, British Columbia, where the family had moved from Ottawa in 1976.

*Ten-year-old Catriona Strang finishing the championship on her Toller, Ch. Shelburne of Jeffery Coldwell, Westerlea's foundation bitch.
Photo by Don Hodges.*

BIS Ch. Westerlea's White Ensign in his prime.

BIS Ch. Westerlea's Tru-Ray Red Rebel WC CDX TT, pride of Jem Kennels. Always handled by owner Brenda Stephens. Photo by Alex Smith.

Tip was not only the foundation sire for the Westerlea line, but in June 1980, he became the second Toller to win an All-Breed Best in Show. Tip was No. 1 Toller that year and second the following year, and he still holds the record for leading sire of champions with seventeen. He also became famous as "the tree-climbing Toller" when this activity, brought about by the lodging of a retrieving dummy in the top branches of a pine in the Strang backyard, was noted in *Dogs in Canada* and the *Canadian Children's Magazine*. The latter article was part of a series written by Alison to promote and publicize "Canada's Own All-Round Dog," the Westerlea slogan for many years.

Tip was bred to Ch. Sundrummer's Seawitch (Lucy). The first Tip/Lucy litter produced four champions, among them BIS Ch. Westerlea's Tru-Ray Red Rebel WC CDX TT, owned by Ken and Brenda Stephens of Lindsay, Ontario. Rebel had a distinguished career, including first Toller to win an All-Breed Best in Show in eastern Canada, Top Show Toller in 1983-84, and tops in Obedience for 1984. This was the only time one dog has held both titles in the same year. Rebel was also an influential sire in Ontario.

A younger full brother to Rebel, BIS Ch. Westerlea's Red Duster, upheld the family honor with an All-Breed Best in Show win in 1987. Handled by owner Sheila Paul, Sailor was Top Toller for 1986-87 and became the first Toller to place in Sporting Group at the Ottawa Show of Shows, finishing third. The Ralston-Purina Show of Shows is Canada's premier dog show, as every entrant is an All-Breed Best in Show Winner.

The Tip/Lucy influence continues in Lucy's outstanding daughter, Dual BISS Ch. Westerlea's Bonny Bluenose, a leading Toller brood bitch with sixteen champion offspring, including a Best in Show and Specialty winner, an OTCh. who also has a WCI, several High in Trial winners, and a number of Group placers and Best Puppy in Group/Show winners. Bonny herself won two NSDTR Club of Canada Specialty shows, a number of Group placings, and several Best Puppy in Groups.

Tip and Lucy are also major forces in the pedigree of another big-winning dog that was bred by Mac and Joan Noullett of Campbell River, British

Crusader of Jeffery Coldwell "Bigs" and his two top-winning kids, BIS Ch. Westerlea's White Ensign and Ch. Jalna's Eager Boots CDX TT, at the first Toller Specialty in Regina, 1979.

BIS Ch. Sandycove at Westerlea WC CD at two years of age.

One of four champions from the first Tip/Lucy litter, Steve Abbott's Ch. Westerlea's Flying Fox.

Columbia — BIS Ch. Sandycove at Westerlea WC CD. Sandy held the record for the most points scored by a Toller in a single show season (2,070 points earned in 1990) until 2012 when Can Grand CHEx, Am Grand Ch. Readyfor Going to the Max CGN WC RN AGNJS piled up an amazing 3,736 points at CKC shows. Sandy, handled by co-owner Susan Kish, not only became the fifth Toller to win an All-Breed Best in Show, but went on to to win Sporting Group First at the Show of Shows. Sandy was in the top three Conformation Tollers for four consecutive years. In 1990, he sired Nos. 2, 4, and 9, while his 1991 record was even better — No. 2 himself, he sired Nos. 1, 3, 4, and 5.

Sandy and Bonny have produced ten champions, several also with Obedience and Field titles. Most notable is BIS BISS Ch. Westerlea's Ilo at the Well CD, who holds the record for Toller puppy wins with nine Best Puppy in Group and two Best Puppy in Show. Ilo, owned and hunted by Jay Attwell of Bristow, British Columbia, went on to an outstanding adult career, placing as Top Toller in 1989 and 1991. His 1991 career included an All-Breed Best in Show, a Specialty Show, and a Show of Shows Group third. Not far behind came his litter brother, Ch. Westerlea's Clan Chieftain CDX, owned by Doug and Andrea Mills of Maple Ridge, British Columbia. Buddy was Top Show Toller in 1993, after being in the first five for four consecutive years, and was also Top Obedience Toller in 1992.

Two Westerlea bitch puppies sent to Denmark in 1982 were the first Tollers to go as breeding stock to Scandinavia. Others have since followed to Denmark, Finland, Sweden, and Austria. A number of today's Toller kennels have Westerlea dogs as their foundations.

Total Canadian titles recorded for Westerlea dogs to the end of 1995 is sixty show champions, forty Obedience titles, eight in Working Certificate programs, and the only Toller with a Tracking Dog Excellent degree, Westerlea's Outfox the Fox CD TDX, owned and trained by Laura Norie of Quesnel, British Columbia.

ARLINE AND DUNCAN MACDONALD
Ardunacres Kennel

Arline MacDonald's attention was first drawn to Tollers by an advertisement in the 1976 *Dogs Annual*. The following year, her husband, Dunc, surprised her with the gift of their first Toller, Tantramar, who came from the Aitkens' Coltriev Kennel. Tanta proved to be an excellent pet, and Arline and Dunc became hooked on Tollers. After moving to Aldergrove, east of Vancouver, British Columbia, they acquired their foundation bitch from Wileen Mann. Ch. Sundrummer's Ardunella CD. Ardun, bred to Casey, produced the first Ardunacres litter in 1982. Unfortunately, a year later, Ardun panicked during a severe thunder-

Foundations for Ardunacres, Ch. Sundrummer's Ardunella CD and Ch. Jalna's Quest for Glory CDX.

Ch. Ardunacres Call Me Ikea, a versatile Toller belonging to Dunc and Arline MacDonald.

storm and disappeared. Despite unremitting efforts to find her, nothing was ever learned of her fate. Ardun left a fine legacy, however, as all of the eleven Ardunacres champions descend from her.

Several dogs from MacDonald breeding have Obedience degrees, most notable being OTCh. Larl-Be-Gingembre Magic, the first Utility Obedience dog in British Columbia. He is owned and trained by Jack and Dallyce Patterson of Victoria, British Columbia. His dam, Ardunacres Gingembre, probably has had the biggest influence on the MacDonald line, because she is the dam of several champions in Canada and overseas. Another good competitor is Pat Townsend's Ch. OTCh. Ardunacres Outward Bound, Top Obedience Toller for 1994.

Arline's favorite was Ch. Ardunacres Call Me Ikea CD, a wonderful ambassador for the breed with her appearances on flyball teams, at many public displays, and, above all, in her role as a therapy dog.

MORE RECENT WESTERN BREEDERS

Several newer breeders came on the British Columbia scene in the 1980s. Steve and Diane Abbott of Castlekeep Kennel are best remembered for Ch. Castlekeep's Magic of Merlin (Gunner), winner of Best Puppy at the 1983 Specialty Show. Several of Gunner's offspring have gone to Scandinavia, among them Cinnstar's Ruffed Grouse, who was Toller foundation for the very successful Zeiban's Kennel in Finland.

DOBIRSTEIN

In the early 1980s, field trialer John Dobirstein married Joyce Wood in Edmonton, and Joyce took over management of John's Toller, Ch. Sundrummer's Valentine Luke, on whom she put Championship, Utility, WC, and Tracking Dog titles. Luke and Joyce were a great team, and Luke is the only Toller to hold *all* these titles. When John died in an accident, Joyce took over his boarding kennel and has since gone on to specialize in Tollers.

Her first bitch came from Hettie Bidewell; she then purchased a male of Westerlea/Jalna breeding. There are a number of Dobirstein champions, including Ch. Dobirstein's Golden Bubbles CD, Best of Winners at the 1993 Specialty. Every Toller puppy that Joyce has kept holds a championship and at least a CD, and some also have WCs.

In 1985, Joyce sponsored the Dobirstein Award in memory of her husband. A plaque is given to any Toller holding a Championship, an Obedience

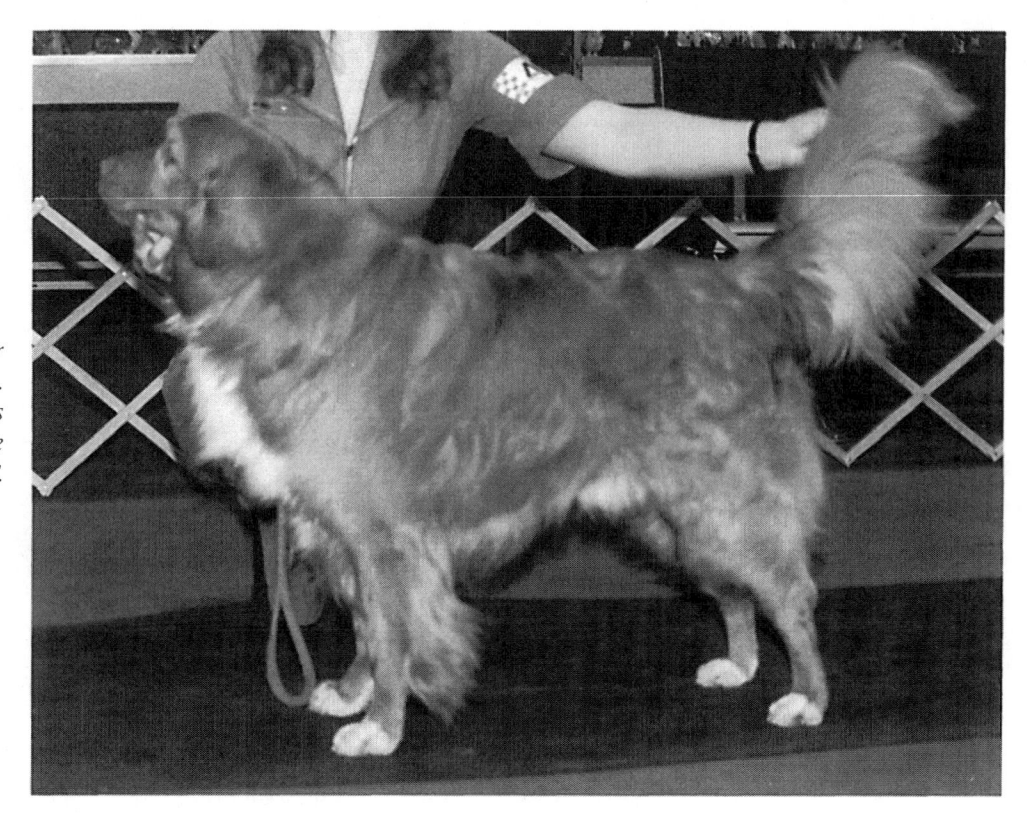

The most titled Toller of all — Ch. OTCh. Sundrummer's Valentine Luke WC TD TT.

All of Joyce Dobirstein's own Tollers have titles. Here is Joyce at the line of a WC test with Ch. Chakim-KY's Suntime Sparkle CDX WC TT.

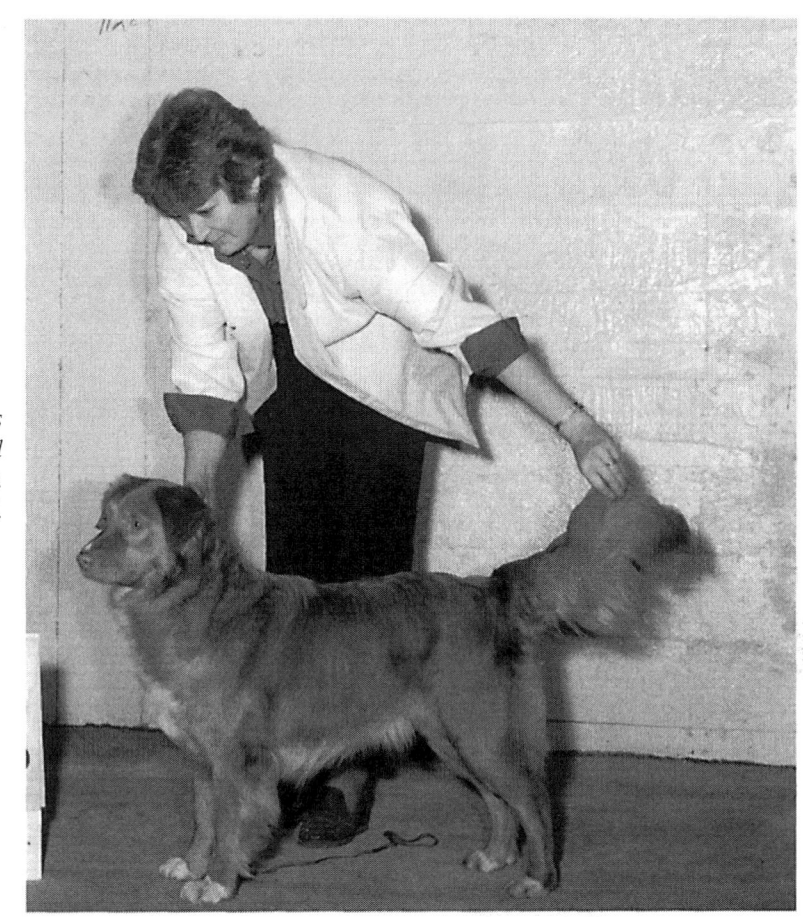

Joan Noullett and her Ch. Westerlea's Summer Sunset, a winner in the ring and dam of a Best in Show Toller. Photo by Russ Hellard.

Gerry Wong's good winner and brood bitch, Ch. Ardunacres Gingerbread Girl, and her son, Ch. Starway's Mr. Leon, keep watch at home.

Lynda Martin enjoys a scenic outing near her home in Sooke, British Columbia, with (left to right) Ch. Westerlea's Colony Blueprint CD, Ch. Westerlea's Cedar Barque, and Tayann Lady of Shallot.

degree, and a Working certificate. This offers an incentive to Toller fanciers to maintain the breed's natural instincts as versatile working retrievers.

SANDYCOVE

Joan and Mac Noullett bought their first Toller in 1981 as a pet, but after breeder Alison Strang kept six-month-old Buffy for a few days, she encouraged Joan to show her pride and joy. In a short time, Buffy became Ch. Westerlea's Summer Sunset, who will go down in the record books as dam of BIS Ch. Sandycove at Westerlea WC CD and his brother, Ch. Sandycove's Gold Horizon WC CD. Both of these dogs feature in the pedigrees of good winners over the past eight years. Before Buffy's death early in 1995, Joan and Mac closed their Sandycove Kennel in Campbell River, British Columbia, but they still maintain a keen interest in the breed.

STARWAY

One day in 1984, Gerry and Doris Wong of Port Coquitlam, British Columbia, went to look at a seven-day-old litter of Tollers at Ardunacres Ken-

Ch. Ardunacres Cheekeye, foundation bitch for Frank Boutilier's Tollbreton Kennel in Burnaby, British Columbia. Photo by Bob Cossar.

nel and ended up buying a puppy. This little pup grew up to become the biggest Ardunacres winner in the Canadian show ring, Ch. Ardunacres Gingerbread Girl, who made a number of Group placements. Ginger, a great show girl with an outstanding temperament, has spent most of her life making friends for Tollers with Gerry, who now breeds under the Starway prefix.

COLONY
Lynda and Richard Martin first met Tollers back in 1977 when Richard's mother, Peggy, was commissioned by Kwakiutl artist Doug Cranmer to find him a Toller. Peggy visited Westerlea Kennel with Richard and Lynda, who were immediately fascinated with the little red dogs and determined to have a kennel of their own "one fine day." Pride of place as foundation bitch for Colony Kennel goes to Ch. Westerlea's Colony Blueprint CD, who won the Brood Bitch Class at the 1993 National Specialty Show held in Edmonton, Alberta. Lynda also bred Ch. (Can. Am.) Colony's Lennoxlove Victoria WC CD, foundation bitch for Lennoxlove Kennel in upstate New York. In 1989, when Lynda was editor, *Toller Talk* was awarded a prize by *Dogs in Canada* as best club newsletter.

TOLLBRETON
Frank and Roberta Boutilier's Tollbreton Kennel was named in honor of Frank's home territory, Cape Breton Island. Best-known Tollbreton dog is Ch. Tollbreton Honey for Westerlea WC, whose first litter has definitely made waves in eastern Canada.

With these breeders, old and new, and several others just entering the breeding game, the Toller is very much alive and well in the west!

Riga pounds the surf.
HR AKC/CAN/NSDTRC-US CH Vermilion's Rah Rah Ramona CD RE SH WCX MX MXJ,
owned and bred by Kathy Koebensky-Como and Jamie Como.

5
Tollers Come to Upper Canada

The Toller took a little longer to make his presence felt in Canada's heartland, or Upper Canada as it is still known in the Maritimes, but the recent great increase in Toller numbers in both Ontario and Quebec more than make up for a slow start.

The first Toller in Ontario to attract public attention was Littleriver Tru Ray Rusti WCX, bought as a pup by Ray Stephens of Scarborough from the Jeffery Coldwell Kennel. Ray hunted Rusti and then decided that he would like to try him in field trials. Rusti earned several Certificates of Merit in Junior classes and went on to become the first Toller to place in Qualifying Stakes. This led to an invitation to run in the annual Canadian National Sportsmen's Shows indoor field trials in March 1982, at that time the largest in North America. This was the first time that a Toller had been so honored. Both main Toronto newspapers ran articles about the little Toller that placed fourth in one of the trials, running against the cream of the more usual retriever crop.

Rusti unfortunately was monorchid, so he was never bred. However, the memory of his accomplishments is still green with those who were in the fancy at the time.

In 1980, Ray acquired a male from Westerlea Kennel and also bought a bitch puppy from Ann Penner of Burlington, Ontario. This puppy was Ch. Liscot's Tru Ray Dynamite WC, who in 1982, trained by Ray, became the first Toller to win the newly established CKC Working Certificate title.

KEN AND BRENDA STEPHENS
Jem Kennel

Ray Stephens's male pup went to live with his brother Ken and sister-in-law Brenda, because the Scarborough municipal limit was two dogs, and because Ken and Brenda were enamored of Rusti. Ken and Brenda eventually bought the puppy, and he grew up to be one of Ontario's best-known Tollers, BIS Ch. Westerlea's Tru Ray Red Rebel WC CDX. Rebel stands in third place for sires of champions and heads the list of Obedience title-holder sires at seventeen.

Rebel was hunted by Ken and shown by Brenda. This was a perfect combination that reached its culmination when Ken and Rebel got their limit of ducks on a Friday, then Brenda stayed up very late for a marathon bathing and grooming session to prepare Rebel for the show ring the following day — November 10, 1984. By the end of that day, Rebel had become the third-ever Toller, and the first in eastern Canada, to win an All-Breed Best in Show. This magnificent

Littleriver Tru Ray Rusti WCX and baby Rebel. Taken at home of owner Ray Stephens.

win capped a long string of Group placements that made Rebel Top Show Toller for 1983 and 1984. Rebel also had been busy in the Obedience rings and Field tests, as he had earned his CDX and WC by the time he went Best in Show. Brenda was his trainer and handler.

Ken and Brenda established Jem Kennel in 1984 and bred numerous litters until the early 1990s, when the pressure of teaching three daughters at home put the dogs on the back burner. Jem Tollers are to be found in pedigrees both in Canada and the United States, and it was from Jem that the first two Tollers went to England in 1987.

ANN PENNER
Liscot Kennel

Ann Penner bought her first Toller, the future Ch. Sproul's Argyle Angel CD, from Sproul Kennel when she was living in Quebec.

When the Penner family moved to Ontario, Ann bought a male from John and Mary Sproul, Ch. (Can. Bda.) and OTCh. Sproul's Angus Macbeth WC. Gus, Top Toller in 1982, amassed a string of titles that has only once been surpassed in Canada, by Ch. and OTCh. Sundrummer's Valentine Luke WC TD TT, in Alberta. Gus also proved that an old dog can learn new tricks when, just to keep him busy, Ann asked Cathy Herring to train him for his Working Certificate and he passed at his first try at the age of nine years.

Ann registered her Liscot prefix about the same time the family moved to Ontario and produced foundation stock for several new Ontario breeders.

TERRY MCNAMEE
Rosewood Kennel

Terry McNamee was living in Manitoba when she bought her first Toller from Rena Cap in 1976, Ch. Jalna's Eager Boots CDX TT, who was No. 1 Obedience Toller in 1981-82. Boots's first litter belonged to Rena and was whelped in Manitoba, but in 1984, Terry bred Boots to Gus and the resulting litter was the foundation for Rosewood Kennel. It included Ch. Rosewood Air Marshall WC CDX TT (Rory), Group placer, Ch. Rosewood Admiral of Liscot CDX TT FbDCh. (Ditto), and Ch. Rosewood's Allie McGuire, whose name appears in several Scandinavian pedigrees.

Ch. Jalna's Eager Boots CDX TT, Terry McNamee's foundation bitch for Rosewood Kennel. Boots was twelve when this photo was taken by Bob Berry.

Boots's son, sired by Ann Penner's Gus, Ch. Rosewood's Air Marshall WC CDX TT, photographed at nearly five years of age.

In 1989, Ditto had the honor of being the first Toller to place in the Top Ten Sporting Dogs for Obedience. Boots and Gus were the first Tollers to pass the newly devised Temperament Test (TT) in the mid-1980s, and Ditto was an early winner of the Flyball Dog (FbD) title.

PAULA AND IRVIN COLLIER
Colliers' Kennel

The Colliers entered the list of Toller breeders after they acquired an adult bitch, Ch. Duchess Nova of Foxdown, from the Jeffery Coldwell line. While Duchess was completing her championship, they bought a male from the Sprouls, Sproul's Highland Scotty, a litter brother to the first Best in Show Toller. From this beginning, they bred their first litter, which included Collier's Cabot Trail McGRR, first Toller for Kirk and Anne Norton of Illinois, who later bred under the Cabot Trail prefix.

When Duchess was killed by a snowplow, the Colliers managed to track down her brother, Foxdown's Sable Lucky, for use at stud. They also bought a female from the Nortons and a male from Jalna. Pressure of work forced the Colliers to reduce their breeding operation, but not before they had sent a bitch to Sweden, Collier's Maple Leaf Ambassador, who helped in the development of the Toller there. The Colliers have also sent breeding stock to the United States, Finland, and the United Kingdom.

LILLIAN GREENSIDES AND KAREN WRIGHT
Kylador Kennel

The mother-daughter team of Lillian Greensides and Karen Wright already had begun a Golden Retriever breeding program in the Toronto area when they began to notice Tollers that were appearing at shows in slowly growing numbers during the last half of the 1980s. After purchasing their first Toller from Westerlea, Lillian and Karen were busy members of the host Toller group at the 1988 CKC Centennial Toller Specialty. There they fell in love with the eventual winner, Ch. Westerlea's Bonny Bluenose, and with Ch. Sandycove at Westerlea WC CD, who earned a Group Fourth at the prestigious All-Breed Centennial Show.

In early 1989, a Sandy/Bonny puppy duly arrived to become the Toller foundation bitch for

Kylador Kennel, Ch. Westerlea Kylador's Sea Gypsy CD TT FbDCh. In 1990, Gypsy was followed by a pup from Bonny's last litter, Ch. Westerlea's Chance for Kylador CD, who went Best of Winners at the 1991 National Specialty, and whose son broke Ontario Toller records in 1994.

Karen and Lillian had the good fortune to be offered a mature male, Ch. Fancysrun Formula One (Nelson), and he finished his championship in short order.

Foundation bitch for Lillian Greensides and Karen Wright, Ch. Westerlea Kylador's Sea Gypsy CD TT.

Above, Right:
Ch. Kylador's Debonair Rob Roy, first back-to-back Best Puppy in Show with proud breeder Lillian Greensides. Photo by Alex Smith.

Left:
Gypsy's partner in several Kylador litters, Ch. Fancysrun Formula One TT (Nelson), a Rebel son.

The biggest Kylador winner to date is a Nelson/Gypsy grandson, BISS Ch. Kylador's Debonair Rob Roy, owned by Donna Houlton of Ottawa. In 1994, Robbie entered the record books by becoming the first Toller to win back-to-back Best Puppy in Show and the first Toller Best Puppy in Show in Ontario. He also earned Fourth in Group at the Pedigree Puppy of the Year Awards at the end of the year, was Top Toller for 1994 and winner of the 50th Anniversary Toller Specialty in 1995, which had the largest-ever entry.

Lillian and Karen run their dogs in flyball, train for WC tests, and compete in Obedience.

COLIN AND JACQUIE RILEY
Rideau Kennel

In 1989, Colin and Jacquie Riley rescued a Toller that had spent his first three years tethered to a heavy chain. Thanks to the Rileys's loving care and his own temperament, this dog went on to become Ch. Laird Rankin of Rideau, who earned several Group placements in his show career. Tug was No. 7 Toller in 1991, while his brother, Ch. Fancysrun Red Dragon of Rideau, finished No. 5 in 1992.

The brothers, who descend from Littleriver stock, often competed against each other in the ring. They swim and play together at the Rileys' lakeside home outside Perth in eastern Ontario. The Rileys subsequently purchased a bitch from Littleriver Kennel, and the first Rideau litter was whelped in 1990. Perhaps the most famous dog of their breeding is Bonnie Lass Chelsea of Rideau CDX, who has been a consistent high scorer in numerous Open Obedience classes, despite being stone deaf. Owners Paul and Barbara Henry have been very successful in their hand-signal training of this intelligent, responsive Toller.

QUEBEC: LA BELLE PROVINCE

SUSAN AND PAUL KISH
Foxgrove Kennel

Tollers were relatively unknown in Quebec until BIS Ch. Sandycove at Westerlea WC CD arrived from British Columbia at the Dorval home of Susan and Paul Kish late in 1989. Sandy's initial short visit has lengthened into a permanent stay,

Jacquie Riley, left, and Joan Dunster both own Ch. Fancysrun Red Dragon at Rideau CD, shown taking Best of Winners at a Quebec Booster Show.

Susan Kish introduced Sandy to real snow during his first winter in Quebec in 1990.

and he has really helped to put Tollers on the Quebec map. The year 1990 was a banner one for Sandy and Sue, when Sandy smashed point records, won an All-Breed Best in Show, and finished by gaining Group First at the Show of Shows.

Susan and Paul established their Foxgrove Kennel in Ste. Lazare with Ch. Westerlea Elias' Tidal Wave WCX CD FBDCh. (Chelsea) as their own foundation bitch. Chelsea has burned up the Field Test scene ever since she was a puppy, and she is the youngest Toller to earn all three titles in the CKC Working Certificate Program. Sue, whose training talents had previously been centered in Obedience, realized that Chelsea had tremendous field potential, so she turned to hunting-dog trainers Norm and Adrienne Bordo for help in the subsequent field successes of Chelsea and her later Tollers.

In 1993, Sue put a WC title on yet another British Columbia bitch, Ch. Tollbreton Honey for

Susan Kish puts field degrees on two dogs on the same day, Ch. Westerlea Elias' Tidal Wave WCI and Ch. Tollbreton Honey for Westerlea WC.

Residents at Wilfrid and Dianne Drouin's Bernache Kennel in Quebec: (left to right) Ch. Kylador's A Penny from Heaven, Ch. (Can. Am.) Westerlea's Cheers to Bayrevel, and baby Elverbredd's Blazing to Bernache.

Westerlea, who, bred to Sandy, gave Sue her first Toller litter. This record-breaking litter contained, at the end of 1994, a Best Puppy in Show winner that went on to earn a WCX; two WC winners; two that earned CDs in three consecutive trials; and four champions.

BERNACHE

Wilfrid and Dianne Drouin lived next door to Susan and Paul Kish in Dorval for a number of years, and their daughters Suzanne and Helene spent almost as much time there as at home. When Sandy arrived in Dorval, he created an instant fan club on the Kish's street, with the Drouins as his greatest admirers. So much did they enjoy Sandy that they decided to begin breeding Tollers themselves. Their first acquisition was Ch. Westerlea Cheers to Bayrevel, a Sandy/Bonny daughter that came from Philadelphia. Cheerio was soon joined by a puppy from Kylador that grew up to be Ch. Kylador A Penny from Heaven CD, trained and shown to her titles by Suzanne and Helene.

When the Kishs moved to Ste. Lazare in 1992, the Drouins found a house nearby and now are happily engaged in producing Tollers under their Bernache prefix. Bernache is a true family affair, as both Suzanne and Helene help train, groom, and show the dogs as well as look after puppies.

After a period of struggle to have their little red dogs taken seriously, breeders in Ontario and Quebec have created an ever-growing interest in their Tollers and compete in nearly all aspects of the dog game.

A hunting future awaits this Sagewood puppy, bred in Wisconsin by Patty and Paul Beran. Photo by Heussner.

6
The Americans Come Calling

The Hon. Vince Pottier surely aroused interest in Tollers south of the border by taking his dog Gunner to various sporting demonstrations. In fact, it is quite probable that a number of hunters bought Tollers because of Gunner. However, no lasting influence came to the United States until nearly forty years later.

In 1977, an American publication, *Dogs Magazine*, carried a lively article by Cynthia Carter about tolling dogs, in particular those at Wileen Mann's Sundrummer Kennel. Response to this article was amazing, and *Toller Talk* editor Larry Levsen was swamped with letters. One writer was Barb Charais, who already bred Golden Retrievers in Wisconsin. Barb was referred to Sproul Kennel, and in 1978, her first Toller bitch, Ch. Sproul's Kinsman's Cedar Fox (Cedar) arrived. She was a full sister to the first All-Breed Best in Show Toller, Ch. Sproul's Highland Playboy CD, and Ch. (Can. Bda.) Ch. and OTCh. Sproul's Angus Macbeth WC TT.

Late in 1978, an advertisement for Obedience trials in Nova Scotia caught the eye of Sue Van Sloun when she was perusing a dog magazine at her Massachusetts home. Sue and her husband, Neil, decided to attend these trials and found their lives changed forever. While waiting for their Labrador's turn, they were entranced by a little red dog performing an almost flawless routine. Sue was struck with the happy attitude of the dog and asked a steward the question she was to hear so often in the future: "What kind of dog is that?" The steward proudly told them that this was a real Nova Scotian dog, a Toller, and gave them Mary Sproul's address, adding that Springhill would be on their way back home.

In Springhill, Sue and Neil were surrounded by dogs just like the one they had seen in Halifax, and they were hooked. Sproul's Celtic Charm arrived the following year, the first of a number of Sproul dogs imported by Sylvan Kennel. Thus the prime movers who established the Toller in the United States, Sue Van Sloun and Barb Charais, began their saga.

Sue joined the Canadian Toller Club in 1979, and soon she and Barb Charais had a list of American Toller owners or anyone even expressing an interest. Laura Grossman, who obtained her first Toller in 1977, wrote an early response. Laura soon was actively promoting the Toller in the United States and became a major American breeder.

Meanwhile, in 1979, Mary Sproul sent two litter brothers to Joe and Jane Ryan in Missouri. The Ryans then purchased a bitch from Avery Nickerson. In December 1980, the first recorded American-born litter of Tollers arrived at the Ryans' Chalk Bluff Kennel. One male from this litter, Chalk Bluff Redwood Jack, went on to make history as the foundation stud of Sylvan Tollers.

In 1980, Sue flew out to visit Barb Charais, and the pair drove up to Canada. They visited Jim and Linda Barnes in Regina, Wileen Mann (who by then lived in Manitoba), and Rena Cap. It was on this trip that Sue and Barb first thought of starting an American Toller Club.

UNITED STATES REGISTRATIONS AND THE AMERICAN TOLLER CLUB

Major stumbling blocks to American Toller breeding were the lack of recognition of the Toller by any registering body in the United States, and Canadian Kennel Club rules requiring that puppies eligible for CKC recognition had to be whelped in Canada or be of a breed recognized by an approved kennel jurisdiction. Apart from the Ryans, early litters were whelped in Canada. The Van Slouns sent bitches to Sproul Kennel in Springhill, while Barb Charais flew Cedar to Westerlea to be bred to Tip. Cedar remained in British Columbia until her litter was old enough to travel. Barb made the long trip west to take her pick from the litter and then flew home to Wisconsin with the pup and Cedar. When that pup was bred, Dave and Barb had to pack her into a camper and drive to Canada, where the first and only Kinsman Toller litter was whelped in a parking lot. So traumatic was the experience for both dog and owners that Barb decided never to breed another Toller litter.

When Kirk and Anne Norton's foundation bitch was ready for her first breeding, the Nortons had to make a round-trip drive of 1,000 miles to have her bred in Ontario, then return to the home of Paula and Irvin Collier, also in Ontario, for the whelping. The drive home was repeated when the puppies were three days old — an uncomfortable, upsetting, and exhausting ordeal for bitch and owners. All the pups were fine, but the experience was one that the Nortons, like the Charais', had no wish to repeat.

Laura Grossman's first two Toller litters were whelped in British Columbia with help from Alison Strang and Steve Abbott. Laura vividly recalls feeding a ten-day-old litter on the plane home, to the keen interest of her fellow passengers.

When the American Toller Club was formed in 1984, these breed pioneers campaigned for the Canadian Kennel Club to accept American-born puppies of an all-Canadian breed. Much correspondence flew back and forth. Dr. Richard Meen, at that time CKC president, expressed personal interest, and, at the end of 1985, U.S. club president Sue Van Sloun and U.S. members John Hamilton and Marile Waterstraat finally sat down in Toronto with the Canadian Toller Club secretary and treasurer and CKC registrar, Mrs. Dorothy Walker, to hammer out an agreement.

CKC acceptance of American-born Tollers in 1986 depended upon the U.S. club maintaining a Stud Book that would eventually be acceptable to the American Kennel Club (AKC) as well as to the Canadian Kennel Club. American-born Tollers would first have to be registered by the NSDTR Club (U.S.A.), which the CKC proceeded to recognize as the official U.S. Registry for the Toller. Once a Toller was registered in the United States, Canadian registration could follow. This was a major step for the Toller on both sides of the border, because it widened the number of dogs available for breeding. This was an especially important point for a breed with a very small gene pool. Dogs born in one country could also compete in the other.

A distinct advantage to the Toller not having AKC recognition was the ability of the NSDTRC (U.S.A.) to form its own rules. Chief among these was the stipulation that a Toller must pass a field test before becoming a Club Champion.

The American Toller Club has grown from a handful of fanciers to a substantial membership of over 850. After several years spent going through preliminaries, full American Kennel Club (AKC) recognition of the Toller came in 2003 and the official U.S. Toller Club is known as NSDTRC(USA). As required by AKC rules, a National Specialty show is held annually, rotating around the country. The club continues to hold its own field tests, but other trials are held under AKC auspices.

In 2000 a committee was struck to draw up a Standard acceptable to the AKC. The existing CKC Standard was largely followed but there are some differences, mostly following AKC requirements. A club vote on the Standard was approved by the membership in April 2001 and was accepted by AKC upon the 2003 recognition. This Standard is found on pp.109-110.

An interesting aside here notes that AKC was the latest to recognize the Toller. The body which controls canine affairs in most of the world's countries, the Federation Cynologique Internationale (FCI) granted recognition to Tollers back in the late 1980s after a number of Tollers had been imported to Scandinavia from Canada. The venerable Kennel Club gave British Tollers import and show registrations in 2001, but it was not until 2013 that the full privileges of Challenge Certificate and champion status was granted.

NEIL AND SUE VAN SLOUN
Sylvan Kennel

Sue Van Sloun remains the chief mover and shaker on the American Toller scene. She continues to campaign the Toller in every avenue open to a rare breed in order to increase public awareness.

She bred and owned the first Tollers to acquire three championships — the Canadian, the NSDTRC (U.S.A.), and the States Kennel Club (SKC). These were won by Sylvan's Maritime Mariner (Jib) and Sylvan's Kinney Brook Swan (Ginger). Sue has attended every Canadian Specialty Show since 1983, and in 1991, Ginger took Winners Female while the daughter of another Sylvan bitch was Best Opposite Sex. In 1993, Sue had the great satisfaction of seeing her young male, Ch. Sylvan's Blaise of Thunder, awarded Best of Winners at the Edmonton Specialty to finish his Canadian championship, then go on to take two Group Thirds and a Group Fourth before going home. He was No. 3 Toller in Canada that year. Blaise capped these feats by taking Best of Breed at the third American National Specialty in 1994.

The year 1995 was a banner one for Blaise, who won no less than four Bests in Show at American Rare Breed Association shows and was seventh overall ARBA dog, coming from twenty-

Doyenne of American Tollers, Sue Van Sloun, at a NAHRA Trial where Sylvan's Tanner Brown was the first U.S. Toller to achieve a Started ribbon.

two group placements, eleven of them Firsts. He was also given an Award of Merit at the Halifax 50th Anniversary Specialty show. It is fortunate that Blaise sired several litters before meeting with a fatal accident early in 1996, just prior to beginning field training.

Before the advent of Blaise, Sue was proudest of Sylvan's Tanner Brown, Am. Can. CD, WC, the first Toller to receive a North American Hunting Retriever Association (NAHRA) Started Certificate and also the NAHRA Brass Band, awarded to a dog that successfully completes four Started tests in one year. Tanner, who is Neil's favorite hunting dog, is also the first American-born Toller to go High in Trial at a Canadian Obedience trial.

Sue Van Sloun, doyenne of the American Toller, has carved out an unforgettable niche for herself in the annals of the breed.

LAURA GROSSMAN WHITE
Cinnstar Kennel

Laura Grossman White first saw Tollers in 1976 while competing in Obedience trials in Canada with her Shelties. Laura came up to British Columbia again the following summer and this time ran into Alison and Catriona Strang, who were showing Shelley and one of her puppies. Laura ordered a male from Shelley's next litter that was sired by Ch. Crusader of Jeffery Coldwell CD. Her puppy, Ch. Westerlea's Cinnstar Eric, won a Puppy Group in Alberta. He was proving a very promising field dog when a foxtail seed that he had inhaled lodged in his lungs and began the infection that killed him.

In 1980, Laura got a bitch puppy from the first Tip/Lucy litter (Tip was Eric's litter brother) that went on to fame as Can. Mex. Ch. Westerlea's Cinnamon Teal, Can. Mex. CD, Am. WC. Teal was Winners Bitch at the second Canadian

Above:
Sylvan's Blaise of Thunder completes his Canadian Championship in style at the 1993 Edmonton Toller Specialty, bred and owned by the Van Slouns and handled by Maureen Kershaw. Photo by Mikron.

Right:
John Hamilton and Ch. (Can. Am.) OTCh. Sylvan's Rusty Jones Can. Am. WC, Can. CD TT, needs almost a full page to list all his titles. Rusty was the first to win a rare breed show and was the first U.S.-born Toller to gain a Canadian championship.
Photo by Stonham Studio.

Left:
"Ian," Can. Mex. Ch. Cinnstar's Ian of Little River, Can. Mex. CD, CACIB, U.S. WC. Owned, bred, and trained by Cinnstar Litle Rivers Laura Grossman.
Courtesy Laura Grossman.

Below:
Litter of Tollers from the Cinnstar Little Rivers Kennel, Laura Grossman.
Courtesy Laura Grossman.

National Specialty Show in 1983 and became foundation bitch for Laura's Cinnstar Little River Tollers. She was also the first Mexican Toller champion and CD winner.

In 1986, Laura flew to Doug Coldwell's Little River Kennel in Nova Scotia to breed Teal to Solidaire of Jeffery Coldwell CD. The resulting litter included the dog that eventually became the first Toller ever to gain points toward a Field Trial championship in North America. Ch. (Can. Mex.) Cinnstar's Ian of Little River, Can. Mex. CD, Am. WC, made history in 1989 by placing second in Open at the Alberta Field Trial Club Trial, with Laura, who had trained Ian almost entirely herself, handling. Ian later took a Fourth Place in another Alberta trial before retiring from trials in 1992.

Laura, who was president of the American Toller Club from 1989 to 1992, always has emphasized working ability in her breeding program, whether for Field or Obedience. The number of Cinnstar Tollers happily working attests to Laura's success. After some three years' absence from the Toller scene, Laura is once more back in harness, working and breeding her dogs in Texas.

JOHN HAMILTON AND MARILE WATERSTRAAT
Lennoxlove Kennel

John Hamilton and Marile Waterstraat, who live near Rochester, New York, first came across Tollers when Marile, a school librarian, happened upon Kurt Unkelbach's *The American Dog Book*. On the cover were four beautiful, sturdy little dogs standing on a rock above a swirling sea. These were none other than dogs from the Jeffery Coldwell Kennel. Marile's reaction was typical: "*A what?*" but she instinctively felt that this would be the hunting dog for which John had been searching.

John and Marile began to read the advertisements in every dog magazine they could find and eventually saw one for Sylvan Kennel. From here it was but a short step to the arrival of a dog that would go on to make breed history in the United States and eventually bear the title Ch. (Can. Am.) Can OTCh. Sylvan's Rusty Jones Can. WCX Am. WC, CD, TT. From that day, John and Marile, along with Sue Van Sloun, have been the linchpins of the American Toller group.

Rusty, a record-breaker every step of the way, was sired by Chalk Bluff's Redwood Jack and hence was ineligible to compete in Canada until 1986. The little guy with the jaunty air has a whole string of American firsts to his credit — first Toller to win a Rare Breed show, a feat that he managed twice; one of the first to gain Started Dog status with NAHRA; and first U.S.-born Toller to finish a Canadian championship. He also gained a Canadian Obedience Trial Championship and a WCX.

Rusty won his Rare Breed Best in Show before the NSDTRC (U.S.A.) put its awards programs in place, so in 1995 the club voted to grant Rusty his American championship, as he had fulfilled all requirements. Such a gesture toward a great old dog reflects the pride that all American Toller owners feel in Rusty's accomplishments.

Hunting was always Rusty's first love, and he and John have completed the NAHRA Intermediate level. His field ability has been passed on in good measure to his son, BISS Ch. (Am. Can.) Bhalgair of Lennoxlove Can. WCI CDX, Am. WC

John Hamilton and Lennoxlove foundation bitch, Ch. (Can. Am.) Colony's Lennoxlove Victoria, Am. WC CD, Can. WC CD TT, wait for the gun at a WC trial.

CD. Val has his own strong ideas as to how things should be done. "Every gray hair I have has been put there by Val," Marile once lamented. Val relented long enough to achieve several field titles, then allowed Marile to steer him to Best in Show at the first NSDTRC (U.S.A.) Specialty Show in 1989.

In 1989, John and Marile purchased the bitch that was to become their foundation, Ch. (Can. Am.) Colony's Lennoxlove Victoria, Can. Am. WC CD TT. Vicky was kept busy accumulating titles and working in the field but finally whelped the first Lennoxlove litter in 1993. One of the pups grew up to become Ch. (Am. ARBA) Lennoxlove's Jasper Jones Esq. Am. WC CD Can. WCI CD, who continued the family tradition by winning a Rare Breed Best in Show early in 1995. He also went Best of Winners at the 50th Anniversary Canadian Specialty.

Marile became U.S. club president in 1992, while John served as treasurer from the club's beginning until 1992. Tireless and selfless work for the Toller is the mark of this indefatigable couple.

KIRK AND ANNE NORTON
Cabot Trail Kennel

Kirk and Anne Norton honeymooned in Nova Scotia and were enamored of all things Nova Scotian. Therefore, when they saw a tiny notice in *Dog World Magazine* for the Toller, they set about tracking one down. They found, as so many have since, that buying a Toller puppy entailed much searching and long waits.

In 1980, the Toller grapevine brought the Nortons to the notice of Paula and Irvin Collier in Ontario, who had recently whelped their first Toller litter. Because the Nortons had always obtained their previous dogs from family friends, they were somewhat surprised by the quizzing they received from Paula, and Anne wondered if she was adopting a baby rather than a dog. Marveling that a breeder could be so conscientious and caring, the Nortons adopted the same methods when they became breeders.

Collier's Cabot Trail McGrr cemented the Nortons' love of Tollers, and they set about acquiring a bitch, Ch. Westerlea's Cabot MacKenzie CD, foundation for their Cabot Trail Kennel. MacKenzie's first breeding, in 1985, was to BIS Ch. Westerlea's Tru Ray Red Rebel WC CDX TT, with pups going to form foundations for several kennels in Ontario and the United States. The male kept by the Nortons, Ch. Cabot Trail's Laird McEwan CD, blind-retrieved four mallards from dense swamp during the very first hunt of his puppyhood. MacKenzie was listed as the top-producing dam of Canadian champions for 1988, the first U.S.-owned Toller to earn this honor.

Anne and Kirk Norton were active members of both the Canadian and American Toller clubs, with Anne serving for several years as editor, of *Quackers*, the NSDTRC (U.S.A.) newsletter. Kirk developed a revision to the Canadian Club constitution that was adopted in the mid-1980s and provided invaluable assistance to a new constitutional committee set up in 1992.

Dog breeding operations at Cabot Trail came to an end with the tragic death of Kirk Norton in 1993, but Anne still retains her love of Tollers.

PAUL AND PATTY BERAN
Sagewood Kennel

Paul and Patty Beran pursued Tollers when they could not find a sound Golden Retriever that would do all they wanted. They waited almost a year before being able to get a Toller from the kennel of their choice but found the wait worthwhile when Ch. Westerlea's Audacious Wave Am. CDX Can. CD (Lacey) immediately stole their hearts. Lacey's first litter, sired by Ch. OTCh. Westerlea's Mountain Echo WCI, made a notable Toller first when it was featured in a stunning photograph on the cover of the April-May 1991 issue of *Gun Dog Magazine*. This litter included the winner of the 1992 U.S. Specialty, Ch. Sagewood's Silver Shadow, as well as High Scoring Toller in Obedience at the 1991 Canadian Specialty, Ch. Sagewood's Lonetree Auburn WCI CD.

In 1989, Sagewood Kennel welcomed a Sandy/Bonny son — Ch. (Am. Can. SKC ARBA) Westerlea's Sagewood Admiral CD. Cody appeared in a spectacular color photo on the front of the United Kennel Club (UKC) publication *Bloodlines* when that magazine featured the Toller in a full-length article. Cody also won fame by going Best in Show at the American Rare Breed Association Windy City Classic, probably the country's most prestigious show for non-AKC breeds, in 1992.

The advent of young Jeffery Beran in 1993 widened the Berans' horizons beyond dog breeding, but Sagewood will surely remain a respected name in American Toller circles for a long time to come.

*Left:
Westerlea's Audacious Wave, "Lacy," as a pup. Courtesy Paul and Patty Beran, Sagewood Kennel*

*Below:
Am. Can. Ch. Westerlea's Sagewood Admiral, owned by Patty Beran; breeder, Alison Strang, Westerlea Kennel. Photo by Paul Beran.*

Ch. Westerlea's Sagewood Admiral CD, TDI "Cody," and Can. SKC Ch. Westerlea's Audacious Wave SKC Can. CDX, NSDTR (USA) BRT "Lacy."

A litter of Sagewood Kennel NSDTR pups. Courtesy Paul and Patty Beran, Sagewood Kennel. Photo by Bob Heusner.

GRETCHEN AND GEORGE BOTNER
Tradewinds Kennel

The Botners' introduction to Tollers came during a long search for a replacement for the family Keeshond when they saw a tiny advertisement in *Dog World Magazine*. Little did they realize how much a phone call to Sylvan Kennel would change their lives. Their first Toller, Sylvan's Keesha, arrived at their Florida home in 1985 and was followed by a bitch — Cinnstar's Carolina Wren (Roxie) — from Laura Grossman's California kennel. Roxie was foundation for the Botner's Tradewinds Kennel. Her litter, sired by BIS Ch. Sandycove at Westerlea WC CD, was whelped late in 1988 and contained two bitches that already have left their mark on the breed in the United States. One is their own Ch. (Am. SKC) Tradewinds Saltwater Taffy CDX. The other is OTCh. (Can. Am.) Tradewinds Dusty Jamoca CDX Am. UD, who, as foundation bitch for Nelson and Evelyn Williams' Lonetree Kennel, already has produced several fine dogs, including the winner of the 1993 Canadian National Specialty.

Gretchen Botner's greatest contribution has been in the area of Toller promotion in the United States, where she has worked tirelessly for many years. She was thrilled to have an article on Tollers published in *Dog World Magazine*, accompanied by a color cover of the Canada Post Toller stamp.

Gretchen Botner will do anything to promote Tollers and also have fun! Gretchen dressed Tradewinds Ain't Misbehavin' in suitable costume for the Halloween Toller meeting in Denver in 1993.

Life off the west coast of Florida gives Gretchen Botner's Tollers plenty of access to water, even if it is warmer than the Bay of Fundy. Tradewinds Kennel foundation bitch, Cinnstar's Carolina Wren, is at left; her daughter, Am. Ch. Tradewinds Saltwater Taffy Am. CD is at right.

NELSON AND EVELYN WILLIAMS
Lonetree Kennel

Nelson and Evelyn Williams are setting a fine example for "newer" American Toller breeders to follow, because they stress Toller versatility. Evelyn read an article about Tollers in 1976, but twelve years elapsed before she remembered the breed when the family was ready for a new dog. Fortunately, Gretchen Botner had a puppy for sale from her first Tradewinds litter, and Dusty duly arrived at the Williams's Iowa home. She was soon followed by Abby.

These bitches went on to become OTCh. Tradewinds Dusty Jamoca Am. UD — the first Toller to hold Utility titles in both the United States and Canada — and Ch. (Am. Can.) Sagewood's Lonetree Auburn WCI CD. Abby, who is proving to be an excellent field dog, passed a difficult NAHRA Started Test at eleven months of age. She is only the third Toller to pass the United Kennel Club Hunting Retriever Club (HRC) Seasoned Test, a feat that she accomplished in 1993.

Dusty, High Scoring Toller in Obedience at both the 1991 Canadian and the 1993 American Toller specialties, is the dam of BISS Ch. (Am. Can.) Lonetree"s Barnstorm'n Jake, Am. WC CD Can WCI CDX. Sired by Ch. Harbourlights Rip Tide, Jake has been making waves ever since he was brought out to shows and field tests as a youngster. He was the youngest dog to pass the American Toller Club Natural Instinct Test (now called the BRT or Basic Retrieving and Tolling Test), when he was only eight months old, and was also awarded Best Puppy in Show at a States Kennel Club (SKC) All-Breed show when he was eleven months old. Jake passed all three HRC Started Tests in which he was entered between twelve and sixteen months.

Jake's biggest achievement came at his fabulous weekend in Edmonton, Alberta, in September 1993 — the weekend of the sixth Canadian National Specialty. By the time it was finished, Jake had been acclaimed winner of the Specialty, earned All-Breed High in Trial at the Edmonton Kennel Club Obedience Trials the same day, and was the only Toller to pass the WC Test the following morning. Jake's feat was the talk of the Toller world.

Evelyn Williams of Michigan hit the jackpot with her first Lonetree litter, as it contained Ch. (Can. Am.) Lonetree's Barnstorm'N Jake WC CD, a big winner in several disciplines on both sides of the border. Photo by Alex Smith.

SUE DORSCHEID AND MIKE ELMERGREEN
Springvale Kennel

Many fanciers spend years trying to either purchase or breed an outstanding dog, one that will leave a mark on its breed. Some of these people might think it unfair for a rescued dog, the proverbial ugly duckling, to turn into a swan. Good deeds, however, *do* bring their rewards. Sue and Mike had their compassion more than amply rewarded when the dog that they rescued from an uncaring home turned out to be a dog that would win a Best in Rare Breed Show, earn his American Championship, be a fine sire, and, above all, prove to be a loving and faithful companion and tireless hunter. Such is Ch. (Am. Can. SKC) Harbourlights Rip Tide Am. CDX WC. He was bought by Sue and Mike from his original owners, who purchased the dog from Harbourlights Kennel, and went on to become foundation sire for their Springvale Kennel.

Rip has sired several litters, many of which are outstanding for their field abilities. One, the Williams's Jake, was the most notable Toller for 1993 in both the United States and Canada. Jake came from Rip's first litter, and when news spread of how pleased the Williams were with their puppies, Carol and Burt Elias in Arizona decided to send their Ch. Westerlea's Sprig of Holly to Rip. One of the resulting puppies was Ch. Westerlea Elias' Tidal Wave WCX CD FbDCh. Chelsea has more than upheld Toller honor in the field with owner-trainer Susan Kish of Quebec.

Lady Luck struck again when Sue and Mike purchased a bitch puppy from the Berans' first litter. This was BISS Ch. (Am. Can. SKC) Sagewood's Silver Shadow Am. WC CD. Not only was she Mike's favorite hunting partner, but she also won the second U.S. National Specialty in 1992. The first Springvale litter was born at the couple's Wisconsin kennel in 1993.

LEE ANN AND JOE GLEASON
Cayuga Kennel

The Gleasons, who farm in upper New York State, have strong ties with Paula and Irvin Collier in Ontario, from whom they obtained all foundation stock for Cayuga Kennel. Their foundation bitch, Collier's Magnum Load Dory, has produced a number of winners, including Cayuga's Lashbrook P.C., who has had several Group Firsts at U.S. Rare Breed shows, and Cayuga's Lashbrook Mia Jewel, Best in Show Puppy at two shows where P.C. topped the Group. Lee Ann also piloted her homebred Cayuga's Hanford Way, then owned by Paul Marx, to Best Opposite Sex, Winner's Dog, and Best in Sweepstakes at the 1992 U.S. Toller Specialty Show. Dewey is now an ARBA Champion.

*A Tradewinds Kennel litter, age seven and one-half weeks.
Courtesy Gretchen Botner.*

*A sixteen-week-old puppy retrieving with enthusiasm. "Bid,"
now AKC CH Vermilion's Bold Bid at Bodanna JH WC, owned by Max Hamilton
and bred by Kathy Koebensky-Como and Jamie Como.*

7

Back To Europe

DENMARK

In the early 1980s, Nete Wunsch, whose Tueholt Kennel in Denmark has produced internationally winning Dachshunds for more than twenty-five years, came upon an article about Tollers. Intrigued, Nete enlisted the help of Flat-Coated Retriever breeder Finn Lange to try to find out more about the breed. Their chance came when the late Ed Dixon, noted Canadian judge and long-standing CKC board member, judged in Denmark in 1981.

Nete and Finn set up a meeting with Ed, who had long been a supporter of Tollers. Ed answered myriad questions and also provided Nete and Finn with the then slim list of Canadian breeders. Nete and Finn sent out letters, including one to Alison Strang. In the summer of 1982, two bitch puppies made the long flight from Vancouver to Copenhagen, and thus began a trickle of Scandinavian imports that has since swelled to quite a flow.

The puppies, sired by BIS Ch. Westerlea's White Ensign ex Jalna's Quillo Quest, were DKCh. Westerlea's Red Tilly and Westerlea's Lucky Toller. An article by Nete, with full-color photographs of the pups, soon appeared in *Hunden*, the Dansk Kennel Klub (DKK) magazine, and a translation was reproduced in the Swedish counterpart, *Hundsport*. Soon, Nete found herself besieged with calls and letters from all over Scandinavia.

Tilly became foundation bitch for Nete's Tueholt Tollers. Meanwhile, Westerlea sent a brother and sister in early 1983 that became DKCh. Westerlea's Brass Toller and DKCh. Westerlea's Red Shona, littermates to Ch. Westerlea's Bonny Bluenose. Shona became the first Toller ever to place in the Gundog Group in Europe. Lucky was bred to Brass, and two of the resulting pups were the first Tollers to go to Sweden.

Brass and Tilly's first puppies arrived in October 1984. This landmark litter, the first to be whelped in Europe, was soon given a boost by the importation of Sproul stock to augment the gene pool. Things progressed when the Federation Cynologique Internationale (FCI), which governs purebred dog activities in more than fifty countries, recognized Tollers in 1982, enabling them to be shown in any FCI country.

Nete's next big excitement came with the first championships for homebred Danish dogs, brothers from that first litter, DKCh. Tueholt Red What A Surprise (Spookie) and DKCh. Tueholt Red Wish Come True. World Shows are held annually in Europe, with Best Dog and Best Bitch winners entitled to call themselves World Winners. The first two such Tollers were Brass

The first Harbourlights Tollers to go to Europe about to embark on their long flight, with new owners Ewa Jonsson, left, and Megg Brautigam at Toronto airport. Harbourlights Perky Peppy is with Ewa, and Harbourlights Laddie Buck is with Megg. Photo by Terry McNamee.

Ch. Westerlea's Coast To Coast CD, the last son of Ch. Danny Boy of Harbourlights, went to Nete Wunsch in Denmark in 1985 and became an influential sire there, as he has also been in Canada.

DKCh. Westerlea's Red Shona, one of Nete Wunsch's early champions, first Toller to take a Gundog Group placing in Europe, in 1984.

An historic win, first Toller to win an FCI Gundog Group, was made by DKCh. Tueholt Red What A Surprise for breeder/owner Nete Wunsch in 1986.

and Tilly in 1985, but there have been quite a few more since those early days. One is Spookie, who made more history when, in 1986, he received the first FCI Gundog Group First ever awarded to a Toller.

In 1985, Ch. Westerlea's Coast To Coast CD (Coaster) was sent to Nete, originally for one year. Coaster, however, was so happy in his new Danish home that it was decided to leave him there and keep his son Sandy at Westerlea. Despite an accident that made him unfit to show, Coaster sired a number of litters for Denmark and Finland, as well as for Canada.

Tollers at home at Kurt and Ann-Marie Henriksen's Shaggy Toller's Kennel in Herning, Denmark. Left to right, they are Ardunacres Diplomat, Zeiban's Number One Flyer, Shaggy Toller's Ayla-L-Ayla, and Bright Flower's Chief.

Nete's second Toller litter, whelped in March 1985, included a bitch, DKCh. Tueholt Red Bright Flower (Wicky), who became the foundation for Frede and Jonna Hansen's Bright Flowers Kennel, which now has exported dogs to Holland, Austria, and Finland. Bred to Coaster, Wicky produced DKCh. Bright Flowers Ambassadeur, a World Winner in Dortmund in 1991. That same year, the Hansens arranged to buy a bred bitch, Ardunacres Toll Free, from the MacDonalds' kennel in Canada, stipulating that she be bred to the Top Winning Toller of 1991, BIS BISS Ch. Westerlea's Ilo at the Well CD. A male from this litter remains at Bright Flowers, and another has ably carried the Toller banner in Holland. Bright Flowers also had previously imported a MacDonald male, Ch. Ardunacres Fantastic (Tucker), an influential sire in Denmark and Finland.

Kurt and Ann-Marie Henriksen were introduced to Tollers by the Hansens, from whom they purchased their first Toller, DKCh. Bright Flowers Chief. They then imported another Ardunacres bitch, Ardunacres Diplomat, in 1991. In 1993, the first litter was born at their Shaggy Toller Kennel from Diplomat and a son of Red Bright Flower. Kurt started a newsletter for the young Danish Toller Club, which he helped to form.

Danish Toller fanciers now have their own Tolling test, largely drawn up by one of the two original importers of Tollers, Finn Lange in co-operation with those who run field tests. Numbers have grown more slowly in this historic land but the club is very active in shows, obedience and now field, and quite often hold their own club shows.

SWEDEN

Tollers first arrived from Denmark in 1984 after Nete Wunsch's *Hundsport* article aroused so much interest. Ingegerd Nordstrom and Tore Olsson brought in two Brass/Lucky sisters and named them Fraisy and Flyingtoller. They took their kennel name from the latter. While these two bitches sat out the four-month quarantine required in Sweden, Birgit and Folke Fantenberg imported the first bitch to come from Canada, Ardunacres Sandy Wonderful, who was also the first registered Swedish Toller.

Three Jalna imports were next to arrive — Jalna's Gentle Giant, a male, and two bitches, Jalna's Quips 'N Quotes and Jalna's Onolee Over the Ocean, all bought by Flyingtollers Kennel.

*Left:
SUCH Riverduck of Drögsta (Leif), Ewa and Anders Jonsson's great all-around champion, whose get are having a tremendous influence on the Swedish Toller.*

Below: Midsummer's Eve is a great festival in Sweden, and even the dogs get dressed up! Here is Larl-Be Spirit of Ardunacres in her festive finery.

These were quickly followed by two bitches, Ardunacres Maple Leaf and Larl-Be-Spirit of Ardunacres, purchased in 1984 by Gunhild Kjellberg of Candlelight Kennel. At the same time, Ulla Hagglund of Birdcherry Kennel imported Jalna's Oneka the One 'N Only, a full sister to Onolee Over the Ocean. Within one year, the Swedish Toller population had risen to nine, and more were to follow.

Kjell Berghed was on a fish-buying trip for his import/export company to Canada's west coast in 1985, carrying instructions from his wife, Lena, to see if he could find any of the new Canadian dogs that she had heard about. Kjell had the names of several West Coast breeders, but only one was home when he telephoned. Duncan MacDonald took Kjell's call and excitedly told Arline that a gentleman from Sweden was coming the next day to see their dogs. It just happened that the MacDonalds had recently taken back a male, Ch. Ardunacres Call Me Ugly (Prince), from their first litter and were happy to let him go to Sweden. The deal also included a young male and a bitch puppy, Larl-Be Finis Renard and Ardunacres Chimo. When Kjell

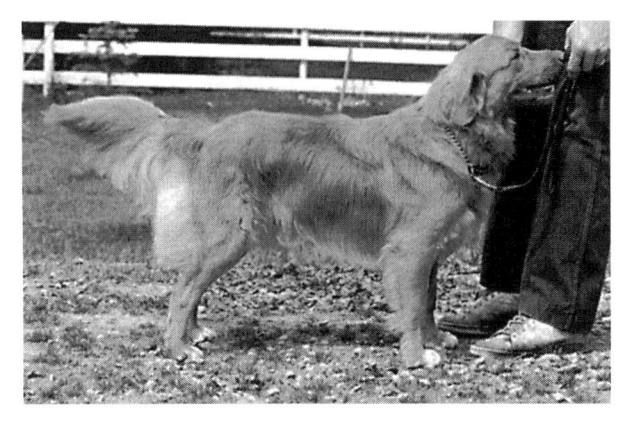

Above: Ch. Ardunacres Call Me Ugly, one of Kjell Berghed's three dogs, has exerted an influence on the Toller in Sweden.

Left: Ardunacres Maple Leaf was one of the first Tollers to be sent from Canada to Sweden and has been a fine brood bitch for Gunhild Kjellberg's Candlelight Kennel.

A Leif daughter, LP Benili's Hekla (Candy), won the 1993 Swedish Toller Specialty for owner Lena Toftling and also placed in the field trials.

Four dogs that have all won high merits in both shows and field trials line up for the camera. They are, left to right, Rävtässens Micmac, SUCH Riverduck of Drögsta, SUCH Drögstas Cat-Ri-Ona, and Drögstas Rödräv, a Leif-MicMac daughter.

Drögstas Papageno brings in a large seagull, a bird that is often used at Swedish trials. Mascot is a big winner in trials and shows for owner Gillis Gustafsson.

returned to Sweden from his trip, an article in a trade newspaper appeared with the headline "100,000 Salmon and Three Dogs." Prince has since sired a number of litters and won Best in Show Stud Dog at a large Swedish show in 1991. Kjell and Lena are still happily breeding Tollers at their beautiful Kanadickens Kennel in southwestern Sweden.

The next figure in the Swedish Toller story is the late Ewa Jonsson, who has exerted by far the greatest impact on Swedish breeding. Ewa, with her husband Anders, was already well known for the field-trial line of Labradors developed at Drogsta Kennel. In 1986, Gunhild Kjellberg arranged to lease a male bred by Ann Penner in Ontario, Ch. Liscot's Turn the Page WC, whose sire was BIS Ch. Westerlea's Tru Ray Red Rebel WC CDX TT, and dam Liscot's Crown Jewel. Page was sent to Drogsta for field training and became the first Toller to place in Swedish Field Trial Open Stakes, a feat that he accomplished in 1987. He also sired several litters before being diagnosed as having progressive retinal atrophy (PRA), an inherited eye disease. He returned to Canada with the Jonssons when they came to the 1988 Centennial Specialty in Toronto, but so close was the bond formed between Page and Ewa that, when Page died, his ashes were sent to the Jonsson farm at Kolmarden for burial.

The Jonsson visit to Canada was crucial to the future of Swedish Tollers, because Anders and Ewa also traveled to Avery Nickerson's Harbourlights Kennel. Once Avery had satisfied himself that his visitors were real hunters, the sky was the limit. After negotiations were completed to purchase an adult male and female, Harbourlights Laddie Buck and Harbourlights Perky Peppy, Ewa was told by Avery to make her own choice for a breeding from which they would receive the pick male. Ewa, with her experienced breeder/hunter eye, selected Harbourlights Scotia Boy and Harbourlights Foxy Amber, and, in 1989, the result bounded out of quarantine to take the Swedish Toller world by the tail and give it a vigorous shake.

The Jonssons suspected that they had a fine-looking hunting demon on their hands, and SUCH (Swedish champion) Riverduck of Drogsta (Leif) proved them correct, becoming the first Toller to achieve a full Swedish Championship. To achieve this, a dog has to place first or second in Open Class in two official Svenska Kennelklubben (SKK) Retriever Field Trials as well as be awarded a CACIB (this is the International Show equivalent of a Challenge Certificate upon which FCI championships are built). Leif, with two CACIBs, was also the winner of the annual Swedish Toller Club Specialty Show in 1992 and Best Opposite Sex in 1993 to his own daughter, LP (an Obedience Degree) Benili's Hekla, who has since passed an Open Field Test.

Swedish field tests require a dog to retrieve birds from water and to track and retrieve birds and rabbits that have been planted in dense cover. The dog is also tested on marked retrieves.

Harbourlights Nifty Nicky accompanied Leif on the trip to Sweden, and the four dogs sent by Avery Nickerson have had a far-reaching effect on the Toller in Sweden. The other full Swedish champions to date, all owner-trained, are Leif daughter SUCH Drogstas Cat-Ri-Ona, owned by Aji Franzen; and Laddie Buck sons SUCH Drogstas Papageno (Gillis Gustafsson), SUCH River Ducks Edward (Mona Lignell), and SUCH INTUCH NORDUCH LP Birdcherrys Autumn Clear Air (Eva Boman). Dennis not only has an impressive string of titles, Swedish, International, and Norwegian Champion, but also was winner of the 1995 Swedish Toller Specialty.

Toller owners are also showing considerable interest in Obedience. Winner of the Obedience Trial at the 1993 Toller Specialty was Simonstorp's Blissful Bonny, a Leif daughter out of a bitch sent from Rosewood Kennel in Ontario to Lena Berglund. This same bitch, owned and trained by Fredrik Ahs, was Best of Breed at Sweden's largest show the following December.

The NSDTR Klubben of Sweden was formed in 1986, with Ewa and Anders Jonsson in the forefront of the organization, along with Sanna Astrom, Gunhild Kjellberg, and Lena Berghed, to name but a few. In compliance with SKK rules, the club set up a Breeding Advisory, consisting of Ewa Jonsson and Toller breeder/veterinarian Megg Brautigam, to assist members with planning breedings.

Dog breeders in Sweden are strictly controlled by the SKK, which requires all veterinarians to send copies of health checks direct to SKK. Here the results are tabulated, published in special biannual *Stud Book* supplements, and incorporated into official pedigrees. The farsighted SKK refuses to register puppies from parents that are not cleared for certain conditions like hip dysplasia and PRA.

The Swedish Toller Club set about fund raising and even successfully tapped the Canadian Consulate in Stockholm for funds. The Swedish club took the first steps towards official tolling tests, sanctioned through the Swedish Spaniel & Retriever Club – first held in the early years of the millennium. These are enormously popular and now draw large entries. The tests consist of a tolling section, followed by water work and ending with the free search of birds and game in forested areas. These tests are now being held in Denmark, Germany and Finland.

FINLAND

Growth of the Toller in Finland has also been explosive since 1985, when the first dogs, Jalna's National Newswoman and Jalna's No No Nanette, journeyed from Rena Cap's Jalna Kennel to Tea Janhonen's Golden Fox Kennel on the little island of Emsalo, southeast of Helsinki. These litter sisters were joined the following year by a male from Nete Wunsch's kennel in Denmark. Tueholt Red Buffalo Bill has been the most influential stud in Finland, and many of the country's big winners are his descendants. The same year saw other imports arriving: Flyingtollers Linda from Sweden to Birgitta Kajander (Nordwart Kennel), and Cinnstar Zeiban's Ruffed Grouse (Ruffy) from Laura Grossman in California to the late Jari Maki's Zeiban Kennel. This latter bitch has put a remarkable stamp on

One of Tea Janhonen's many winners, Golden-Fox Pamina, is owned by Britt-Marie Sundquist. This photo illustrates the Toller in Finnish Retriever Club promotion. Photo by Mirja Tuominen.

Tytti, Bertta & Jigi, three Tollers in Finland, demonstrate the intense focus so characterisic of the breed.

Cinnstar's Zeiban's Ruffed Grouse was the biggest-winning Toller bitch in Finland and is one of the top brood bitches there. Ruffy was owned by Jari Maki and was bred by Laura Grossman in the United States.

the Zeiban Tollers. No other kennel anywhere produces such uniform dogs, many of which bear a close resemblance to Ruffy, regardless of the stud.

Tea Janhonen also has the distinction of having bred the first litter of Finnish Tollers, which arrived in May 1986. The following year, two litters, totalling sixteen puppies, were born. In 1988, the floodgates began to open, with four litters and twenty-four pups registered.

The year 1990 proved to be the year of Canadian imports, with nine Tollers coming from the breed's homeland, four from Sweden, and two from Denmark. In 1991, there were no fewer than 193 new registrations, and total registrations at the end of 1994 numbered well over 700.

The Finnish Toller Club, or Novascotiannoutajat, founded in 1990, now has more than 400 members and publishes its own quarterly news bulletin. The Finnish Kennel Club (Suomen Kennellitto or SK), like that of Sweden, requires parents of a litter to clear for hips and eyes before puppies can be registered. More than 300 Finnish Tollers have been X-rayed, with roughly three-quarters clearing. About the same number have been checked for eyes, but the failure rate is lower.

One of Finland's major winners, Golden-Fox Jamboree, who also placed in field trials. Bred by Tea Janhonen, he is owned and handled by Minna Jatkola.

Nordwart Gos is one of the big-producing sires bred by Birgitta Kajander. Photo by Mirja Tuominen.

Tollers have been a hit on the show scene in Finland, but fewer have passed Hunting Tests. This situation undoubtedly will be rectified as Toller owners become more knowledgeable about retriever training. SK Hunting Tests call for a dog to retrieve birds from the water, and birds and rabbits on land. Dogs are also checked for their social behavior toward people and other dogs and must not demonstrate any gun-shyness. A dog must pass a Field Test and obtain three Challenge Certificates in the Conformation ring before he can become a full Champion. The present full SK Champions, seven dogs and six bitches, and their owners are:

Fin. & Int. Ch. Golden-Fox Jamboree
    Minna Jatkola
Fin. Ch. Damiikan Bailador
    Arto Tiainen
Fin. Ch. Damiikan Blessed
    Kati Jaaskelainen
Fin. Can. Ch. Nordwart Cajun
    Sanna/Eila Rantanen
Fin. Ch. Nordwart Kassandros
    Hanna Laasenen
Fin. Ch. Openbays Bariton
    Arto Kylmala
Fin. Ch. Westerlea's Kitimat Mox
    Mirja Tuominen
Fin. Ch. Flyingtollers Lucky Queen
    Janina Sommarlund
Fin. Ch. Nordwart Fama
    Mika Lehto
Fin. Ch. Nordwart Goggie
    Taija Hepojarvi
Fin. Ch. Nordwart Kleio
    Taija Hepojarvi
Fin. Ch. Openbays Fallon
    Taija Helpjarvi/Pia Tasa
Fin. Ch. Openbays Gilly Flower
    Taija Hepojarvi

Obedience enthusiasm is high among Finnish Toller fanciers, while litter brothers Totemin Paroni and Totemin Ponzo work for Finnish customs as drug-detecting dogs. Tracking is another growing activity.

One of the biggest show winners in Finland for several years was Golden-Fox Jamboree, a dog that also passed a Working Test. It is obvious that the dual Toller is certainly to be found in Finland. As the Toller Club sponsors training classes for Field, Obedience, and Show, the numbers of versatile Tollers are bound to increase.

NORWAY

The Toller in Norway is developing along the same lines as in Denmark, with slowly growing numbers and, to this date, only a few breeders. The first Toller to come to Norway, NUCH Flyingtoller Boomer, was sent to Magnor Rasmussen in 1986 from Sweden. Boomer was soon followed by Norway's biggest-winning Toller to date, NUCH (Norwegian Champion) NVCH (Tracking Title) Candlelights Fisherman at Fraser, with more than twenty-five CACIBs from Norway and Sweden for owner Helge Solberg. He was also Best Opposite Sex at the large 1994 Swedish Toller Specialty.

It was not until 1989 that another breeding line was introduced by Helge Solberg with the advent of NUCH NVCH Ravtassens Tonkawa from Sweden. Parents Harbourlights Laddie Buck and Harbourlights Perky Peppy were in Swedish quarantine when the litter was born.

Norway and Sweden both impose quarantines so that dogs can pass freely from one country to the other. Two dogs have come from the United Kingdom, also a quarantine country — Lyonhouse Ewan Stuart and Winfren Vulpecula Rex. Ewan went to Unni Solberg of Sunlit Kennel, who also owns several bitches imported from Flyingtollers, while Rex is with Magnor Rasmussen.

The first Toller to win a Best in Show in Norway was Sunlit Glory Garret, owned by Linda Nilsen, and bred by Unni Solberg.

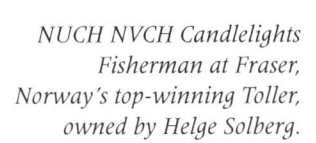

NUCH NVCH Candlelights Fisherman at Fraser, Norway's top-winning Toller, owned by Helge Solberg.

In 1993, Gudrun and Steinar Hansen had Alison Strang bring a male puppy for them from Canada when she traveled to Scandinavia to judge. Westerlea's Canadian Rockies spent the four-month quarantine period in Sweden together with another puppy, Westerlea's Rodrav of Drogsta, a male destined for Ewa Jonsson in Sweden.

Unni Solberg took two bitches to the 1993 Swedish Toller Specialty and went home with First Prize in the Breeder Class for five of her dogs. These included Best Female No. 2, NUCH Flyingtollers Florette Mary; her daughter, Sunlit Florence Caya, who won the nine- to fifteen-month Bitch Class of twenty-five entries; and a young male with a First Prize, Ann Helen Brandal's Sunlit Enchanting Emil To Avonlea, the first puppy to win a Best in Show Puppy Award in Norway. Unni repeated her record-breaking triumphs at the Swedish Specialties in 1994 and 1995.

A major retriever show is held every fall in Norway. The 1993 show was momentous for the small Norwegian Toller family, as Best in Show went to none other than a Toller, Sunlit Glory Garrett, who went all the way from the Junior Classes to his historic win. Well-known Norwegian All-Breed judge Rodi Hubenthal declared Garret the best Toller that he had ever seen, which added to the thrill for Garret's owner, Linda Nilsen, and breeder Unni Solberg. Garret is by Lyonhouse Ewan Stuart from Flyingtollers Beata.

Norwegian Toller affairs are ruled by the Norsk RetrieverKlub and more fanciers are becoming active in all aspects of Toller activities.

UNITED KINGDOM

Tollers have been slower to take hold in Britain, most likely because of Britain's stringent quarantine laws. Also, an incident that occurred at the National Gundog Championship Show in 1981 may have played a role. To give the crowd a laugh amid the serious business of judging gundogs, show organizers dreamed up a class for Nova Scotia Duck Tollers in which stuffed toy animals were substituted for dogs. Canadian Toller fanciers, who at that time were working hard to have their breed accorded equal status with other retrievers, interpreted this joke as a slight to the breed. Acrimonious letters were exchanged between Canadian fancies and writers for a British dog magazine. As a result, none of the Canadians felt the slightest urge to promote the Toller's future in Britain.

Nevertheless, several British dog publications have, over the years, made brief mention of Tollers, including a nice piece in the 1980s in *Dogs Monthly* from information sent by ten-year-

Lyonhouse Alexander Stuart is from one of the first English Toller litters born in quarantine, from a Harbourlights bitch leased by Avery Nickerson to Geraldine Flack.

Harbourlights Douglas Stuart of Lyonhouse was imported by Miss Flack from Nova Scotia. He is a full brother to the big Swedish winner, SUCH Riverduck of Drögsta.

Britain's top-winning Toller and top Import Register dog for 1993, is Ken and Sheila Rees's Lyonhouse Colin.

Lyonhouse Alexander Stuart

Nacton Decoyman John Norris with four of his Nova Scotia Duck Tolling Retrievers, which he presently uses to lure ducks to be tagged. Courtesy John Norris.

old Joanne Hudson of Vancouver, an avid dog fancier who often visited Westerlea Kennel. An action photo of Tip accompanied the article.

Miss Geraldine Flack was the first person to introduce Tollers to Great Britain. She has a nephew living in Nova Scotia and had seen some Tollers while on a holiday there. One of her physiotherapy patients told her of an article that she had read wherein a veterinarian, extolling the Toller's virtues, had expressed surprise that no one in Britain had brought any specimens over from Canada. She was impressed when Miss Flack told her that she had actually seen these dogs in their native province. Thus primed, Miss Flack decided to initiate her Lyonhouse Kennel.

In 1988, Miss Flack flew to Ontario and purchased two pups, a male and female, from Jem Kennel in Lindsay. Despite the loss of all of their papers en route, Nigel and Flora were safely installed in quarantine outside Bristol, where Miss Flack visited them regularly, making the long trip every week from her home in Godalming, Surrey. After six months, they were released but were immediately sent to kennels in Abergavenny, Wales, for training, which, given the circumstances, got off to a slow start.

Nigel was found to have an undershot jaw, a condition that necessitated removing him from a breeding program, but Flora proved a promising gundog. Miss Flack told her nephew in Canada of her need for other breeding stock and was sent the address of Avery Nickerson. The indomitable lady thereupon set out for Yarmouth and bought a two-year-old male, Harbourlights Scotia Duke. During her visit, she was offered lease of a bred bitch that could be flown to England, have her litter there, and then be

Decoymans Piper V.D. Echtinger Grift, one of John Norris's dogs imported from Holland and co-owned with Mrs. Audrey Ellis.

returned to Canada. The puppies, having been born in quarantine, would be free to go to homes earlier than imported pups.

Harbourlights Nova Nipper had an even more eventful trip than Flora and Nigel, as her crate was loaded upside down and the pregnant bitch flew all the way to England in disarray. No wonder she whelped early and lost three of her pups. The remaining four were registered with the Kennel Club as Lyonhouse Angus Stuart, Alexander Stuart, Arabella Stuart, and Elizabeth Stuart. They became the foundation for nearly all subsequent British breeding, along with Duke, Flora, and a bitch imported by Michael French from Colliers' kennels in Ontario. In addition, there is Harbourlights Douglas Stuart of Lyonhouse, imported in 1989, a litter brother to the great Swedish champion, Riverduck of Drogsta.

Miss Flack was very canny in the placing of her dogs, trying to ensure that a number will be worked and shown, and exported dogs to all four Scandinavian countries and Switzerland.

A big winner in British show rings was Lyonhouse Colin (Toddy), owned and shown by Ken and Sheila Rees. Tollers could be shown only in what is called an Import Register Class, and at the end of 1993, Toddy was declared Best Import Winner for the whole of Britain. Ken and Sheila have traveled throughout the United Kingdom to show Toddy and thus publicize Tollers and now are having fun with Agility.

Ken and Sheila Rees were among thirty fanciers who gathered for the inaugural meeting of the fledgling British Toller Club in 1993, where Miss Flack was elected life president in honor of her service to British Tollers. Dave and Babs Harding were elected chairman and secretary and are now publishing the club newsletter, aptly named *Nova News*.

The most exciting newcomer to emerge in England is John Norris, who is in charge of one of the last Decoys in England. It seems only fitting that Tollers should return to one of their probable roots in East Anglia and be worked once more along the pipes of the Nacton Decoy in Suffolk. John and his family occupy a picturesque house on a large estate, which he helps manage along with his work as Decoyman. With miles of trails and several very large ponds, it is an ideal place to breed and train gundogs.

John's breeding stock began with Winfren Vulpecula Meg from Michael French and Oldhobans Mary Mac from Ann Findlay. He brought in a young male from Holland, Decoyman's Piper V.D. Echtinger Grift. John's two bitches were making names for themselves and for the breed in official Working Field tests until the Kennel Club ruled in 1994 against Import Register dogs taking part in its trials. A disappointed John now runs his dogs in unofficial tests and is determined that his Tollers shall go to working homes.

2013 was a red-letter year for Tollers in the UK as the Kennel Club gave the breed the full privileges of the award of Challenge Certificates leading to full KC championships.

AND THE REST

Tollers are becoming better known in Holland, with breeding stock initially coming from Jalna and Ardunacres kennels in Canada, followed by dogs from Bright Flowers Kennel in Denmark. Linus Bos established Kennel von Echtinger Grift with Ardunacres Winnie of the West and is beginning to work with Swedish breeders, as well as with John Norris in England.

Bright Flowers Caesar and Bright Flowers Champ are brothers belonging to Gerhard and Marjetta Roscher of Austria. They were bred in Denmark by Frede and Jonna Hansen.

Gerhard and Marjetta Roscher have plans to breed Tollers in Austria with dogs imported from the Hansens in Denmark. They have had showring success with brothers Bright Flowers Champ and Caesar; a young bitch from Finland, Absolutis Nutty Solera; and a 1993 bitch from Canada, Westerlea's Red Sun Over Austria. With this varied foundation, Toller breeding should get off to a good start in Austria.

Elsbeth Wittwer's Objibway Kennel in Switzerland has been responsible for several Toller litters, and Elsbeth is a tireless promoter of the working Toller. She puts out an informative quarterly newsletter, published in both German and French, and wrote the section on Tollers for a small book, published in 1995 in Germany, on the Curly-Coated Retriever and the Toller. Elsbeth and her husband also travelled to Nova Scotia for the 1995 Toller Specialty and Field Tests.

AUSTRALIA

In 1990, Marilyn Kellie, a Canadian citizen living in Australia, heard about Tollers and thought it her patriotic duty to introduce Canada's dog to her new homeland. She wrote letters to a number of sources and was offered a pair of Tollers from Ardunacres stock. So began the long saga of shipping the pups to Australia, via Hawaii, for a total of *nine* months in quarantine. Missionsview Shilo of Kelmark went to his first show two weeks after getting out of quarantine and was awarded a Challenge Certificate by a Canadian judge. Shilo was soon joined by Ardunacres Jetlag to Kelmark, and in 1993, the first litter of Tollers was born in Australia.

Tim and Sara Coombes fell under the Toller's spell when they were exhibiting their German Shepherds at a show and happened to meet Denise Sandow with some of the little red newcomers. Tim and Sara have subsequently crossed Australia promoting the Toller and travelled across Canada, visiting breeders, before attending the Anniversary Specialty Show in Halifax, Nova Scotia, in 1995. Their first import, Aust. Ch. Lyonhouse Agnes, arrived from the United Kingdom on Christmas Eve in 1994, in whelp to Lyonhouse Douglas Stuart. Fluffy stole the hearts of all who saw her before her untimely death early in 1996, and her two large litters more than doubled the Australian Toller population.

More recent breeders include: Therese Kropman, Aprilraine; Andrea Nixon and Terry Johnson, Fionavar; Kim Walker, Tarshona; Sandra Goldsmith, Micmaq; Glenda Forster, Glenmave; Sandi Gee, Ptolomy; Denise Jacoby, Ximinez; and Z. Macdonald, Zirius. Emma Simon, Lidlriva, was the breeder of the first Toller Grand Champion, Aust Grand Ch Lidlriva Gingerbread Man (Teddy) and the first Toller retrieving Champion Aust Rt. Ch Lidlriva Onyx Gundi (Gundi).

Since this book was first published, Toller populations have increased in many areas of the world. It is beyond the scope of this book to document all of the growth and development of the breed. Additional European and Australian dogs are pictured elsewhere in the book and in the color section at the end of Chapter 12.

Grand Champion Aprilraine Maggie Rose, The United Retriever Club Show, BIS runner-up, bred and owned by Therese Kropman of Australia.

8
The Toller Personality

An amazing personality and remarkable spirit are dominant traits in the Nova Scotia Duck Tolling Retriever. Intelligent, obedient, and good-natured, this hardy little dog is easy to train and a pleasure to have as a companion. With an innate eagerness to please, a Toller will quickly and happily master any feats that he is capable of performing once he has grasped the concept of what is expected of him. A Renaissance dog among retrievers, he is as versatile as he is quick witted.

This razor-sharp intelligence is evidenced in the number of Tollers earning Companion Dog (CD) and Companion Dog Excellent (CDX) titles at an early age and by their success in mastering sports such as flyball, tracking, and scent hurdling. Frequently compared to the Border Collie, a canine reputed to have the problem-solving ability of a twelve-year-old child, the Toller is as swift to master any new situation or circumstance that might suddenly confront him.

This ability to cope makes the Toller an excellent traveling companion. Not only does he take up less space in a vehicle, he readily adapts to hotels, motels, camps, cottages, and even tents. City, village, forest, or marsh — as long as a Toller is with the master to whom he has wholeheartedly devoted himself, this compact little dog is always at home.

TOLLER PROTECTIVENESS

Anne and Kirk Norton of Cabot Trail Kennel enjoy relating their experiences with their Toller named Cabot, especially when it comes to his instinctive sense of protecting his mistress from danger. Anne relates:

Cabot seemed aware that I couldn't swim. Whenever we went into the water together, he always kept an eagle eye on me. If I went out to a place that he judged was too far, he would swim out and circle me until I grabbed onto his middle. Then he would tow me back to shallow water. Once he felt I was safe, he would go about his own business. Kirk, my husband, had been a competitive swimmer in high school and taught Red Cross water safety as an adult. Cabot never once swam out to rescue Kirk. Kirk even tried pretending to be drowning once to see what Cabot would do. Cabot simply watched him for awhile, then turned back to his frog hunting.

I really enjoyed "riding" him back to shore when he came to rescue me; it was a neat feeling once we'd both figured the best way for me to cling to him without sinking him or interfering with his own movements. However, I soon realized he wasn't doing it for

Arthur Forrester's daughter with Ceilidh. Photo by Arthur Forrester.

Tollers and kids: recipe for fun!

Stephanie and Nicholas Botner getting Tradewinds Saltwater Taffy ready for a sunny day in Miami, Florida. Courtesy Gretchen Botner.

fun but because he genuinely felt responsible for me and was truly worried. As a result, I stopped doing it. He seemed relieved, but I missed that intimacy with him.

This acute awareness also makes Tollers excellent watchdogs. When strangers come into the vicinity, a Toller immediately lets his master know with a few of his famous foxlike barks and yelps.

But while they are good watchdogs, they most definitely are not guard dogs. A Toller is too good-natured and too people-loving to take on such a violent task.

TOLLERS AND CHILDREN

This good-natured aspect of the Toller personality renders them desirable companions for children. Tollers frequently visit schools, providing some children with their important first contact with animals. The laid-back, fun-loving nature of Tollers ensures that these visits will always be reassuring, pleasant experiences.

While *adult* Tollers are excellent companions for children, Toller *puppies* are not always suitable for the very young or for toddlers. The reason is simple. Toller puppies enjoy gnawing on toes and fingers — all in play — but they can at times produce a painful pinch. The new Toller owner should not despair, however, because this behavior disappears at about seven months of age once adult teeth are in place.

TRAVELS WITH CABOT
By Anne Norton, Cabot Trail Kennel

I was taking a trip from Illinois to Rhode Island to visit my aunt. I was going alone, so my husband Kirk determined that he'd feel safer if I took Cabot, who was just a year old at the time and gentle as a lamb. But he could look like a guard dog if he had to.

We had a brand-new car that had just been serviced, but just outside Syracuse, New York, suddenly every light on the dash lit up, something under the hood squealed, and the car stopped dead. We were only a few miles from a large dealership, but it was Saturday and the repair shop was closed until Monday. As a result, Cabot and I ended up in the downtown Holiday Inn on the sixth floor in Syracuse for three days.

It was his first car ride with a total stranger (the tow-truck man), his first big city, his first elevator, first motel, and certainly his first cab

Collier's Cabottrail McGrr CD, the dog that made a hunter out of his master. Courtesy Anne Norton

ride and first car repair shop! But he was a trooper throughout, partly due to his personality and partly due to his formal obedience training. For instance, when we got onto that "first" and very full elevator, he was visibly ill at ease until I told him to sit. A simple word, but it was something that he understood amidst so much that was confusing to him. He sat instantly at my heel, and his unease seemed to disappear completely.

At the repair shop on Monday afternoon, I was even more grateful for the obedience. I had all my baggage and his, which we'd brought over in a cab, and I still had to struggle with the paperwork involved in getting my car back. In an effort to cope, I found a relatively unbusy spot in the middle of the noisy, smelly shop, put all my stuff down, and commanded him to Down next to it. He obeyed immediately and stayed for almost ten minutes while I conducted business way across the huge room from him.

Cabot and I never did get a CDX; trials were just fun to him. But his whole life, when it was crucial for him to obey commands, he always did, and with great contentment.

Kirk Norton of Cabot Trail Kennel with Ch. Sproul's Celtic Casey CD. Courtesy Anne Norton.

One reason why these dogs get on so well with children is because of their fun-loving nature. A Toller lives by a simple credo: I love everybody and everything; therefore, everybody and everything must love me.

TOLLER TOUGHNESS

The hardy little Toller lives much of his life in joyful leaps and bounds; indeed, it is his uniquely animated movements that make him a Toller and not just another retriever. He is so intense in his activities that he becomes oblivious to other things — even pain. High-powered and happy, a Toller can hit the waters of lakes and streams either in August's clammy heat or November's icy chill with equal zest.

Kirk Norton described one outing that he and his wife Anne had in the bush with their dogs.

Our Tollers are part of our family. They do everything with us. A typical vacation for us means canoeing in Superior Provincial Park, near WaWa, Ontario. We load our five Tollers

Above:
Can. SKC Ch. Westerlea's Audacious Wave SKC Can CDX, NSDTR (US) BRT "Lacy," owned by Paul and Patty Beran, Sagewood Kennel. Courtesy Patty Beran.

Below, Left:
Tollers will go anywhere.

Below:
Tollers are kids at heart.
Courtesy Cathy Thompson, Royal Palms, Florida.

Rob Van Ryswyk's Toller, one of a growing Toller population in Holland, sits at the alert. Jalna's Bryher From Manitoba was bred by Rena Cap, by Ch. Jalna's Firefox ex Ch. Jalna's Brazen Brat.

into the canoe with us and the camping gear — usually the gunwales are understandably near the water line — and off we go.

The last time we camped at Mijinimungshing, however, we encountered a disaster. It was a rainy evening. I noticed that Cabot was standing at the door of the tent, asking to go to bed. I told him that it was too early. Then I noticed that something wasn't right. Moving closer in the dim light, I realized that the skin on his leg was all around his ankle like an oversized, worn-out sock that will not stay up.

Cabot behaved like a typical Toller. He didn't complain. Since it was sunset — about 10 p.m. on a Friday night — and to get him to a vet would entail an hour's paddle in the dark and a three-hour drive over roads heavily traveled by moose, I was forced to use my knowledge of first aid. Cabot, tough little

The annual British Columbia Toller Fanciers' picnic: ten minds with a single thought, while the Sheltie eggs them on. Photo by Kerry Beaulieu.

A BRAVE LITTLE TOLLER
By Heather Molloy

My husband dreamed of a hunting dog that would complement his zeal for hunting and the family's desire for a pet, and he realized this dream when Alison Strang of Westerlea Kennel provided us with a Toller pup that grew up to be Can Ch. Westerlea's River Lady.

On September 26, 1990, Lady showed just how much of a champion she was and how dedicated she was to those she loved. I had returned home from work so tired that my shoulders ached. I tried to take a nap but couldn't get comfortable. Lady never left my side — she sensed before I did that something was very wrong. My husband was out on an errand, and my mother-in-law, who lives with us, was having her evening snooze. I decided to rest my sore muscles in a relaxing jacuzzi. Still Lady did not leave my side.

In the next few minutes, I experienced terror beyond imagination. Pain of intense proportions reached my chest and left arm, neck, and shoulder. I knew what was happening. My nurse's training told me that I was having a severe heart attack. My left side was useless. I was in trouble. I had to get out of the jacuzzi and get help. No one would have heard me even if I could shout. I had to get out of the tub and get to a phone.

Lady got me out of the tub. She braced her small body on the side of the tub, and I grabbed her chest with my right hand. By our combined strength, I made it. Lady never left me after that moment. She lent herself to me and I drew strength from her presence and physical contact. When I moved, she led the way; when I rested, her body was my pillow. I crawled a few feet at a time, then had to stop and rest. Lady and I worked our way to the stairs, and I managed to edge halfway down before my strength gave out.

Lady stays with Heather during her recovery.

Lady's voice was my voice. She barked so loudly and frantically that my mother-in-law woke up. Finding me collapsed naked on the stairs, resting my full weight on the little dog, she called 911. Lady still didn't leave me even when the firemen and paramedics worked to save my life. Only when I was put in the ambulance and she wasn't allowed to get in did she relinquish her position beside me.

The thought of Lady's warmth as I lay on the floor was reassuring to me for the six weeks I remained in the hospital. As we all know, time is very precious to people suffering heart attacks. I know that without the little Toller's help that night, I would have died. When I got home, Lady was glad to see me, but to her, what she had done was all in a day's work. That work gave me the rest of my life.

This story is dedicated to our memory of Lady. On September 19, 1992, she died of cancer. Lady made an irreplaceable impact on our lives. She was a brave little Toller who enriched our lives by her presence.

Lady

A frolic in the snow is enjoyed by Ch. Kylador's A Penny From Heaven CD, left, and her mate, Ch. Westerlea's Digby Schooner, visiting from the Calgary home of owners Web and Cindy MacDonald.

Toller joie de vivre... Can.Ch. Jagador Rainkist Coastal Livin'.

creature that he was, let me work on his injured leg with no anesthetic and never once whined. The next morning we finally got him to a vet.

Another of our Tollers, Casey by name, once severed an artery in his leg. In spite of the fact that there was blood everywhere, he wanted to keep on playing.

SENSITIVITY

The tough yet tender Toller, however, seems innately sensitive to when he must curb his exuberant nature in deference to the needs of those around him. As a result, many Tollers have proven to be excellent visitors to senior citizen homes and hospitals. With the very young and elderly, the Toller behaves with the gentleness and attention that the situation demands.

"They're just pleasant little red dogs," Erna Nickerson aptly reported. "They get along perfectly with my grandkids. And at night, they're quite willing to curl up at my feet and go to sleep."

FEARLESSNESS

Toller historian Colonel Cyril Colwell did find one flaw in the Toller personality that could prove disastrous to the little dog himself.

"For the reason that he [the Toller] does not sense danger, many of the best of the breed have been accidentally killed by trains, trams, motor cars, and trucks," he wrote. And the dog's apparently complete lack of vertigo can also lead to death or injury as the result of falls in spite of his almost catlike agility.

Gretchen Botner of Tradewinds Kennel also found that this lack of fear, coupled with the Toller's overpowering desire to retrieve, could prove dangerous.

> *I live in the hot South, and I face a potential hazard that many northern [Toller] owners wouldn't think twice about — alligators! I almost lost my first Toller to a seven-foot alligator in a lake deep in the Everglades west of Miami, where we lived for thirteen years.*
>
> *She was my first retriever, and we were having a family picnic. Of course, she was in and out of the water fetching sticks that my son and daughter were throwing for her. All of a sudden, there appeared a gator. My husband forgot to take into consideration that a Toller ALWAYS retrieves what is thrown. Knowing that if you throw something large at a gator, it will more than likely swim off, he did just that. And much to our horror, we watched our Toller go after it!*
>
> *The large stick landed in front of the gator's snout, and so did Keesha. The gator's mouth opened, then closed. The gator went down, the stick went down, and so did Keesha. To say that there was a lot of commotion on the shore would be minimizing the situation. However, the next instant, up and out of the water flew Keesha, howling all the way as she "walked" — or should I say "ran" — on the water all the way to the shore and deep into the woods.*
>
> *After a little discussion and lots of hugging and crying, we packed up, and it was quite a while before we went back to the Everglades with our Tollers. Now we always look before we throw.*

When not retrieving birds, Tollers love to play with and retrieve balls and toys. Photo courtesy of Cheryl Tomayer.

FIRST TOLLER
By Gail MacMillan

Within minutes a flight attendant was handing me a small, beige cage that had a pair of the most intense blue eyes I'd ever seen staring out at me. And when I opened the door, the most adorable ball of tan-colored fluff in the world tumbled out to seize my thumb and give it a nice, firm welcoming nip.

Almost immediately, Chance proved to be no chance at all. She was a definite winner. At 49 days, true to Avery Nickerson's forecast, she was retrieving in the house like a little trooper. Toddling determinedly and as fast as short puppy legs could go across our living room and down the hall after a ball, Chance left no doubt that she was born to retrieve. And by the time she was three months, the commands of sit, down, and come were a piece of cake. She was even staying, although not consistently, and beginning to understand hand signals and whistle commands. Her willingness to please was amazing. The only rules that had to be followed conscientiously (as Avery Nickerson had said) were to incorporate training into the dog's naturally playful nature and to be lavish with praise.

Socially, Chance was a great hit right from the day she arrived. She went to school during the month of June with our daughter, a third grade teacher, and became unofficial mascot of a local amateur baseball team. Her gregarious personality soon made her social puppy of the year wherever she went and showed us she would be an excellent family pet and companion when not out on a hunt. She loved people and life, and she showed it in leaps and bounds.

During the summer we took her to our camp and introduced her to water and marsh. From our old Lab she quickly learned about retrieving in and under the water and developed a jealous need to outdo the "old guy" when both went after a stick. In September we took her hiking in the mountains. At first we were a little apprehensive about letting her off her leash. After all, she was an inexperienced pup and the rocks were sharp and steep. We soon saw that our fears were ill-founded. Leaping from cliff to cliff, scrambling around the mossy faces of waterfalls with catlike grace and ease, our pup quickly assured us she had enough mountain goat know-how to lay our worries to rest. Flushing upland game in such terrain would be a cinch for our Toller. Later she climbed up onto a picnic table bench and politely waited to be served her lunch at her own place . . . a genuine lady even with mud on her face.

My husband brought home a partridge to see how five-month-old Chance would react. At first she merely circled the fresh kill, sniffing and looking it over apprehensively. Then we had our old Lab demonstrate how the bird was to be picked up and carried. That was all she needed to see. Within five minutes she was carefully carrying the bird toward the house. A week later we took her to the marsh to see how she would react to the sound of a shotgun. My husband looked at Chance and we settled in the long grass beside him. I nodded, he turned, aimed, and fired. Chance didn't so much as blink. Instead, she looked up alertly at Ron. What now, she seemed to ask.

The following week Ron took her on her first serious hunt across a wide expanse of peat bog. With very little training, she even did her act of capering about on the shore to attract ducks. She demonstrated that she has all the ingredients necessary to make a first-class hunting dog.

A veritable red flash, full of energy, possessing the endurance of a retriever twice her size, Chance is as amazing as she is beautiful. In her first year, Chance has already proven that she is, indeed, "the finest hunting companion on four legs."

HISTORY IS MADE!

Lineup for the very first Toller Specialty anywhere, held in Regina, Saskatchewan, in the summer of 1979.
Show organizers Mary and Larry Levsen are standing behind. From left to right are Dorothy Jacob and her two sons with Jiggs of Sundrummer, Ch. Sundrummer's Calais Rose and Sundrummer's Rebel Marksman; Murray Yarema handling Ch. Jalna's Eager Boots; Rena Cap with Jalna's Legendary Love; Wileen Mann and friend with Ch. Sproul's Highland Commander and Ch. Coltriev Drummer Boy; Alison Strang and Sheila Paul with Sundrummer's Seawitch and Ch. Westerlea's White Ensign; Doug Coldwell and his sister Deanna Jeffery with Ch. Crusader of Jeffery Coldwell and Royal Flush of Jeffery Coldwell; Linda and Jim Barnes with Sproul's Highland Playboy and Craigie's Classy Cassy; Daphne and Barry Craigie with Ch. Sproul's Merry Maiden and Craigie's Constant Comment, and Brian Finlay with Sundrummer's Acadian Sunrise.
An interesting note is the presence of the first two Tollers to win Best in Show the following year. Ch. Sproul's Highland Playboy was the very first Toller Best in Show winner, followed less than a month later by Ch. Westerlea's White Ensign.
It should be noted that not all of the dogs entered in the Specialty were available for this photo.
An amazed ring steward exclaimed: "Twenty-two Tollers and they all look alike!"

9

An In-Depth Look at the Standard

A Standard is the blueprint for any given breed. It is a written description of an ideal specimen and is what a dog is judged against in the show ring.

The original Toller Standard was written by Colonel C. W. Colwell when he was making arrangements to have the Toller recognized by the Canadian Kennel Club (CKC) in 1945. Many Toller fanciers in Yarmouth disagreed with the heights and weights given in the original Standard, and they were also disturbed by descriptions lessening the white markings held so dear by tolling men in southwestern Nova Scotia.

The committee formed in 1979 to revise the CKC Standard took these views into account so that when the resulting version came into effect January 1, 1982, a majority of fanciers felt that it was a much-needed improvement on the original. When the Toller was accepted into the Federation Cynologique Internationale (FCI) in 1982, the revised CKC Standard was adopted for FCI countries, and the fledgling Nova Scotia Duck Tolling Retriever Club (United States) also used the Canadian Standard. The NSDTR Club of Canada has voted to accept a few minor changes, but these will not become official until the Canadian Kennel Club adopts them. The NSDTRC (USA) will then cut and paste this revised Standard to conform to AKC rules.

CANADIAN KENNEL CLUB BREED STANDARD FOR THE NOVA SCOTIA DUCK TOLLING RETRIEVER

ORIGIN AND PURPOSE

The Nova Scotia Duck Tolling Retriever was developed in Nova Scotia in the early 19th century to toll (or lure) and retrieve waterfowl. The tolling dog runs, jumps, and plays along the shoreline in full view of a flock of ducks, occasionally disappearing from sight and then quickly reappearing, aided by the hidden hunter, who throws small sticks or a ball for the dog. The dog's playful actions lure the curious ducks within gunshot range. The dog is then sent to retrieve the downed bird.

Comments

Nothing much can be added here, as the preceding chapters deal with the development and history of the Toller and the writings on tolling techniques.

GENERAL APPEARANCE

The Toller is a medium-sized, powerful, compact, balanced, well-muscled dog; medium to heavy in bone, with a high degree of agility, alertness, and determination. Many Tollers have a slightly sad expression until they go to

BIS Ch. Westerlea's Tru Ray Red Rebel CDX WC bred by Alison Strang; owned by Ken & Brenda Stephens.

work, when their aspect changes to intense concentration and excitement. At work, the dog has a speeding, rushing action, with the head carried out almost level with the back and the heavily feathered tail in constant motion.

Comments

The General Appearance section of any Standard is really a short précis of the breed. A desirable addition here would be: "Structure of the ideal Toller should indicate an anatomy that enables the dog to do his work, both retrieving and swimming, in an effortless, efficient way."

The use of the term "compact" has aroused queries in the past. The *Oxford Dictionary* has this definition: "Closely or neatly packed together," wording that should not be confused with "short bodied." The Toller is a "compact" retriever in a body smaller than those of the other retrieving breeds, rather like a "compact" car. He is a remarkably powerful retriever for his size, but "powerful" should not be interpreted to mean "the bigger, the better."

Nothing is said about ratio of length to height in the Toller Standard, but it would be safe to say that most Tollers are slightly longer from point of forechest (prosternum) to pinbone (ischium) than from the highest point of withers to the ground. This should be spelled out in the Standard. A really square dog will not have the required reach and drive, because his body will be too short to allow proper freedom of movement, but an overly long back or loin is also a bad fault.

Balance is of prime importance in any breed, requiring correct proportions of head and neck to body, height to length, bone and substance to frame, and angulation of forequarters to hindquarters. Each part should flow smoothly into the next, with no one part showing any exaggeration. The Toller is a moderate dog in shape, size, and appearance, with nothing exaggerated.

The original Standard called for a dog "very heavy in bone," and this was lessened in the revision. A dog of very heavy bone may not have the degree of agility called for in the Stan-

Typical Toller concentration and enthusiasm for a retrieve.

dard, but agility is not just a matter of bone. It is also a matter of musculature and determination. General consensus, however, seems to be that medium, or moderate, but strong bone is ideal for the Toller. In this way, Tollers that are really heavy in bone and overall structure are to be penalized in the show ring, as are specimens that are very fine boned, with accompanying lightness of frame, thus lacking the called-for substance.

Many show judges look for bright, happy Tollers. However, the description of a "slightly sad expression" was included in the original Standard and is still applicable to a number of Tollers today. A show judge will never see the "rushing action" and "intense concentration" described, but anyone who knows the Toller at work or even at play will instantly recognize these traits. Moderation is the key to the Toller except in working attitude. Tollers should not be moderate in their enthusiasm to retrieve.

Historically, the Toller was bred for a slight resemblance to the Eastern Red Fox, at a distance. A foxy expression is often looked for, but to take the vulpine analogy to its logical conclusion would require a dog with pricked ears, black legs, and a very snipey muzzle!

Faults

Dogs of too heavy or too fine bone, with either too much or not enough substance. Dogs lacking balance or proper proportion.

TEMPERAMENT

The Toller is highly intelligent, easy to train, and has great endurance. A strong and able swimmer, he is a natural and tenacious retriever on land and from water, setting himself for springy action the moment the slightest indication is given that retrieving is required. His strong retrieving desire and playfulness are qualities essential to his tolling ability. Loving and playful to his family, he can be reserved wth strangers without being aggressive or overly shy. Aggression is not to be tolerated.

Comments

The Toller's native intelligence and inborn instincts to do the job he was bred for *are* strong, and he often resists efforts to instill other methods of working.

A highly charged retrieving drive is often allied with a calmer attitude to life when the dog is not at work. Tollers that "bounce off the wall" may make dandy hunters if they can sit still in a blind, but they are not ideal house companions. A self-confident, exuberant, enthusiastic, stylish retriever that is also calm at home is the ideal.

Breeders and judges alike must guard against aggression. It is not a typical Toller trait, although the Toller *is* like other dogs in matters of territory or sex.

Faults

Shyness or aggression.

SIZE

Ideal height for males over 18 months is 19-20 in. (48-51 cm); females over 18 months, 18-19 in. (45-48 cm). One inch (3 cm.) over or under ideal height is allowed. Weight should be in proportion to the height and bone of the dog. Guidelines are 45-51 lb. (20-23 kg) for adult males; bitches, 37-43 lb. (17-20 kg).

Comments

When these heights and weights were determined, the original Standard, which decreed a minimum of 20½ inches (52.5 cm) as ideal for an adult male, was the blueprint. Most Yarmouth tolling men strongly disagreed with this section, asserting that the true Yarmouth Toller was a far smaller dog. It was therefore decided to reduce minimum heights and corresponding weights. Nineteen to 19½ inches (48 to 49.5 cm) is ideal for a mature male and 17½ to 18 inches (43.5 to 45 cm) for a full-grown bitch. Deviations from these sizes could be penalized according to the amount of the deviation. Present weights would have to be reduced in accordance with the lesser size and preferred medium bone, approximately 3 pounds (1.5 kg). It must *never* be forgotten that the Toller is the smallest of all the retrievers.

Faults

Deviations from ideal size should be penalized according to the amount of deviation.

COAT AND COLOR

The Toller was bred to retrieve from icy waters and must have a water-repellent double coat of medium length and softness with a softer, dense undercoat. The coat may have a slight wave on the back, but is otherwise straight. Some winter coats may form a long, loose curl at the throat. Featherings are soft at the throat, behind the ears and at the back of the thighs, and forelegs are moderately feathered. While neatening of the ears and feet is permitted, the Toller should always appear natural. Colour is various shades of red or orange with lighter featherings and underside of tail, and usually at least one of the following white markings — tip of tail, feet (not exceeding beyond the pasterns), chest, and blaze. A dog of otherwise high quality is not to be penalized for lack of white. The pigment of the nose, lips and eye rims should match, and be flesh coloured, blending with coat, or be black.

Comments

The Toller must have a thick, water-repellent double coat of medium length and texture, neither as hard as that of a short-coated breed nor as silky as that of a Setter. Hair on the skull and muzzle is short and fine. Tollers have varying textures and lengths of coat. A short, dense coat can be water-repellent but will probably not keep out the cold as well as a slightly longer but dense coat. The thickness of the coat is more important than the length, but there must be a soft, dense undercoat except when the dog is in summer coat. An overabundance of coat can create a problem in the water and with burrs, but the water-shedding properties are what determine the best water coat, not the length. The topcoat should feel very slightly harsh to the hand but not really hard, nor should it be overly soft or silky. There is no oily feel to the coat as there is in some other water breeds.

Tollers are beginning to appear in the show ring with coats that are brushed up and back-combed, moussed, and blow-dried. This is a corruption of a true Toller coat and should be penalized. The coat may be slightly wavy but should otherwise lie fairly flat and straight. Featherings (the soft hair found behind the ears and at the back of the thighs) should not be too profuse. Those behind the ears are usually trimmed for show. Many Tollers have thick "culottes," and these should not be trimmed.

Whiskers are important to any dog but especially to one that may be used for hunting. Toller whiskers should not be trimmed for cosmetic reasons only.

The section on color is a bit unclear. Perhaps the best description of an ideal Toller color is "bright, coppery red," keeping a piece of brightly polished copper in mind. Many fanciers love a dark red color, but care must be taken to avoid an Irish Setter red. Orange is a difficult color to define; keep in mind the orange of an orange belton English Setter or a Brittany Spaniel. Featherings are almost always lighter than the rest of the coat. The Toller is a red dog, not pale fawn or almost the color of a Weimaraner. These colors do occur in the breed, but they should be discouraged. There have been documented instances of a lighter-colored dog being used to toll ducks on a very dark, overcast day, but the color should be a pale red-gold rather than light fawn or mousey silver.

Because the primary job of the tolling dog is to attract the attention of rafted ducks, white markings are a definite aid and are a Toller trademark. A dog with no white is very rare, and some white is almost essential for true Toller type. The Standard clearly states where these markings should be but does not demand that all dogs have all markings. Nearly all Tollers have some white on the feet and chest. A white tail tip is highly prized and is most noticeable when the dog is afield. A white blaze is attractive but not essential. The Standard does not penalize a dog for lack of white, but good white markings could make the difference between two dogs of otherwise equal quality.

The words "not above the pasterns" have caused a lot of argument in the fancy. Some maintain that dogs with even a tiny bit of white above the top of the pasterns should be discarded for show. Here, as everywhere, common sense should prevail. A little white above the top of the pastern, if it is on the inside of the leg, does not detract from the dog's appearance. A solid white leg, almost up to the brisket, however, is to be discouraged. Some earlier experimental breedings produced pups that resembled long-tailed Brittany Spaniels — white with red markings. By limiting the amount of white on legs as well as disallowing white on the trunk of the dog, breeders hope to avoid producing such pups in the future. The Toller is supposed to bear a slight resemblance to a fox, and foxes most certainly are not red and white. Rather, they are varying shades of red with white around the mouth extending to the chest, and sometimes they have white on their tail.

A flesh-colored nose has become something of a Toller trademark, but the Standard allows dark brown and black. The darker the dog, the darker the pigment can be. All pigment must, however, match.

Faults

Any color other than varying shades of red or orange; patches of black, gray, or silver in coat; open, standoff coat; coat too short or too long; lack of undercoat; coat not lying fairly flat or overgroomed. White on trunk of dog or extending beyond top of pasterns all around the leg. Nose, lip, and eye-rim pigment not matching or blending with coat, unless black. If the latter, then all must match.

BIS BISS CKC IKC NSDTRC-USA AKC CH Vesper Mariner Coupe De Vale JH AX AXJ WCI VCX, "Schooner," owned by Deb Gibbs, bred by Diana Semper.

*First AKC Sporting Group Winner
First AKC Multiple Group Winner
First AKC BIS Winner 2003
First Westminster Kennel Club BOB Winner 2004
NSDTRC-USA National Specialty Winner 2007
AKC Eukanuba National Invitational BOB Winner 2006
IABCA Best In Show
Pedigree Award Winner 2003*

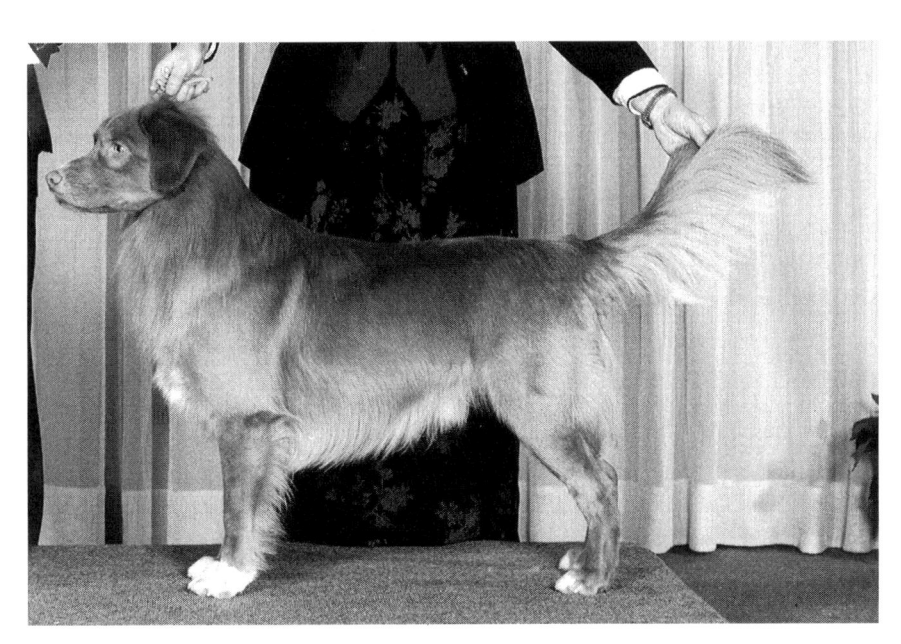

This lovely charcoal drawing of a generic Toller head captures the alert, friendly expression called for in the Standard. Copyright © 1995 by P. Burtch Symons.

HEAD

Skull: the head, which should be in proportion to the body size, is clean-cut and slightly wedge-shaped when viewed from above. The broad skull is only slightly rounded, the occiput not prominent and the cheeks flat. Length from occiput to stop should roughly equal that of stop to tip of nose. The stop is moderate. Muzzle: tapers in a clean line from stop to nose, with the lower jaw strong but not prominent. The underline of the muzzle runs almost in a straight line from the corner of the lip to the corner of the jawbone, with depth at the stop being greater than at the nose. Hair on the muzzle is short and fine. Whiskers are not removed. Nose tapers from bridge to tip, with nostrils well open. Colour should blend with that of the coat or be black. Mouth: lips fit fairly tightly, forming a gentle curve in profile, with no heaviness in flews. The correct bite is tight scissors, full dentition is required. Overshot by more than 1/8 inch, under shot and wry mouth are highly undesirable. Jaws are strong enough to carry a sizable bird, and softness in mouth is essential. Eyes set well apart, almond shaped, medium-sized. Colour, amber to brown. Expression is friendly, alert and intelligent. Flesh around the eyes should be the same colour as the lips. Ears triangular, rounded at the tips, medium-sized and carried in a dropped fashion. They are set high and well back on the skull, with the base held very slightly erect so that the edge of the ear is carried to the side of the head. They are well feathered at and behind the fold, with short hair at the tips.

Comments

Measurements can be misleading because Tollers vary so much in size. It should be stressed that the head is clean-cut, slightly wedge-shaped, with moderate stop and flat cheeks. The skull should not be too domed. Ideally, it is only slightly rounded. Nor should it be overly broad. Size of head must be in proportion to the dog's body and should be neither too fine nor too heavy, too large, nor too small. Measurement from occiput to midstop should roughly equal that from midstop to nose, but a slightly longer muzzle is an asset when it comes to picking up a bird — providing the muzzle is not snipey and the jaw is strong enough to hold a goose or large duck.

It should be mentioned here that the Toller, even though not a big dog, is a slow-maturing one. Therefore, it is not uncommon to find young males with fairly narrow skulls. Judges might bear this in mind when assessing puppies and young adults.

The Standard omits to mention in this section that the nose may be flesh colored. This is very common in Tollers and gives the dog a distinctive look. A dark flesh blends well with a coat of correct color. The same cannot be said for a very bright pink nose, which sunburns easily. Darker-red Tollers often have brown noses, which blend well with their coats. Tollers with black noses should also have black lips and eye rims. It is important that the nostrils be large and well open — this allows the dog to breathe while carrying a large bird or when swimming.

The Standard is quite specific about the correct bite. A level (or pincer) bite is not penalized, but care should be taken if such a dog is to be bred. Remember that the lower jaw in puppies grows faster than the upper jaw, which means

An In-Depth Look at the Standard

Examples of Good Toller Heads, All Different, but All Typical.

Small, pointed, folded ears change the dog's entire expression. This dog also lacks proper angulation, and the tail is too curled.

that if a puppy has a really tight scissors bite at seven to eight weeks, the finished jaw may actually be slightly undershot — and this is a disqualification. A scissors bite is definitely best for getting a proper grip on a bird without causing damage. The underjaw should not be weak, too receding, or too fine. A strong underjaw is required for retrieving. A soft mouth would be almost impossible to judge in the show ring but becomes very evident when the dog is in the field — hunters do not appreciate mangled birds!

Eye color should also blend with the coat. A light or yellow eye gives a hard expression, which is not typical. Many Toller puppies go through a stage where the eye has a greenish tinge. This is simply a phase on the transition to amber. Many young puppies have eyes of quite startling blue. The more pale the blue, the lighter the adult eye will be.

The "friendly, alert, intelligent" expression called for could be in conflict with the "slightly sad" look described in General Appearance, but it certainly is the preferred expression for showing, as well as being the most pleasing. Some Tollers have a round eye. This is incorrect, because an almond-shaped eye is called for. The eye also should not be prominent but well set into the socket. Any looseness of lids is a serious fault in a hunting breed, because seeds could become lodged behind the lid.

The correct Toller ear is somewhat triangular with rounded tips, lying fairly close to the head and of medium size. This is preferable to small, pointed, folded ears, which stand out from the head and spoil the soft expression. Ears also should not be too wide, long, and houndlike.

Faults

Skull too wide, too narrow, or too round; abrupt stop; cheeks not flat; muzzle too short, overly long, or too snipey; loose flews; overshot or undershot bite; missing teeth; weak underjaw; eyes too large or too small; round or prominent eyes; loose eyelids; nose, eye rims, and eyes not of prescribed color; bright pink nose; ears too small and folded, or too large and houndlike.

NECK

Slightly arched, strongly muscled and well set on, of medium length, with no indication of throatiness.

Comments

The Toller is not an elegant dog. While he should not have too short a neck, neither should the neck be overly long, thus losing strength.

The neck should be long enough to show some arch and must be very muscular in order for the dog to carry a large bird.

Faults

Neck too weak, long, short, or stuffy. Swan or ewe neck.

FOREQUARTERS

Shoulders should be muscular, with the blade well laid back and well laid on giving good withers sloping into the short back. The blade and upper arm are roughly equal in length with the upper arm well angled back under the body.

Elbows should be close to the body, turning neither in nor out, working cleanly and evenly. The forelegs should appear as parallel columns, straight and strong in bone. The pasterns are strong and slightly sloping. The strongly-webbed feet are tight and round, with well-arched toes, thick pads and strong nails, and are in proportion to the size of the dog. Dewclaws may be removed.

Comments

The whole front assembly should be muscular, but care must be taken that muscles do not become overly developed underneath the shoulder blades, a condition known as "loaded shoulders." This tends to push the elbows out of alignment, resulting in the dog being out at elbow and probably turning the front feet inward as he moves.

Fronts are a problem area in the Toller, with many having shoulder blades that are too upright, or, even more commonly, a short, steep upper arm. This results in lack of forechest and in the whole front assembly being too far forward on the dog, with consequent lack of good reach of the front legs. The blade and upper arm roughly equal in length, with the upper arm well angled back under the body, is correct. In conjunction with the desired angulation of between ninety and ninety-five degrees, this will produce a good forechest and an overall good front—something to be prized as it is relatively uncommon.

Straightness of bone, as well as strength, is to be sought in the legs. Many Tollers have slightly crooked front legs. Quite a few Tollers are too short in the legs for these to be in balance with the body, and some are too leggy. The pasterns are shock absorbers for the front — if they are too upright, they do not absorb well enough, and if they are too long and sloping, they do not have the required strength. As in everything, moderation is the key.

Feet are very important. Look for fairly round, tight feet with good thick pads and strong nails. A dog with poor feet, thin pads, or splayed toes cannot do his work properly. Strong webbing is essential for swimming.

The removal of dewclaws from the front legs is very common in dogs which are going to be shown, and the possibility of a torn dewclaw can be very messy. However, recent thinking about dewclaws tends towards the desirability of leaving them alone, as it has been often observed that a dog uses front dewclaws to help grab onto uneven or uphill ground. If, however, dewclaws are removed it should be done at birth, or some prefer to do it around day three.

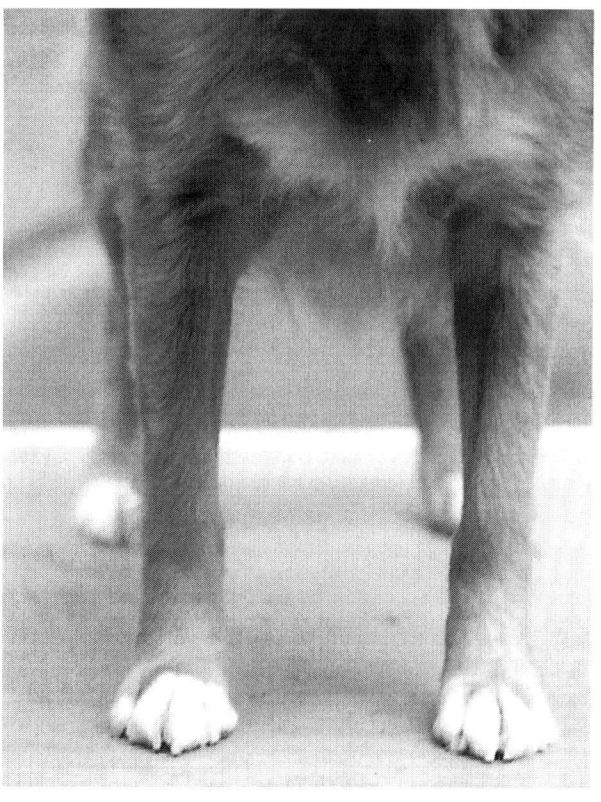

Excellent straight legs and strong medium bone. The feet are tight and fairly round.

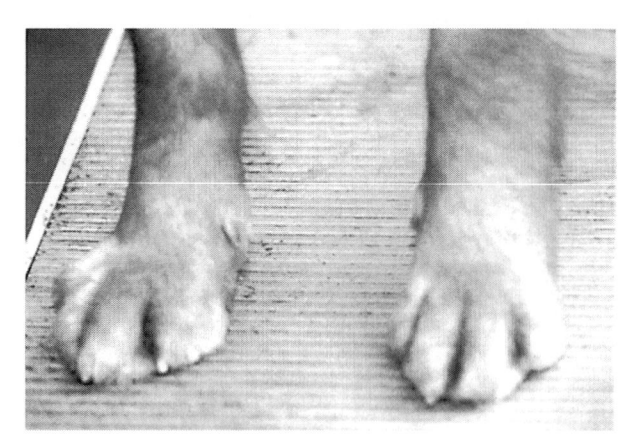

Feet are tight and round, with thick pads. Pasterns are strong. Dewclaws have not been removed on this Swedish import.

Faults

Shoulder blades too upright or too short; upper arms not in balance with blade, either too short or long or too open; loose elbows; crooked front legs; legs too short or too long for balance with the rest of the body; pasterns too upright or too long and sloping; splayed or paper feet (flat, thin feet, not well arched); hare feet (elongated toes, not well arched).

BODY

Deep-chested with good spring of rib, brisket reaching to the elbow. The back is short and straight, the topline level, the loins strong and muscular. The ribs are well-sprung, neither barrel-shaped or flat. Tuck-up is moderate.

Comments

Good width, as well as depth of chest, is needed to give room for heart and lungs, but an overly wide chest can also push the elbows out of alignment. The ribs should be well sprung but not barrel-shaped. They should be somewhat egg-shaped, tapering at the ends, thus allowing room for the organs that they are protecting. Good depth of chest is required, and a shallow body is a bad fault except in an immature dog.

Many Tollers show a pronounced rise over the loin and a fairly steep croup. This gives a low tailset, which is incorrect. There is usually a slight rise over the loin so that the topline is not absolutely level, but a strong, short back with well-extended ribs and a muscular, not overly long loin, is called for. Such an assembly is the best transmitter of power from the rear to the front. Conversely, a loin that is too short will hamper freedom of movement in the rear.

Some Tollers have rather weedy bodies and a lot of tuck-up, giving a whippetlike appearance that is atypical. Others are too heavyset throughout, and a number are too short in the leg for their length of body, or vice versa. Moderation and balance are, as always, requisite. An agile, strong dog is required.

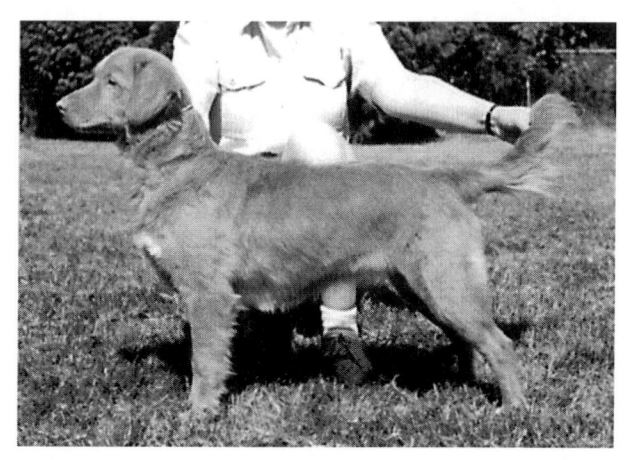

This young bitch, although out of coat and looking long and immature, shows excellent bone and substance and fine front and rear assemblies.

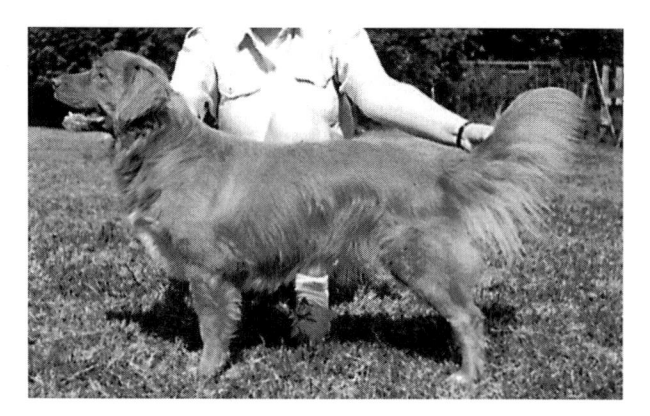

A good illustration of a strong, "compact" bitch.

Faults

Shallow brisket; chest too narrow or too wide; ribs flat or barrel-shaped; sway or roached back; uneven topline with rear higher than withers; croup too steep or too flat; low tailset; loins too long or too short, slack loins; too much tuck-up.

A well-balanced bitch from Finland, Zeiban's California Maid, owned by Jaana Heinonen. She has lovely, straight legs, good feet, a compact body, and very good angulation front and rear.

Comments

The Toller rushes out to retrieve sticks when tolling, often coming to a sharp halt or making very quick turns. He is also a strong swimmer. All of this activity calls for strength and soundness throughout, but particularly in the rear, from where impulsion initiates. The Toller should have strong, sound hind legs supported by powerful muscles and strong bones. If front and rear angulation and bone lengths are roughly equal, the dog is in balance structurally.

A swimming dog will push his front legs out to the side almost as in a breast stroke, with the toes spread wide. The webbing is thus extended to help pull the dog through the water. At the same time, the hind legs kick backward with a powerful thrust, propelling the dog forward. This power, coming from a correctly angled pelvis and strong musculature, is also necessary for proper economical movement on land.

An excellent example of balance, lovely neck, good front with strong, straight bone, correct round feet, and an excellent strong rear.

HINDQUARTERS

Muscular, broad, and square in appearance. Rear and front angulation should be in balance. Thighs are very muscular, upper and lower sections being approximately equal in length. Stifles are well bent and hocks well let down, turning neither in nor out. Dewclaws must not be present.

An example of an excellent, strong rear, with strong bone, perpendicular hocks, and good musculature.

Many Tollers do not have particularly well-let-down hocks, and many are high on hock. Trying to lengthen the second thigh often results in reduced strength of rear; therefore, moderation would again seem to be the answer. Balance between the upper and second thighs, powerful muscles, and strong bone will give the required strength. A few Tollers lack angulation in the hock area, an almost inverted condition that is a distinct fault.

A good turn of stifle is needed for the second thigh to transmit forward thrust. A strong, driving rear is essential, but it must be accompanied by matching good reach in front.

Rear dewclaws are rare in the Toller. If they are present at birth, they should be removed for the same reasons as given for removing front dewclaws.

Faults

Lack of strength in rear; cow or barrel hocks; weak musculature; thigh assembly not in balance; straight stifles or hocks with little angulation; pelvis angled too flat or too steep; too high on hock; rear not square in appearance from behind; rear dewclaws.

TAIL

*Following the natural, very slight slope of the croup, broad at the base, luxuriant and heavily feathered, with the last vertebra reaching at least to the hock. The tail may be carried below the level of the back except when the dog is alert, when it curves high over, though **not** touching, the back.*

Comments

The tail is a Toller's crowning glory if it is as the Standard describes — full and bushy rather than feathered like that of a Setter. When the dog is working, the tail lashes back and forth in excitement. This is one of the main attractions to incoming ducks. A white tip is a definite asset and is highly prized, but it is not absolutely essential. A short tail will not have the full mobility necessary to a tolling dog.

The tail should follow the very slight slope of the croup and should not be set too low. It should be very broad at the base in order to act

Firefly Fauna shows high curved tail carriage so typical of Tollers at the alert.

as a rudder. A tail reaching at least to the hock might appear too long on a short-legged dog, but the importance of a full tail to the tolling process should never be forgotten.

When the dog is trotting, the tail ought to be carried above the level of the back. A fairly high carriage is preferred, but the tail must not curl over and touch the back when the dog is gaiting. When the dog is really alert, the tail comes over the back in an inverted C. This is a real Toller trademark but may not be seen in the show ring because the dog is seldom at full alert in such a situation.

Faults

Tail too short or stringy; too narrow at the base; kinked; set too low; carried too low, or too high, curled over touching the back; shaped and/or scissored tails.

GAIT

The Toller combines an impression of power with a springy, jaunty gait, showing good reach in front and a strong driving rear. Feet should turn neither in nor out and the legs travel in a straight line. As speed increases, the dog should single-track, topline remaining level and covering ground with economy of movement.

Comments

It is perhaps difficult to combine a springy, jaunty gait with smooth, powerful reach and drive. Many Tollers appear to mince around the ring with small, quick steps, denoting lack of reach and drive. Tollers are swimmers and retrievers and should move with smooth, strong, ground-covering strides, although they are not intended to range widely but rather to stay close to the hunter until sent to toll or retrieve. There is no need for the dog to cover ground to the extent of a Setter or Pointer, but economy of movement *is* necessary, avoiding both lack and overabundance of reach and drive.

As the dog increases speed, the legs come in under the body to maintain static balance, and the inside toes will touch an imaginary central line, not the whole foot. The hind leg should reach forward the same distance as the diagonal front leg. All four legs should extend the same distance.

Faults

Too little or too much reach and drive; paddling; crabbing; toeing out or in; failure to single-track at speed; topline not fairly level.

Two excellent examples of correct movement.

Top: This Halifax field dog exhibits beautiful side gait.

Bottom: Can. Am. Ch. Anando Off Center Toller Tyson gaiting in the ring. Tyson won BOB at Westminster in 2009.

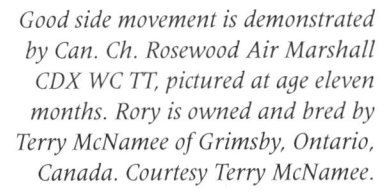

Good side movement is demonstrated by Can. Ch. Rosewood Air Marshall CDX WC TT, pictured at age eleven months. Rory is owned and bred by Terry McNamee of Grimsby, Ontario, Canada. Courtesy Terry McNamee.

FAULTS

Dogs more than 1 inch (3 cm) over or under ideal height
Overshot bite
Tail too short, kinked, or curled over, touching the back
Lack of substance in adult dog
Dish- or down-faced
Abrupt stop
Large, round eyes
Nose, eye rims, and eyes not of prescribed color
Bright pink nose
Splayed or paper feet, down in pasterns
Open coat
Roached, sway back, slack loins
Tail carried below level of back when dog gaiting

Any departure from the foregoing points should be considered a fault and penalized according to the degree of deviation.

DISQUALIFICATIONS

White on shoulders, around ears, on back of neck, across back or flanks
Silvery coat, gray in coat, black areas in coat
Lack of webbing
Undershot bite, wry mouth
In adult classes, any shyness
Butterfly nose
Overshot by more than one-eighth inch
Any color other than red or orange shades

It would be desirable to see faults incorporated into the body of the Standard at the end of each section. Many kennel jurisdictions are doing away with disqualifications, their Standards simply stating the ideal, followed by: "Deviations from this ideal are to be penalized according to the amount of deviation." Numerous judges have commented unfavorably on the number of disqualifications in the present Standard.

SHR AKC GCH NSDTRC-USA CH QuinnCreek's Montana Premier CDX RN WC JH TDI VCX, "Baxter," bred by Terri Krause, owned by Gary and Elizabeth Boryczka and Terri Krause.

NOVA SCOTIA DUCK TOLLING RETRIEVER CLUB (USA) STANDARD

I General Appearance

The Nova Scotia Duck Tolling Retriever (Toller) was developed in the early 19th century to toll, or lure, and retrieve waterfowl. The playful action of the Toller retrieving a stick or ball along the shoreline arouses the curiosity of the ducks offshore. They are lured within gunshot range, and the dog is sent out to retrieve the dead or wounded birds.

This medium sized, powerful, compact, balanced dog is the smallest of the retrievers. The Toller's attitude and bearing suggest strength with a high degree of agility. He is alert, determined, and quick, with a keen desire to work and please.

Many Tollers have a slightly sad or worried expression when they are not working. The moment the slightest indication is given that retrieving is required, they set themselves for springy action with an expression of intense concentration and excitement. The heavily feathered tail is held high in constant motion while working.

The Nova Scotia Duck Tolling Retriever Club (USA) feels strongly that all Tollers should have these innate working abilities, and encourages all Tollers to prove them by passing an approved Nova Scotia Duck Tolling Retriever Club (USA) field test.

II Size, Proportion and Substance

Size: Height at the withers—males, 18-21 inches. The ideal is 19 inches. Females, 17-20 inches. The ideal is 18 inches. Bone is medium. Weight is in proportion to height and bone of the dog. The dog's length should be slightly longer than height, in a ratio of 10 to 9, but should not give the impression of a long back.

III Head

Skull: The head is clean-cut and slightly wedge shaped. The broad skull is only slightly rounded, giving the appearance of being flat when the ears are alert. The occiput is not prominent. The cheeks are flat. The length of the skull from the occiput to the stop is slightly longer than the length of the muzzle from the stop to the tip of the nose. The head must be in proportion to body size.

Expression: The expression is alert, friendly, and intelligent. Many Tollers have a slightly sad expression until they go to work, when their aspect changes to intense concentration and desire.

Eyes: The eyes are set well apart, slightly oblique, and almond in shape. Eye color blends with the coat or is darker. Eye rims must be self-colored or black, matching the nose and lips. Faults: large round eyes. Eye rims and/or eyes not of prescribed color.

Ears: The high set ears are triangular in shape with rounded tips, set well back on the skull, framing the face, with the base held slightly erect. Ear length should reach approximately to the inside corners of the eyes. Ears should be carried in a drop fashion. Ears are short-coated, and well feathered only on the back of the fold.

Stop: The stop is moderate.

Muzzle: The muzzle tapers in a clean line from stop to nose, with the lower jaw not overly prominent. The jaws are strong enough to carry a sizeable bird, and softness in the mouth is essential. The underline of the muzzle is strong and clean. Fault: dish face.

Nose: The nose is fairly broad with the nostrils well open, tapering at the tip. The color should blend with that of the coat, or be black. Fault: bright pink nose. Disqualification: butterfly nose.

Lips, flews: Lips fit fairly tightly, forming a gentle curve in profile, with no heaviness in the flews.

Bite: The correct bite is tight scissors. Full dentition is required. Disqualifications: undershot bite. Wry mouth. Overshot by more than 1/8 inch.

IV Neck, Backline, Body

Neck: The neck is strongly muscled and well set on, of medium length, with no indication of throatiness.

Backline: Level. Faults: roached or sway back.

Body: The body is deep in chest, with good spring of rib, the brisket reaching to the elbow. Ribs are neither barrel shaped nor flat. The back is strong, short and straight. The loins are strong and muscular, with moderate tuck-up. Fault: slack loins.

Tail: The tail follows the natural very slight slope of the croup, is broad at the base, and is luxuriant and well feathered, with the last vertebra reaching at least to the hock. The tail may be carried below the level of the back except when the dog is alert, when it is held high in a curve, though never touching the body. Faults: tail too short, kinked, or curled over touching the back. Tail carried below the level of the back when the dog is gaiting.

V Forequarters

Forequarters: The shoulders should be muscular, strong, and well angulated, with the blade roughly equal in length to the upper arm. The elbows should work close to the body, cleanly and evenly. When seen from the front, the foreleg's appearance is that of parallel columns. The pasterns are strong and slightly sloping. Fault: down in the pasterns.

Feet: The feet are strongly webbed, slightly oval, medium in size, and tight, with well-arched toes and thick pads. Front dewclaws may be removed. Faults: splayed or paper feet.

VI Hindquarters

Hindquarters: The hindquarters are muscular, broad, and square in appearance. The croup is very slightly sloped. The rear and front angulation should be in balance. The upper and lower thighs are very muscular and equal in length. The stifles are well bent. The hocks are well let down, turning neither in nor out. Rear dewclaws must not be present. Disqualification: rear dewclaws.

VII Coat

The Toller was bred to retrieve from icy waters and must have a water-repellent double coat of medium length and softness, and a soft dense undercoat. The coat may have a slight wave on the back, but is otherwise straight. Some winter coats may form a long loose curl at the throat. Featherings are soft and moderate in length. The hair on the muzzle is short and fine. Seasonal shedding is to be expected. Overcoated specimens are not appropriate for a working dog and should be faulted. While neatening of the feet, ears, and hocks for the show ring is permitted, the Toller should always appear natural, never barbered. Whiskers must be present. Faults: coat longer than medium length. Open coat.

VIII Color

Color is any shade of red, ranging from a golden red through dark coppery red, with lighter featherings on the underside of tail, pantaloons, and body. Even the lighter shades of golden red are deeply pigmented and rich in color. Disqualifications: brown coat, black areas in coat, or buff. Buff is bleached, faded, or silvery. Buff may also appear as faded brown with or without silver tips.

Markings: The Toller has usually at least one of the following white markings—tip of tail, feet (not extending above the pasterns) chest and blaze. A dog of otherwise high quality is not to be penalized for lack of white. Disqualifications: white on the shoulders, around the ears, back of the neck, or across the flanks.

IX Gait

The Toller combines an impression of power with a springy gait, showing good reach in front and a strong driving rear. Feet should turn neither in nor out, and legs travel in a straight line. In its natural gait at increased speeds, the dog's feet tend to converge towards a center line, with the backline remaining level.

X Temperament

The Toller is highly intelligent, alert, outgoing, and ready for action, though not to the point of nervousness or hyperactivity. He is affectionate and loving with family members and is good with children, showing patience. Some individuals may display reserved behavior in new situations, but this is not to be confused with shyness. Shyness in adult classes should be penalized. The Toller's strong retrieving desire coupled with his love of water, endurance, and intense birdiness, is essential for his role as a tolling retriever.

Disqualifications:
Butterfly nose.
Undershot bite, wry mouth, overshot by more than 1/8 inch.
Rear dewclaws.
Brown coat, black areas in coat, or buff. Buff is bleached, faded or silvery. Buff may also appear as faded brown, with or without silver tips.
White on the shoulders, around the ears, back of the neck, or across the flanks.

Approved by vote of the Nova Scotia Duck Tolling Retriever Club (USA) April 23, 2001.

10
The Art of Tolling

The Finest Hunting Companion on Four Legs

> Tho' gay and winning in my gait
> I'm treacherous as a viper.
> Follow me and sure as fate,
> You'll have to pay the piper.

When H. C. Folkhard wrote this jingle for his book *The Wildfowler* (1864), he was drawing a comparison between the legend of the Pied Piper and the little piper dogs so long used to attract waterfowl in Europe. Today, his poem might just as aptly apply to their likely descendants, the Nova Scotia Duck Tolling Retriever.

A TREASURY OF TOLLING AND TOLLER TIPS

Toward the end of his life, Avery Nickerson compiled advice and reminiscences for a book on tolling that he hoped to produce. To our loss, death came before this project could be realized, but some of the information that he relayed to dedicated hunters and sporting writers follows.

* * *

Courtesy Lynda Dickson-Martin

Tolling is a very simple method of luring wildfowl within gunshot range and is almost foolproof, providing the duck hunter is fortunate enough to have access to a reasonably large body of water isolated from the traffic of boats and other commotion that normally disturbs resting waterfowl. In this ideal situation, the tolling procedure is as follows:

Get ready for the upcoming season in early autumn by building blinds on the shore, keeping in mind that points that jut out beyond the regular shoreline are best for tolling. In other words, get as close to the birds as you possibly can before starting to "play" the dog. Evergreen thickets along the shore facilitate entry to the blind without disturbing the birds. If there are open areas that make undetected entry impossible, build a fence with boughs or bushes that blend in with the existing ones. String a reasonably strong line (synthetic material is best) back from the blind, attach this line tightly to stronger trees, and then, with smaller twine, fasten branches and bushes to the larger line. Then hunters can sneak into the blind undetected.

Next step is to make a tolling run for the dog. Depending on location, you may want to play the dog from the right or left side of the blind, or, perhaps, on either side. This last method is possibly the best, particularly on a point where the birds may be resting on one side or the other. Always remember that no obstructions should hinder the ducks from recognizing the dog, and make sure nothing is in the way that might affect the dog's speed and agility. Twenty feet of shore is plenty to "show" the dog.

When decoying ducks, it has been my experience that hunter and decoys should be set upwind. Not so when tolling, where the wind factor is the exact opposite to that of decoying. The blind should be downwind. Why? First, I firmly believe that ducks and geese can smell humans, and we also know that they have a keen sense of hearing. The most important reason, however, to be downwind is the fact that the wind and waves give the birds considerable help in making up their minds about which way to go by giving them an extra push in the desired direction, especially when there is a light to strong breeze blowing. Being both fascinated by the tolling dog, and unobtrusively propelled by the elements, before they are aware of distance they are up against the shoreline with others coming in and crowding them.

After the blind has been prepared as described, the hunter and his dog sneak in and settle down. When a flock of birds appears, allow them time to settle before attempting a toll. Once the hunter is confident that the birds are relaxed, he throws a stick out onto the shore for the dog. Like a dancing flash of flame, the little red dogs make a neat retrieve. Such initial retrieves are referred to as "playing the dog," a deceptive term since at this point a Toller is working in earnest. It was only the dog's prancing, dancerlike gait that gave rise to this expression.

During this orchestrated playing, obedience is essential. The dog is never allowed to caper aimlessly about the beach or show any interest in the birds. If, as sometimes happens with a young or inexperienced Toller, the dog pauses to sniff or explore before returning to the blind, a long lead or line should be attached to his collar to draw him back. Using this method, the hunter does not have to reveal himself, and the dog is quickly broken of a habit that can easily ruin a hunt.

Once in a while, a young Toller will show some interest in the birds, but it is easy to break him of this. Just scold him a bit or, if he actually drives a flock away, punish him, but not severely. These dogs are bred to be much more interested in retrieving and really only focus on the birds as objects to retrieve — they don't try to catch them. It is a good idea to take a young dog to the blind a few days before you plan to hunt with him, to familiarize him with the new surroundings. This will reduce his need to explore new terrain when it is essential that he not pause to do so.

In Yarmouth County, ducks usually stay on freshwater lakes near the sea and fly out to the mudflats to feed on eel grass. After these feeding forays, the birds frequently stay a good distance offshore. Only the antics of a prancing, well-trained Toller will lure them within range. It may take only one retrieve or a good number to

The beginning of a hunt, the Toller is in the blind. All photos this page and next courtesy Nicholas Karas.

The Toller goes after a tossed stick when ducks appear at rest.

Retrieving the stick.

The ducks move closer.

The Toller ignores the approaching birds.

Returning to the blind.

The Toller after another stick when the birds stop moving.

Bringing in more and more birds.

Safely back in the blind before shooting begins.

The Toller in action! Retrieve that bird!

Retrieving birds.

The end of a successful hunt.

catch the birds' attention, but once they spot the dog, they will usually start to move enthusiastically toward him. Only if the birds hesitate does the hunter "show" the Toller again.

Once the birds are well within gun range, the hunter makes certain that his Toller is safely back in the blind with him and on a sit stay command before he shoots. Afterward, his little red-coated companion will happily retrieve the kill and is then rewarded with the customary pat and praise that is always his due after a successful toll. One word of warning — if the same flock of ducks is tolled *too* often, the birds get wise to the game and will refuse to come in to the dog.

We have been considering the ultimate with regard to the tolling procedure. Now let's deal with the not-so-ideal situation. I recall one instance when two other hunters and I were in a rock blind decoying whistlers and bluebills. Three bluebills came over the decoys and two hit the water dead. My Toller, Cindy, was in the water making the second retrieve when about one hundred more came toward us. They noticed the dog with the bird, flared off a bit, and then set down about one hundred yards offshore. Another, larger flock zoomed in and settled with the other ducks about two to three gunshots away.

Cindy retrieved her bird to the blind while the bluebills just sat and watched. We were without a stick or other object to throw, but our empty shells were there, and almost immediately she was in action again retrieving the spent cases. Within three minutes, all the watching birds were in easy range and we were finished for the day.

Eldon Pace told of hunting after a hurricane while the waves were still very high. He shot two ducks and sent his Toller to fetch them. Because of the height of the waves, the dog could not get through them, so after several attempts, she looked around and spotted a high rock some distance down the shore. She raced to this rock and scrambled with difficulty to the top, from where it was no effort for her to jump over the nearest wave and swim out to the duck. She then repeated the performance for the second duck. Ever after, if this dog had to retrieve from rough water, she would look for a high rock.

Waterfowling with a Toller generally works best on "bluebird" (calm, clear) days, with a high tide. At such times, decoys are not effective, but tolling works well. However, areas where tolling works best are becoming few and far between, with rising populations and burgeoning vacation homes occupying previously fine tolling areas.

* * *

In the mid-1980s, an article by Avery Nickerson appeared in Toller Talk *describing one of his early tolling experiences with Dick Crowell, the man whom Avery considered the grand master of the art of tolling. The following excerpts are taken from this article, considered to be one of the most descriptive pieces written on the subject.*

When the ducks and geese are sitting rafted within visible distance of the shore, the degree of excitement I experience is no less than the first time I went duck hunting more than fifty years ago.

As the dawn reflected the morning light, the whistle of wings, the short, sharp, clucky quacks of the blacks, combined with the talking of the Canadas, were answered by the "come in — we're here" of the already-setting relatives on the lake. By the time one could see from shore to shore, there were several thousand ducks and hundreds of geese, and the flocks were still appearing over the woods with wings set. The noise was almost deafening from the calls of the setting to the flying birds.

Needless to say, a young boy could not understand why we were just sitting and waiting with this many birds in front of us. When I could not stand it any longer, the question was asked and I was abruptly told that there was no hurry, as the birds weren't going anywhere. I soon learned that the birds were coming to the lake for fresh water and to wash the salt from their feathers after spending the night feeding on the mudflats.

"The more rested they are, the better tolls you get," Dick explained.

As the sun came up over the trees, the mist that hugged the water dissipated. I was allowed to peek through a hole in the blind about the size of one's wrist, and there I saw, out on the lake, what Dick estimated were 10,000 Black Ducks and geese.

In the meantime, the master had been whittling the bark from several six- to eight-inch pieces of hardwood saplings and placing the pieces close to his feet. He ordered us only to shoot when he counted to three.

As Dick picked up a stick from the ground, his little bitch Nettie braced and trembled. The stick was thrown out about twenty feet, and the little dog retrieved it with lightning speed. The heads of the birds came up, and, within seconds, there was a movement toward Nettie accompanied by an excited variety of quacking. Ducks were soon within thirty feet of the blind and coming from all quarters. I was bubbling over with anxiety — why wouldn't he let us shoot? I later learned that Dick Crowell was not interested in how many ducks he could kill but what he could do with this many birds while they were turned on to little Nettie.

It seemed to me to be forever, with ducks and geese even crawling up the shore of the lake, but then the count came . . . one, two, three . . . and soon it was over. We were not allowed to shoot cripples, as the injured birds would swim to the islands and crawl onto land. With a dog like Nettie, Dick would account for every one after the remainder of the birds had left for the feeding grounds. Now it was Nettie's turn again, and with very little instruction, the retrieves were made like clockwork.

* * *

Sporting-dog writer Jerome B. Robinson gave an apt description of the dogs developed during Avery Nickerson's lifelong involvement with Tollers in an article for Sports Afield.

Today's [tolling] dogs have an unusually high degree of intelligence and a particularly animated retrieving style. . . . They dart and dash about with the excitement that some terriers exhibit, and they display an eagerness to retrieve that surmounts that of the more popular retriever breeds. . . . When the shooting is over, the tolling dog will hit the water and chase down cripples with all the determination of a Chesapeake Bay Retriever, deliver his ducks with the merriment of a Labrador, and look as pretty as a little Golden Retriever while he's at it.

New Tolling technique!
Jem's Cajun Fox CDX,
bred by Ken and Brenda Stephens;
owner/trained by Tom and Deb Vaida.

11

Field Training the Toller

While various articles in sporting magazines have tried to describe tolling, all are remarkably silent on how a dog is prepared for his life's work. It appears that very little attempt at formal training was made in earlier days, and even later proponents seem to have confined their training largely to basic obedience, with emphasis on instant obedience to commands such as sit, stay, and come. Avery Nickerson would bring a puppy into the house at seven weeks and encourage him to retrieve by rolling a ball.

Children were encouraged to play with puppies by throwing objects for the pups to retrieve. The dogs that showed the most retrieving enthusiasm generally made the best tolling dogs. The accepted way to train a Toller was to make a pet of him and allow children to throw sticks for him to retrieve.

The use of sticks as objects to retrieve is anathema to most gundog trainers, one reason being that they feel the dog will bite too hard on a rigid object, thus encouraging a hard mouth. Nova Scotians, however, train tolling dogs with fairly short sticks, because these will be used in the tolling process. They believe that, because the dogs are small, with small mouths, they are more inclined to grab a bird by the neck or the wing where they can get a better grip, thus avoiding puncturing the bird's body.

Some old articles tell of taking a young dog out on a toll with an older, experienced tolling dog (Hemeon) and claim that the young one learned by watching. There are many stories of dogs of other hunting breeds learning in this same way.

All experienced Toller lovers agree that it is essential to keep training fun for the Toller, incorporating play sessions right along with training and making lavish use of praise. The basic keys to Toller training are play, praise, consistency, and tone of voice. Tollers have their own very strongly defined sense of how they should work and do not take readily to being taught different methods — unless, of course, the trainer is highly creative.

If a hunter wishes only to toll or pleasure hunt with his dog, the training can be fairly simple. But in today's competitive dog scene, a number of field tests are offered to retriever owners, many of whom will not be hunters but are eager to train their dogs to work with birds. It is a great help to have had previous training experience, either for field work or obedience. Toller owners will do well to remember that most of the tests are very different from the work the Toller was originally bred to do and

Harbourlights Highland Chance retrieves a pheasant in the field. Courtesy Ron MacMillan.

require a degree of training not necessary for tolling. There is a marked difference between a dog reaching a peak of excitement while tolling birds, then jumping in to retrieve them, and a dog being brought to line and immediately directed to go out and bring in a cold, dead bird.

The best trainers are usually born, not made, but all of them work hard to hone their skills. One such trainer is Toller owner Susan Kish, who began field training her Tollers shortly after obtaining her first puppy. Sue came to field work with an extensive background in obedience training and dog therapy work. In the remainder of this chapter, she details her training philosophy and outlines the early stages of the program that she has developed, with the help of gundog trainers Norm and Adrienne Bordo, to transform her Tollers from fuzzy puppies to eager and successful trial contestants. Sue runs her Tollers at various levels of the CKC Working Certificate Program and the new Hunting Tests, as well as at tests of the North American Hunting Retriever Association (NAHRA) and the American Toller Club.

HOW TO FIELD TRAIN YOUR NOVA SCOTIA DUCK TOLLING RETRIEVER
By Susan Kish

Training the Toller begins at a far younger age than most owners realize. A puppy is born a blank slate, and his personality is developed with everything that he encounters as he matures. In the whelping box, he hears his first noises and has his first contact with humans. He learns what stress is as he is handled by people unknown to him and when he enters a new environment unfamiliar to him. Probably the largest stress for a young pup is leaving his littermates behind when he goes to his new family.

TAKING YOUR PUPPY HOME

In his new home, the puppy develops rapidly. This blank slate is soaking up all of these new experiences. Without realizing it, you are training your new puppy from the moment you pick him up. His first car ride could very well be the trip that he makes home with you. Try to make it a positive experience. Reassure him, talk to him softly, and if it is to be a long trip, remember to stop at regular intervals. When you enter your home, don't allow other people and pets in the house to overpower him. Introduce family members to the puppy by asking them to sit on the floor with him, at the puppy's level. Don't allow young children to pick up the puppy, and don't allow anyone to be rough with him.

EARLY DEVELOPMENT AND SOCIALIZATION

The next couple of weeks are critical in your puppy's development. He will be encountering many new experiences each day. He must learn to be clean in the house, walk on a leash, and be accepting of unfamiliar people. Socialization — taking your young puppy to new places to hear and see new things — is very important. But he should not be exposed to areas where lots of other dogs pass through until he has had at least two distemper injections and three parvo vaccinations, usually around twelve weeks of age. So you must be careful in choosing the areas in which you wish to socialize your puppy. Shopping centers are usually good places. I often sit outside with my puppy on a short leash and allow people to pet the puppy and talk to him. The puppy learns that strangers are gentle people and that people are to be trusted. The puppy is also exposed to the sights and sounds of a busy environment. Taking the puppy for frequent short car rides also helps him to become comfortable in this environment.

TEACHING BASIC COMMANDS

Now is also the time to teach basic commands. The first command that I teach my puppies is to come when called. Say the puppy's name in a happy tone to get his attention, then follow it with "Come." Run backward, and the puppy will usually chase you. The puppy should be well rewarded for this behavior with lots of pats and attention when he gets to you. Get down on one knee and make a fuss over him. Always keep the "come" word happy so that your puppy continues running to you.

If you are going to whistle train your puppy, now is a good time to introduce the whistle. Give the whistle one long blast, then two short blasts, followed quickly by "Come." Again praise the little guy for returning to you. Use lots of enthusiasm. You want him to think that he has just performed some kind of amazing feat. Repeat the exercise as your puppy becomes interested in other things. Whistle and call him. You will soon have a puppy that will return from a distance on the blast of the whistle. This is so much nicer than having to yell for him and is invaluable in field training.

TRAINING AS BEHAVIOR SHAPING

A word of caution here. Training is behavior shaping. Every time you interact with your puppy, you are shaping behavior. If you allow your puppy to stand up on you and you pat him, you are reinforcing this behavior; if he barks at the door so that you will let him in, you are teaching him to bark to come in. This may be acceptable if you wish to act as a doorman for your dog. I prefer my dogs to remain quiet outside, and I like to choose when they come in. If you feed your puppy from the table, you are teaching him to beg for food.

Ch. Kylador's Andebaran Destiny CD TT, a Nelson-Gypsy daughter, out field training.

What I want to stress is that *everything* you do with your dog — especially a young dog — is training. When you interact with your puppy, you are training him. Training is also confidence building, because you are teaching your puppy that yes, he can do what you requested, and that it really *is* easy to succeed. Teach all new exercises in increments, and make it easy for your puppy to succeed.

TRAINING AND YOUR TOLLER'S PERSONALITY

There are many ways to train a dog, and lots of them are very good (see list of recommended reading for training books). For a Toller owner, however, a word of caution. Tollers are extremely smart, learn very fast, and do not like constant repetition. They also can become sulky when they have had enough. Keep your training sessions short, and do not perform too many repetitive drills. If your dog has done a good job, quit while you are ahead. Keep your training sessions fun, be consistent with what you expect from your dog, use lots of praise, and maintain your patience and sense of humor.

BEGINNING RETRIEVING TRAINING

Field training can start at a very young age. Hopefully, your puppy was introduced to wings and short retrieves before he left his breeder. When you get your puppy home, let him settle in and bond to you. Then you can continue with the wings and short retrieves. It is important to wait until your puppy has bonded with you if you expect him to return the object to you.

Pick a confined area in which to work. A hallway, with all of the doors shut, works well. Kneel on the floor, hold the puppy on your lap, and get his attention. A good retrieving toy for a young pup is a knotted sock or a tennis ball. When he is interested in what you are going to throw, toss the object five to ten feet in front of him, releasing him at the same time. When he reaches the object, praise him immensely, and coax him back to you by clapping your hands or running backward. If the area is small enough, the puppy will usually run back toward you because he has nowhere else to go. As he gets nearer, stoop down to his level, catch him, and praise him, but *do not* remove the retrieving object. This is his prize. Allow him to hold it for a short while as you tell him what a terrific job he has done. As you are praising him, say, "Good puppy, Hold," and pat him for a job well done. Hold will be taught later, but now is a good time to start teaching this word association. Repeat the retrieves only three or four times. You are working for success, and a few good ones are best. As in all training, you want to leave your puppy wanting more.

If your puppy is retrieving enthusiastically in the confined area, you can move into a larger area. You can now lengthen your retrieves, but do it gradually. If you find that your puppy is heading in another direction with his retrieving object, put a line on him to coax him back to you. Never let your puppy repeatedly run away when retrieving or you will teach this undesirable behavior. Put him on the line and coax him back — do not drag him back. The puppy usually just needs a little convincing at this stage. If you consistently ask him to return to you, you will shape the behavior needed for more advanced work.

BUMPERS AND WINGS

As soon as your puppy is big enough to carry a bumper (usually by ten weeks), this can be used for all future retrieving training. But remember — the bumper is not a toy. Do not leave it out where the puppy can get to it and chew on it.

Wings can now be taped onto the bumper for your puppy to retrieve. Go back to very short retrieves when you introduce these new bumpers so that you can see how your puppy handles the wings. If he tries to tear the wings off the bumper, give him a firm "No," place the bumper gently in his mouth, and run backward. Never let a puppy tear at the wings. If he is more interested in eating the wings than in retrieving the bumper, remove the wings until your puppy is force fetched, an exercise that occurs after six months of age.

Foxgrove's Natural Edge retrieving at 7 weeks of age. Bred by Sue Kish and owned by Donna Lahaise.

Mother and daughter work together. Ch. Sundrummer's Seawitch and Ch. Westerlea's Bonny Bluenose.

WING-CLIPPED PIGEONS

I introduce my Toller puppies to wing-clipped pigeons between eight and ten weeks of age. I do this for two reasons. First, it helps in choosing the birdy puppy, and second, it introduces the puppy to live birds during a very important period in his development. At this age, a puppy cannot hurt the pigeon.

Kneeling on the ground, I have the puppy focus on the bird thrower, who goes ten or fifteen feet away and tosses the bird into the air. The puppy is immediately released and usually goes tearing after the bird. Puppies will show different reactions. Some will eagerly pick up the bird and carry it, others will tentatively chase it and check it out, and the odd few will ignore it. One session on live birds is all that a young dog needs. They can be reintroduced after the force fetching is done.

INTRODUCING YOUR PUPPY TO TERRAIN

A young dog should also be introduced to the terrain in which he will be asked to hunt. Once your pup has had adequate vaccinations, take him out to the fields and woods for a walk. Wear your boots, because you are going to lead your puppy through some puddles and muddy areas. Take the pup out of the car on leash, and once you have gotten away from any traffic areas, turn him loose. Walk and encourage him to explore different areas as you go. Walk through thick cover as well as open areas. Pick out some muddy areas and walk through them. Try to cover as much varied terrain as possible.

Water can be introduced to your puppy at a very young age. Encourage your puppy to enter the water, but *never* drag him, push him, or throw him into the water. Make the introduction a pleasurable experience. Pick a warm day and warm water — water that you yourself do not mind entering. Play with your puppy along the shore. Walk a short distance into the water and call him to you. One way that has always worked for me if the other method fails is to cross a narrow stream and call the puppy. Puppies do not like to be left behind and will cross to be with you. Make a big fuss as he crosses the stream and when he gets to you. Some dogs are just natural swimmers and will not hesitate to enter water, while others will need some encouragement. Do not despair if your puppy will not enter the water the first time. Just keep the experience pleasurable and do not scare your puppy.

The future Ch. (Can. Am.) Westerlea Cheers to Bayrevel shows that a pup is not too young to bring in a bird.

BIS Ch. Sandycove at Westerlea retrieves a pigeon during WC training.

Steady your puppy by bending to his level and holding him around the chest. Make sure that he is watching the gunner, then give your puppy a verbal command, "Mark." Have the gunner yell, "Hey, Hey," and toss the bumper into the air in a nice arc. As soon as the bumper hits the ground, release your puppy. As the puppy picks up the bumper, whistle him to you and race backward ten feet. Because he is on a line, you can direct him to you in case he has other ideas.

Repeat the same retrieve, having the bumper land in the same area, with you in your new position that is a few feet longer. You are lengthening your retrieve while building your puppy's confidence, because he is always going into the same area to pick up the bumper. Three or four retrieves are plenty for a training session. Yes — your puppy wants more — but his attention span will start to wander, and success is what you are after.

Jared Howard with Bandit after a successful hunt. Courtesy Jeff Howard.

LENGTHENING THE RETRIEVES

By this time, your puppy is now used to varied terrain, is retrieving from short distances, and is learning to swim. It is time to start lengthening his retrieves.

Field training requires several people if you are to lengthen your retrieving distance. At this point, you will need a gunner — someone who will stand out in the field and throw the bumpers for you. A big mistake that trainers make at this point is not running the puppy on a long line. With the dog on a line, you can make sure that he will come back to you and not head in another direction. It is easier to prevent bad habits than correct them.

Have the gunner stand out in the field where your puppy can see him. Bring your puppy to the area from which you will be sending him. At this stage, you should be working on a clear field with little, if any, cover. The goal is a successful retrieve, not a long hunt that will discourage the puppy.

INTRODUCING YOUR PUPPY TO GUNFIRE

Introduction to gunfire can begin once your puppy is retrieving well in the field. The gunner in the field will now yell, "Hey, Hey," and immediately fire a .22 blank. With the gun being at a distance, the pup should not become gun-shy. Gradually move the gunner closer, always watching your puppy to make sure that he is comfortable with the gunfire that close. When your pup has no problem with the .22 blank at close range, move back out into the field and introduce a .20 gauge in the same sequence. The puppy will soon associate the sound of the gun with the retrieve. When gunfire is introduced in this way, your puppy should not become gun-shy.

FORCE FETCHING

I am a firm believer in force fetching a Toller. It is impossible to properly go through the full sequence in this chapter, and I would like to refer readers to James Spencer's book, *Training Retrievers for Marshes and Meadows*.

Force fetching can begin as soon as your pup has his full set of adult teeth. In force fetching, the pup is taught to pick up and hold on command. For those who firmly believer that Tollers are natural retrievers, I will not disagree with you. What my force-fetched Tollers give me is a perfect retrieve with delivery to hand at all times. When my dogs are sent, they do not quit and do not mouth the birds. Force fetching virtually eliminates a hard mouth, because the dog is taught what is expected of him when he is retrieving birds.

Force fetching is also a confidence builder. The dog fully understands what is expected of him. He must pick up the bird gently and carry it to his master without chomping on it or dropping it and must hold it until he is asked to give it up. A dog that is not force fetched is working on the hope method — you hope that he will bring it back to you. This works well for some, but for those who want a nice crisp pickup and delivery to hand, read Spencer's book.

GETTING YOUR PUPPY OFF THE LINE, LENGTHENING RETRIEVES, AND INTRODUCING MORE COVER

Your pup is now force fetched, comfortable with gunfire, and retrieving with a gunner, and he has been introduced to water. It is now time to get serious. Some basic obedience training should have occurred along with the field training. Your pup knows what come means and is returning to you with the bumper, because he is

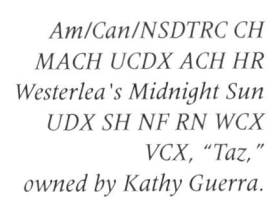

Am/Can/NSDTRC CH MACH UCDX ACH HR Westerlea's Midnight Sun UDX SH NF RN WCX VCX, "Taz," owned by Kathy Guerra.

on a line and thus is patterned to what you want. Now is the time to get him off the line, lengthen out the retrieves, and get him into more cover.

With your pup sitting beside you on a check cord (a three-foot cord that you can use to steady him), have him locate and mark on the gunner. Call for the shot, wait for the bumper to land, count to three, and send your puppy. He should be eagerly retrieving and picking up the bumpers at this point, and if he is force fetched, he will bring them back to you without playing with them.

If your puppy has been force fetched, birds can be introduced without your worrying that your puppy will play with them on the return. Pigeons are best on land, because they are not too big for a young dog to carry with confidence. Again, you use the same sequence of having your puppy locate the gunner, calling for the shot, and sending the dog. If you have been thorough in your training and have not cut corners, your puppy will deliver to hand.

Cover can be introduced for your puppy to run through, but it is best to have the bumper land in open areas until he has enough confidence to run through cover for the retrieve. There is no sense in making things too difficult all at once.

When introducing retrieves into cover, it is best to keep the distance short. What you want is a successful retrieve, and this can be accomplished in several ways. One of the best is to place several bumpers in the cover where the bumper is to be thrown so that once the pup gets into the area, he is more likely to find a bumper even if it is not the one thrown. Which bumper he retrieves is not important. A successful retrieve is what matters to build confidence. Again, only do a few at a time and then quit. Vary your terrain with each training session. As his confidence builds, start stretching out the length of the marks. Always keep in mind that your Toller is watching the gunner from an eye level of less than two feet. When setting up marks in cover, get down to his eye level to see if he can actually see the gunner and the trajectory of the fall of the bumper. Don't send him to retrieve something that he could not have possibly seen.

Harbourlights Highland Chance with a pheasant after a successful hunt. Courtesy Ron MacMillan.

WATER RETRIEVES

Serious water retrieving is always trained after the puppy is very confident about land retrieving. This is done for several reasons. Before asking a puppy to retrieve in water, you want to be sure that he is very comfortable swimming distances. Water is a harder medium than land in which to retrieve, and it takes longer to get to the mark. Thus, the dog must remember the mark for a longer period of time. And it is harder to make a correction in the water than on land. If my dog quits on land, I can lead him to the bumper. I prefer not to have to swim with my dog to a bumper, but I have done it.

The puppy can do short — and I stress short — water retrieves as soon as he is reasonably comfortable in the water. However, do not throw a bumper farther than he can comfortably swim or you will have a puppy that refuses a retrieve. There is not a lot you can do about this that will be positive.

When setting up your first water retrieves, it is important to pick an area from which to work that will discourage bank running. Dogs can be taught to take angled entries, but this is not the goal right now. Just try to keep it very simple and straightforward. Have your puppy back on the long line. It is usually easier to use a line that floats, because it will not sink and become tangled around the puppy's legs.

Start with fairly short retrieves in open water — that means no cover for the dog to swim through and no cover where the bumper lands. Use white bumpers, because these will be easier for the puppy to see. Have the puppy mark on the gunner, and call for the throw. Wait several seconds, then send the dog. Because the puppy is on line, feed the rope out behind him as he swims. The rope will ensure that, once your puppy has the bumper, he will return to you and not swim to the opposite shore or somewhere downstream on his return. Again, you are trying to prevent mistakes instead of having to correct them.

Watch your puppy carefully as he approaches the shore on his return. Many dogs will drop the bumper as they exit the water so that they can have a good shake. One way to prevent this is by meeting your puppy at the water's edge and taking the bumper before he exits the water. Another is by running away from shore as he gets close. This is the same as when you did early puppy retrieves, where you ran backward and the puppy chased you. The most foolproof method is to force fetch your puppy, because a puppy that has gone through this training has learned to hold until delivery to hand. I cannot say enough about the problems that force fetching prevents.

As your puppy becomes proficient with these water retrieves, you can start lengthening them. But watch your puppy for signs that you are pushing him too far. If a young dog refuses to enter the water, you may be asking too much from him. Remember — you are working on success, not on marathon retrieving sessions. Do only a few retrieves at a time and keep things successful. When your puppy is retrieving successfully and is not hesitating about turning and coming back to you, you can remove the line.

COVER IN THE WATER

When introducing your young dog to cover in the water, you may want to shorten up the retrieves if possible. Again, keep in mind that confidence building is the name of the game. The puppy must now remember the area of the fall, because he will not see it while he is swim-

Rusty and his son Val, Ch. (Can. Am.) Bhalgair of Lennoxlove Am. Can. WC, Can. CDX, both love the field best. Here they are winning Intermediate NAHRA ribbons.

ming. In the open water, the white dummy sat on top of the water and made it easier for the puppy. Warn the gunner to be ready to assist the puppy if he quits. This can be done by calling, "Hey, Hey," and throwing a rock into the area of the fall, or by throwing another bumper into the water right where the first one fell. You do not want your puppy to quit. If he needs help, redo the same mark again. He now knows where the dummy is and will be more confident his second time out. With each successful retrieve, you are building your Toller into a buddy that will be an asset when you are out hunting.

DECOYS

Because hunt tests call for dogs to work through decoys, your Toller must learn that decoys are not toys and should not be retrieved. This is trained on land by placing out several decoys. Walk your puppy on leash and allow him to check out the decoys, but do not allow him to pick them up. If he does, say "No," and correct him with the leash.

After your puppy is familiar with the decoys, have him retrieve a dummy thrown next to them, and have him run through them to retrieve a dummy thrown farther away. Because he has never been allowed to play with them or retrieve them, he should lose interest.

Do the same drill on water. Set the decoys out close to shore, and allow your puppy to see them. They will be viewed as just another part of the scenery, and your puppy should completely ignore them when working. In training, set up marks where the puppy has to retrieve through the decoys, to the side of the decoys, and in among the decoys.

INTRODUCING YOUR TOLLER TO BOATS

Tollers that are to be used for hunting need to be introduced to boats and must learn to retrieve out of them. Good boat manners start the first time the pup enters the boat and is asked to stay quiet in his designated area. The puppy must learn to retrieve off of the side of the boat and re-enter on a ramp at the back of the boat. A dog that is retrieving well usually has no problem adapting to this situation.

TRAINING MISTAKES

It seems that the more dogs I train, the less mistakes I make and the more I learn. One of the most common mistakes made by many Toller owners is not immediately curtailing the

Harbourlights Taffy Pull, the first NSDTR to earn 40 UKC/HRC championship points to put the title HR in front of her name. Bred by W. Avery and Erna Nickerson, owned by Alan and Janet Wagner, Pacific, Missouri. Courtesy Janet Wagner.

The first Toller to have gained points in a licensed field trial, Ch. (Can. Mex.) Cinnstar's Ian of Littleriver Can. Mex. CD, is owner-bred, trained, and handled by Laura Grossman.

Cinnstar's Southern Fundy Fox US WC, owned, bred, and trained by Laura Grossman White.

A young puppy belonging to Laurie Geyer, Skylark Tollers, retrieves a Teal. Photo courtesy of owner.

Ch. Rosewood Air Marshall CDX WCTT "Rory"; owner/breeder Terry McNamee, Rosewood Kennel. Photo by Terry McNamee.

Age is no barrier. Bonny at age ten. Courtesy Johan Adlercreutz.

screeching Toller. A Toller puppy has an intense desire to retrieve and often lets out a horrible noise, anticipating his turn, or complaining because it is not his turn. This sounds very much like an infant in distress and is very high pitched. Some Tollers are gifted with this lovely sound, and from others it is never heard. A Toller that learns that this is acceptable behavior is almost impossible to be made quiet.

The first time — the very, very first time — your puppy utters this awful noise, hold his nose and say, "Quiet." This is supposed to work in theory. However, I have found that my best retrievers almost lose their mind when another dog is working, and the only way I was able to keep my Jenny quiet as a puppy was by putting a bark collar on her until she learned to stay quiet while other dogs were working. Was this cruel and unjust punishment? I don't think so. It did not take this dog very long to learn to stay quiet, and I am now able to work her alongside the other dogs without the collar. A dog that screeches will not make much of a hunting companion, because he will screech when the ducks come in and when you shoot at them, and he will screech even louder when you miss. Not a very pretty picture.

Another common mistake is throwing a tennis ball or bumper for several dogs at once. What happens is that the fastest and most aggressive Toller returns with what is thrown and usually tosses it at your feet. He runs back anticipating the next throw. What have you done? You are accepting a dog running to retrieve and coming back empty, because only one dog can come back with the ball. You are accepting a dog tossing the thrown object at your feet and immediately leaving again. You are also blowing the confidence of the other dogs that don't get to retrieve and are working at ruining them. All in all — not a pretty picture. If you plan on having a good working Toller with good line manners and delivery, please play with your dogs individually.

Another mistake that new Toller owners can make is treating their dog like a Labrador Retriever. Tollers are a lot more unforgiving than other retrievers and are better compared to Spaniels. Although many Toller breeders profess that Tollers should never be given any type of harsh correction, I have found that when it is delivered at the right moment, with praise following for the new behavior, a dog reacts just fine. When a dog becomes too sulky in training, I place him back on the truck and let him watch me work the other dogs.

I have found and hopefully stressed throughout this chapter that repetitive drills will not work with this breed. The Labrador will do

> **WHICH DUCKS TOLL?**
>
> Toller historian Colonel Cyril Colwell once made a survey of experienced waterfowl hunters and arrived at the following conclusions regarding the tollability of various species.
>
> Dusky Mallards: One of the best to toll
> Widgeons: Will toll
> Whistlers: Difficult to toll, slow and wary
> Teals: Easily tolled
> Mergansers: Will toll with heads erect and necks straight out; cannot keep them away; in fact, a nuisance
> Butter Balls: Will toll well
> Pintails: Yes
> Sea Ducks: Moody, sometimes will toll (opinions differ here)
> Coots: Moody, do not appear to notice dog, sometimes will come in slowly  
>
> Blue Wings, Black Ducks: Splendid and come in very fast
> Bluebills or Broad Bills: Splendid, will toll with heads erect and necks straight
> Scaups: Can be tolled
> Red Heads: Inquisitive
> Old Squaws: Will toll
> Canadian Geese: Occasionally

things over and over again, while the Toller will say, "I've done it right — let's get on to other things."

A trained Toller is truly an asset on a hunting trip. Chelsea, my thirty-five-pound bitch, has brought in a nine-pound goose that she carried, not dragged, back. She has also proven to be an excellent pheasant dog, both as a flusher and retriever. Toller hunting stories abound, and Tollers are brave enough to tackle most hunting situations. However, it is the responsibility of the gundog owner to learn to recognize the dog's limits and not keep him in extremely cold water constantly without a chance to dry. With his reduced body mass, he will chill earlier than a larger retriever. If you can recognize your Toller's limits, he will make a fine companion for most hunters.

These outstanding etchings by Lynn St. Clair Stubbs show excellence in head, type, and movement.

12
The Versatile Toller

Tollers can do it all. They are fine hunting dogs and the ever-growing number of multi-titled Tollers shows that they excel in hunt tests, obedience, agility, tracking, flyball, scent hurdling, rally and dock diving. A few Tollers have even been used for skijoring, a combination of cross-country skiing and sled-dog racing.

The bright, lively, agile and alert Toller, with tireless retrieving drive, has a temperament that helps make him such an all rounder. These same attributes make Tollers invaluable companions for active families which enjoy hiking, biking, swimming, boating, camping and cross-country skiing. In the 1989 Canadian statistics for winning dogs, all five of the top-placing show Tollers also held at least one other title, a record for any sporting breed.

OBEDIENCE

Many Tollers have done extremely well in formal obedience competitions, but care must be taken to keep training creative by varying exercises and making frequent changes of routine. Repetition bores the thinking Toller.

In both Canada and the USA, obedience competition is divided into three main levels of difficulty: CD (Companion Dog); CDX (CD Excellent or Open); UD (Utility Dog). Classes are divided: trainers who have not earned an Open or UD title compete in A; B is for those whose dogs have these titles, and also any professional trainers. In Canada dogs gaining UD are titled OTCh (Obedience Trial Champion).

In the USA, however, dogs must first earn a UD title, then accumulate points from Open and Utility classes before OTCh can be earned. An Obedience Master may then be earned for scores of 190 or better from the Open B and Utility B

MOTCH CH Foxgrove's Circle of Life SH, WCX, RE, "Taffy." Owners/breeders: Diane Loiseau and Sue Kish. Taffy was the first toller bitch to obtain the MOTCH title in obedience.

131

classes. AKC also has a Grand Master title for which dogs can have OGM after their names. The Grand Master Obedience Trial champion title is the highest of all: points are awarded for a minimum score of 195 in both Open and Utility classes at the same trial on ten separate occasions under ten different judges; a High in Trial must be achieved in at least one Open and one Utility class.

Both AKC and CKC now offer a Pre-Novice test for beginning obedience, an introduction to regular competition. AKC lists pre-titles for those working at differing levels. United Kennel Club also features popular obedience tests run on similar lines.

European obedience tests are quite different. When two American-owned dogs competed at Crufts, owners John and Marie Simonson had to learn completely new exercises for the huge trial. John was on the U.S. team with his Eddy, while Canadian-born Marie was part of the Canadian team with Eddy's son Winston—a nice international effort!

The late CAN/AKC/NSDTRC(US)CH AKC OTCH CAN MOTCH Westerlea's Sir Edmund UDX4 OM1 MH US/CAN WCX,VCX, ROM, "Eddy," owned by John and Marie Simonson, represented the USA as a member of the 2010 World Cup Obedience Team at Crufts. He was 3-time Canadian National Toller Specialty High in Trial for Obedience (2003, 2007, 2011) and High in Trial at the USA National Toller Specialty (2010). He was one of a few all-breed retrievers to earn an AKC Championship, Obedience Trial Championship and a Master Hunter Title, and to date the only Toller to earn that combination of titles.

HUNT AND WORKING CERTIFICATE TESTS

Although Tollers are first and foremost hunting dogs, early training methods did not place much emphasis on such niceties as delivering to hand, sitting to deliver or taking a straight line out to a bird. As with obedience, trainers must be creative and not allow their dogs to become bored. A sense of play is a basic ingredient in Toller makeup so all training should be kept fun. Many hunters do not wish to fine-tune their dogs, but for those who do there are now various tests that are an integral part of the dog game.

The first organization dedicated to preserving and enhancing hunting retriever skills was The North American Hunting Retriever Association (NAHRA), established in 1984. Dogs compete in tests simulating typical hunting scenarios with distances and conditions encountered by most hunters. NAHRA still supports clubs throughout the USA and Canada.

AKC and CKC both established Hunt Tests in the 1990s, and both have rules for fair tests under fair conditions. Each dog which passes the test earns a "leg" towards a title. The basic test is Junior Hunter (JH), going on to Senior Hunter (SH) and finishing with Master Hunter (MH). CKC also has a Grand Master Hunter title (GMH), which is basically a MH test passed ten more times. These land and water tests are very popular with hunters and non-hunters alike—hunters enjoy spending a summer at dog sports which keep their dogs fresh, while non-hunters gain field experience helping to enhance their dogs' original purpose. As in all types of hunt tests, dogs are evaluated for natural retrieving desire, memory, marking ability and obedience to handler commands.

The United Kennel Club (UKC) enjoys a big following with its popular hunting, obedience and conformation tests. Field titles awarded in escalating levels of difficulty are SHR (Started Hunting Retriever); HR (Hunting Retriever); HRC (Hunting Retriever Champion), and GRHRC (Grand Hunting Retriever Champion).

The mid 1980s saw the introduction of the Working Certificate tests in Canada. The WC entry title was designed to help evaluate basic

SHR NSDTRC/AKC/UKC CH Water's Edge Stings Like a Bee UD WC FDX VCX, owned by Dan Rode.

instincts, and more refinements were incorporated into the WCI and WCX tests. Level of difficulty is a little below that required for Hunt Tests but WCX is similar to SH. These are one-day tests easy to put on as adjuncts to a Specialty Show.

Right from its start the American Toller Club, formed in 1984, required a basic instinct test for all its champions. From this has grown a very strong field Toller community, with the club still holding its own tests in addition to those of the AKC. A very basic tolling sequence is an important part of these club tests.

European Toller fanciers also have their own variations of tests, mainly based on those set out by the organization which controls dog activities in well over three-quarters of the world, the FCI (Federation Cynologique Internationale). The Swedish Toller Club formulated the first set of rules for separate tolling tests, starting in 2000, and these are spreading across Scandinavia. In Sweden the tests became official in 2007 and are now run by the Swedish Spaniel and Retriever club (SSRK) with three levels: Beginners, Open and Elite, the latter for dogs achieving two first prizes in the open class from two different judges.

"Winston," AKC/CAN/NSDTRC-US CH CAN OTCH Kilcreek's Sir Winston UDX, OM1, MH, US/CAN WCX, CAN UD, VCX, owned by John and Marie Simonsen.

GMH CH OTCH Redadict Road Runner WCX AGN AGNJ ADC, US WCI. Josh was imported into Canada from Finland. He is the only Show & Obedience Trial CH, Grand Master Hunter, & Agility titled Toller to date (2013). Owner Sue Kish, breeder Annina Nurmikivi.

The tolling test starts with the handler throwing dummies left and right from behind a blind, sending the dog to retrieve after each throw. Multiple land and water marks with birds follow, and higher levels also include blind retrieves. All tests end with a Free Search segment, something which North Americans could well emulate. Various game animals and birds are spread out over varying distances, usually in wooded areas, and the dog is simply sent by the handler to find and retrieve every one. There are no marked retrieves, no directional handling, just the dog using its nose and following its instincts.

MASTER HUNTERS

Canada

The first four are all owner/breeder/handled by Sue Kish:

1) GMH Ch. Foxgrove's This Bud's for you WCX CDX – first MH Toller, 4th GMH of any breed; 2) *Ch. Foxgrove's Raisin Cain QFTR WCX CD Am. MH WCX* (only Toller to earn a Qualifying title in Licensed Field Trials in 3 trials, earning a 3rd, 2nd, and a First, to qualify); 3) *Ch. Foxgrove's Sea Spray MH WCX CD Am.WCX*; and 4) *Foxgrove's Annie Get Your Gun MH WCX*.

GMH OTCh. Ch. Redadict Road Runner WCX AGN AGNJ ADC – bred by Annina Nurmikivi, owner/handler Sue Kish.

OTCh Foxgrove's Whirling Dervish MH WCX NSDTRC(USA) WCX AGN AGNJ – bred by Sue Kish, owner/handler Diane L'Oiseau.

GMH Ch. Redland's Ahoy There Seabright WCX – bred by Sandra Bruce, Shelley/Steve Hutt, owned by Sheila Fee, handled by Sue Kish.

Ch. Seabright's Start Me Up MH WCX RN NSDTRC(USA) WC – bred, owned by Sheila Fee, handler Sue Kish.

Can.Am.Ch. Javahill's I'm a B'liever Can.Am. MH WCX CD – bred by Linda Fitzmaurice/Meredith Noreen, owner/handler Donna LaHaise.

Ch. Kare's Red Hunter MH WCX CD NSDTRC(USA) WCI – breeder/owner/handler Derek Dunn.

Am.Ch. Redrock's Straight Shooter Can.Am.MH NSDTRC(USA) WCX – bred by Dominique Jolley, owner/handler Nancy White.

Redland's Pegasus Decoy MH WCX CD NSDTRC(USA) WC – bred by Sandra Bruce, owner Steve Hutt who handled to his last four MH passes, trained by Sue Kish.

Can.OTCH Ch. Brandywine Highlander Shaye MH WCX NSDTRC(USA) WCX – bred by Patricia Kinsley, owner/handler Donna Houlton.

USA

HRCH Am.Can.Ch. Springvale's Roy'll Flush MH WCX CDX – First US MH, owner breeder handler Sue Dorscheid.

MHR Westharbour's Admiral Halsey MH CDX Can. MH CDX – Second, one week later, bred by Rick/Cynthia Richardson, owner handled by Nancy White.

Skylark's RePete Adventure MH AX AXJ OF RN BN NSDTRC WCI VC – bred by Laurie Geyer, owner handler Mary de Lamerens. All titles put on by Mary with her first field dog!

Shamrock's London MH NSDTRC WCX – bred by Jean Gilroy, owner/handled by Jason Cyr.

HR Am.Can.NSDTRC CH Vermilion's Twist'n Torque MH MX MXB MXJ MJB WCX – bred/owned by Brody Koebensky/Kathy Koebensky-Como

Am.NSDTRC CH Manitou Aqueus All Spruced Up MH WCX AX AXJ – bred by Cynthia/Grant Lindemer, owner handler Danika Bannasch.

AMGCH/CKC/NSDTRC CH Cedar Fog Midnight Seduxtion MH UD MX MXJ XFRN WCX VCX Can. WCI – bred by Betsy Fogg, owner/handled by Kathy Guerra.

Leylines Beautiful Swimmer MH WCX – bred by Francine Kaplan, owner handled by Jeff Tinsman/Ruth Richards.

Am.Can.NSDTR CH Westerlea's Hey Now MH Am.Can.WCX NSDTRC WCI – bred by Alison Strang/Linda Moran, owned by Laura Hamilton. Iko was handled by Butch Higgins to his AKC JH, SH, and MH titles, then Laura took over for his US club and all 3 Canadian Working Certificates.

Am.Can. NSDTRC CH Javahill's I'm a B'liever MH WCX CD – bred by Linda Fitzmaurice/Meredith Noreen, owner handler Donna LaHaise.

Springvale's Home Grown MH WCX CDX RA AX OAJ - breeder, owner, handler Sue Dorscheid.

HR AKC/UKC NSDTRC CH Springvale's a Ton of Fun MH WCX Can WCI – bred by Sue Dorscheid, owned by Kelly Barry/Sue Dorscheid.

Chesagrove's Micmac Scout MH WCX CGC – bred by Shirl DeVore, owner handled by Robert/Ann Callender.

Am.Can.NSDTRC CH OTCH Kilcreek's Sir Winston MH Am.Can.WCX UDX OM1 VCX Can.UD - bred by Julie Hanson/Donna McClellan, owned by Marie/John Simonson, handled by Marie – her first field dog.

Foxgrove's Red Storm Rising MH WCX – bred by Sue Kish, owner handled by Tony Hunt.

Am.Can.NSDTRC CH Redrock's Straight Shooter MH WCX – bred by Dominique Jolley, owner handled by Nancy White. Shooter also qualified with a 2nd place at licensed field trials, handled by Sue Kish.

CH HR Lonetree's Neon Storm MH AKC UKC CDX Can.CD RE OAJ – owner bred/handled by Corinne Williams.

Can.GMH Ch. Foxgrove's Raisin' Cain MH WCX Can.QFTR WCX CD – breeder/owner handled by Sue Kish.

Am. Can.NSDTRC CH MOTCH Westerlea's Sir Edmund Am.Can.MH WCX UDX4 OM1 VCX – bred by Alison Strang, owner John/Marie Simonson, handled by John. Eddy was John's first-ever dog.

Springvale's Blitz for All Seasons MH WCX CDX OA OJ – bred by Sue Dorscheid, owner handled by Ritu Bala.

Note: Winners up to the end of 2013 are included above.

AGILITY

Agility, the fastest growing dog sport all over the world, attracts thousands to watch dogs and handlers run a course against the clock, rather like those of show jumping only tailored to dogs. Courses include seesaws, tunnels and jumps of varying heights, plus weave poles which high-level dogs run through with dizzying speed. Begun in UK in the 1970s, agility competitions are a landmark event at such huge shows as Crufts and the World Shows. AKC and CKC both have agility programs—Agility Association of Canada (AAC) and United States Dog Agility Association (USDAA), both using the same equipment but with slight differences in rules.

Tollers are eminently suited to agility and owners are finding trials a great way to build a dog's confidence and develop a rapport between dog and handler which carries over to other forms of dog work. Specific standards are required for games of Gamblers, Jumpers, Pairs and Snooker on courses designed by the judge of the day.

Agility titles are seemingly endless and far too numerous to be listed here. Everything agility can be found at www.cleanrun.com.

FLYBALL

This once popular sport appeared to have taken a back seat to agility, yet in 2009 alone over 350 tournaments were hosted by 137 US and Canadian clubs for the North American Flyball Association (NAFA). Modifications to equipment have meant that there are fewer serious injuries today, but dogs become extremely excited at these trials and can easily get out of control. Four dogs run in relay down a course of four hurdles to a specially constructed flyball box, trigger a tennis ball and return carrying the ball over the jumps to the starting line, where the next dog takes over.

Points are given for time; 20 points for Flyball Dog (FD) title, 100 points for FDX and with 500 points a dog becomes a Flyball dog champion (FbDCh). A very dedicated flyball enthusiast can earn a Silver Milestone certificate with 10,000 points and a Gold Milestone with 15,000 points. A 20,000 point dog will received an engraved plaque named after the first dog to reach this level, the Doberman Onyx.

Ripper clearing an agility jump at the AKC National Agility Finals. Photo courtesy of Terry Simons, Flyingdogagility.

"Annie," owned by Cheryl Tomayer, Torlan Tollers Reg'd, clears the tire jump in agility. Photo courtesy of owner.

"Chive," NSDTRC/AKC CH Skylark Chive at Water's Edge WC VC FG40K MBM IRONDOG, owned by Dan Rode and Lori Anderson, catching the ball at the training box (above) and going over a jump on the flyball course (below). Photos courtesy of Dan Rode.

RALLY

Rally Obedience, fast growing in popularity, comprises a combination of exercises from Canine Good Citizen to a bit of obedience and agility, and holds tests for dogs and handlers which are both fun and energizing. Each team moves at its own pace between 10 to 20 stations, depending on the level of test. Communication between handler and dog is encouraged and requirements are not as rigorous as those of formal obedience.

Rally was designed to produce dogs trained to be well behaved at home, in public and in the presence of other dogs. There are three levels: Novice (RN), Advanced (RA) and Excellent (RE). There is also a Rally Advanced Excellent (RAE) in which a team has to qualify in both Advanced and Excellent in ten trials.

The American Association of Pet Dog Trainers (APDT) is open to any dog and handler and is not limited to registered dogs. Canada has its own branch, along with the Canadian Association of Rally Obedience (CARO) and CKC Rally. There are many opportunities to win titles, including Puppy and Veteran. UK Rally, started in 2010, puts much emphasis on judges providing competitors with standardised, objective and fair tests. Rally is also appearing in Continental Europe.

DOCK DIVING

This exciting sport is gaining popularity in parts of the USA and Canada, with sanctioned training facilities springing up. Dogs race along an entry board of varying length then leap into a long pool in quest of a retrieve which is thrown where the handler thinks the dog will land. Some retrieves are snatched in mid-air. Water dogs such as Tollers love this sport, which consists of Big Air (a long jump); Extreme Vertical (High jump); Speed Retrieve and Iron Dog, which is for dogs that have achieved the highest score in the other three. More information can be found at *www.dockdogs.info*, which lists upcoming events, affiliated clubs and much more.

A Toller dives off the dock in a Dock Diving competition. Dogs jump into the water to retrieve a dummy and winners are chosen accordng to the length of the jump. Tollers are a natural for this competition.
Photo © J. Soria Pet Photography.

TRACKING

Hunting dogs have natural tracking ability, but tests of both CKC and AKC have formalized this into two levels of ability: Tracking Dog (TD) and Tracking Dog Excellent (TDX). Tracks of varying hours' duration are laid with some hidden articles to be found. In addition the tracks are also crossed at some points. Laura Norie of BC with Westerlea's Outfox the Fox (Sly) holds the honour of having the first Toller to earn TDX. Sly was also the youngest Toller to earn these titles.

Tracking tests were included in some of the early U.S. Toller Club's shows, with the first title going to Diana Semper's Sagewood's Vesper Belle Starr TD. European field tests have always contained a Blood Trailing test, another tracking variation.

OTHER ACTIVITIES

Tollers are tremendously versatile and can be found competing or participating in many types of activities. Dan Berg and Piper do Avalanche Rescue. Ellen Jackson trained her Toller to compete in lure coursing, a sport normally reserved for hounds. Undoubtedly there are more Tollers participating in unique activities.

UJJ Hylander's Lennoxlove Something About Meri, owned by Ellen Jackson, lure coursing. Photo © DreamEyce Studio.

CONFORMATION

Dog shows lend highest profile to winning dogs, but they may be the hardest for a novice to understand. The main purpose of dog shows is to find the best physical specimens of each breed entered, with judges using written Breed Standards as guidelines. Many deride such shows as mere beauty contests, but the Standards spell out the ideal for each breed and often contain useful information regarding the breed's origin, purpose and type. In North America there are seven different groups of breeds, with dogs bred for

"Colin," Ch Westerlea's Bold Venture, from one of Alison's last litters. While the tracking venue hasn't been the most popular one with Toller folks, the dogs love it. This is just another example of Toller talent! Photo courtesy of owner Terry Miller.

similar jobs being grouped together. Best of Breed winners go on to compete for the seven Group awards—Tollers compete in the Sporting Group with all the other gun dogs. Near the end of each show Group winners parade into the ring for the ultimate award, Best in Show. In the last few years a Reserve Best in Show has also been awarded, thus providing some consolation to a runner-up. In Canada puppies earning Best Puppy in Breed also compete for Best Puppy in Group; the final judging is for Best Puppy in Show. Some shows also have competitions for brace and veteran in show.

In reality, dog shows are giant elimination contests, going from maybe thousands of competitors at major shows down to the one BEST in SHOW dog.

Hettie Bidewell of Saskatchewan was the first person to take Tollers into the Canadian show ring in the 1960s, then Mary Sproul, Roberta Mackenzie, and Jim and Deanna Jeffery in the Maritimes joined in. One of the objectives of showing Tollers then was to have the breed accepted for its own virtues and be treated as an equal with all the other Sporting breeds. As time went on good-natured jokes about "bastard Golden Retrievers" and "little mutts" gradually disappeared.

CANADIAN BEST IN SHOW

Newcomers to Tollers might find it hard to understand the wave of excitement that swept the tiny Toller world when not one but two Tollers won Canadian All-Breed Bests in Show in 1980, thus setting the seal of showring acceptance for the breed. The honour of being the first Toller ever to place so high went to effervescent "Mork," *Ch Sproul's Highland Playboy CD*, whose historic win on June 1 in Battlefords, SK, was awarded by William Brennan to ecstatic owners Jim and Linda Barnes of Regina. The whole building erupted into pandemonium when Mork was selected as he had won a wide following at Prairie shows. Mork, bred by Mary Sproul in Nova Scotia, began his impressive show career with a Best Puppy in Group in 1979, and went on to become a consistent Group placer, earning Top Toller in 1981. He was also a key member of a Regina scent-hurdle team after he retired from the show ring.

June 28 was another red-letter day, when the second BIS was awarded to *Ch Westerlea's White Ensign* in Chilliwack, BC. A burst of cheering and applause greeted Virginia Hampton's choice of Tip with his regular handler, Sandra McFarlane. Breeder/owner Alison Strang had nursed a seemingly impossible dream of taking her own homebred Best in Show Toller back to her old home kennel club in Ottawa for Canada's premier dog show, the Purina Show of Shows, where every entry holds a BIS. As it is, both BIS Tollers upheld breed honour in Ottawa that year, and some future BIS Tollers followed.

1984 *Ch. Westerlea's Tru-Ray Red Rebel WC CDX*, owned by Ken & Brenda Stephens, bred by Alison Strang – a Tip son and full brother to

1987 *Ch. Westerlea's Red Duster*, owned by Sheila Walker, bred by Alison Strang.

1990 *Ch. Sandycove at Westerlea WC CD*, owned by Alison Strang, bred by Joan Noullet - a Tip grandson, then his son,

1991 *Ch. Westerlea's Ilo at the Well CD*, owned by Jay Attwell, bred by Alison Strang.

1994 *Ch. Sproul's Happy Higgins*, owner/bred by Mary Sproul – and then his son,

1995 *Multi BIS Ch. Sehi's Little Breton*, bred by Dr. Robert McNeil, owned by Dennis & Geralyn Tobin. (Eleven Best in Shows are claimed for Breton.)

Ch. Sproul's Highland Playboy was the first all-breed Best In Show Toller, 1980. Owned by Jim and Linda Barnes.

1994 Canadian National Specialty BOB was BISS Sylvan's Blaise of Thunder, owned by Sue Van Sloun and Sylvia and Neal Plante, bred by Sue and Neil Van Sloun.

BISS Ch. Berdia's Electra Ice Storm CD WCI JH AGI US WC, winner of the 2007 Canadian Specialty. Owner handled by Laura Norie, bred by Bernard Barber. Photo by Hershberg.

"K2," BIS GCH Vermilion's K2 of Edte, owned by Cheryl Chapman; bred by Kathy Koebensky-Como and Jamie Como.

BISS OTCH CH NSDTRC CH Kylador's Karma Kamelia WCX CGN AKC CD NSDTRC WC AKC ThD, owned by Lillian Greensides. Photo © Freeze Frame Photography.

MBIS BISS CAN/AM CH Kylador's Bustin Thru Th'Reeds CGC JH CD ADC AGI WCI ROMX, owned by Christine Jones and bred by Lillian Greensides.

BIS BISS GCH Pikkinokka's Lightning Bug won the 2011 US Specialty for Canadian breeder Til Niquidet; owner Stacy Einck-Paul and Nanci Mages.

2000 *Ch.Beinnbhreagh's Aces are Better*, a Breton grandson, owner/bred by Dennis & Geralyn Tobin.

2000 *Ch. Ruaview's Cape Breton Schooner*, another Breton son bred by Sheila Fee/Jan Stevens, owned by Gale & Martha Ashbaugh.

2004 *Ch. Sproul's Remshag*, owner/bred by Mary Sproul.

2006 Dual BIS *Can.Am.GrCh. Kylador's Bustin' Thru th'Reeds, JH WCI CD CGC ADC*, bred by Lillian Greensides & Karen Wright, owned by Christine Jones.

2008 *Can.GrCh.X Am. GrCh. Pikkinokka's Stormtide Barnaby RN TDI CGC CGN*, bred by Til Niquidet, owned by Kerri VanEaton.

2011-13 *MBIS MRBIS MBISS BISS(N) Can.GrChX Am.GrCh. Readyfor Going to the Max WC RN AGNJ*, bred by Jamie Klein, owned by Christina Calado. (Four BIS, seven ReserveBIS.)

2012-13 *MBIS MBISS(R) Can.Am.Ch. Roaneden's Int'l Harvester JH WC CGN*, Owner-bred by Christine and Rob Jones. (Seven CKC BIS, 1 UKC BIS.)

2013 *Can. GrCh. Vermilion's K2 at Tala of EdTe CGC*, bred by Kathy Koebensky-Como & Jamie Como, owned by Cheryl Chapman.

CANADIAN SPECIALTY SHOWS

Although the Toller is a native of Nova Scotia, an important place in their development is Regina, Saskatchewan. For it was there in 1974 that a small but enthusiastic band of Toller lovers formed the NSDTR Club of Canada, led by Larry Levsen who founded and edited the club newsletter *Toller Talk*. Several years later talk of holding the first-ever National Specialty show began, and in **1979** this dream came true. Spectators were excited by the most Tollers in one place anyone had seen. "Twenty-two Tollers and they all look alike!" was an amazed reaction heard at ringside as the entrants filed in. Founding members Joanne and Ron Saxby had the thrill of seeing their own *Ch. Todd of Alin Decaro CDX* declared the winner by judge Ed McNeill.

The next Specialty was not held until **1983**, in London, Ontario, and was notable for entries from across Canada, in addition to the first contestants from the USA. Knut Egeberg selected Alison Strang's homebred Tip, *BIS Ch. Westerlea's White Ensign*, as Best in Specialty and Best Stud Dog.

Expo year in Vancouver **1986** saw a giant show staged at BC's new showcase dome, the site of the next Specialty. Over 40 Tollers were topped in her first Specialty win by Alison Strang's homebred bitch *Ch. Westerlea's Bonny Bluenose*. Judge was Newfoundland breeder Kitty Drury who reportedly coined the "bastard Golden Retriever" remark heard so often at early Toller shows. Here she spoke of the breed's fine attributes and was delighted at the quality of the entries. Another highlight was the presence of Mr. and Mrs. John Colwell from Halifax, who presented a large trophy for Best in Specialty in memory of John's father, Col. Cyril Colwell, the man responsible for having the Toller recognized by the CKC in 1945. Early Toller breeder Hettie Bidewell was also welcomed.

1988, the CKC Centennial year, seemed appropriate for the next Specialty, part of a glittering show in the palatial Metro Toronto Convention Centre. This ran concurrently with the World Congress of Kennel Club meeting, to whose delegates Alison Strang spoke about Tollers during a symposium on Canadian dog breeds. Once more Alison's *Bonny Bluenose* was placed at the top by Megan Nutbeem over more than fifty entrants.

In **1991** the fifth Specialty went back to the Maritimes at Fredericton, New Brunswick, next door to Nova Scotia. Bonny's son *Ch. Westerlea's Ilo at the Well CD*, owned by Jay Attwell, was chosen by Betty Peterson for Best in Specialty.

An American-bred and owned Toller swept the board at the **1993** Specialty in Edmonton, AB. Judge James Kilgannon chose Evelyn Williams' *Am.Can.Ch. Lonetree's Barnstorm'n Jake WC CD Can.WCI CDX*, and this feat was capped not only as high scoring Toller at the obedience trial but by completing a WC the following day. Owner, trainer and handler, Evelyn bred some fine early American Tollers before succumbing to cancer far too early in life.

In **1995** the fiftieth anniversary of CKC recognition of the Toller was marked with a then-record entry of eighty Tollers from all parts of North America and by a formal proclamation making the Toller Nova Scotia's Official Dog, to match the iconic Bluenose schooner. However, judge John Kearley went outside the Maritimes for his Best in Specialty, *Ch. Kylador's Debonair Rob Roy*, bred in Ontario by Lillian Greensides and Karen Wright, with Donna Houlton as co-owner.

Later Specialties

1997 Cambridge, ON – *Dual BISS Ch. Kylador's Debonair Rob Roy CD.* Judge Archie Warnock,
1999 Surrey BC – *Ch. Littleriver's Delhaven Dancer,* bred/owned by Douglas Coldwell. Judge Leslie Rogers,
2001 Cornwall, ON – *Ch.Seabright's Red Alert* bred/owned by Sheila Fee. Judge Thom Nesbitt,
2003 Calgary, AB – *Ch. Kylador's Karma Kamelia CDX WCI,* bred/owned by Lillian Greensides & Karen Wright. Judge Virginia Lyne,
2005 Halifax, NS – *AKC/CKC MBISS AKC/CKC NSDTRC-USA Ch. Littleriver's Decoy Dancer CGC CD CDX JH.* bred by Douglas Coldwell, owned by John & Corinne Beckner. Judge Waren Hood.
2007 Surrey, BC– *Ch. Berdia's Electra Ice Storm CD WCI JH AGN SMADC RA-MCL,* bred by Bernard Barber, owned by Laura Norie. Judge Tom Alexander.
2009 Kitchener, ON – *Ch. Anando Off Center Toller Tyson,* bred by Doug & Andrea Mills, owned by Tanya & Gabe Bergamo. Judge Ainslie Mills.
2011 Calgary, AB – *MultiBIS MBISS(R) Ch. Ready-for Going to the Max WC CGN RN,* bred by Jamie Klein, and co-owned with breeder by Christina Calado. Judge Jeffrey Pepper.
2013 Fredericton, NB – *Can.Gr.Ch Am. Bronze Gr.Ch. Tollerpride Gathering Storm,* bred by John & Heather Gordon, co-owned with Rick Fearon. Judge Jan Buchanan.

The Canadian Toller club had voted, before 2011, to have separate titles for National and Regional Specialty shows, due to a number of Regional Specialties which had become popular but were for only one region, whereas a National is exactly that. Titles now are BISS(N) and BISS(R). Compiling these lists brings home how the dog world is changing. There are now so many more chances for titles that some dogs' registered names with titles take up more than one line in a catalogue or book like this one. Sometimes one wonders how much further this trend can be taken.

U.S. SPECIALTY SHOWS

Before AKC recognition came to U.S. Tollers in 2003, American fanciers got their show fix at venues of the UKC or American Rare Breed Association (ARBA) shows, as well as club events. In October 1984 fanciers met in Timonium, MD, at an ARBA show to form the U.S. Toller Club. Imagine their jubilation that day when the first Toller to win Best in Show was John & Marile Waterstraat's evergreen Sylvan's Rusty Jones. Rusty, bred by Sue Van Sloun, later took a second BIS, thus writing his name large in U.S. Toller annals — in fact the club Versatility award is named for him.

The U.S. Club eventually grew to where thoughts of holding a club Specialty took hold. The first U.S. Specialty was in **1989**, again in Maryland, with Rusty's son *Ch. Bhalgair of Lennoxlove* (Val) winning for owner/breeders the Waterstraats. The show went south to Carrollton, GA in **1992** when Sue Dorscheid won with *Ch. Sagewood's Silver Shadow CDX WC,* bred by Patty Beran. In **1994** Sue Van Sloun's homebred *Ch. Sylvan's Blaze of Thunder* took top honours in Ann Arbor MI. New England saw the **1996** show in New Bedford MA, where once more John & Marile Waterstraat were given the nod for BIS with their homebred *Ch. Lennoxlove's Bronze Trinket WC CD,* a Val granddaughter. Carol and Paul Milbury came out on top in **1998** with their homebred puppy *Driftwood's Coastal Clipper* at Appleton WI, and again in **2000** with *Ch.Driftwood Rose WC CD.* Finally in **2002** came the last club show, topped by *Dominique Jolley's Ch.Cayuga's Lucky Charm WC ,* bred by LeeAnn Gleason.

Since AKC recognition, an annual National Specialty show has been held as AKC rules demand. Then began a special time dominated by a Canadian dog bred in Nova Scotia by Douglas Coldwell. Owned by Corinne Beckner, *AKC/NSDTRC/CAN MBISS CH. Littleriver's Decoy Dancer* won in **2004, 2005, and 2006**, in Alabama, Oregon and Wisconsin. Not content to rest on laurels which also included the 2005 Canadian Specialty in Halifax NS, Corinne and Decoy went on to earn an impressive string of titles, JH, UDX, CGC and also agility awards, despite the demands of a family of eight children!

The **2007** Specialty, held in Syracuse NY, was won by a dog who became famous in U.S. Toller annals as the first Toller All-Breed Best in Show winner, Jeff and Deb Gibbs' *BIS Ch. Vesper Mariner Coupe de Vale JH AX AXJ WCI*. Breeder was Diana Semper.

2008 saw the winning debut of an Australian-bred, now officially *Am.GrCh/ CAN/NSDTRC(USA) BIS BISS Javahill Top Gun Am.Can.CD WC VC*. Maverick was bred by Terry Johnson and Andrea Nixon and owned by Linda Fitzmaurice and Meredith Noreen. Maverick has had enormous influence on the Toller in the USA and leads statistics for stud dog and number of U.S. champions.

Girl Power came in **2009** with *Ch. Manitou's Granturismo JH WC* at the Huntsville, TX, show. Tori is owner-bred by Grant and Cindy Lindemer.

At Lake Elmo, MI, in **2010** the winner was *GrCh. JavaHill Steal My Heart RA JH WC*, bred by Linda Fitzmaurice and Meredith Noreen, and owned by Paul Soderman. Now a GrCh NSDTRC(USA) & CAN CH JH WC Can. RN JH WCX Dual BISS, Nicholas triumphed again at the **2012** Specialty in Albany, OR.

Sandwiched in between came *GrCh. Pikkinokka's Lightning Bug*, who won the **2011** Specialty in Kissimee, FL, for Canadian breeder Til Niquidet and owner Stacy Einck-Paul, who lives in Virginia.

In **2013**, the National Specialty in Syracuse, NY, resulted in a great win for yet another JavaHill dog, this time *Am. Can. GCh. JavaHill Surf2 An 8Second Ride BN Can. WC CGC*. Bred by Linda Fitzmaurice, April Pasko and Terri Krause, Wrangler was owner-handled by young Kendyl Schultze from California. He also went BOB at Westminster Kennel Club in 2014 and was the first Toller ever to make the cut in Sporting Group at Westminster.

AKC BESTS IN SHOW

In July 2003 U.S. Toller fanciers were thrilled when Deb and Jeff Gibbs' handsome boy *Ch. Vesper Mariner Coupe de Vale* earned the first AKC All-Breed BIS. For some years "Schooner" really

GCH NSDTRC-US CH Vermilion's Ram'n Jam'n Rosco of TnT CD RN WCI, owned by Hugo Hietapelto and Kathy Koebensky-Como, taking Best Puppy 2012 NSDTRC-US.

set the type for U.S. Tollers and is a credit still to his owners and breeder Diana Semper.

A long wait came before Linda Fitzmaurice and Meredith Noreen's *BIS BISS GCH NSDTRC-US/Can CH Fionavar JavaHill TopGun Am/Can CD, WC, VC, ROMX*, "Maverick," came out on top in a California show in 2008. The following year a Maverick son, *Am.Can.Ch. Javahills's Backwoods Boy RN*, won also in California. Bred by Linda Fitzmaurice & Meredith Noreen, "Ranger" is owned by Phyllis McDonald. JavaHill was on a roll as in 2010 another Maverick son, *Dual BISS Ch. Javahill Steal My Heart WCX JH CD RE* (Nicholas), won BIS for owners Paul & Amy Soderman of California.

Then in 2011 came two Toller BIS, California again the setting for the first bitch to take an AKC BIS, *GrCH CAN/NSDTRC-US CH Javahill Surf N' Aloha Sun JH AM WC CA*, bred by April Pasko and Linda Fitzmaurice and owned by April.

Near the end of 2011 Stacy Einck-Paul's *GrCh. Pikkinokka's Lightning Bug* won BIS in Florida and then another in mid 2013, this time in Mississippi. Flash was bred in Canada by Til Niquidet.

NOTE: *Winners are listed for both the USA and Canada up through the end of 2013.*

EUROPE

European shows often have well over 3-4,000 entries and lack of statistics makes it impractical to list all wins. However mention must be made of what is still the largest single win made by a Toller anywhere. One of Finland's major shows is held at Lahti, outside Helsinki, and in 2007 a Toller went Best In Show in an entry of 4,538 dogs—a mid-sized show in Finland! One of the earliest Toller breeders, Mirja Tuominen, has had many good wins, but nothing matches this triumph for her Allan, *BIS INT. FIN. CAN. Ch. NORDW-05/EURW-06 Siphra's Fire at Kitimat Can. WC,* who also placed Group Fourth at the 2006 European Winner show in Helsinki. Although whelped at Mirja's home, Allan was bred by her close friend Britt-Marie Sundquist, who for some years has produced world class Pharoah Hounds but earlier also enjoyed a very successful Toller career.

Another big Finnish winner is *FIN Ch.W-09 -10 -12, DK SE(U)Ch. WW-10, WW-11FINW 09 10, FRW-11, HeW -11 -12 Fireheart Kid Sundance,* who was bred by Anja Laakso and owned by Saija Lampinen. Ramon has won three All-Breed BIS, one in 2011 and two in 2012, but Saija is proudest of his Group Third placing at the 2010 World Show in Denmark. Ramon is the only Toller to have placed in Group at a World Show as of 2013.

INT FIN CAN CH Siphra's Fire At Kitimat CAN WC, was Best in Show in an entry of 4,538 at Lahti, Finland. Bred by Britt-Marie Sundquist and owned by Mirja Tuominen, Allen was by Fin Ch Nordwart Kassandros, from Multi Ch Westerlea's Tornado At Siphra.

"Wrangler," Am Silver GCH Can GCH **Javahill Surf2 An 8 Second Ride** Can WC CGC, won the 2013 US National Specialty and was Best of Breed at Westminster in 2014. Owner Handled by Kendyl Schultze.
Owned by Kendyl Schultze, Linda Fitzmaurice, and April Pasko. Bred by L. Fitzmaurice, A. Pasko and Terri Krause.

Can Am GCH **TollerPride Gathering Storm**, winner of the 2013 Canadian National Specialty, was bred by owners John and Heather Gordon, co-owned by Rick Fearon. Storm was handled by Darcie Cantor.

"Worf," Multi BISS Can CH **Seabright's Red Alert** WCI JH AGX AADC SGDC CD, bred and owned by Sheila Fee, shown winning the NSDTRC Canada Specialty in 2001. Photo © Alex Smith Photography.

Multi BISS AKC/Can/NSDTR-USA/ARBA GCH SR **Driftwood's Coastal Clipper** RE CD WCI JH Can WC, owned by Dr. Paul E. Milbury, Ph.D., CFII. BISS NSDTRC National Specialty Show in 1998. BOB at AKC Eukanuba National Championships in 2005 and 2006.

BIS BISS CKC IKC NSDTRC-USA CH **Vesper Mariner Coupe De Vale** JH AX AXJ WCI VCX, "Schooner," owned by Deb Gibbs, bred by Diana Semper. NSDTRC-USA National Specialty Winner 2007; 1st AKC Sporting Group Winner; 1st AKC Multiple Group Winner; 1st AKC BIS Winner 2003; 1st Westminster Kennel Club BOB Winner 2004; AKC Eukanuba National Invitational BOB Winner 2006. "Schooner was purchased to be an agility and hunting dog and those qualities are what carried him in the breed ring. He won BIS on a Sunday afternoon. We headed home where Jeff was waiting to head out for a pheasant hunt with buddies. Schooner limited out on pheasant that week," according to his owner.

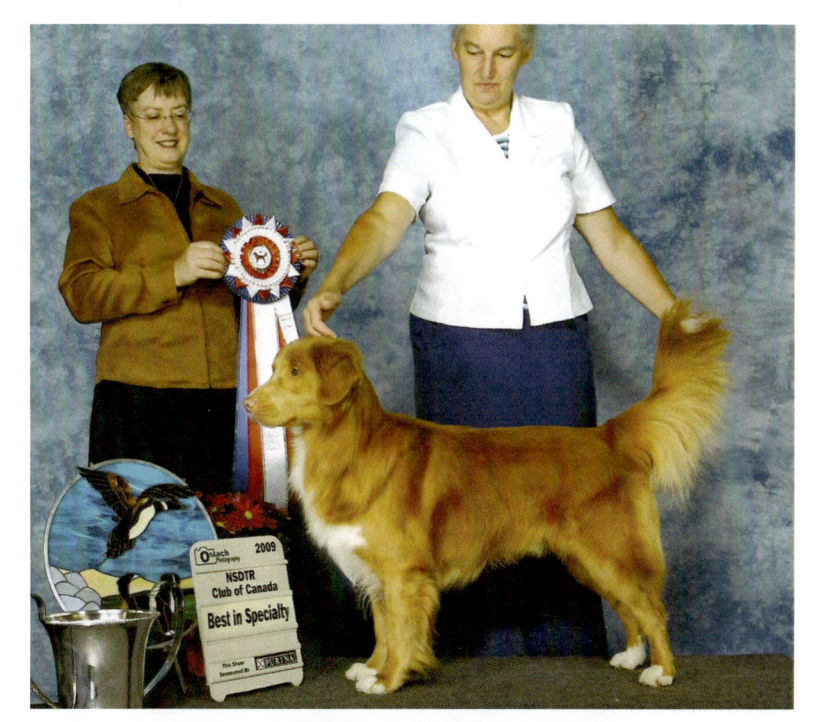

BISS (N) CH **Anando Off Center Toller Tyson**, 2009 Canadian National Specialty winner, and BOB Westminster KC 2009. Owned by Gabe and Tanya Bergamo. Bred by Andrea and Doug Mills and Joy Hill. Photo © Oslach Photography.

"Harvey," MBIS MBISS MBPIS BPISS Am GCH Can GCHEx **Roaneden's Int'l Harvester** CGN WC JH, the top winning Duck Tolling Retriever in Canada with 11 CKC All Breed Best in Shows in 2013, Ranking #6 All Breeds and #1 Sporting Dog in Canada (*stats by Canuck Dogs). He also has a UKC BIS win and 3 Best in Specialty Show wins (one as a puppy). Bred/owned/shown by Christine Jones.

MBIS MRBIS BISSN MBISS Am GCH Can GCHEx **Ready-for Going To The Max** CGN WC RN AGNJS winning BOB at Westminster in 2012. Owners: Christina Calado and Jamie Klein; Breeder: Jamie Klein Photo © Fritz Clark

Top Left:
AM/NSDTRC USA CH **Aqueus Hop To It** MH WCX NA NAJ, owned and bred by Danika and Michael Bannasch, handled and trained by Danika, is the youngest AKC CH MH Toller at 2 years, 4 months of age.
His dam (right), HIT **Aqueus Dutch Wood Polish** MH WCX MX MXJ CD earned her MH the same weekend. She was bred by Danika and Michael Bannasch and owned, trained and handled by Kathy Gibson.

Top Right:
GMH CH **Foxgrove's Raisin' Cain** QFTR CD US/Can WCX Am MH, owned by Sue Kish. Raisin is the most Field Titled Toller in Canada – the only Toller to hold the QFTR title and also a Grand Master Hunter.

MACH HRCH AKC/Can/NSDTRC-US CH **Vermilion's Twist'n Torque** CDX RE MH MXB MJB WCX VCX CGC Can JH WCI. Breeder-Owners: Kathy Koebensky-Como and Brody Koebensky. Photo by Cathy Kishel.

"Val," BISS NSDTRC/Can CH **Bhalgair of Lennoxlove** NSDTRC CD, Can CDX, NSDTRC WC, Can WCI. Bred by Al Haden; owned by Marile Waterstraat and John Hamilton.

148

AKC BIS GCH Can/NSDTRC-US CH **Javahill Surf N' Aloha Sun** JH AM WC CA. Breeder/owner Linda Fitzmaurice. Photo © Holloway.

Above Left: BISS CH **Kylador's Debonair Rob Roy** CD CGC, "Robbie," won the Canadian Specialties in 1995 and 1997. Breeder/owner handled and trained to all titles by Lillian Greensides.
Photo © Alex Smith Photography.

Above Right:
BISS GCH CH **Manitou's Granturismo** CD RE JH WCI, a bitch, went BISS at the US National in 2009. Owner/Breeders: Cynthia K. and Grant Lindemer. Photographer: RealTime.

Right:
BISS NSDTRC CH **Lennoxlove's Bronze Trinket** RE NSDTRC/Can CD WC VCX ROM was BOB at the 1996 US National Specialty. Bred and owned by Marile Waterstraat and John Hamilton

"Jouni," FIN MVA MV-98 S MVA KANS MVA V-00 **Siphra's Indiana Jones,** owner/trained by Minna Jatkola in Finland, bred by Britt-Marie Sundquist. One of his sons was imported into Canada and has had a big influence on the breed in both Canada and the USA. He was one of two brothers who won Finland's premier award for retrievers with high titles in both show and field.

Toller's Delight Running Dakota. DKCH (Danish Champion), DEVDHJCH (German Youth Champion), DEVDHCH (German Champion), KLBCH (Danish Club Champion), INTCH(u) (International Show Champion), NORDJUV04 (Nordic Youth Winner 2004), NORDVV12 (Nordic Veteran Winner 2012), KLBV05 (Toller of the Year (Bitch) 2005), KLBV06 (Toller of the Year (Bitch) 2006), KLBV12 (Toller of the Year (Bitch) 2012). Breeder/Owners: Gea Bos & Lars Møller.

Aus GCH **Lidlriva Almond Nougat** ET. Owner, Kim Walker; breeder, Emma Simon. 5 Group 1st wins, 12 Group 2 wins, Multiple Class in Group and Class in Show wins, BOB at Sydney, Canberra and QLD Royals, Won NSW State Finals Junior Handlers Competitions multiple times. He has appeared on television and danced in a respite centre for early onset dementia sufferers. Photo by Jacob Booth.

Toller's Delight Midnight Blue, DKCH (Danish Champion), DEVDHCH (German Champion), KLBCH (Danish Club Champion), NLCH (Netherland Champion), INTCH(u) (International Show Champion), VV02 (World Winner 2002), Breed winner Danish Kennel Club 2002 and 2003, KLBV02 (Toller of the Year (Bitch) 2002, 2003 and 2004.
Breeder & Owner: Gea Bos & Lars Møller, Toller's Delight Kennel, DK. Photo © Nina Helander

Andbjerg's Adonis Rufus, DKCH (Danish Champion), KLBV12 (Toller of the Year (Dog) 2012).
Breeder: Hanne Cramer Jørgensen, DK. Owner: Nina Orvokki Helander, DK.

Fireheart Kid Sundance BIS BISS C.I.E. DK CH SE U(u)CH EE CH FIW-09 FIW-10 HeW-11 WW-10
WW-11 FRW-11 DKW-12 HeW-12 FIW-12 NORDW-13 FIW-13 SEW-13 Owner Saija Lampinen.
So far, Ramon is the only Toller to place in group, a third, at a World Show.

*Eng CH **Trevargh the Entertainer at Brizewood**, top winning Toller in the UK with 67 BOB (including twice at Crufts) and 7 BIS. Owned by Dave and Babs Harding and Elaine Whitehill; handled by Elaine. Bred by Gareth & Sandra Hawkins.*

*Best in Show winning Aus. GCH **Fionavar Danger Zone**, owned and bred by Andrea Nixon and Terry Johnson of Brisbane, Australia. Photo by Mayfoto.*

13

Toller Good Citizens

THERAPY DOGS

One of the most heart-warming trends in recent years is the emergence of the use of animals, especially dogs and cats, to aid physically or mentally disadvantaged people. Success is well documented. Several organizations in North America are doing sterling work in the field, setting up criteria for therapy dogs, sponsoring seminars and workshops, and providing information and counseling to those wanting to participate in this useful and rewarding field.

Service dogs do more than play a vital role in the treatment of humans sick in mind or body. By showing what can be accomplished to help human beings in need, these dogs are providing an effective rebuttal to the anti-dog sentiment that is so prevalent in our urban environment.

Edith Latham and her brother Milton were pioneers in the exploration of the human/companion animal bond, and in 1918 they established the Latham Foundation for the Promotion of Humane Education. The foundation still exists today and is continuing to inform people of the interdependence of all life, to document the bond at work, to report on current research, and to encourage the establishment of further study programs. From this foundation have sprung most of today's dynamic organizations that promote the companion animal and human bond.

Pet Partners (formerly the Delta Society) is also active throughout North America with a thorough program for certifying dogs or cats for pet therapy. Their program has established a training manual to educate volunteers regarding the specifics of pet therapy. These include information on what type of patients the volunteer may meet, how to approach a blind person or an individual with Alzheimers disease, how to manage a dog near a wheelchair, and how to evaluate visits. The society maintains an extensive library and devotes much of its resources to education as a pet partner. See the Appendix for the address of this and other therapy organizations.

Human Animal Bond Association of Canada (HABAC) is dedicated to improving the quality of life for the elderly through human-animal relationships. Although it is HABAC's intention to eventually encompass all groups interested in promoting the human-animal bond, present resources require that the organization focus on only one aspect. In 1994, HABAC decided that the needs of the elderly should be the first to be addressed.

HABAC sponsored the first large international conference on the human-animal bond in Mon-

The exuberant Toller seems to know instinctively when to control his vivacious nature in deference to those around him. Tradewinds Dawn of Struan owned by Eric Johnson. Courtesy Eric Johnson.

treal in 1992 and followed this up with another in Vancouver in 1993. One of the presentations at the Montreal conference was on dogs in therapy, given by Gordon Travis, R.N., who carries out extensive therapy work with animals at St. Peter's Hospital in Hamilton, Ontario. Gord has had excellent results using a number of different Tollers in his program. At present, five staff members at St. Peter's own six Tollers, which is probably a breed record. The hospital's therapeutic recreation department has Tollers working eight-hour shifts five days a week, and Gord generally brings another Toller to work with him on a behavioral health unit. According to Gord:

> In general, we have found Tollers to be excellent at working one on one with our clients, because Toller nature is good for working in close proximity to patients who might display aggression. Our main aim is

Gord Travis' therapy dogs, including three Tollers: Caper, Cricket, and Ditto.

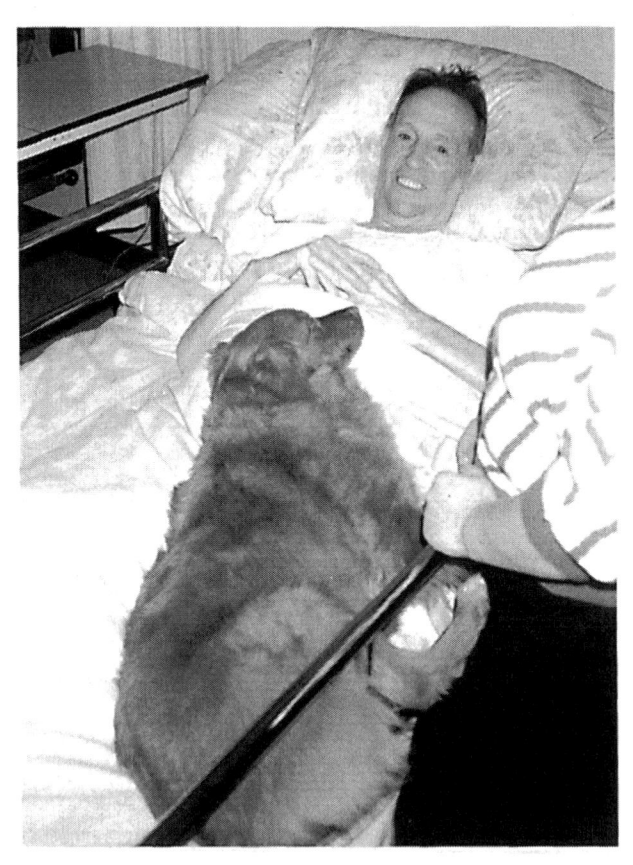

Ikea brings a smile to a bedridden patient in Langley, British Columbia.

to increase the socialization skills of our patients. Research is full of incidents where patients have responded to a dog but never to a person. Therapy dogs can also be used to help increase the range of motion of a particular limb simply by throwing a ball and having the dog retrieve it. Just having patients pet the dog or feel the texture of its coat brings some movement. We feel that the unusual color of the Toller makes a natural attraction for people. The presence of the dog also often stimulates a flood of old memories, which is a very positive step.

Gord also takes his dogs to other hospitals as well as to schools, youth groups, and nursing homes, where he receives much positive feedback.

Terry McNamee of nearby Grimsby has also done therapy work with her Tollers and had several registered with Therapy Dogs International, one of the organizations that oversees formal registration and training of dogs used in therapy.

International organizations have provided impetus on a more local level for groups doing valuable work in their communities. All groups are always looking for more volunteers and would welcome Toller owners.

CANINE GOOD CITIZENS

All of the therapy organizations now base their selection of animals to be used on the AKC's Canine Good Citizen Test, introduced in the late 1980s in an effort to educate dog owners about training their pet to be a better citizen. This was a positive step in the fight against growing anti-dog sentiment and legislation all across North America. The purpose of the test is to demonstrate that the companion dog can be a respected member of the community and can be trained and conditioned to behave in the home, in public, and in the presence of other dogs in a manner that reflects credit on the dog and its owner.

Left: Jumping through the hoop. Knowing a few tricks comes in handy for therapy dog work. Courtesy Diana Semper.

Above: Jalna's Zippy Zinfandel CD (M) is the first Toller to be awarded his AKC Canine Good Citizen Test. He is a dual-registered Therapy Dog TDI, TDInc. Courtesy Diana Semper.

Below: Benili's Ghats practices his concentration for drug detection in Quebec.

The ten sections, which must be passed to earn the CGC, are:

- Appearance and grooming
- Accepting a stranger
- Walk on loose lead
- Walk through a crowd
- Sit for exam
- Sit and down on command
- Stay in position (sit or down)
- Reaction to another dog
- Reaction to distractions
- Dog left alone

Any AKC club or other qualified dog-training organization may hold the CGC test, and use of the test is on the increase. This test will either supplant or enhance the CKC-sanctioned Temperament Test already in place in Canada. There are already instances of municipal organizations requiring dogs to hold a CGC certificate in order to be allowed off-leash in certain areas.

Tollers in both the United States and Canada have already won their spurs as Canine Good Citizens or Temperament-Tested dogs.

SERVICE DOGS

Although their numbers are small at present, Tollers are beginning to take part in differing types of service activities. At least one Toller has been trained in British Columbia as a hearing dog by the Pacific Assistant Dogs Society. Boots was donated to the society when he was six months old by his breeder, Olga Hymers.

Tollers are generally thought to be too small to act as guide dogs for the blind. However, one very large puppy was donated by breeder Bernie Barber in Ontario and graduated from the Canadian Guide Dogs for the Blind training establishment near Ottawa.

A new venture for Tollers is in the field of drug detection. Dogs in Finland and Sweden were already in use when a Swedish dog, imported into Canada in 1993, went into training with Canada Customs at Rigaud, Quebec. Customs officers heard about Toller abilities and thought that they would make ideal detector dogs, but wanted to obtain an older dog with some training in hunting. Benili's Ghats (Thai) was trained through youth level of Swedish field tests before coming to Canada and seemed an ideal candidate. He breezed through the drug-training program and is now living and working happily with handler Paul Beaulieu in the Vancouver area. He was even seen on television during the 1994 Commonwealth Summer Games in Victoria, British Columbia, inspecting the baggage of incoming athletes and spectators.

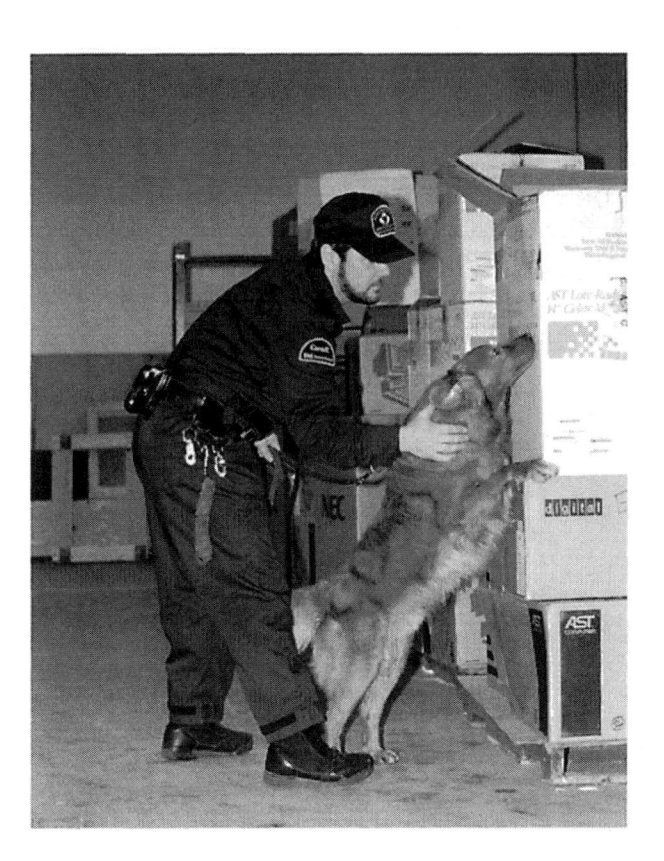

On several occasions, Paul and Thai have worked with their American counterparts, and Thai always impresses people with his scenting ability and agility. Where the heavier Labradors and Goldens have to be lifted to search high places, Thai can spring up on his own. One of Thai's sons, Westerlea's Douanier (Spookie), was sent as a young puppy to head trainer Michel Gaudet at the Rigaud facility and is reported to be progressing extremely well as an active drug detector. Recently, Spookie joined his dad in making one of the largest cocaine busts in Canadian history and was shown on Vancouver television.

Another Thai son, from his first Canadian litter, was accepted at the beginning of 1995 by the Canadian Avalanche Rescue Dog Association as an avalanche rescue dog in training. Bernache's Show Boat (Sherpa) and his owner Ken Matheson of Kamloops, British Columbia, spent an intensive five days of preliminary training and evaluation before they were admitted into the full CARDA training program. Dog and handler must train as a mountaineer team with year-round tracking, retrieving, obedience, agility, and endurance. Ken, who has owned several Tollers, hopes that the next CARDA session will see him and Sherpa validated as an avalanche rescue team in western mountain country, where deep winter snows, steep, rugged slopes, and dense scrub vegetation present demanding challenges to both dog and handler. These conditions are not for the unskilled or faint-hearted.

Left: Working together to detect contraband drugs are Swedish import Benili's Ghats, better known as Thai, and his handler/partner Paul Beaulieu of Canada Customs. Photo by Yvonne Rodney.

Dogs know when they have done especially well in competition, regardless of the event!

*Above left:
Can. CH Jagador'S Rainkist Nomia CD RA WCX JH Am WC Fdx Sadc enjoys competing in Agility.*

*Above right:
AKC BIS, GrCH CAN/NSDTRC-US CH Javahill Surf N' Aloha Sun JH AM WC CA poses with her Best in Show ribbon. Photo © Vavra Photography.*

*Below right:
Ch. Westerlea's Betsy Sunshine WCX JH CD proudly displays the bird she retrieved. Photo by Ann Lockley,*

14

Showing Your Toller

When Tollers first came into the show ring in the late 1960s, presentation was quite casual. As is often the case in Europe today, most exhibitors simply walked in with their dogs after giving them a brush and maybe a bath and hoped for the best. As the popularity of showing increased, and people with experience in other breeds came into Tollers, presentation became a matter for study and work.

Several early breeders insisted that the dog be shown in what they called natural condition — long-haired fuzzy ears, untrimmed feet, and all. In the late 1970s, famed handler/trainer Martha Covington Thorne coined an unforgettable phrase in one of her monthly columns in *Dogs in Canada*:

> *If Tollers are to compete with other show dogs, they must be presented in proper condition with pride. It does nothing for the promotion of Tollers to have them come into the ring looking like flying wombats in moult!*

Some present-day exhibitors have taken this so much to heart that there is now a grave danger of overgrooming Tollers, which is almost as bad. Here, as elsewhere, moderation is the key.

There used to be a certain amount of debate on the correct way to hold a Toller tail when stacking the dog in the ring. Some maintained that the tail should be held high and curving over the back in an inverted C. This was to try to emphasize natural Toller tail carriage when the dog was at full alert. This presentation worked for dogs that had very good toplines, but because these are not always easy to find in Tollers, it often looked clumsy and emphasized tailset faults. Others preferred to hold the tail stretched out in a straight line from the end of the croup, like Golden Retriever exhibitors.

Perhaps the most commonly used tail position is achieved by gently grasping the tail near its end and raising it well above the topline. Try to give the tail a slight curve to produce a small, less-exaggerated version of the C-carriage. If your dog's tail has a good white tip, do not hide this with your hand; rather, emphasize such an asset.

SHOW TRAINING

Toller puppies are trained for the show ring in the same fashion as most other sporting breeds by being taught to gait properly, hold a stack, and stand still with an alert expression. This is usually achieved by early table training accompanied by the use of bait.

Ch. Sproul's Highland Playboy, with owner Linda Barnes, getting ready for a show. Playboy is the first Best in Show Toller.

Ch. Westerlea's Clan Chieftain CDX, one of the "accidental" Sandy/Bonny litter, proving he is no mistake, either in show or obedience. Owned by Doug and Andrea Millis. Handled here by Cynthia Merkley. Photo by Stu Wainwright.

Tollers make wonderful companions for kids past the toddler age. Here, Darcy Beecroft, age five, takes a First in Junior Handling with Sandy. Photo by Linda Lindt.

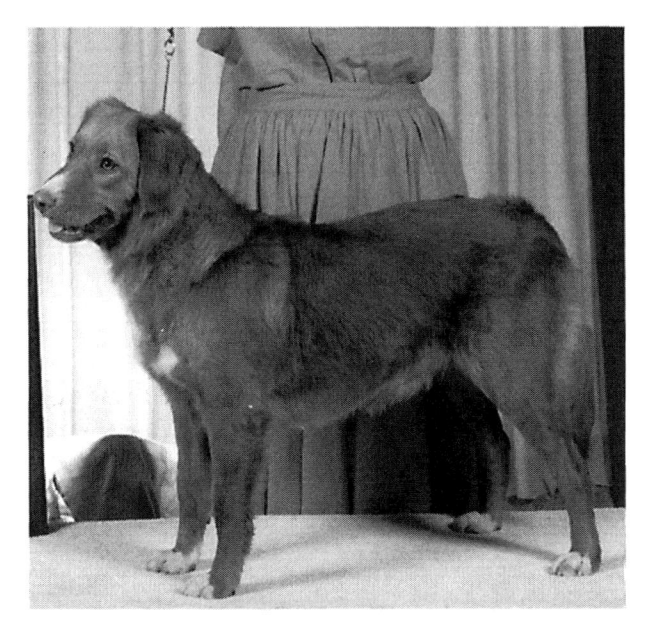

A triple champion wins big at a Canadian Specialty. Sue Van Sloun's Ch. (Am. Can. SKC) Sylvan's Kinney Brook Swan was Winners Female in Fredericton in 1991. Photography of Distinction.

BAITING

The best baits are big chunks of liver or pepperoni sticks made for dogs. Some dogs do not like these, and if your Toller will bait better for cheese, then use that. Other dogs show best for a squeaky toy, although this must be used with extreme discretion as it can be annoying to other exhibitors.

Baiting is used simply to keep your dog sharp, not to feed him a meal. You can either let your dog have a nibble after he is stacked, or stack your dog, move around to his front, and kneel in front, whichever keeps him looking the best. Many dogs love to jump and catch liver thrown to them, and this makes them active and alert.

HOW TO MAKE LIVER BAIT

To make liver bait, buy one or two pounds of liver. Bring to a boil, then simmer for about fifteen minutes. Rinse off the scum and cut into good-sized chunks. Arrange these on a cookie sheet and sprinkle with salt and/or garlic powder. Bake at 250 F until the tops are dry, then turn them over and repeat. Let cool and store in the freezer.

Train to bait by playing games with liver and by having your puppy accustomed to stacking on a table, where you will use bait as a reward when he does what you want. When he learns that the bait is kept in a pocket, you can get his alert attention simply by waggling your fingers inside your pocket. This is a useful trick if you happen to show under a judge who does not allow bait in the ring.

One of Marangai Kennels's homebred winners, Ch. Marangai Mail Order Annie, bred and owned by Vic Dunphy and Heather Connors-Dunphy. Dennis Photography.

STACKING

Accustom your puppy to stacking, first on a table and later on the floor. Breeders who show their dogs will probably have done some table work with their very young puppies. Continue to place them on a table every day, and praise them when they stand. Do not try to put your pup into a perfect stack right away, but praise him for standing and reward him with a treat. You can gradually place his feet where you want them, telling him "Stay" and "Show" and rewarding him with bait. If the dog braces or leans backward, you can place his hind feet at the back edge of the table and let his hindquarters fall over the edge. Put him back, give him a treat, and try again. A steady backward pull on

Kristina May with Ch. Westerlea's Crimson Crusader CD. This is the preferred tail hold. Photo by Linda Lindt.

Above: A high but attractive way to hold the tail. Hellard Photo.
Left,: A high tail position, but Dorothy MacDonald knows her Ch. Westerlea's Krugerrand looks good this way. Photo by Linda Lindt.
Below: Inverted C tail carriage, which does not enhance the dog's appearance. Mikron Photo.

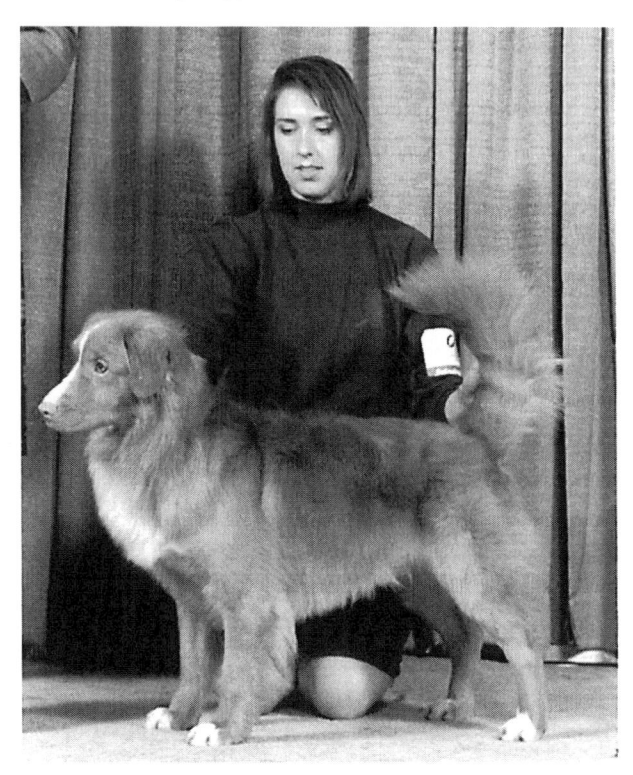

Three dogs and three different tails! All could look better! Mikron Photo.

the tail, followed by a quick release, will often result in your dog leaning forward into a proper stance. Do only a little work at each session, and be sure to keep all training fun for your dog.

Once your show prospect is steady on the table and knows the commands stand, stay, and show, you can try him on the floor. Do not allow his feet to move, but reward a stack with a quick treat, reaching out to your dog rather than having him jump toward you.

If possible, practice setting up your Toller in front of a mirror so that you can see what he looks like from a judge's point of view.

LEASH TRAINING FOR SHOW

Leash training for show involves teaching your dog to trot steadily and brightly beside you so that his movement is shown to best advantage. Do not let him gallop or pull. Reward him with a treat when you come to a halt, and use your baiting technique to have him look alert. Always use a show collar and leash for these sessions, and soon your puppy will know that this means *fun*! Learn the various ring patterns, and practice doing neat turns and changing the leash from one hand to the other. Watch the professional handlers at shows. Many of their techniques are so smooth that they are undiscernible to any but a very practiced eye. Nevertheless, you can get a good idea of how a dog should be handled.

SHOW-HANDLING CLASSES

Most sizeable communities will have at least one person giving show-handling classes. These are a good investment for you and your puppy, provided that the classes are not too big and noisy, with too many distractions, and that the young dogs are not kept constantly showing for an entire hour. The best teachers use short sessions interspersed with instruction on showing techniques and dress, how to make entries, and other show tips. The pups are allowed to socialize with each other and are kept alert and lively.

MAKE SHOWING FUN

Try to remember that your dog is the same, win or lose, and that the day's results are only one judge's opinion. Showing is supposed to be a hobby, not a matter of life and death. Try not to take results too seriously, and make showing fun for your dog. Then you can both enjoy yourselves. A rapport with fellow exhibitors and a sporting attitude, win or lose, will gain you good friends and good times.

GROOMING

One of the first questions asked by many newcomers to Tollers, particularly those planning to show their dogs, is how to groom. A number of breeders give advice with each new puppy and a brief demonstration of techniques for brushing, ear cleaning, and nail clipping. More detailed information is necessary for those interested in showing.

The Toller is a natural-looking dog and should appear for any activity with his coat neat, clean, and tidy. Shun overgrooming, which includes moussing, blow-fluffing coats that ought to lie flat, and excessive trimming. This includes any scissoring and shaping of the tail and trimming of the often-profuse Toller culottes. Trimming of ears and feet should be done at least one week before a show to give the coat time to settle and the outline time to soften.

SUPPLIES

Cynthia Merkley, who has been grooming dogs since she was a child and who has shown a number of Tollers to championships, kindly consented to take an ungroomed dog and demonstrate the basic steps. Cindy emphasized the importance of correct, high-quality equipment. Here is her list:

Steel combs: Large for body hair; small for ears, head, and between pads. They should have both wide and narrow teeth.

Steel combs. ©Johan Adlercreutz.

Brushes: Pin, for body coat and line brushing. Slicker, to brush up hair between toes. Bristle, for finishing and polishing coat.

Left to right: Bristle brush, pin brush, nail clippers, and slicker brush. ©Johan Adlercreutz.

Scissors: Steel thinning shears with teeth on one blade only; teeth range at least thirty-five to forty depending on the size of the shears. Cindy uses large shears for trimming shaggy hair on ears and feet and small shears for ears; straight shears for trimming ears, hocks, and pasterns; small, blunt-ended scissors for trimming pads.

Left to right: Small and large thinning shears, blunt-end scissors, and large straight scissors. ©Johan Adlercreutz.

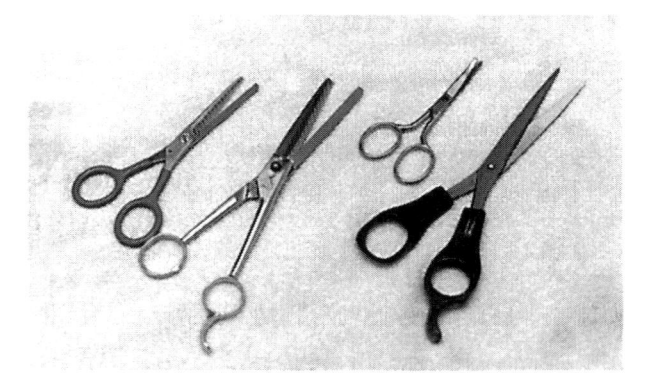

BEFORE: An ungroomed Toller, Barney.
©Johan Adlercreutz.

AFTER: Barney, a new dog!
©Johan Adlercreutz.

Some groomers also use a fine stripping knife for ears. These are obtainable in both right- and left-hand models.

It is useful to have a grooming table or grooming top that fits on top of a dog crate. Rubber matting or a nonslip mat laid out on a table, countertop, or freezer top will do instead.

STEP ONE

Brush the dog lightly to remove any embedded dirt, seeds, or burrs, and check for parasites, skin irritations, or cuts. Now bathe your show candidate. There are dozens of good dog shampoos, formulated especially for various types and colors of coats. Be sure to use one of these, not a shampoo made for humans. Lather the dog thoroughly, making sure that no soap gets in the eyes, and squeeze the lather all through the coat, down the legs to the feet, and also through the tail. It is very important to rinse well so that all traces of shampoo are removed. Dry the dog thoroughly, making sure that the insides of the ears are clean and dry. A light blow-drying is helpful, but continuous use of a blow-dryer will only harm and dry out the coat.

STEP TWO

Mist the coat lightly with water from a spray bottle before grooming. This prevents the coat from tearing or hairs from splitting. Brush the coat upward and outward from the body in the direction opposite the way in which the coat falls naturally. Then, beginning at either the head or the tail, or with the dog lying on his side, brush the coat back into place, one line at a time, making sure that the brush reaches right down to the dog's skin. This is known as line brushing. Do this all over the dog's body, then brush out the neck ruff, the tail, the pants, and the leg fringes. This procedure should also be incorporated into regular grooming sessions.

STEP THREE

Trim the nails (this should be done regularly in order to keep the quick fairly short). Most nails have a slight curve, and they should be cut above the start of the curve. Most Tollers have light nails, which makes the job quite easy because you can see the quick. In case you cut the quick, have some KwikStop or similar product handy to staunch any bleeding. Then comb

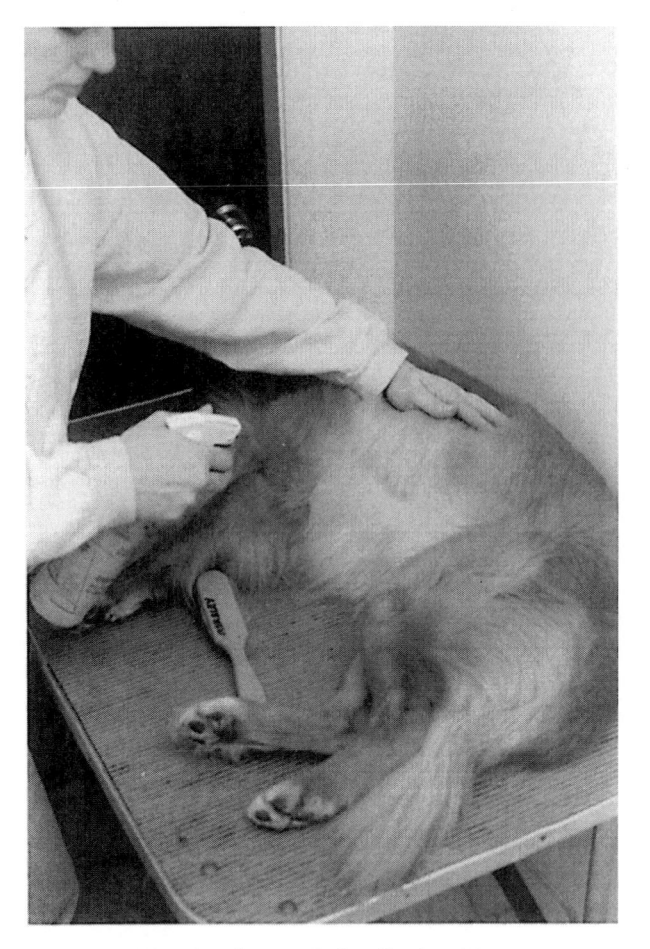

Spraying the coat before line brushing.

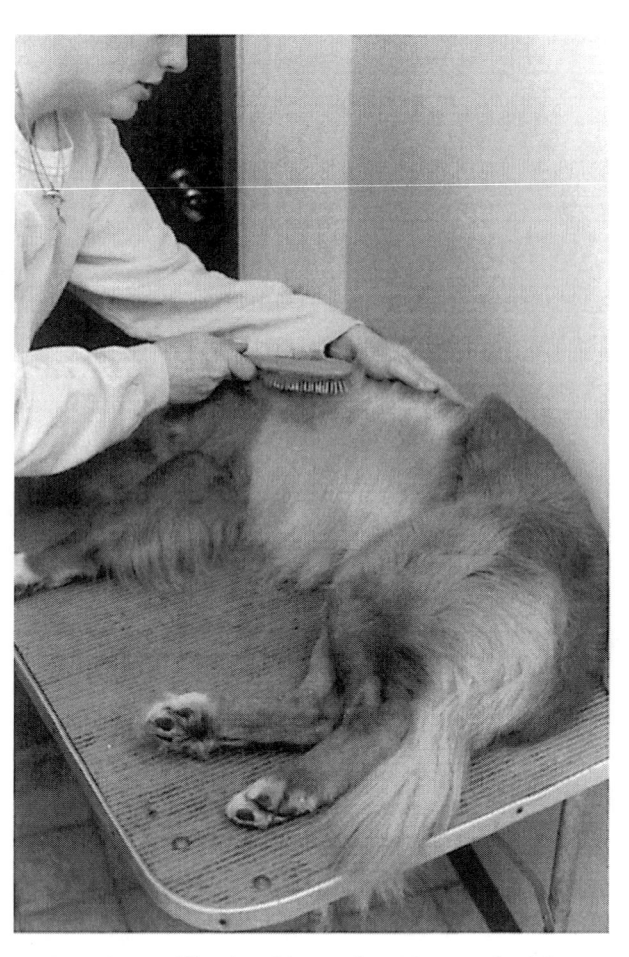

Second step of line brushing — brushing coat back into place in the direction the hair grows.

Untrimmed foot.

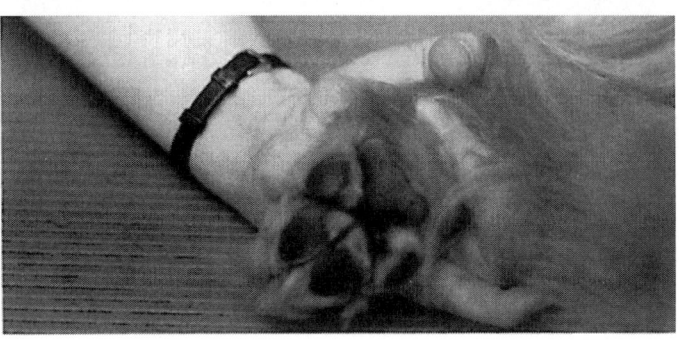

Untrimmed pads.
All photos this page © Johan Adlercreutz.

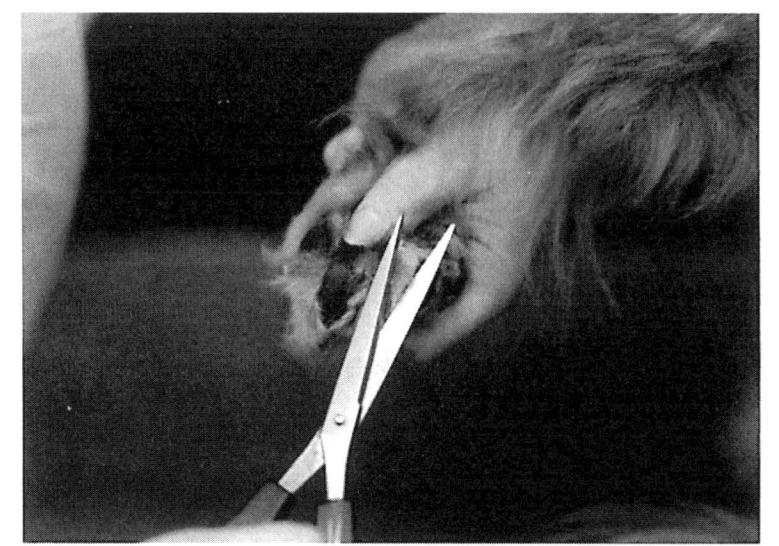

Trim hair between pads.

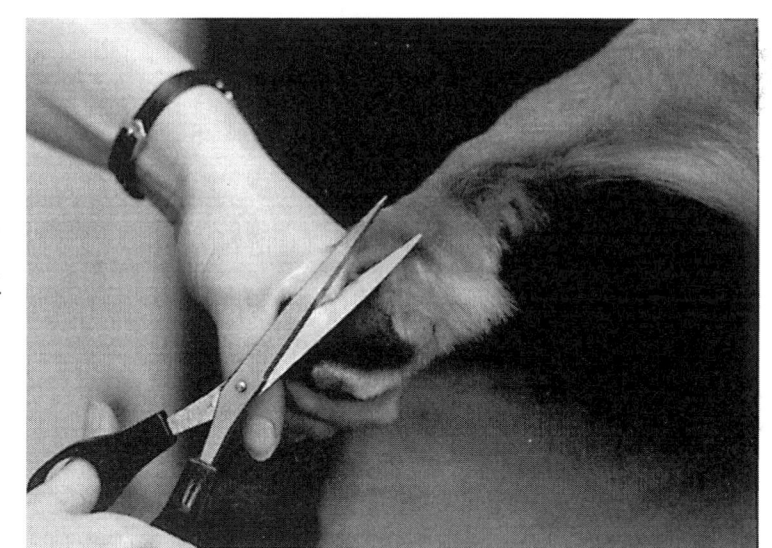

Trim around the edge of the pad.

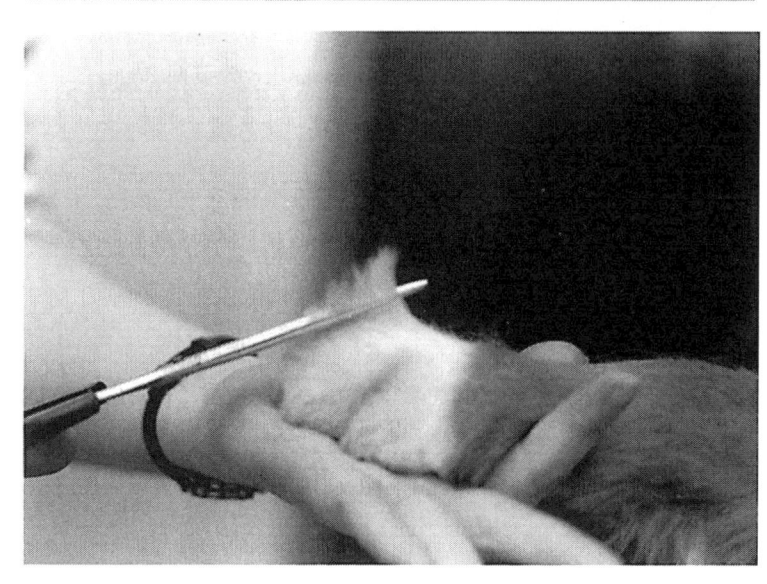

*Trim hair from between the toes.
All photos this page ©Johan Adlercreutz.*

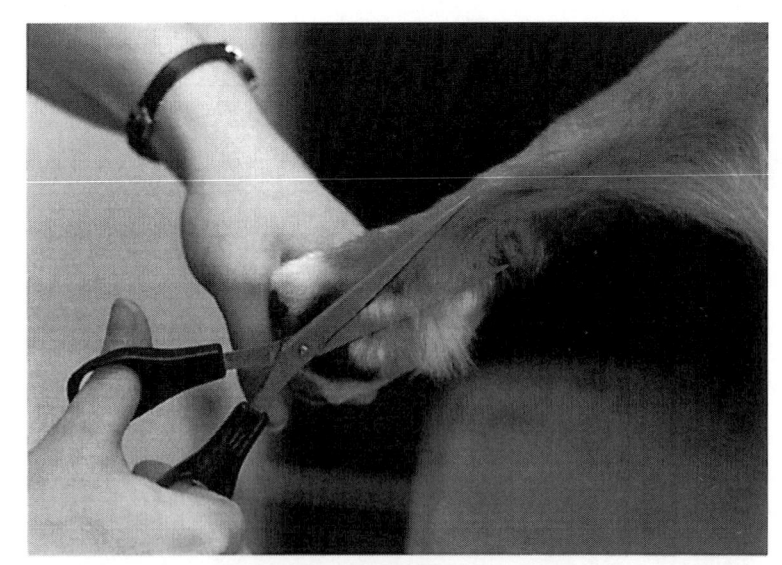

Trim excess hair on pastern, slanting back into the feathering.

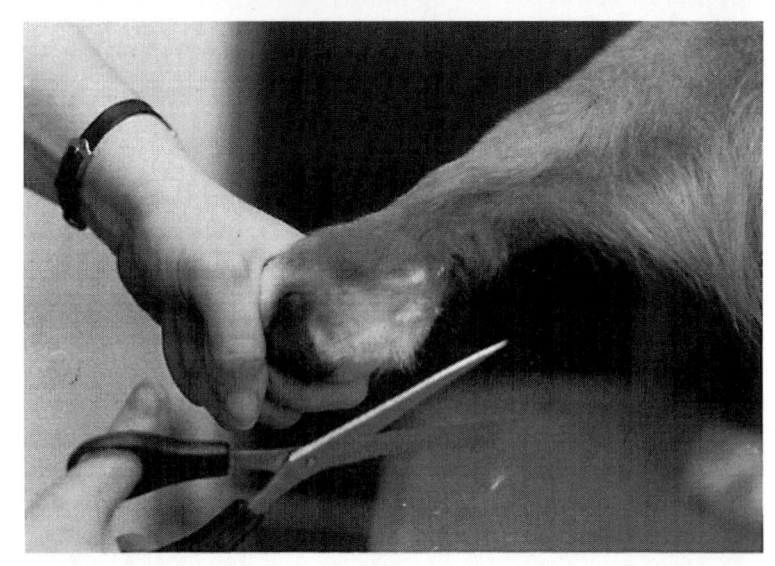

Finishing off pasterns.

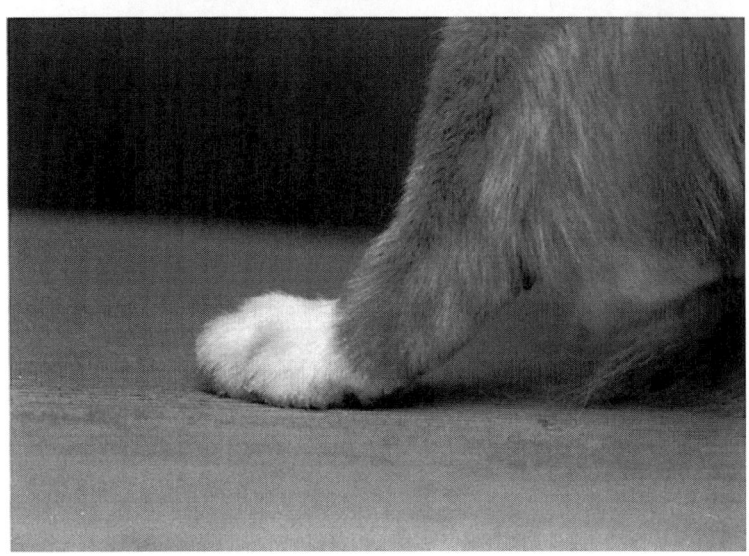

A finished foot.
©Johan Adlercreutz.

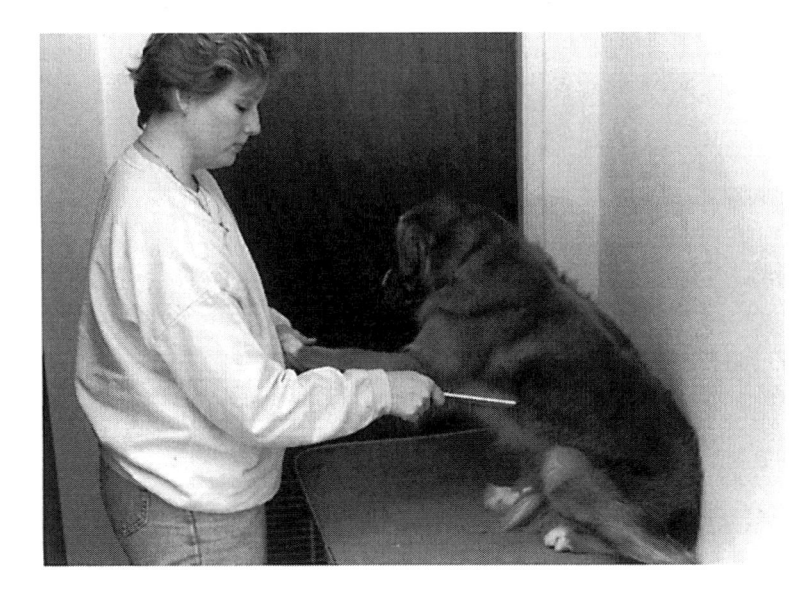

Comb the leg feathers and the hair under the elbows.
©*Johan Adlercreutz.*

or push up excess hair between the toes so that it can be trimmed away with either straight or thinning shears.

Now trim away the hair between the pads on the underside of the foot, using blunt-tipped scissors to avoid nicking the skin. This will give the foot a neat look and will help the dog on slippery surfaces. Trim around the feet with sharp, straight scissors, emphasizing the round look for the front feet. Hind feet are a little longer and thinner. Trim pasterns to the button just above the foot with thinning or straight shears, giving them a neat but not shaved appearance.

If you live in a northern climate, it is unwise to remove all of the foot hair in the winter, especially if the dog lives outdoors. However, feet certainly do look much neater if most of the excess hair is trimmed away.

STEP FOUR

Tidy hair on the hocks by combing the hair outward, then trimming with straight scissors in a neat line, parallel to the hock, working from foot to hock joint. This task is made easier if you lift the hind foot. Hair on the hocks should be about one-half inch long when the job is finished. If the dog is fairly fine boned, leave the hair standing out from the hock. Trim the hair more closely and comb it into place if the dog has larger bone; otherwise the extra fringe may make the dog look too heavy.

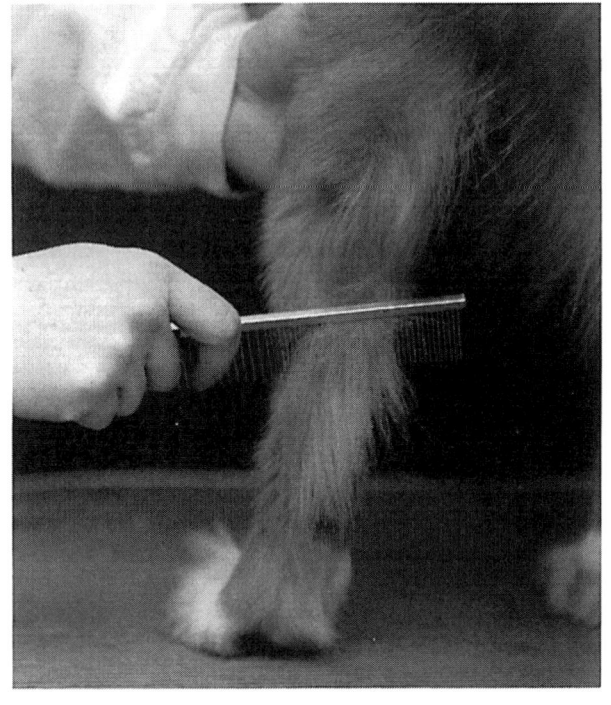

Comb the hair on the hock.
©*Johan Adlercreutz.*

STEP FIVE

Comb all ear hair well, then trim around the ear with straight scissors to give a neat outline. Excess hair can be trimmed with thinning shears. Be sure to make only one cut at a time, then comb out the cut hair. This way, you can shape the hair and also make sure that you are

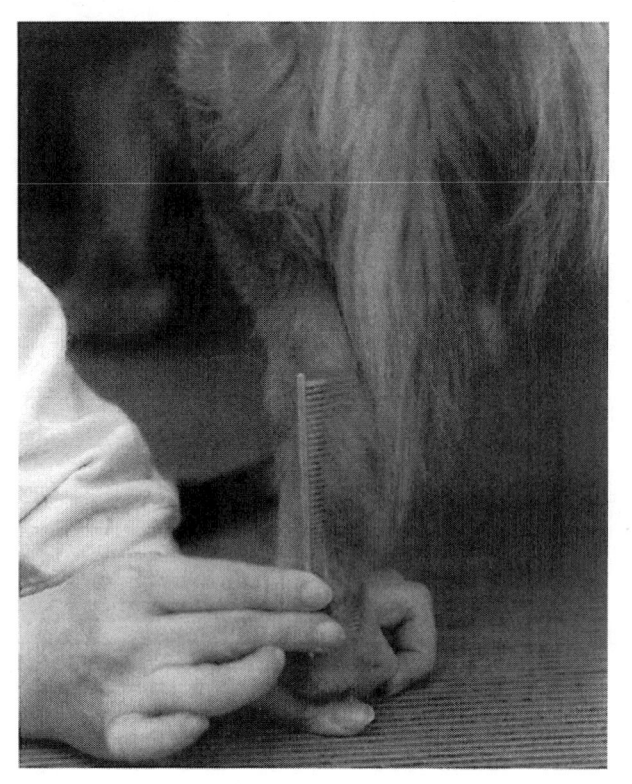

*Comb hair to one side and trim,
then to the center and trim,
then to the opposite side, cutting the ends
in a vertical line as you comb.*

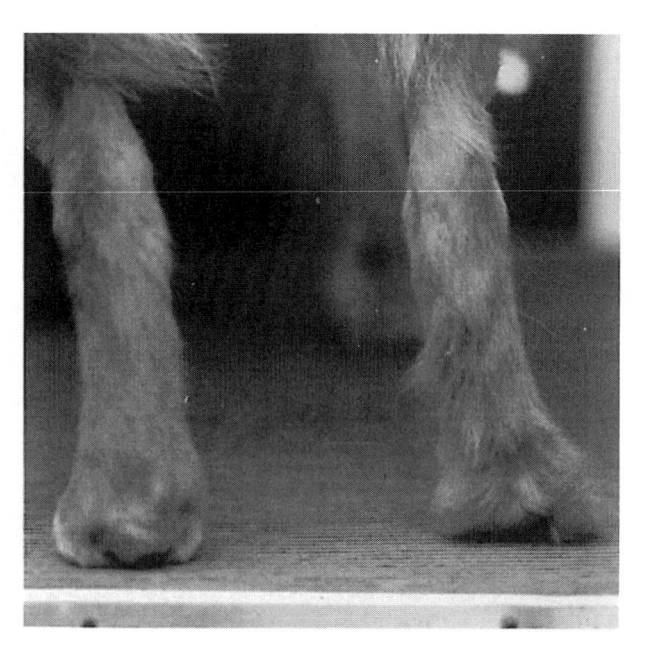

*Hock trimming.
Left is trimmed; right needs attention.*

All photos this page ©Johan Adlercreutz.

not cutting too much. If you prefer, you can strip excess ear hair with a fine stripping knife or with your fingers. Any heavy feathering behind the ears should also be reduced with thinning shears, but some of the longer, straggly hair can best be removed by hand plucking.

Next, trim away some of the hair from inside the ear flap and just below the ears, being careful not to nick the skin (blunt-tipped scissors will help here as well). The ultimate aim of ear trimming is to give the dog's head a tidy appearance while avoiding an overly trimmed or shaved look.

Comb the hair in front of the ear . . .

and thin it.

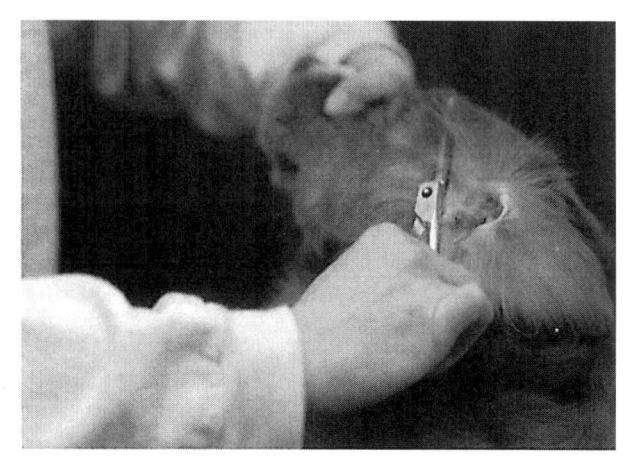

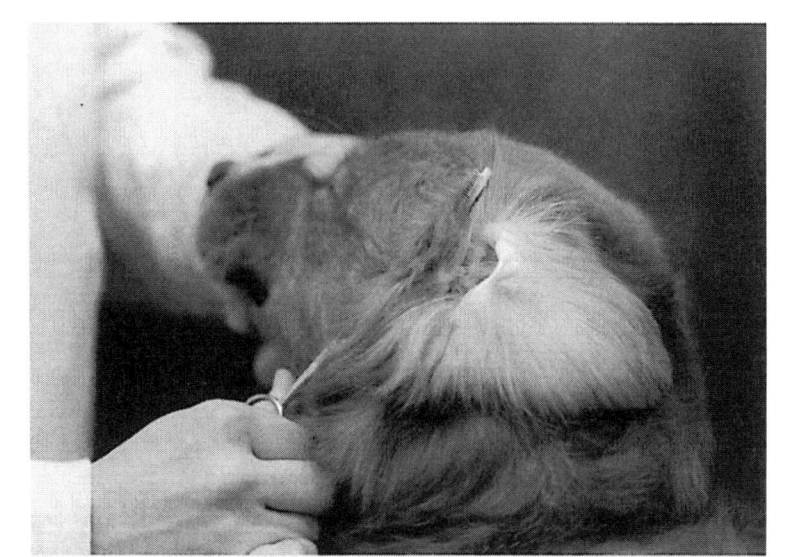

Trim hair inside ear.

A neat look for inside the ear.

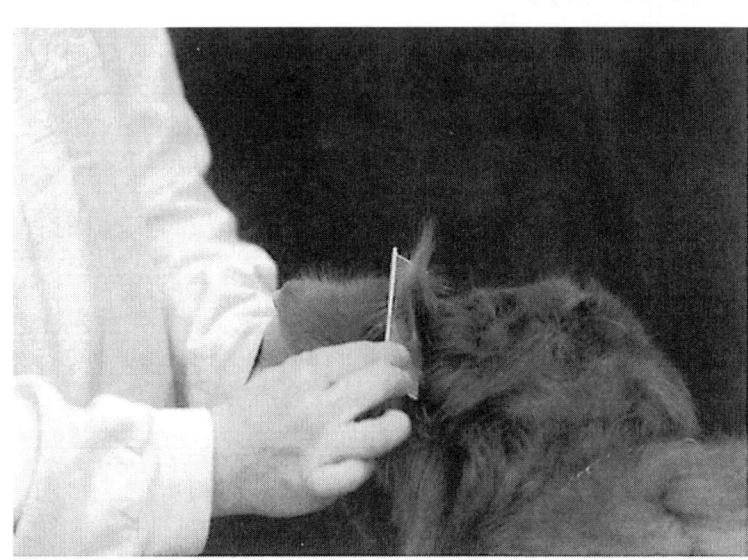

Comb the hair on top of the ear so that it stands up.
All photos this page ©Johan Adlercreutz.

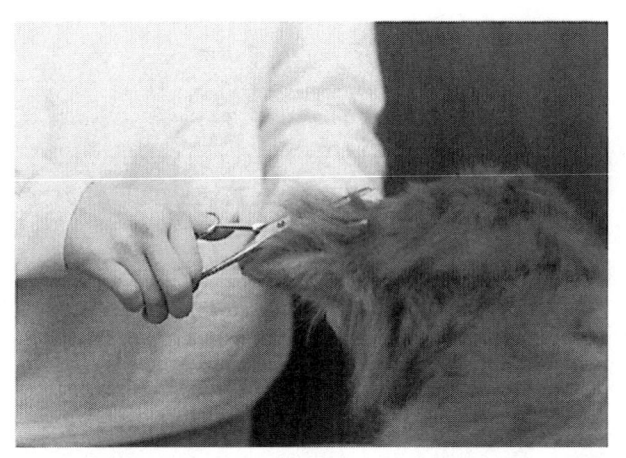

Thin excess hair on the top of the ears.

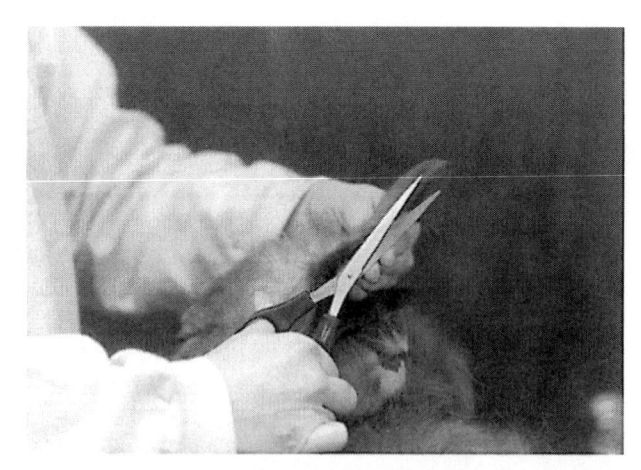

Trimming around the ear flaps.

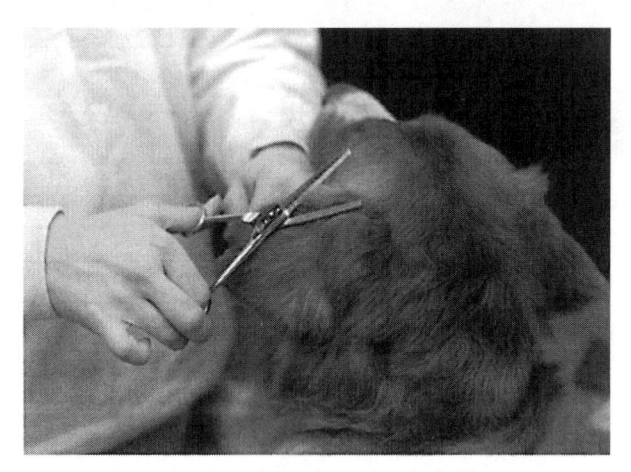

Blend ear fringe into the topskull.

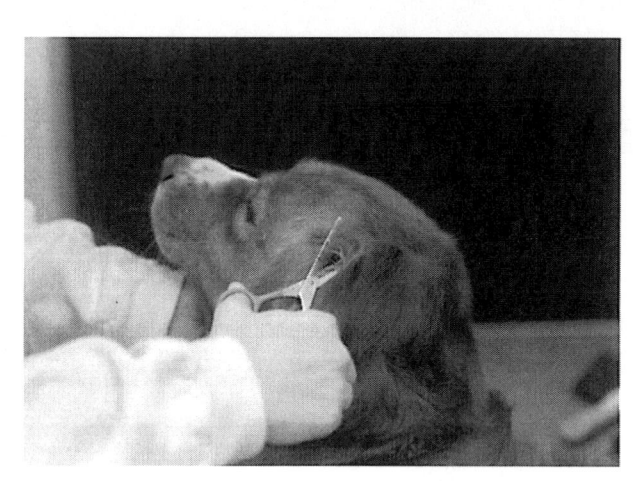

Clip off uneven hairs in front of ear and blend into frill.

STEP SIX

Final polishing of the coat is best accomplished by vigorous brushing with a bristle brush. When not grooming for an actual show, many people like to use a capful of therapeutic bath oil in a spray-bottle of water, because this helps oil the coat from the outside. The addition of a little canola or other vegetable oil in the food will do the job from the inside. Too many baths will dry out the coat, robbing it of natural oils.

Various coat conditioners are on the market, but no amount of grooming takes the place of a naturally good coat. Nor can grooming alone replace the bloom on a coat, which is brought to full glory by a combination of good health and proper conditioning, grooming, and exercise, coupled with a correct diet. There is an old adage that says, "Coats are bred, then fed."

WHISKERS

Most Toller exhibitors do not trim the whiskers on their dogs. Tollers are hunters, and many dogs that are shown are also used in the field. Whiskers act as antennae and should not be trimmed.

Barney thanks Cindy as she finished the job.
All photos this page ©Johan Adlercreutz.

Ch. Woodsway's Arcadia Red CD, owned by David C. Wood of Springhill, Nova Scotia.
Best of Winners at the NSDTR National Specialty, 1983.
Courtesy David C. Wood.

*Ch. Red Russel of Jeffery (center) is flanked by two of his mates,
Ch. Forette Jeffery of Overton (left) and Chin-Peek Wee Lady Susan.*

15

In Sickness and in Health

Tollers are pretty hardy dogs; indeed, they would had to have been to survive in the harsh climates and rugged way of life of their originators. They have a wash-and-wear coat and good hunting instincts and can take care of themselves. Mary Sproul tells how one of her early bitches, Happy Holly of Harbourlights, escaped from their kennel and lived in a semi-feral state for more than a year. Happily for the breed, she finally decided to return from the wild, and she went on to become ancestress of many of today's well-known Tollers.

GENERAL CARE

Day-to-day care of the Toller is the same as for any other dog and encompasses lots of love, good nutrition, good grooming, and regular veterinary checkups. It is not the purpose of this book to detail comprehensive general care, because so many books are available (see List of Suggested Reading). A few general recommendations are in order, however.

At least once a month, check your dog's nails and trim them if they are too long. Be sure to keep your dog's teeth clean by regularly wiping them with a face cloth dampened either with diluted hydrogen peroxide or plain water, or use one of the special canine tooth-care products that are now available. Your dog will love the treat of hard shank bones or nylon substitutes, as well as raw vegetables (such as broccoli stalks and carrots) and hard biscuits. Feeding kibble without too much liquid added also helps keep teeth in good condition. Shank bones are the only bones recommended, because Tollers can crunch up a large knuckle bone quickly, and pieces may become lodged in the intestines, causing blockage. Dogs cannot destroy the very hard shank bones, which also contain valuable marrow.

Ears should also be checked for any odor and cleaned out to make sure that there is no brown, odorous deposit deep down. Regular use of an ear wash helps keep the ears free of yeast infections. An effective and inexpensive ear wash is made by combining one part surgical wash such as Betadine or Hibitane with one part white vinegar and six parts plain water. Put the mixture into a bottle with a small opening, such as an old shampoo bottle. Squeeze a small amount of liquid into the ear canal, then massage the base of the ear well to make sure that the wash

---

* Much of the information in this chapter was provided by Janice Madjanovich, DVM.

penetrates the canal. Leave it for a moment (trying to make sure that your dog does not shake all the liquid out of his ear), then clean it out with a cotton ball, just as far down as you can comfortably reach. Never probe deep down into the ear canal with a sharp object, such as a Q-tip, because you may puncture the eardrum. Make sure that the ears are dry when you finish.

Periodically, examine your dog's skin for a healthy, pink appearance, foreign objects, fleas, or ticks. You can thus catch any moist hot spots before they grow too big. Also look for irritations, redness, or cuts. Check the condition of your dog's pads and run your hands over his entire body to check for any lumps or bumps that should not be there.

A SPECIAL PRECAUTION REGARDING FOXTAILS

If you live in an area where foxtails are common, be on your guard against these lethal little grass seeds. They are barbed at the tips and can work their way underneath the skin, enter the bloodstream, and cause considerable damage. One very promising young Toller died after a foxtail lodged in his lungs and set up a massive infection. After hunting or just running your Toller in areas where foxtails are to be found, check your dog thoroughly for foreign objects, especially around the feet, ears, eyes, nose, and mouth.

Right: Shaking off after a dip. Photo courtesy of John Gordon, Toller Pride Kennels.

Below left: Photo courtesy of Laurie Geyer, Skylark Tollers.

Below right: The chase! Photo courtesy of Jamie Klein, Readyfor Nova Scotia Duck Tolling Retrievers.

RETRIEVER EMERGENCY KIT

Product Needed	Use
Topical germicide	For cleansing of wounds, lacerations, burns
Nonadhesive dressing	For direct application to tissue, and dressing of wounds prior to bandaging
Emetic (Syrup of Ipecac or dilute hydrogen peroxide)	To induce vomiting
Antihistamine	To prevent allergic reaction to a sting
Anti-inflammatory (ASA recommended)	For stiffness, soreness
Sugar source (corn syrup)	To increase blood-sugar level
Antibiotic eye ointment	To treat eyes for mild injury
Germicidal and anti-inflammatory ear solution	To clear up sore, inflamed ears
Saline eye cleanser	To flush eyes for easier removal of grass seeds
Antidiarrhea preparation	To control diarrhea caused by stress or change of water

OTHER MATERIALS TO INCLUDE:

Scissors — both bandage and round-nose
Rectal thermometer
Surgical blade
10 3 x 3 gauze pads
2 rolls vet-wrap
1 roll surgical tape

Hemostat
Forceps
Tweezers
Q-tips (long)
Coins (phone) or cellular phone

REMEMBER: CONSULT A VETERINARIAN FOR ANY PROBLEM THAT PERSISTS FOR MORE THAN 24 HOURS.
(This kit was originally set up by the late Dr. Ben Schmidt for use in seminars. Consult your veterinarian for specific products.)

FIRST-AID KIT

If your Toller sustains a serious injury while away from home, are you prepared? A course in first aid and CPR would be a big help, and it is also wise to keep a comprehensive first-aid kit for dogs at home. If you hunt dogs or work them in field tests or any outdoor activity, carry a small pocket kit and keep a more extensive kit in the car. Rotate the contents to keep them fresh, and include a first-aid reference in the kit, although you should know how to use the items before an emergency arises.

COMMON HEALTH PROBLEMS IN THE TOLLER

Anyone asking about general health problems of the Toller ten years ago would have been told that there were hardly any. That, however, was before the present Toller population explosion. Because the dogs mainly go back to the same few that were registered in the 1950s and 1960s, the gene pool is quite small. Generations of close breeding have taken a toll, as undesirable recessive genes have been unmasked in the process.

Armed with this knowledge, current and future breeders have the task of trying to remove these genes with sound, sensible breeding practices, while not losing the essential Toller in the process.

When a particular problem occurs widely, breeders tend to zero-in on this affliction, to the exclusion of others. There is a real danger of losing many fine attributes that make up breed character and type while trying to eradicate a problem. There is more than one serious health concern in Tollers to which breeders should be alert, particularly health problems that are life-threatening.

AUTOIMMUNE DISEASES

Many of the diseases that affect Tollers are due to failure or abnormal function of the dog's immune system. A very sketchy outline is necessary for the understanding of these diseases, but more detailed knowledge will have to be sought elsewhere.

The immune system may be considered in two parts that are actually intertwined and that work together. The first is nonspecific (or innate) immunity, which protects the body against foreign organisms without having to identify the invader. The second is specific immunity, in which the immune system recognizes a particular foreign material (antigen) and acts against it.

Nature has set up many barriers as defense mechanisms against invading disease agents. Fatty acids on the skin, continual shedding of the outer layer of skin cells, and the presence of natural bacteria make it difficult for harmful agents to gain entry. The mucus secreted by the linings of respiratory and upper gastrointestinal tracts also contains antimicrobial chemicals and traps foreign particles. In the respiratory tract, tiny hairs (cilia) move in waves to carry these particles to the back of the mouth, where they are swallowed, only to be killed by the low pH of the stomach.

If these barriers are breached, the next line of defense is inflammation, which may result from injury or infectious agents. A complicated chemical reaction ensues that finally results in the destruction of the invaders. The complementary system is a complex group of proteins that is activated by bacterial toxins. they are able to punch a hole in the membrane surrounding a microbe, thus causing its death.

Autoimmune disease occurs when an immune response develops to antigens produced within the animal's own body. Some diseases involve complex reactions between antibody and antigen, which then stimulate inflammation and tissue injury. In addition to many antigen-related factors, there is evidence that failure of suppressor networks is involved in the development of autoimmune diseases. The fact that autoimmunity occurs with increased frequency in certain lines, breeds, or families has led researchers to conclude that there is a genetic base for these problems.

Clinical problems arising from autoimmune injury are usually related to the locations of the antigens. Where the antigen is localized in a specific tissue or organ, the problem is usually organ-specific; for instance, autoimmune inflammation of the thyroid gland (thyroiditis), leading to hypothyroidism, and autoimmune inflammation of the adrenal gland (adrenalitis), which causes a condition commonly called Addison's Disease. Where the antigen is present in many tissues, the autoimmune response can result in problems with kidneys, joints, and skin.

These are the principal autoimmune diseases affecting Tollers:

Systemic Lupus Erythematosus: A multi-systemic condition causing arthritis, kidney disease, anemia, and many forms of dermatitis.

Polyarthritis: Arthritis affecting multiple joints, manifested by shifting lameness due to pain; heat, swelling, and pain in several joints.

Hemolytic Anemia: Anemia due to acquired defects of red blood cells.

Autoimmune Skin Disease: Results in blisters and ulcers of the skin and mucous membranes.

Thyroiditis: Responsible for about 50 percent of hypothyroidism in dogs.

Adrenalitis: Cause of hypoadrenocorticism (Addison's Disease).

It is thought that genetic predisposition, infections, and environmental factors may all be involved in the development of autoimmune diseases.

CANCER

Cancer in dogs, as in humans, can take various forms. Many older Tollers have succumbed to cancer, possibly in about the same ratio as those in other breeds. It is interesting for ordinary dog owners to speculate on what goes into the dog food they buy or what falls out of the sky as acid rain or other forms of pollution. There are strong indications that human cancer is most prevalent in areas that have high levels of industrial pollution, so it would not be illogical to expect animals to show the same effects.

Many dogs suffer from tumors, both benign and malignant. The benign tumors may be removed safely, while malignant tumors are treated with surgery, chemotherapy, or radiation. Lee Ann Gleason, Toller owner and breeder, reports that research is being done in Rochester, New York, on bone-marrow transplants for dogs with lymphosarcoma.

Vigilance pays off in combating this dread condition and in helping our Tollers live longer, healthier lives. In this, as in all other matters of Toller sickness and health, it is necessary to work in close consultation with your veterinarian. After your family, he or she is, and should be, your dog's best friend.

FLEA ALLERGY DERMATITIS

Many Tollers living in coastal and warmer areas of the continent suffer from various forms of flea-bite allergy. When a flea bites a dog, it injects saliva into the tissue, provoking a local inflammatory reaction that causes itching and irritation. In some dogs this goes further when a chemical in the flea saliva reacts with collagen in the dog's skin to form an antigen to which the dog's immune system becomes hypersensitive. The result is flea allergy dermatitis (FAD), the most common cause of dermatitis in dogs and cats.

Allergy susceptibility is known to be inherited, and dogs with other allergies may be prone to developing FAD. Tollers that tend to suffer from immune-related diseases appear to have a high incidence of FAD, which has developed in dogs as young as one year of age. Onset between three to six years is more common in colder climates, where exposure to fleas is seasonal. A Florida study has shown that dogs with intermittent exposure to fleas react more severely than do animals with constant high exposure.

The primary symptoms of FAD are small, solid, raised skin lesions that crust over. These

Left: Peanut, owned by Alison Strang, all dressed up for the holidays.

Right: CH OTCH MOTCH Westerlea's Sir Edmund UDX4 OM1 MH WCX VCX ROM. John Simonson and Eddy "hugging" after Eddy was declared overall winner of High in Trial in four obedience trials at a large show at Spruce Meadows, Alberta.

Six in a row. Photo courtesy of Laurie Geyer, Skylark Tollers.

are accompanied by a reddening of the skin, typically on the lumbar region near the tail, on the backs of the thighs and belly, and, to a lesser extent, on the flanks and neck. Secondary symptoms include abrasions, hair loss, and broken hair due to scratching and chewing by the dog because of the intense itching. Acute moist dermatitis ("hot spots"), pustules, and excess sebaceous-gland secretions are also common.

You can detect fleas on your dog by using a very fine flea comb and noting the presence of flea dirt in the coat. Absence of fleas does not rule out FAD, because fleas spend much of their time off the dog and only jump on to have a meal.

Not only must you treat your dog for the skin condition, but you must also treat the environment. This means ridding both dog and premises of fleas by using sprays, foggers, and dusts. Regular vacuuming will help remove flea eggs and larvae indoors, and special preparations are now available containing microencapsulated insecticides that kill eggs and larvae over a period of time.

Once you have tackled the symptoms on your dog, you must keep him free of further infestations by using shampoos, sprays, powders, dips, collars, or oral treatments. It is wise to discuss these fully with your veterinarian, because he or she will be able to assess the best methods for your dog.

Unfortunately, there are no flea repellents that are 100 percent effective. Many breeders rely on brewer's yeast and/or garlic, but neither have been conclusively proven effective. A solution (one and one-half ounces per gallon of water) of Avon's Skin-So-Soft® has been touted as being effective, with better results being obtained from a stronger solution that, unfortunately, leaves a greasy feel to the coat.

You may want to try a few drops of pine oil (*not* Pinesol) added to a capful of therapeutic bath oil in a spray bottle of water for regular grooming. Pine oil in a *very* dilute solution, brushed into the coat, is a harmless way of killing fleas on young pups, unless you can crush the little devils between your finger and thumb.

HYPOTHYROIDISM

Hypothyroidism is a disease of the thyroid gland causing underproduction of thyroid hormone. More than 90 percent of the occurrence in dogs is due to dysfunction of the gland itself (primary hypothyroidism). The two major causes of this primary condition are lymphocytic thyroiditis, also known as autoimmune thyroiditis (see above), and idiopathic atrophy (wasting of the gland for unknown reasons). The end result of both forms is the same, i.e., a reduction in the amount of thyroxine (T4) being produced.

Hypothyroidism most often affects dogs in the four- to ten-year range, with classic symptoms including symmetrical hair loss, increased skin pigmentation, skin thickening (especially around the face and eyes), weight gain, lethargy, mental dullness, cold intolerance, and infertility. However, many hypothyroid dogs display none of these symptoms.

A basic blood test (T4) will sometimes reveal low levels of thyroxine, but is not highly reliable in that many outside factors can contribute to a low T4 level, including medications and the dog's current state of health. The test currently considered to be definitive is the Thyrotropin (TSH) Stimulation Test, where serum T4 concentrations are measured before and after administration of the thyroid-stimulating hormone, thyrotropin. A typical hypothyroid dog shows a low initial T4 concentration that does not increase significantly after stimulation. The test is administered over several hours and is considerably more expensive than the T4. However, it is also much more accurate.

About 50 to 60 percent of hypothyroid dogs have antibodies to thyroglobulin (a thyroid-specific protein). These antibodies are also present in some euthyroid (normal) dogs, and it is possible that such dogs are in the early stages of autoimmune thyroiditis. Testing for thyroglobulin antibodies may, therefore, be a means of screening for early hypothyroid disease. Also, since some normal dogs related to affected animals have a relatively high incidence of thyroglobulin antibodies, testing for these antibodies has potential use in genetic screening.

Hypothyroidism has been identified as an inherited disorder. Some breeds are more susceptible than others, and familial patterns show up within breeds. Pedigree analysis in an affected Borzoi family found lymphocytic thyroiditis to be an autosomal recessive trait. There is also a possibility, not yet scientifically proven, that there is a relationship between hypothyroidism and the bleeding disorder, von Willebrand's disease, and, possibly, epilepsy.

SEIZURES

A seizure is a frightening event for anyone witnessing it for the first time, but it is the most common neurological reason why dogs are seen by a veterinarian. Despite its awesome appearance, a seizure is not usually an emergency situation, and owners who are aware of what happens and can stay calm may play a big role in helping the veterinarian diagnose the cause of a seizure.

Many animals become very apprehensive when they feel a seizure approaching. An observant owner will recognize these signs — pacing, whining, hiding, or excessive affection. Dogs usually fall on one side, the legs stiffen due to muscular contractions, then they begin to jerk due to alternating cycles of muscular rigidity and relaxation. Dogs can appear to "foam at the mouth" due to excessive amounts of saliva, and they usually lose consciousness for a short period. The animal may urinate, defecate, or vomit. After the dog regains consciousness, he may continue to make paddling movements with his legs. Most dogs will be confused, disoriented, and uncoordinated for a short while and will be hungry and thirsty when they do recover.

Many seizure disorders are caused by diseases other than epilepsy. Brain disorders include tumors, infections, head trauma, and congenital defects, and the brain is also affected by certain toxins. Other causes of seizures are viral, bacterial, or fungal infections, the best known of which is distemper.

Hypoglycemia, or low blood sugar, is one cause of seizures, and very small dogs or puppies may have hypoglycemic convulsions after a bout of diarrhea. Working or hunting dogs may have a seizure within an hour after heavy exercise if they have not been fed. This situation can usually be remedied by giving a light meal early in the morning and by carrying snack food as emergency rations.

If no underlying cause for the seizures is found, the diagnosis will then be epilepsy, which is an hereditary disease.

HERITARY DISEASES IN TOLLERS

CATARACTS

Opacities of the lens occur in a number of different forms, several of them hereditary. They do not appear to be a major concern in Tollers, but several cases have been diagnosed as posterior pole cataract, which does not cause blindness but which *is* hereditary. There have also been a few Tollers initially diagnosed as having cataracts when what in fact was seen was a failure of the membranes present at birth to dissolve. This usually happens soon after birth, but in a number of Tollers, they persist as a small opacity. Common procedure followed in these instances is to wait for at least one year before retesting. If the opacity has not changed in any way, it is probable that there is no true cataract, but the condition must continue to be monitored over a period of time.

Specialists believe that some cataracts are inherited from a simple autosomal recessive gene. ("Simple" here means one single gene, and "autosomal" means not sex-linked.) Sex-linked diseases are transmitted only by the female. Recessive genes are often masked by dominant genes, except when the animal's genetic makeup for a single trait has only recessive genes.

Dr. Keith C. Barnett wrote an interesting paper titled "Eye Disease in the Dog," which was published by the *Gaines Progress Bulletin* in 1976. He described the effect of recessive genes: "Recessive means we have dogs that are affected, those that are unaffected, and that big group in the middle, the carriers: transmitters of the gene but never themselves becoming affected."

Dr. Barnett classified juvenile cataracts, which have occurred in Tollers, as caused by a simple autosomal recessive gene. This type always results in blindness. Posterior pole cataracts are, according to Dr. Barnett, a result of a dominant gene of variable expression (meaning that some cataracts look and are different from others), but these different types are all due to the same gene.

EPILEPSY

Epilepsy accounts for nearly 70 percent of all seizure disorders. Once an animal begins having epileptic seizures, which usually start between six months to five years, a regular pattern will emerge. In most cases, teamwork between owner and veterinarian will result in successful management of an epileptic pet for many years. However, epilepsy is also suspected as one manifestation of autoimmune disease.

Veterinarians at Ontario Veterinary College (OVC) have noted a disturbing increase in the incidence of epilepsy among Tollers. Because the condition seems to run along familial lines, epilepsy must go on the list of disorders that breeders should guard against when planning matings.

CANINE HIP DYSPLASIA

So much has been written and said about canine hip dysplasia (CHD) that it is sometimes difficult to sort fact from fiction. Tollers are relatively free of this partly hereditary, partly environmental condition. However, there has been an increase in known incidence since records began to be kept, because some of the earlier breeders

*Brooke peeking.
Photo courtesy of Jamie Klein,
Animal Health Technologist
Ready for Nova Scotia Duck Tolling
Retrievers*

were reluctant to have their dogs X-rayed. Hip clearing has become more standard practice in the last fifteen years, and now most Toller breeders are careful about using only certified-clear stock.

The hip joint is a ball-and-socket joint and ideally should consist of a round ball fitting tightly and deeply into a round socket. Put simply, the essence of hip dysplasia is a poor fit between the ball and socket. An X-ray of a badly dysplastic hip will usually show a shallow socket and a flattened, misshapen ball, with a resulting poor fit between the two. Outward signs of hip dysplasia include stiffness when rising, evidence of joint pain, and awkwardness in the dog's gait. Sometimes a severely dysplastic dog will show no signs of the disease due to extremely good musculature that holds the hip joint in place.

For many years, the standard method of hip evaluation has been X-rays of the hip structure, with the dog usually anesthetized, or at least sedated, in order for the proper position to be maintained. The Orthopedic Foundation for Animals (OFA) in the United States classifies four degrees of dysplasia and will also certify as clear any animals with an excellent, good, or fair rating. In some of the more popular breeds, a fair rating is looked on askance, but many experts believe that the differences between the OFA passing grades is minor. Ontario Veterinary College at Guelph, Ontario, and Western College of Veterinary Medicine in Saskatoon, Saskatchewan (WCVM) both give hip clearances in Canada. The majority of Canadian Toller breeders use OVC, while some send X-rays to OFA.

OFA requires that the dog be at least two years of age, as does WCVM, while OVC experts believe that at eighteen months, many dogs have reached maturity of the skeletal structure. OVC will, however, issue clearance at eighteen months only if the hip joints are of extremely good conformation. Otherwise, a further X-ray six to eight months later is advised.

In the past couple of years, a new method has been perfected to test dogs as young as sixteen weeks of age for susceptibility to CHD. Specialists at the University of Pennsylvania School of Veterinary Medicine have devised a program to evaluate what they call "the hip-joint laxity" of young dogs. Radiological studies have shown that the greater the laxity, the greater the likelihood of the dog developing CHD. The genetics of hip-joint laxity and CHS susceptibility suggest that by using this new technique, the incidence of CHD can be reduced. More than 100 centers, named PennHIP™, have been set up, and it is hoped that the opportunity for expanded tests will confirm their findings.

Many orthopedic experts now believe that progeny testing is the best way to reduce the incidence of CHD, but it is difficult due to the lack of puppies readily available for follow-up and X-rays. Progeny testing relies on the type of hip joints that the sire and dam are known to produce and places slightly less emphasis on the status of the parents' hips. Most breeders, however, still place their faith in clear X-rays of sire and dam, a method which, though slow, has been proven over the years to reduce the incidence of CHD. If, however, clear sires or dams produce several affected offspring, it would be wise to discontinue breeding them.

CHD has been established as being polygenic in its makeup, that is, caused by many different genes. This is what makes it so difficult to eradicate. Many specialists also feel that environment plays a strong role in the development of the disease but that the genetic predisposition must be present in the dog as well.

Many orthopedic and regular veterinarians now caution breeders and owners against the use of high-protein puppy foods for long periods. This warning applies more to those with giant breeds, because it is believed that large doses of high proteins serve to promote too-rapid bone growth. This is not really a problem in a dog the size of a Toller, but many experts feel that the newer puppy foods can do as much harm as good and that a high-quality adult kibble serves just as well.

PROGRESSIVE RETINAL ATROPHY (PRA)
Dr. Charlotte Keller, assistant professor in ophthalmology at the Department of Clinical Studies of the University of Guelph's Ontario Veterinary College, has kindly given permission to reprint a short article that she wrote for the Fall 1992 issue of the Toller Club magazine *Toller Talk*:

"PRA is a slowly progressive disease which affects the retina with its photoreceptors, the cells needed for vision. It causes atrophy, or

Toller puppies get their first introduction to water. Photo courtesy of Sue Kish.

degeneration, of these cells which results in blindness. PRA affects the photoreceptors for night vision and later also the cells for day vision. The dogs therefore experience night blindness first and later become completely blind. Both eyes are always affected simultaneously. The onset of the disease and the time interval between night blindness and complete blindness varies widely amongst different breeds. So far, no treatment is available to stop the progression of the disease.

In all the breeds examined, PRA is inherited in an autosomal recessive pattern. This means that a dog affected with PRA acquired two affected genes, one from each parent. It also means that both parents of an affected dog have to be either carriers or affected themselves. Each time an affected dog is bred it passes on a bad gene to each puppy and therefore produces carriers. If a carrier is used for breeding, half of the puppies will be carriers. If two carriers are bred together, half of the puppies will be carriers, a quarter will be affected with PRA, and a quarter will be free of the PRA gene.

It is pretty well established that most Tollers affected by PRA will show signs of the disease between the ages of four and five, but there will always be the one which confounds this neat assumption. No one knows how many Tollers went blind in the old days as, if they did, the cause was probably put down to old age.

PRA-affected dogs can be recognized by two different examination techniques, the ophthalmoscope and the electroretinogram. The advantage of the ERG is the earlier detection of the disease. PRA can be diagnosed by ERG months or even years before changes can be seen in the back of the eye using an ophthalmoscope. This allows elimination of an affected dog from a breeding program before diseased genes have been spread and more blind dogs produced."

* * *

When Dr. Keller gave permission to use her PRA article, she was asked to make an educated guess regarding the approximate age at which PRA will show up in Tollers. She replied, "From the relatively large number of Tollers I have ERG'd, I feel comfortable saying that by three years of age affected dogs have obvious problems. Therefore, I would expect to see definite abnormalities showing up before seven years."

Night blindness is one of the first visible signs of PRA, leading some eye specialists to suggest that earlier detection could be made by owners simply by turning their dog loose in an unfamiliar, darkened room. If the dog constantly bumps into furniture or other objects, it is likely that his night vision is affected. This unscientific method of PRA detection is not likely to find wide favor, but it might be useful for giving an early indication that something is wrong with the dog's vision.

GENETIC TESTING FOR BREEDING STOCK

Since 1996 when this book first appeared in print, a number of tests have become available to significantly change the way responsible Toller breeders manage their breeding programs. Testing is now mandatory through Toller Club Codes of Ethics and most breeders submit evaluation forms to Orthopaedic Foundation for Animals (OFA) and Optigen for their breeding stock. Tests include those for various forms of progressive retinal atrophy (PRA) type prcd for Tollers; Collie eye anomaly (CEA); juvenile Addison's disease (JADD), and cleft palate (CP1).

Early in 2002 both North American Toller Clubs made the exciting announcement *"PRA*

Has Had Its Day!" Ever since veterinary ophthalmologists discovered PRA in Tollers a few years previously, breeders had put promising dogs out of their programs when it was discovered with the use of an electroretinogram (ERG) that they were either affected or carriers for the eye disease. Eye specialists were insistent that carriers — those that test positive or have a positive parent or offspring — should not be used for breeding. Then exciting news came from the Baker Institute of Animal Health at Cornell University that a DNA blood test was being developed, thanks in part through generous donations from the Van Sloun Fund for Canine Genetics started by Toller fanciers Sue and Neil Van Sloun. With this news came many donations from delighted and relieved Toller lovers, both Toller Clubs, and the Morris Animal Foundation. Sue Van Sloun, who with Marile Waterstraat had spearheaded specific Toller research at Cornell, was awarded the Baker Institute's 1998 Arthur F. North Jr. Canine Service Award.

On Feb. 1 2002, Optigen Laboratory LLC began accepting and processing blood tests to determine the PRA status of Tollers. This has continued up to the present, with Optigen offering special discounts during certain periods to keep down costs to breeders, many of whom test puppies before they are placed. It is now quite easy to find out whether each pup is Pattern A (clear); B (carrier) or C (affected), thus eliminating guesswork from a breeding program with respect to prcd, the only form of PRA in Tollers which results in blindness. Two A dogs bred together will produce all clear puppies; A to B will produce some clear and some carrier but no affected dogs. Using the Mendelian ratio, C can even be bred to A, there will be some carriers and some affecteds but within a few generations it is possible to breed no more affected dogs.

All went well until CEA was found in Tollers around 2005, thus reinforcing the theory that there is a lot of collie in Toller origins, as CEA is mainly a collie disease. Optigen already had a CEA test for the collie breeds, which is now also used by Toller breeders worldwide. CEA, technically known as choroidal hypoplasia (CH), is a recessive disorder causing abnormal development of the choroid, a layer of tissue under the retina. Tests can be done at a very young age, but there is no known treatment. In Europe this disorder is known as coloboma, a Greek word meaning 'unfinished.'

Addison's disease, or hypoadrenocorticism, occurs when the adrenal glands fail to secrete hormones necessary to control sodium and potassium levels in the blood. Addisons usually shows up around four years of age or later, but in Tollers this can happen around five months or earlier, and is known as JADD. This form of the disease is inherited as an autosomal recessive with one copy of the mutant gene coming from each parent. In addition, JADD is not completely penetrant, meaning that not all puppies with two copies of the mutation will be affected. The test was developed by a team at UC Davis in California, led by Toller breeder Dr. Danika Bannasch, and is now marketed by OFA.

Another test now available through OFA is that for CP1, or cleft palate. However, there are four different genes for cleft palate and so far only CP1 is available, making it difficult to pinpoint carriers. Mode of inheritance is a simple autosomal recessive, but just because dogs are clear for CP1 does not mean that they do not carry one of the other three genes.

Epilepsy in Tollers has been problematic in various countries for a long time, but now there is a special program to seek solutions by the Neurology Service at Ontario Veterinary College, University of Guelph. Initiated in 2006, the pilot project was completed in 2009. However, further data collection and analysis necessary for success came to a halt with the tragically sudden death of leader Dr. Roberto Poma in 2010. In 2013 Dr. Fiona James, Dr. Poma's only graduate student to work on the project, came back to Guelph to fill his position and carry on this vital task; the main objective is to define common clinical and electroencephalographic seizure patterns in epileptic Tollers. Dr. Hannes Lohi, a canine genetics expert at the University of Helsinki in Finland, is now working closely with Dr. James and a new graduate student, Dr. Kelley Vurik. The NSDTR Club of Canada has voted funds to support this important project. Further information can be found by writing to Dr. James at OVC or emailing: jamesf@uoguelph.ca.

Chase, BISS HIT CH Foxgrove's The Chase Is On SH WCX CDX, a Chelsea daughter who had a large influence on the breed, and her brood of 10 day old puppies. Owner/breeder Sue Kish.

16
The Art of Breeding

One can say that there are proliferators and there are breeders. Proliferators seem to think that they need do little more than mate a dog and bitch of the same breed, sell the puppies to the first comers, then sit back and count their profits. On the other hand, very few careful hobby breeders break even, let alone make a profit.

True breeders choose a breed because they love it and because they want to do their utmost to produce good dogs. Without breeders, there would be no distinctive breeds — merely a lot of mongrels. Toller pioneers suffered many setbacks, but thanks to their persistence, our breed is alive and flourishing today.

The breeding picture has changed considerably over the past twenty years. Back then, the tiny group of Toller breeders outside southwestern Nova Scotia had to work hard to inform the public about the dog's existence. Breeding animals of high quality were few and far between, meaning that breeders outside the Maritimes had to import what they hoped would be good breeding stock from the East. Bitches were flown right across Canada from British Columbia and Saskatchewan to be bred to studs in Nova Scotia, but the gamble was worthwhile and gave new breeding stock upon which to build.

In those days, puppies could be much more than eight weeks old before someone bought them, which meant that breeders had to deal with the need for socialization, training, feeding, and care. Breeding Tollers was, indeed, a labor of love. This is still the case in most instances, but now there is a real danger that the quickly growing popularity of Tollers will lead to an increase in proliferators rather than true breeders.

Breeders of rare breeds often envy those in more popular breeds, thinking that the selection of suitable stock must be simpler with more dogs from which to choose. Conversations with these breeders, however, reveal that many of them feel that they, too, are limited in their choices due to problems in various lines or their dislike of certain types within their breed.

Toller clubs in North America and Europe now produce lists of hip- and eye-cleared stock, and both Canadian and American clubs have established health and genetics committees to work on current problems. Responsible breeders are members of their country's parent breed club, which works to educate future Toller owners about club membership, adherence to a club code of ethics, and health clearances on parents of the puppy that they hope to obtain.

BREEDING SYSTEMS

Many authorities advocate the use of line breeding or inbreeding to set type and reinforce good qualities. Pedigrees show that most of today's successful Toller lines have been produced by close line breeding, when one or two notable individuals appear several times in the first three generations of a pedigree. Breeders have also done a fair amount of inbreeding, the mating of very near relatives. A price is now being paid for these practices by an increase in health problems, discussed in the previous chapter. This is due to the unmasking of heretofore hidden recessive genes in the ever-increasing numbers of Tollers being produced.

Dog breeders speak of the pull of the norm. A majority of dogs in a breed will approximate the average, or norm, with a few above this norm and some below. Just as a quality line is created by concentrating desirable genes in its dogs, breeders can expect a lessening of quality when they use outcross dogs closer to the breed norm. Toller breeders find themselves in the predicament of being unable to safely continue inbreeding and close line breeding until tests to pinpoint carriers of various diseases become available.

Some breeders are trying to rectify this situation by incorporating dogs from other lines in their breeding programs and by limiting repeat breedings. This can result in loss of preferred type, at least temporarily, but the genetic health of a line can be improved by introduction of new genes. Of course, sometimes the old adage, "Better the devil you know than the devil you don't," can apply to dog breeding, but breeders must also take risks if the Toller is to go from strength to strength.

Breeders must have a clear picture in their mind of their "personal blueprint" of an ideal specimen, gained from experience and from study of the breed Standard. They must stick to this ideal through thick and thin, no matter what fads intervene or what is winning. Kennel-blindness has no place here, because breeders must be able to evaluate their own dogs honestly in order to know the strengths and weaknesses of the dogs and also be able to recognize a dog that can correct some of the faults. Breeders should also think ahead when planning matings so that offspring from these matings can be used together in the future to enhance the entire program.

One successful breeding system involves keeping back one or two of the best puppies from each litter for later evaluation. If the pups do not measure up to what is desired, or do not surpass the quality of their parents, they are placed. This system has a great deal of merit in the hands of

A new litter. Notice the identifying collars made with different colors. Photo courtesy Sue Kish.

BIS Maverick with his two AKC Best in Show sons, winning Best Stud Dog at the 2012 National Specialty. He also won it in 2010.

Left to right: Nicholas, BIS MBISS GCH NSDTRC-US/Can CH JavaHill Steal My Heart Am RE JH WC, Can RN JH WCX ; Maverick, BIS BISS GCH NSDTRC-US/Can CH Fionavar JavaHill TopGun Am/Can CD, WC, VC, ROMX, and Ranger, BIS Am/Can CH JavaHill's Backwoods Boy RN.

Courtesy of Linda Fitzmaurice, JavaHill Tollers

an experienced breeder, one with in-depth knowledge of breed qualities necessary for a dog to be a top-class specimen. Pups that do not fulfill the very high expectations of such a breeder will doubtless satisfy one who is slightly less demanding.

SELLING GOOD TOLLERS

While many breeders retain control of some of their best dogs by means of co-ownerships, or by placing pups where they are available for a breeding program, there is a fundamental flaw in keeping the best to oneself. A top breeder should be willing to provide high-quality stock to others starting out, or share the best with another top kennel. The fact that an established breeder asks for a puppy is a compliment. The welfare of the breed as a whole comes before being a top winner. If breeders part only with their second-best, how are others to upgrade? Quality competition will provide stimulus for a top breeder to produce even better litters. No one can take real pride in making champions by defeating only mediocre opposition. In a hunting breed, there is the additional question of how to properly train and evaluate several puppies at once unless help is available or the breeder can devote full time to this task.

BREEDING THE ALL-ROUND TOLLER

The need to produce all-rounders makes it inevitable that some drawbacks may have to be overlooked in order to achieve other necessary attributes. Toller breeders who care about producing dogs that can "do it all" cannot afford to breed solely for one activity. Sacrifices may have to be made in, say, conformation, in order to keep hunting instincts strong, but breeders must seek a balanced mixture of hunting promise, trainability, and construction while also paying attention to temperament. Breed type must always be maintained, and every effort should be made to try to ensure that the same structural faults do not exist in both prospective parents.

As truly high-quality specimens are few and far between in today's Toller ranks, breeders are often faced with having no place to go in efforts to improve their stock. There is a desperate shortage of outstanding stud dogs and brood bitches, as there is a lack of experienced breeders with enough knowledge to make really educated breeding decisions. Some promising newcomers are, however, now entering the breed, bringing with them hope for the future.

THE SWEDISH METHOD

The late Ewa Jonsson, backbone of the Swedish Toller, had some very definite ideas about breeding, cemented after a lifetime of breeding dogs, horses, and cattle. Ewa and veterinarian-geneticist Megg Brautigam hammered out a policy for the Swedish Toller Club that differs quite drastically from North American practices of line breeding. The Swedes have built a wide "breeding base" for their Tollers, and the closest acceptable matings allowed by the club's breeding advisory is between cousins.

The Swedes feel that only now, after ten years, do they have a breeding base sufficiently wide to allow them to begin selecting for individual desirable traits. Most dogs from each litter are bred, because it is felt that each dog has something valuable to contribute. A male is not allowed to sire more than 5 percent of the puppies produced in order to keep genetic variation.

Ewa organized the pedigrees of all Tollers in Sweden using a color-coded system to indicate carriers for certain conditions. The drawback to this system is that dogs farther back in the pedigrees have been labeled as carriers only on the strength of probability from the pedigrees. These dogs are now dead and, because such records were not kept in Canada, the information is suspect.

The Swedish program is given a remarkable boost by the fact that the Swedish Kennel Club closely regulates activities of all dog breeders in Sweden, and everyone is forced to comply. All health checks, both good and bad, are published in the official SKK magazine. This results in a closer spirit of cooperation than is dreamed of in North America, because no one has anything to hide.

Ewa bred for three points only in her program, which has produced winners in both field tests and conformation shows:

1. Health: Some genetic risks have to be taken with dogs farther back in the pedigree, but never with the animal that is actually to be bred. (Some of these risks are, however, beginning to come back to haunt present-day breeders.)
2. Temperament: Choose dogs that are not easily stressed and that have sound, stable temperament; neither too easygoing nor too wild.
3. Hunting ability: Pick only dogs with spontaneous retrieving and hunting ability.

Chelsea, top producing bitch owned by Sue Kish, with some of her kids.
Left to right top row:
Foxgrove's Wave Chaser US CD Can WCX;
"Chelsea," CH Westerlea Elias Tidal Wave SH WCX CD FbDCH US WCI;
BOSS HIT CH Foxgrove's The Chase Is On SH WCX CDX.
Bottom row left to right:
CH Foxgrove's Springvale Windswept CD WC OA NAJ;
GMH HIT Foxgrove's This Bud's For You, US CDX Can WCX ;
HIT CH Foxgrove's Sea Spray MH, US CD, Can WCX

CHOOSE YOUR PARTNERS

The Toller breeder's task would be made easier if the breed possessed high-quality individuals that were prepotent with any breeding partner. There have been successful stud dogs but none that have indelibly stamped their progeny and succeeding generations with their quality, regardless of which bitch they were bred to. It appears that Toller bitches, in general, exert more influence on the breed, even though they produce fewer offspring.

The Brood Bitch

A quality Toller bitch is a pearl beyond price if she produces offspring as good or better than herself when bred to different stud dogs. She should have strong retrieving and water instincts, allied to good or above-average conformation as defined in the Standard. Look for a wide pelvis, because this facilitates easy whelping. A good, equable temperament with strong mothering instincts also are important for a matron.

The ideal brood bitch will whelp good-sized litters of strong, healthy puppies, will produce lots of milk, and will take good care of her brood. The number of puppies is determined by the number of eggs released at the time of ovulation. This number is controlled by the bitch's genetic makeup and state of health. Many Toller bitches go far longer between seasons than bitches of other breeds, and it is fairly common for a bitch to come in season once a year. You must take care in breeding these bitches in case a fertility problem is in the making, but if the bitch has the necessary attributes, she should be tried. You must then watch her daughters to see if they cycle regularly.

Most breeding manuals tell you that the bitch will bleed fairly copiously from the first day of her heat period until about day ten to eleven, with the discharge gradually changing to the color of straw. It is quite normal for Toller bitches to continue bleeding throughout their cycle, with little change in color. The average best days for breeding are days twelve to fifteen, but there is a large variation and you may happen to try to breed one whose optimum days are seventeen to eighteen.

Reddog Ribbon's Elegant Echo, daughter of Ch Skylark's Ribbons for Reddog WCI JH RA CD ThD CGC. Co-owned by Mardie Smith and Renee Rosamillia. Shown at three to four months of age.

A bitch with outstanding retrieving and water instincts is sometimes selected for these traits, despite having less-than-ideal conformation. In this case, put even more care into stud selection. Although the pups will be good hunting dogs, often conformation will suffer and faults will be produced that will be extremely hard to eradicate in succeeding generations.

The Stud Dog

A stud dog can contribute far more to a breed's population than any one bitch. Ideally, he must be an above-average specimen, with strong retrieving and water instincts and a good temperament. He must be in good health, active and sound, with no disqualifying faults. However, the most important consideration is the quality of his offspring, always keeping in mind the bitches he has bred. Stud owners should consider the quality of bitches in field ability, temperament, and conformation contemplated for their males and ask themselves if they really want their good dog's name at the top of the pedigree of such a mating. If the answer is lukewarm or negative, decline the inquiry, remembering that the bitch will probably exert more influence on the litter. If brucellosis is a problem in your area, or in the area of the bitch's home, be sure to have both dogs tested. It goes without saying that all breeding stock be cleared for hips and eyes by the appropriate certifying agencies.

Many factors can affect sperm production, so it is wise to have a sperm count done on any dog considered for breeding. It is customary to take the bitch to the stud, because dogs will be more eager to breed in familiar surroundings. Some young dogs may have to be helped, but most Toller males know exactly what to do when the bitch is absolutely ready. Even young, untried males seem to have this instinct. The big mistake is to expect the male to breed a bitch before or after her optimal time.

Tollers are, on the whole, natural breeders and whelpers, but there seems to be an increasing reliance on sophisticated methods of artificial reproduction. The more we abandon natural methods of breeding, the more we encourage reproductive problems in our dogs. Veterinary medicine has allowed breeders to save puppies that otherwise would not have survived, and these may, in turn, pass on the potential for reproductive troubles to their offspring. Cattle breeders are much more pragmatic — if a heifer of prime breeding, bred to a proven bull, does not produce a calf, she is immediately removed from the breeding program. Shouldn't dog breeders be as strict?

The growing use of frozen or fresh-chilled semen will help alleviate problems of shipping valuable bitches to a stud. It is possible that one day Toller breeders will also be able to import or export semen to and from Europe, where the use of frozen semen is already very well established due to quarantine restrictions. Such exchanges will help widen the Toller gene pool and benefit the entire breed. Progesterone tests and artificial insemination are, of course, required for such matings.

WHAT BREEDERS SAY

In preparation for this book, we sent a questionnaire to established Toller breeders in North America. Many influential breeders, past and present, offered their thoughts about their personal priorities and goals, and what they felt the future holds for the breed. A number of their ideas have already been incorporated into this and other chapters, and we are grateful for their input.

Almost all respondents said that they tried to breed quality, all-purpose Tollers, although some placed higher emphasis on one aspect, such as

Ch. Javahill Steal My Heart winning BIS Puppy. Owners: Amy and Paul Soderman. Breeders: Linda Fitzmaurice and Meredith Noreen. Photo © MyDog Photo.

hunting, than on others. All are worried about health problems in the breed, and most expressed concern about the current rapid growth in breed popularity. All want to avoid a split between show and field Toller types.

PATTY BERAN

We hope that the Toller will remain a fairly rare, sound, versatile breed, with a small number of dedicated breeders, and that we continue to be relatively unadulterated by kennel-club politics, puppy mills, and thoughtless breeders.

GRETCHEN BOTNER

I try to match the Standard in size, weight, and color but feel that too many light-colored Tollers are cropping up. I have worked to keep white markings as a strong part of my Toller type and do not like the black pigment. Color, size, white markings, and pigment-matching coloring are all a strong part of what makes a Toller different from a Golden Retriever.

RENA CAP

I place prime importance on the elimination of genetic problems. Ninety percent of Jalna puppies go to pet and hunting homes, so my most important aim is to produce a healthy puppy with the kind of temperament that allows the dog to live with, and be loved by, its owner to a ripe old age. I see better dogs in the future, free from serious problems, *if* breeders share the bad as well as the good news about their dogs, and if they are selective as to where they place breeding stock.

JOYCE DOBIRSTEIN

All of my pups are sold with CKC nonbreeding contracts, which will not be canceled until hips and eyes are certified, and my own dogs have obedience and/or field degrees — often both. I foresee more Tollers in animal shelters as the breed's popularity surges. Not everyone who is captivated by Toller charms is suited to cope with such an intelligent, sensitive animal. Bored dogs tend to get into trouble if they think they can run the household.

**LILLIAN GREENSIDES
AND KAREN WRIGHT**

Good temperament and health are our main goals. We insist on ERG testing for all of our breeding stock as well as for any bitches that come for breeding, in order to help rid the breed of PRA.

When Toller Hope had eleven puppies, labrador kennelmate Guinle helped out, and they shared the same nest. Gwen Kinney.

A newborn litter. Puppies without unique markings are identified with collars in various colors. Photo courtesy of Sue Kish.

LAURA GROSSMAN

Toller owners must work together and support each other, even if our own personal goals might not be the same, as long as the ultimate purpose is to better the breed. Negative thinking is demeaning to a breed that can win Best in Shows and High in Trials, as well as place in field trials, NAHRA, and Master Hunting Retriever tests. Owners of such dogs must have the time, dedication, and finances to make this happen, and they must have an exceptional dog.

ERIC JOHNSON

In the United States, the primary retriever will always be the Black Labrador, followed by the Golden Retriever. Relative future positions of the other retriever breeds will be determined by what sets them apart from each other, and I feel that the Toller can compete very well. Its smaller size makes it an obvious choice for some, compared to Flat and Curly-Coated Retrievers, Chesapeakes, and Irish Water Spaniels. Its personality is good, and the breed already has a reputation for being an easy keeper and more trainable than some of the other breeds. However, the smaller size means that Tollers just won't ever be truly competitive in traditional field trials, where the bigger dogs can see better and travel the longer distances faster.

SUSAN KISH

The biggest problem that we have today is lack of cooperation between breeders. Unless we all work together, we will not be able to come up with solutions or even understand fully what we have, genetically, in Tollers. We must work to widen the gene pool and should look into bringing dogs into Canada from places like Sweden, although the cost is atrocious.

ROBERTA MACKENZIE

If we ever begin breeding Tollers again, I will aim to produce a foxy-looking dog with much inborn intelligence, strong-willed but trainable, with no traces of shyness. I predict that the Toller could become number-one dog in many countries if the breed is in the hands of careful, caring breeders and owners. The club should be serious about culling breeders and owners, not just dogs.

TERRY MCNAMEE

I place health, good temperament, hunting instincts, and breed type ahead of conformation. Breeders must step back and think about the genetic pedigree of any planned mating. A former Maritime breeder told me that Tollers nearly died out at least twice in the past because of decimation from inherited diseases. If, in ten or twenty years, I have produced only a few more champions but can say that my dogs are healthier, sounder in structure, typier, and better hunters than when I started, I will feel that I have reached my goal of contributing to the betterment of the Toller.

ANNE NORTON

The ebb and flow of Toller popularity over the past half century has left us a difficult legacy of structural and health problems, with wide variations in conformation even within a litter. This is due to the small gene pool, generation upon generation of line breeding, and misinformed breeding practices. Nonbreeding contracts are the best friend that a breeder has, but many are not using them and some owners are ignoring them. I hope that future Toller breeders will look ever more carefully toward their dogs' Canadian Maritime past and strive toward a healthy, sound, compact, intelligent, companionable, eager little red-haired, white-footed waterfowl hunter that is judged in the show ring based upon his conformation to a Standard that emphasizes just that.

JOAN NOULLETT

All breeders have a trust to preserve the Toller. How can we forget those dogs that, as pets, simply gladdened the hearts of their owners — the man who owned many different breeds but felt his Toller was the best dog he ever had, or the elderly lady who declared that her Toller was worth his weight in gold? These are the people who sing the praises of the Toller every day, in layman's language, and I am as pleased to have produced those dogs as I am the champions.

MARY SPROUL

In the beginning, the Toller was a hunting dog, but today the game that he hunts is slowly becoming scarce. The population of ducks and geese has gone from thousands to hundreds in our part of Nova Scotia. The Toller may lose his purpose as a hunting dog, but I feel that the future has a bright side because of the dog's size, intelligence, and devotion.

SUE VAN SLOUN

Although we in the United States have come quite far in a short time, we still have a way to go before we have established a strong breeding stock foundation. I still see a lot of type variation both in Canada and the United States and see more work ahead, rather than a quick end to our rare-breed status and AKC recognition. If you think of the Toller as a breed in relationship to a split-level house, we are still in the basement!

* * *

All of these breeders would agree that hobby breeding has its great rewards, as well as moments of black despair when things do not go right. The rewards usually outweigh the setbacks, as the next chapter tells.

Proud mother Gypsy and her new litter.

Lovely young puppy bred by Krista Wendland, Rainkist Nova Scotia Duck Tolling Retrievers. Photo courtesy of the owner.

17
Diary of A Litter

Sue Kish is involved in all Toller activities — field tests, obedience, conformation, flyball, and agility. She now breeds Tollers under her Foxgrove prefix. A graduate animal health technician, Sue has an avid interest in animal health and genetics. Many thanks go to Sue for this interesting and informative contribution to our book.

Raising a litter of puppies brings with it many responsibilities. The first is being able to realize that not all dogs should be bred, nor should all people be breeders. Before taking on the task of raising a litter, it is important to learn as much as possible about the Toller breed and also have the ability to assess your bitch — both her strong and weak points — in order to find a male to complement her. Her temperament must be sound, she must be a good retriever, she must have no disqualifying faults according to the breed Standard, and she must be certified free of hip dysplasia and heritable eye diseases. You, as the breeder, must have the time available to raise the litter properly, because puppies need lots of time for socialization and handling. If there are problems, the project can become expensive.

Once you have made the decision to breed your bitch and have found a suitable male, the waiting game begins. Bitches come in season once or twice each year, and arrangements for the stud dog should be made well in advance. Once the bitch comes in heat, notify the stud owner and have the bitch tested for brucellosis, a sexually transmitted disease that causes abortion of the fetuses. You must also request a similar clearance for the stud dog. The bitch will usually stand for the male a few days before and after ovulation, and in Tollers, this can be as early as day eight of the oestrus (heat) cycle or as late as day nineteen. You can expect puppies approximately sixty-three days later.

With this in mind, a litter was planned in 1993 between a male and a bitch that I co-owned. Honey (Can. Ch. Tollbreton Honey for Westerlea WC) lived on Canada's west coast with her co-owner, and Sandy (BIS Can. Ch. Sandycove at Westerlea WC CD) lived in St. Lazare, Quebec, with me. Sandy had proved that he puts both coat and bone onto his puppies, and he was also passing on his biddable and outgoing temperament. Honey had more length of leg, needed by Sandy, and could use a little more drive in the hindquarters, which Sandy has. She had retrieving intensity but was a little lacking in desire to please. I felt that these dogs complemented each other, so, with the breeding already planned, Honey arrived from British Columbia in March.

Father and mother, Sandy and Honey.

Honey and I spent the next two months in field and obedience training so that she would be ready to run a WC test in June. This dog had oodles of natural talent and passed with style two days running. Having already attained her show championship, she thus proved worthy of producing a litter. Her hips had been certified clear, and a second eye check was normal. Now the waiting — and this diary—began.

JUNE

Honey is due in season in July, so it is time to make an appointment to administer her yearly vaccinations. To be on the safe side, I will also do a fecal analysis, because she should be free of worms and have a high immunity against disease before she is bred.

JULY 13-17

Sandy has been interested in Honey for the last few days, and now she is standing for him. She looks for him and stands with her tail held to one side when she sees him. She is proving to be an easy breeder, flirting with him and then standing quietly while he mounts her. Breedings took place between July 13 and 17, so I can expect puppies around September 14.

JULY 18-AUGUST 9

Honey's activity level has remained the same for the last few weeks. She is still running several miles each day in the woods and leaps into the water to retrieve bumpers. By week three, however, there seems to be a noticeable increase in her appetite. Normally a slow eater, she is now gobbling food and looking for more.

AUGUST 23

I palpated Honey today, and we are definitely having puppies! The puppies feel like peach pits, but I am unable to guess how many there are. It is time to increase her food intake, and I'll switch her over to a good puppy kibble by week five.

AUGUST 24-SEPTEMBER 9

I am now adding boiled eggs to Honey's diet as well as cottage cheese and liver. It is week six, and she is starting to tire more easily but is still game to run and retrieve. Exercise is an important element in a healthy brood bitch's regime and should not be eliminated, but altered to her tolerance level. I will allow Honey to swim almost daily until the time she whelps, knowing that the water where we exercise is unpolluted.

SEPTEMBER 10

It is time to start taking Honey's temperature twice daily. A drop in temperature, from a normal of around 38.5C (101.5F) to 37C (98.4F) or lower, is normal twenty-four hours prior to whelping, coinciding with the drop in progesterone levels. Honey's temperature today is 37.8C (98.8F).

SEPTEMBER 12

Honey's temperature dropped to 36.8C (97F) this morning, leaving me with the feeling that I will not get much sleep tonight. She displayed little interest in food today and became very restless by suppertime. Tonight we bunk down in the whelping room.

Keeping both Honey's comfort and my own in mind, I installed a cot and radio in the room. Honey has already spent several nights here to get acclimatized to the environment in which she will be spending so much time in the next few weeks. I saved newspapers, and several layers are now lining the whelping box. I've checked my supplies, which include ten white towels, mosquito hemostats, thick thread, a baby scale, a heating pad in a box lined with towels, blunt scissors, and a cordless phone in case I need to call for help.

SEPTEMBER 13

It is midnight and Honey has arranged and rearranged the papers many times. She is restless and asking to go out every half-hour. I am sure that puppies are imminent.

At 12:49 A.M., the first puppy is born — a healthy, loud fourteen-ounce (400 gm) male with a white blaze, four white feet, and a white chest. A great start for the litter.

The next puppy takes almost two hours and is born quite weak at 2:35 A.M.

The puppies come faster after this, with the last of the six born at 4:21 A.M. The puppies, two males and four females, are all looking healthy at this point, but I am concerned for the bitch because the placentas for puppies four and five were not delivered. I have administered twenty units of oxytocin to no avail. Honey's temperature is rising, so I check with my veterinarian and we have chosen to put her on a fourteen-day course of novalexin, an antibiotic that will not be harmful to the puppies.

SEPTEMBER 14-27

Honey's temperature dropped to within a normal limit, which is higher after parturition for a couple of days anyway, but a temperature higher than 39c (103F) signals trouble. Honey's had

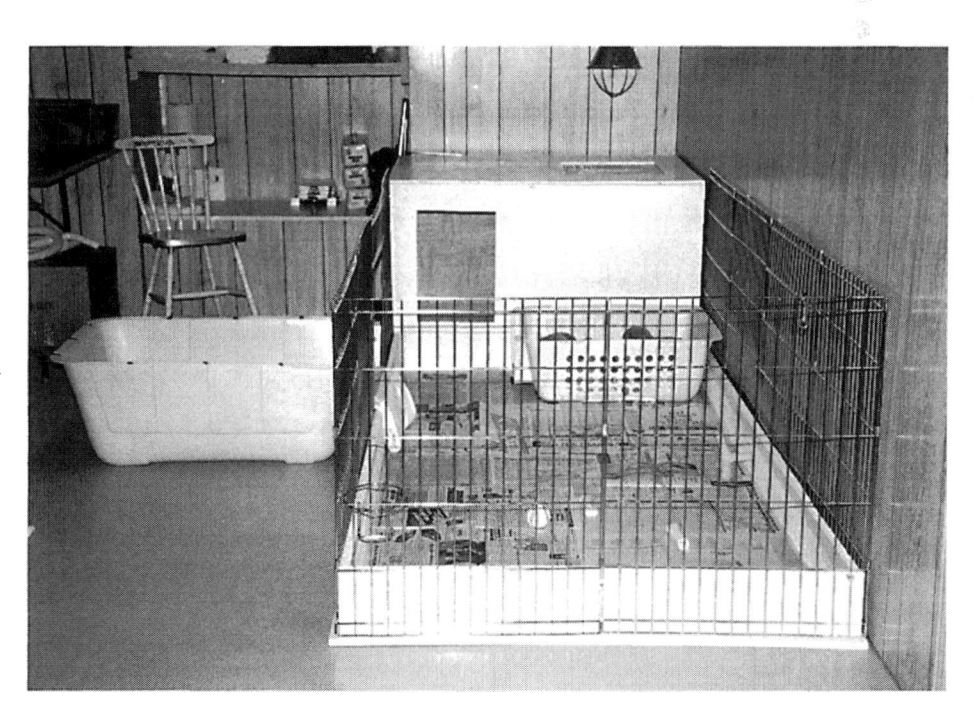

The whelping room is ready.

Newborn pups.

risen to 40C (104F). I had been contemplating an IV drip of penicillin, but this necessity has been eliminated, much to my relief. The puppies are oblivious to my worries, as they are snug in a covered whelping box on a thick, stay-dry liner, in a 37C (80F) environment with a mom that is reluctant to leave them.

During their first two weeks, the puppies need very little care that Honey can't provide. I handle them several times daily, twice a day necessitated by supplementing them with yogurt to offset the effects of the antibiotics that Honey is receiving. I also weigh the puppies daily. I removed the dewclaws at day four and will cut the puppies' nails every five days while they remain with me.

The puppies spend this time eating and sleeping. Directed by their sense of smell, they crawl to Honey for nourishment. During this time, their eyes are closed and they cannot hear. This keeps them in a relatively nonstressful environment. The puppies are learning at a very young age to differentiate familiar from unfamiliar smells. When, at four days of age, a stranger picked up a puppy, the pup snuggled down for warmth. However, if I place my hand near the puppy, he will try to crawl toward me. Although I am not mom, I do represent a smell with which they are familiar.

NEWBORN RESUSCITATOR

For the puppy that appears lifeless at birth, first try to clear mucus collected in the mouth and throat using a very small ear bulb, then wrap the pup in a towel and shake vigorously, holding the pup on his back and cradling him in your hands. Be careful to keep his head supported. You can help matters by placing a drop or two of the following solution on his tongue with your finger or a small eye dropper:

1 teaspoon honey or corn syrup
a few grains salt
½ cup boiled water

Another more drastic method of starting a puppy breathing is to quickly hold him under cold running water, then vigorously towel-dry him. You can also massage his rib cage and breathe into his mouth, covering his nostrils.

Puppies at this age are susceptible to heat and cold and must have the temperature of their environment monitored closely. (A heating lamp that I placed above the box does a nice job, and the puppies can crawl away from the heat as necessary.) By the end of the first week, I am finding the puppies away from the direct heat of the lamp more often than not. Puppies at this age cannot urinate or defecate without stimulation, and they rely on Honey's regular cleaning. During the first ten days, they sleep 90 percent of the time. This litter is spending a considerable amount of time sleeping on their backs, as do many adult Tollers.

WHEN THINGS GO WRONG

If a puppy shows a definite defect, there is no point in trying to save it. There is, however, no harm in extending a helping hand if a pup is small, thus allowing it to compete with more robust littermates for the available food supply. Either tube or bottle feeding for a few days will help smaller, weaker pups to hold their own.

Two-week-old puppies.

Tollers love to lie on their backs, even when nursing puppies.

Roger and Jenny at three weeks.

SEPTEMBER 23-26

Between days nine and twelve, the puppies' eyes start to open, beginning with tiny slits at the edge of the eye and opening fully in two days. Vision seems hazy at first, and it takes a few days until I can see them follow an object with their eyes. The ears open several days after the eyes, and at this point, the puppies are starting to react to sound. By day thirteen, teeth are beginning to appear in the gum line, and the puppies make their first attempts at stepping and scratching. They are definitely more awake than during the first week.

SEPTEMBER 27-OCTOBER 2

The puppies are fourteen days old and are spending almost all of their time away from the heat source, so I am turning off the lamp but am closely monitoring the room temperature, which is 67F by day and 62F at night. By this time, Honey is producing lots of milk, and her food intake has increased from her normal one and three-fourths cups to eight cups of dry kibble plus one and one-half cups of yogurt, one egg, and two cups of milk daily.

OCTOBER 3-10

By the end of the third week, the puppies are able to eliminate on their own and have discovered how to get out of the whelping box. I have

Bee with her favorite toy, three weeks.

placed a box of shavings at the far end of an enclosure that I made from an exercise pen, and within two days the puppies are defecating

Roger on the scales at three weeks.

The puppies get to know strangers and gravitate to kids.

exclusively in the shavings. This makes cleanup much easier and is the start of house training. Honey is now spending less time with the litter but is still concerned about them.

I am starting to introduce food. I keep Honey out of the box for several hours, then place a pan of food in the pen. I put moistened puppy kibble in the blender and make a gruel, which the puppies start to lap up amazingly quickly. I use two stainless steel, eight-inch puppy pans, big enough for food but small enough to discourage the pups from climbing in.

I am now encouraging as many people as possible to come and play with the puppies. Visiting kids have to sit on the floor, and then the puppies are allowed to crawl all over them. I place various toys on the floor, and the puppies are beginning to carry them around on their explorations. I've also introduced duck wings, much to the litter's excitement, but I don't leave them out as toys.

The puppies begin, very slowly, to play with each other around seventeen to eighteen days. I can start to see a pecking order form at this point, with a "boss bitch" becoming evident. She is the fattest puppy, first at the food dish and pushy with her siblings. If she does not want to play, she lets the others know. As the puppies

RECIPES FOR FEEDING AND CARE OF NEWBORN PUPPIES

As the older generation of dog breeders gradually disappears, so do the tried-and-true remedies that evolved when veterinary medicine was not nearly as advanced as it is today. Because most of these methods do not involve chemicals or antibiotics, those interested in more natural methods of raising dogs might like to have a few recipes for the feeding and care of newborn puppies.

Homemade Formula

If you must bottle- or tube-feed a puppy, here is a recommended formula:

1 cup evaporated milk
1 cup boiled water
2 tablespoons light corn syrup
2 egg yolks

Mix all together and give as much as a pup will take every three to four hours. For supplemental doses, give approximately 5 cc per feed. Because one tablespoon equals 15 cc, it is best to mix up a batch and measure accordingly, as 5 ccs is less than a teaspoonful.

Milk-Maker

This is an excellent mixture to keep on hand and feed to your nursing bitch, especially if the litter is large and/or she has had a difficult delivery:

1 can evaporated milk
1¾ cup boiled water
2 pkgs. gelatin dissolved in 1/3 cup cold water
2 egg yolks
1 tablespoon honey

Mix softened gelatin with the boiled water, add honey and then the evaporated milk. Lastly, add the egg yolks, beaten with a little of the milk mixture. Do not feed more than a cupful of the warmed mixture at a time to a dog the size of a Toller. Refrigerate.

Old-Fashioned Diarrhea Remedy

Apple Tea
   Make 1 cup of tea with 1 bag black tea.
   Cook one medium apple with 1-2 tablespoons water, then sieve.
   Toast 1 slice whole-wheat bread until it is burned.
   Scrape charcoal from the toast and add to apple mixture.
   Add tea to the apple mix until it has slow-drip consistency.
   Sieve again.
   Before giving to the pup, coat the mouth with a tiny bit of milk, then place 1-2 cc of apple tea on the tongue.
   Give after every bowel movement.

If the pup seems dehydrated, try this Electrolyte Replacer:
   To 2 quarts (a little less than 1 litre) warm water, add 1 cup brown sugar, 1 tablespoon baking soda, ¼ teaspoon salt, and about 1/2 teaspoon cream of tartar. Mix together and give 1 cc every hour. Amounts would have to be increased for a larger puppy. To test for dehydration, lift the skin on the puppy's neck. If it stays in a ridge and does not quickly sink back into the neck, the pup could use some help. Ringer's Lactate injected under the skin by a veterinarian is the classic remedy for severe dehydration, but the recipe above could help if the condition is not too advanced.

SANDY/HONEY LITTER
September 13, 1993

Puppy	Time (a.m.)	Sex	Weight (oz.)	Afterbirth Present	Cleft Palate	Markings
Roger	12:49	M	14	Yes	None	Blaze, 4 paws chest white
Bugsy	2:35	M	14	Yes	None	4 paws white
Fanny	2:53	F	12	Yes	None	Large blaze, 4 paws, and lots of white on chest, good tip
Bunny	3:24	F	13	No	None	Small blaze, 4 paws, and lots of white on chest, tiny tip
Jenny	4:10	F	12	No	None	Huge blaze, 4 paws, and lots of white on chest, big tip
Bee	4:21	F	11	Yes	None	Tiny blaze, 4 paws, and small white spot on chest, tiny tip

These trees were made just for us to chew!

are starting to chew on things, I am providing nylabones and bleached bones to satisfy this craving.

I am taking the puppies outside for short periods, because the weather is nice. The sights and sounds of the great outdoors are important for their development. At first they are reluctant to stray too far, but each day they get a little bolder. They have also been moved upstairs during the day to a pen in a central atrium area of the house.

OCTOBER 11-17

Four weeks of age and the puppies are trying to run rather than walk around. They also have found their voices with growling and a few yips. They are carrying toys more frequently and are starting to tussle with each other over them. They also will chase a wool ball if I roll it a few feet right under their noses. Some puppies will return it, while others lie down to chew it.

I take them out every few hours while the weather is still good, and the puppies are quickly learning to eliminate as soon as I place them on grass. This is a first step to house training, but there is a long way to go. At this stage they have three meals a day, but Honey still allows them to nurse. Honey loves her babies and is reluctant to leave them for extended periods.

OCTOBER 18-24

The puppies are five weeks old, and I am making a serious effort to wean Honey away from them. They now have full sets of razor-sharp teeth, and Honey is wearing the scars from their nursing. True to her name, Honey will not say no to her babies. By drastically cutting back her food for the past week and increasing puppy feedings to four meals per day, I have been able to decrease Honey's milk supply but not her desire to nurse her puppies. The only solution is to deny her access to them, which I will do little by little over the next week.

I wormed the puppies for the first time at five weeks and will repeat this weekly for the next three weeks. I have started daily sessions with the puppies on an individual basis. We take walks around the property or play fetch on the floor of the playroom. I lie on the carpet, get the puppy's attention, and roll the wool ball a few

Jenny explores the great outdoors.

feet. At this stage all the puppies are chasing it, picking it up, and running somewhere with it. Half of them bring it back to me, and half carry it to their own little den. I also introduced dead pigeons to the puppies, and all raced after them by the second session.

Personality differences are becoming apparent. "Roger" is very confident and will explore on his own. He much prefers the pigeon to the ball and will race out to get it and then leave with it. "Bugsy," the other male, will retrieve anything, run back with it, and curl up for a hug. Out on our little walks, he stays close to me. "Fanny," a very busy puppy, is showing a short attention span and has to be into something different every few minutes. "Bunny," the boss, is turning into an excellent retriever. She will retrieve endlessly, return with it, growl as she holds it, and not let go. She loves to be out on her own and is a wild puppy away from her littermates. She is more reserved when she is with the others. "Jenny" is the naughty puppy that gets into everything, and she is the ringleader of the pack.

This stuff is fun. Nine-week-old Sylvan pups get used to water.

Jenny — a dream come true.

She is self-confident, loving, and full of personality. She spends considerable time pawing at my legs to be picked up. She loves to discover things to chew and is responsible for demolishing more tree branches and digging big holes than all the rest combined. "Bee," a follower rather than a leader, is the most avid retriever and the one that strives to please. She will go to anyone and sit patiently, waiting for attention. She is also the first puppy to find her voice, which she uses often, and is becoming the spokesperson for the entire litter.

The puppies have lots of play periods in the dog room. Obstacle courses consisting of chairs on their sides, tunnels made from boxes, obedience jumps set low to crawl over, and half crates have been put out for them to explore. Toys are plentiful — tennis and squash balls, bones, plastic squeaky toys, socks with balls in them, rope tug toys, and plush toy dogs. They always have something in their mouths.

OCTOBER 25-31

Now the puppies are six weeks old, and the vaccination schedule must begin. I will vaccinate with distemper/measles at six weeks, with modified live parvovirus at six and one-half weeks, with coronavirus at seven weeks, with Intratrach (nasal protection against kennel cough) at seven and one-half weeks, with distemper/parvo/parainfluenza/bordatella at eight weeks, and with corona again at nine weeks.

Weaning is now complete, and the puppies are being socialized and handled as much as possible by many different people. The neighborhood kids were very good about visiting, but

> **REMEMBER:**
> Veterinarians have varying protocols to follow for both worming and vaccinating puppies. Both the American and Canadian Veterinary Medical Associations have online sections for these, but it is also advisable to consult your own veterinarian for up-to-date information and discussion. Current thinking tries to lessen the number of vaccinations given at any one time, but if no vaccinations are given there is a stronger chance of dread diseases such as distemper and parvovirus rearing ugly heads again. Experienced breeders are also a good source of information but each is apt to have strong, sometimes conflicting opinions!

now the puppies are getting boisterous and hang onto the kids' pant legs, chew their laces, and steal their mitts. Only the older ones will enter the yard, while the rest of the kids race along the fence with the puppies running up and down the fence with them. Sometimes a puppy will still manage to steal a mitt through the fence. Trying to catch a puppy carrying a stolen mitt is a challenge!

Differences in temperament are becoming more obvious. Jenny, Bugsy, and Fanny adore the kids and race along the fence to play with them. They all love to be held, but all except Bugsy are too busy to spend time cuddling. Jenny, Bee, and Bugsy are the first to come when called, while Roger and Bunny run the other way when they don't want to come in. Fanny is starting to fall behind the others in weight, because she is always too busy to eat. Noting temperament differences will be important to help match the right puppy with the right owner.

NOVEMBER 1

At seven weeks, the boys weigh nine and one-half pounds (more than four kilograms). Fanny is seven pounds, three ounces (just over three kilograms), Bee and Jenny are nine pounds (just under four kilograms), and Bunny is nine pounds, four ounces (four kilograms).

Today a veterinarian-breeder friend performed a temperament test. He tested each puppy individually to assess reactions in new situations. Jenny stood out as the most forgiving, people-oriented puppy that raced to the tester when called. Bunny was very unforgiving and avoided eye contact. Fanny showed signs of being sound sensitive. Roger was the least sensitive to pain. All have been classified as nice, middle-of-the-road puppies that should do well in a family environment.

It is time to part with the puppies. This will be the hardest part for me, because I have devoted many hours to "my" puppies over the last seven weeks. However, puppies need individual homes at this stage to develop their full potential with one-on-one attention. These puppies have good homes waiting for them where they will be loved and nurtured. As for me, it will be at least another year until I do this again. But I will have Jenny to keep me busy, still digging holes in snow or mud, still chewing what is left of the lower tree branches, and now retrieving pigeons almost as well as her mom. She is just too naughty to part with!

EPILOGUE

Reviewing what became of this litter while sitting at home on a cold, snowy day gives me a great sense of satisfaction. The puppies are now sixteen months old and are all healthy and doing well with their owners.

Roger (Ch. Westerlea's Roving Highlander) is working in obedience after completing his championwith with a five-point booster show Best of Winners. He has been handled exclusively by his teenage mistress, whom he adores. Bugsy (Ch. Foxgrove's Glengarry Rob CD WC) gained his championship quickly with two booster BW wins. He lives with a retired couple who trained him to his CD in three straight trials. He is still as sweet as he was as a puppy and definitely has his dad's temperament. He is also showing lots of natural talent in the field.

Cricket can do it, too!
Ch. Foxgrove's Westerlea Sandpiper WC.

Fanny (Westerlea's African Queen Zizi) is still a very active youngster. She is spayed, is working in obedience, and is running flyball, where her intensity and energy can be focused. Bunny (Can. Ch. Foxgrove's Westerlea Sandpiper WC) has a great family that caters to her every whim, but they are also continuing the training that I began. She did extremely well in the field in 1994, earning her WC as a puppy. She also has a show championship gained with two booster Winners Bitch awards and is working toward her CD and running flyball. Bee (Westerlea's Red Lady Tara) is a much-loved family pet that is also working in obedience.

Jenny (Can. Ch. Foxgrove's On Your Mark Can. WCX CD, Am. WC) is a dream come true. Her confidence and desire to please have come through in everything she does. Jenny earned her championship by seven months of age, undefeated at breed level, with a Best Puppy in Show, two Best Puppy in Group, and two Second in Group placings.

Jenny then went into field training, where she showed intense desire teamed with excellent scenting and marking ability. Her fieldwork was summarized by one judge as "running on more pistons than any dog I have seen before." Jenny passed her WC at ten months and two days, then passed three more times that summer. She also successfully ran in NAHRA Started Gundog tests.

Attending the U.S. National Toller Specialty Show at two weeks over one year of age, Jenny came away with Winners Bitch, Best of Winners, and Best of Opposite Sex honors in an entry of forty Tollers. She also passed her American WC test the following day.

Showing potential to be an outstanding obedience competitor by earning her CD in three consecutive trials, an accurate and speedy flyball dog, and already a member of the Superdogs entertainment troupe, Jenny is the epitome of the versatile Toller.

Cricket, Sue Kish, and Jenny — a working trio.

One year later: Three champions from the litter. Photo by Alex Smith.

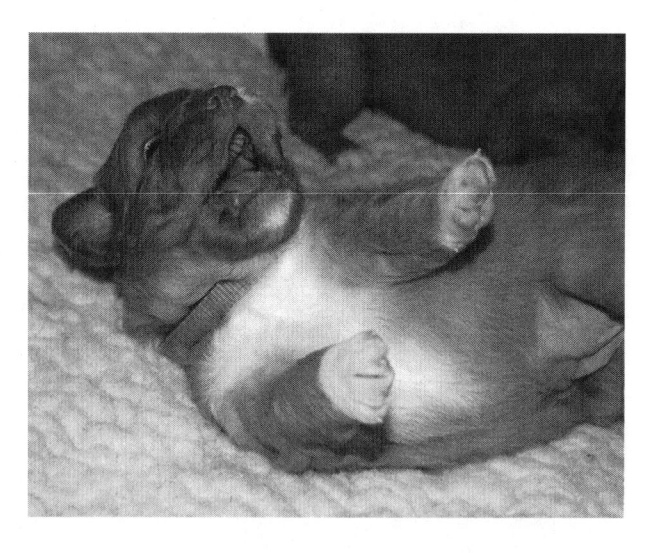

A SELECTION OF PUPPY PHOTOS
Above: (left) Sleeman, 8 weeks, and (right) Stella, both courtesy of Jamie Klein.
Center left: Curry with a disc, courtesy of Dan Rode.
Below right: "Schooner" (BIS BISS CKC IKC NSDTRC-USA AKC CH Vesper Mariner Coupe De Vale) as a puppy, courtesy of Deb Gibbs.

18
Picking the Right Puppy for the Job

Responses from the breeder questionnaire (Chapter 16) also contained interesting observations on the subject of puppy evaluation and what to look for in choosing a puppy for any particular purpose. Almost all breeders agreed that they closely observe the litter from birth, and some maintained that they pick pups at birth and are often proved correct at six to seven weeks. Others prefer to wait, watch, and draw their conclusions from impressions gained over the weeks of puppy care and watching, combined with a more formal evaluation between six and seven weeks of age. Many also use some form of puppy testing.

Gretchen Botner thought that a video record of her early litters would help her in making a final selection as well as provide a lasting record of the litter. She now finds that what appeared on video was not always how a pup actually moved or acted, because so much depended on who was using the camera. Gretchen now thinks that her best way to evaluate a litter is to ask longtime breeders of other breeds to go over the pups at six and again at eight weeks of age. With the help of these knowledgeable people and her growing skill as a breeder, Gretchen feels that her hands and eyes are becoming more educated with each litter. She still thinks, however, that a video record of a litter, showing growth and individual development, is a useful tool when comparing one litter against another.

Dramatic changes can occur in a puppy between six to eight weeks, but many old-timers believe that a pup is closest to his finished conformation at six weeks, before long-term changes in bone length take place.

THE SHOW-RING STAR

When selecting a show hopeful, good to excellent conformation must be allied with proper temperament. The puppy with an outgoing, "hey-look-at-me" air will often win in the show ring even though he lacks something in conformation, while a better-built dog that has less personality may be overlooked. The Toller breed is not one in which show-ring wins are the ultimate aim, but a well-constructed dog will be best equipped to carry out the multiple tasks that are demanded of Tollers.

Here are the physical attributes to look for:

HEAD
- Is the head blocky or fine?
- Is the muzzle wide or snipey, short or long?
- Are the eyes light or dark, wide or close set (small or large)?

Will I make a showdog, Mom? A Kylador puppy, Laker, at three weeks.

- Is the bone heavy, medium, or fine?
- Are the feet round, with thick, tight pads, or are the toes spread out and the pads thin?
- Are the pasterns fairly short and upright, or are they long and sloping? (A very slight slope is desired, but pasterns must be strong.)
- How long is the leg from point of elbow to pastern joint? (This can sometimes give an indication of future short legs if the measurement is much less than three inches.)
- How wide is the puppy's chest? (About three fingers is good for the average Toller puppy.)
- How much forechest (breastbone) can be felt?
* Is the neck of medium length and strong, is it short and strong, is it long and strong, or is it long and weak?
- Is the shoulder layback (angle of the shoulder blade) well angled backward or upright, and is the blade short or long?
- Does the upper arm extend well back under the dog's body so that it lies in a straight line with the highest point of the blade, or is it angled steeply downward, forming a front assembly that is pushed forward, thus hampering free movement?

At six weeks, Ilo had the right stuff—1986.

- Are the ears set high or low on the skull, and are they big or small? (There is a possibility of the ears folding if they are very small and pointed at the tips.)
- Do the teeth meet in a scissors bite, and how tight is that bite? (If they are nearly level at six weeks, there is a strong chance of the dog having an undershot bite at maturity.)

Heads and earsets can be picked out fairly early. A big blocky head will usually stay that way, although muzzles do lengthen out over several months. Fine, snipey muzzles also become apparent quite early. Toller puppy eyes are often a startling blue, although the color will change, first to a greenish hue, then finally to amber. The paler the blue, the lighter will be the adult eye color. Pups with dark pigment will have dark eyes.

FRONT
* When raising the puppy up and letting his front legs drop naturally, do the legs drop straight down, or are they crooked?
- Do the feet turn out?

Before their glory days — Ilo, left, and Buddy as puppies.

- Are the blade and upper arm roughly equal in length?
- Are the shoulder blades well laid on (lying close to the rib cage with not too much width between the blades at the highest point of the shoulder)?
- Do the elbows lie close to the body, or do they stick out and feel loose?

Crooked front legs are a big problem in some Toller lines, and it is unlikely that a young pup with very bowed or crooked legs will ever straighten out. Angulations do not change and are easily determined at six weeks.

BODY
- Is the backbone strong and level, or is there a soft, yielding feel to the back?
- Does the tail flow as a continuation of the croup with only a little drop?
- Does the ribbing extend well back, or is the loin area long (two and one-half to three fingers is good)?
- Does the loin feel strong?

Some toplines that are straight at six weeks can become soft and "dippy" later, but in general, if the back is strong at an early age, it will stay so. Many Tollers go high in the rear during their growth periods, but the topline should be level by one year. A high rear can be forgiven in a pup, but not in an adult.

REAR
- Does the croup angle roughly match the angle of the shoulder blade (placing a thumb on both can give a quick and immediately obvious answer)?
- Is the stifle well turned and strong?
- Are the hocks strong and not set too high?
- Does the puppy set up well on strong hind legs, or is the rear wobbly?
- Do the hocks turn in or out?
- Does the last vertebra of the tail reach the hock, and is the tail wide at the base?

Rears can strengthen with exercise, but in general, rears will remain as they are at the time of evaluation. A weak rear is a serious fault in a sporting dog.

COAT
- Does the coat feel thick, and what is its length?
- Is the color strong and vivid or rather washed out? (Most puppies darken as they grow older; the color of the ears is a good indication of final adult color.)

A future champion learns to pose. Flying Fox (Tod) at twelve weeks.

This puppy bitch shows excellent reach and drive.

- Are the white markings in accordance with the Standard?

There is much variation in puppy coats, but the pup should have a thick coat, regardless of length. Good coats can show up very early, with the better-coated pup having a slight ridge running down the spine even at birth.

As you can see, a working knowledge of dog anatomy is necessary to evaluate puppies properly. Nothing takes the place of an educated eye. Some breeders rely on formal measurements of bone and angles, but these can be noted by experienced eyes and hands. Balance and strength are the keys.

Of course, the most perfectly constructed puppy will not be a true Toller without the proper personality and temperament. These can be developed to their fullest by the environmental conditions in which the puppy grows up. Still, the basics must be in place. A number of puppy tests are available, many of which are used by Toller breeders. Most of the best books on dog raising and training include these tests. Some breeders develop their own tests and have a strong indication of how each puppy will react even before testing takes place.

THE FIELD PUPPY

For a hunting puppy, most breeders place high value on outgoing temperament, allied to strong retrieving drive and love of feathers. He should be a real "go-getter" — playful and aggressive — that should not, however, be so independent that he will not be trainable. For a field test dog this biddability is a must. Otherwise, the pup will not be able to handle the stress of training and competition later. The pup should exhibit no shyness and should have a strong love of water. Many feel that, because they have bred a good hunting dog to an equally adept hunting bitch, most of the puppies will show "the right stuff."

You can test pups in the whelping area with duck wings. Look for the puppy that grabs the wing as if it were the greatest thing on earth. If you have access to pigeons, you can introduce slightly older puppies to a shackled one. Some field trainers dangle a wing-clipped pigeon on the end of a fishing line, because the moving bird is more attractive to pups. Some also place obstacles for the pups to conquer, looking for the puppy that quickly solves the problem.

It is preferable not to choose a pup for field before he is seven weeks old, because the playfulness and aggression do not really develop much before that age.

In evaluating a puppy for hunting, you should note if the pup is fetching between seven and ten weeks of age. Not only is this a prime component of his hunting training, it is also an excellent test of intelligence, trainability, and aggressiveness. At this stage, the pup does not really need to be taught to fetch. If he is a good specimen, he will chase the ball on the first throw and bring it back.

The best place to start is just outside the puppy's pen. Throw a small ball about four to six feet away from the kennel, making sure that the pup has sniffed it first and has seen it thrown. As he goes after it, he will automatically turn back toward his kennel.

The next part is crucial. As he returns, move sideways so that you can grab him gently as he

May I be a field dog, Mom? Photo © PrincePrince Studio, courtesy of Terry Simons

returns. Then pour on the praise. Praise and lots of it is the only reward necessary when training a Toller. Throw the ball again, and this time he will most likely come right back to you. If not, repeat the procedure. If a seven- to ten-week-old pup will not go after the ball immediately, he may not be a good potential for hunting.

Before doing this test, hold the pup, talk to him, and place him on the ground. Then walk around. The pup should very quickly follow at your heels, imprinting himself upon you just as a baby duck will do if taken from the nest at the right time. This imprinting of the pup onto his master is crucial and is the basis of the relationship needed between the hunter and his dog.

THE OBEDIENCE HOPEFUL

When picking an obedience prospect, the middle-of-the-road, eager-to-please puppy is the best candidate. A very dominant pup will not necessarily have the desire to please, which is integral in a good obedience dog. These dogs, however, often do well in the hands of an experienced trainer. Many of the same attributes of trainability will be needed for a dog expected to work in agility and flyball, but this dog will need to show a very outgoing temperament and no shyness, along with an indication of being quick to learn.

THE IDEAL PET

Temperament is the single most important ingredient for a pet puppy. Tollers are *the* perfect dog for an active child, especially boys, because boys love to throw things and Tollers love to retrieve. However, avoid placing a Toller pup in a household where there is a crawling baby or a toddler. Although they are wonderful family dogs, Toller puppies use their teeth in greeting and must be taught that such behavior is unacceptable. While the Toller is learning, young children could be turned off if they have too much contact with needle-sharp teeth. A shy, withdrawn puppy will often blossom when removed from the litter but should not be placed with a large, boisterous family.

A young Toller checks out the scent on a group of utility articles.

FINDING THE RIGHT OWNER

An important part of puppy raising, and one not always mentioned in books, is the matching of a puppy to his eventual owner. Orders for show/breeding/hunting puppies can be filled by proper evaluation. However, which puppy is to go to which pet home is often decided as much by the puppy as by the people. Puppies will often go to one set of prospective purchasers and avoid another, while a different puppy will pick the alternative family.

One breeder uses a system of cards, one for each puppy and one for each purchaser, and plays a game of mix-and-match, based upon puppy personality and the requirements of the purchasers. Good breeders agonize over the placement of each puppy, but there is great satisfaction in seeing a happy family drive off with the new pet in the certainty that this puppy will be perfect for that family. This satisfaction is enhanced over months or years as the initial judgment is confirmed.

Breeders with a lot of experience often get "vibes" about certain prospective customers and report that the only times that puppies have proven unsuitable came after they ignored a tiny question in their minds about the particular people who were taking that puppy. Tollers are not for everyone, and it is often easy to screen out unsuitable owners with a few pertinent questions over the telephone.

INTERVIEWING PROSPECTIVE BUYERS

1. *What do you want a dog for?* Hunting, obedience, show, family pet?
2. *How did you hear about Tollers and our kennel?* The Toller is still rare enough for this to be of interest. Explain that there might be quite a wait for a suitable puppy because of the small number of breeders and the demand. Beware of the buyer who wants a Toller because it *is* rare — this is not of itself a good reason for having one.
3. *How active is your lifestyle?* Does the caller like to boat, swim, hike, camp, etc.? Explain that the Toller is a hunting dog and retriever and needs lots of exercise. The dog does not necessarily have to hunt, but he *must* retrieve.
4. *Do you have a family?* Find out if all family members really want a dog. Does dad think it is a good idea for the kids while mom is less than enthusiastic? Who usually ends up looking after a puppy?
5. *Do you live in a house with a fenced yard?* Tollers are not suitable apartment dwellers, but a townhome with a small yard is acceptable if the owners are aware of exercise requirements. Tollers should never be tied up; a good fence is a *must*.
6. *Have you owned dogs before?* Many mistakes are made with a first dog. Tollers will do best with those who know how to handle dogs because of their sensitivity and high level of activity.
7. *If you live in the area, please come and visit.* Nothing beats personal contact. This gives a breeder the chance to watch the interaction of families with adult dogs and puppies and to assess something about their lifestyle. Fussy housekeepers might not appreciate the Toller double coat shedding on rugs and furniture, and fastidious dressers are not likely to be attracted to a muddy Toller!
8. *Price for a puppy*. This question often does not come into an initial conversation. If price is the first thing a caller asks, do not take the interview any further.

Well-known breeders often have to deal with prospective customers by mail. Some ask for a brief background on the subjects mentioned above. It is more difficult to assess personalities by mail, but, because letters are usually combined with phone calls, placements are, on the whole, successful.

BUYER EDUCATION

It is the responsibility of breeders to produce the very best puppies they can, and also to educate buyers, not only about Tollers but about dog owning in general. You should discuss kennel policies such as the use of a non-breeding contract fully before you and a potential buyer make any agreements. Explain that, because Tollers are still comparatively rare, established breeders have orders for different purposes, and it will not be possible to pick a pup until the litter has been evaluated.

If the buyers live locally, you should invite them to come and visit the litter as often as possible after the pups are about three weeks old. This gives the breeder a chance to observe the interaction of individual puppies with different families and helps socialize the litter.

When the puppy is ready to leave home, the very least that a breeder should do is provide new owners with a puppy-care package containing feeding schedules, hints for general care, and a list of references where interested people can find out more for themselves. Every pup should go with an up-to-date health record containing details as to which vaccinations he has received and when, and dates of wormings, listing the preparation used.

You should provide a five-generation pedigree along with the care package and (a very important item in these days of anti-dog legislation and pet lemon laws) an explicit guarantee in which you spell out exactly what you will be held responsible for should the dog prove to be unsuitable for the purpose for which he was bought. Discuss these items with purchasers prior to when they pick up the pup. Quite a bit

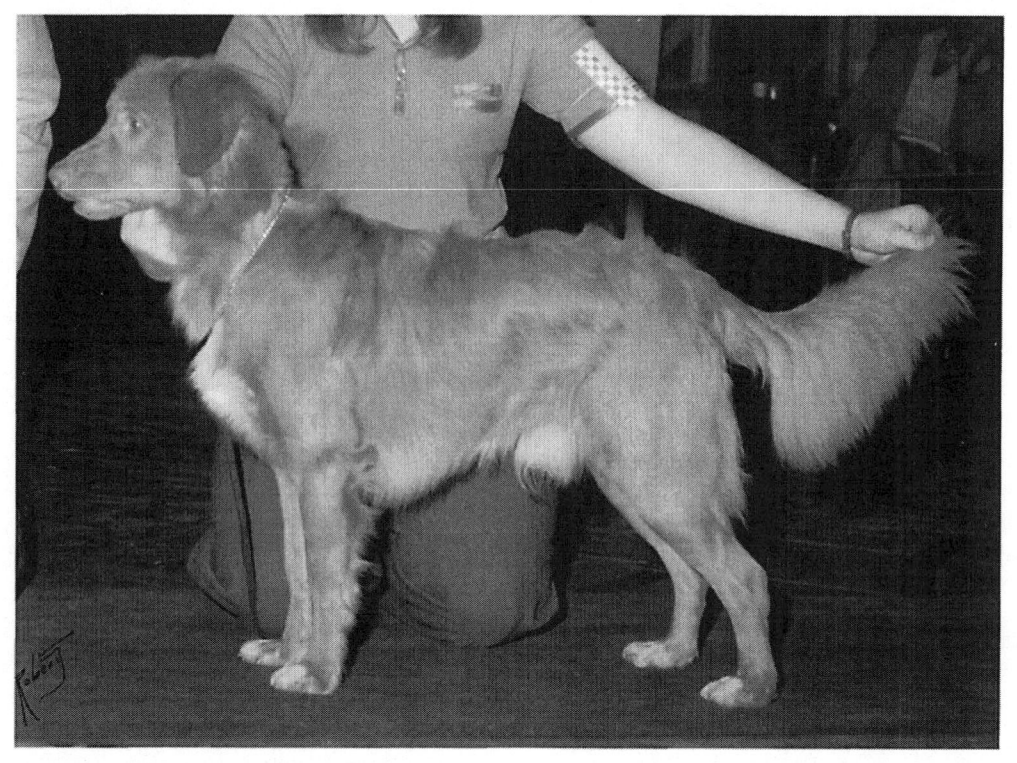

Here is a dramatic example of how a male Toller changes as he matures. In the top photo is Ch. Jalna's Quest for Glory CDX as a teenage male — weedy and out of coat. The same dog is shown in his maturity in the bottom photo, taking a Group placement, as he often did. Courtesy Sheila Paul.

of paperwork is involved in purchasing a purebred dog. Be sure that this is filled out completely before the pup leaves the premises.

New owners also appreciate a short demonstration on how to groom the puppy, cut the nails, and clean the ears. Discuss preferred types of food, and also talk about the desirability of crates for housebreaking and car safety. Recommend types of collars and leashes, feed dishes, and other equipment. For hunting prospects, be prepared to part with some wings and tell the new owner where to purchase puppy dummies.

ADVERTISING AND MARKETING

All Toller breed clubs maintain a list of breeders, and often breeders must abide by a club code of ethics in order to stay on a referral list. It is customary to levy a small charge for a breeders' listing, and referrals will usually only be made to those on the lists. There are numbers of dog magazines in which Tollers can be advertised, but the present high demand means that most established breeders already have long waiting lists. These breeders will often wish to have their kennel represented in the more popular magazines such as *Dogs USA*, *Dogs in Canada Buyers' Guide*, and *Dog Fancy*, even if they do not need the advertising to sell pups.

This is a far cry from early days, but years of promotion have paid off with the dog's growing popularity. Tollers were given an initial boost at displays like the big pet extravaganzas in Toronto, Dog World at the PNE in Vancouver, and the traveling Superdogs shows. Toller owners and their dogs have been attending these shows, plus mall displays put on by local canine organizations, for many years, and they are always big drawing cards. Breed publicity handed out at such shows is often kept and referred to years later when a new family pet is being sought.

A solid breeder-buyer relationship, with contact maintained throughout the life of the dog and often long after, is one of the best ways to educate the public to "buy from a breeder." A good owner is a treasure not to be taken lightly, and breeders should offer continuing after-care for all of their puppies. When all is said and done, breeders are responsible from before birth. A good reputation is not built overnight and can be ruined by carelessness or neglect in a very short time.

Toller puppies love to play hide-and-seek!

A Toller the way a Toller likes to be! Photo courtesy of John Gordon.

19

Toller Pedigrees

This chapter consists of a number of pedigrees selected to include as many representative Tollers as possible.

All the major kennels in Canada and the United States are represented, as are kennels in Europe.

Using these pedigrees, it should be possible to find ancestors to most of today's Tollers.

The dogs represented here are:
1. Harbourlights Scotia Boy
2. Coltriev Drummer Boy
3. Sproul's Mac-a-Doo
4. Sproul's Highland Playboy
5. Westerlea's Tru Ray Red Rebel
6. Westerlea's Ilo at the Well
7. Jalna's Our Only One
8. Rosewood Air Marshall
9. Cinnstar's Ian of Little River
10. Sylvan's Rusty Jones
11. LoneTree's Barnstorm 'n Jake
12. Kylador's Debonair Rob Roy
13. Sehi's Little Breton
14. Drögstas Cat-ri-ona
15. Golden Fox Jamboree
16. Lyonhouse Colin

TOLLER PEDIGREE DATABASE

TollerData, http://toller-l.org/tollerdata/ is an online and interactive pedigree database with approximately 30,0000 dogs from all over the world entered. Conceived and manintained by Eric Johnson, in addition to the pedigrees it has a number of features that make it unique. First of all, the data contained in each dog's record goes beyond a simple pedigree. Present are the health clearances commonly accepted in the Toller world, a photograph of the dog, and several supplemental pedigrees such as vertical pedigrees for hips, eyes and longevity.

The second unique feature is that it allows a user to generate a test breeding. Given a candidate sire and dam, TollerData will generate a theoretical pedigree for that breeding.

Future plans include a modified health record of the dog. The idea behind Toller-Data is that the Toller is now a world-wide breed both in acceptance and breeding. Breeders think nothing of using a foreign dog for a breeding, and buyers aren't afraid of foreign-bred puppies. TollerData provides a single source which uses a universal format.

```
                                                                              |DIGGER
                                                  |MAJOUR OF SCHUBENDORF 540281
                                                  | RED/WHITE              |LASSIE (A)
                              |SCHUBENDORF'S SANDY-
                              | 584077                                      |GEM OF GREEN MEADOWS
                              | RED/WHITE         |GOLDIE OF SCHUBENDORF 529755
                              | 05-07-63          | DARK FAWN/WHITE         |AUTUMN'S CINDERELLA
              |PAT OF SCHUBENDORF--
              | 627514                                                      |DIGGER
              | RED/WHITE                         |MAJOUR OF SCHUBENDORF 540281
              | 03-07-65                          | RED/WHITE               |LASSIE (A)
              |                |SCHUBENDORF'S LADY--
              |                | 584075                                     |GEM OF GREEN MEADOWS
 Sire>        |                | RED/WHITE        |GOLDIE OF SCHUBENDORF 529755
 -----        |                | 05-07-63         | DARK FAWN/WHITE         |AUTUMN'S CINDERELLA
 CHIN-PEEK GOLDEN LUCKY KIM
 736025                                                                     |BUSTER
 GOLDEN RED/WHITE                                 |BIDEWELL'S FLIP-----
 11-10-66                                         |                         |TOOTSIE
                              |CHIN-PEEK SHEP------
                              | 442958                                      |BUTCH
                              | RED/WHITE         |BIDEWELL'S LADY-----
                              | 01-24-56                                    |SANDY
              |CHIN-PEEK LUCKY-----
              | 684481                                                      |BIDEWELL'S FLIP
              | RED/WHITE                         |CHIN-PEEK GOLDEN KIM 442960
              | 07-18-64                          | RED/WHITE               |BIDEWELL'S LADY
                               |CHIN-PEEK GINGER JULIE
===============================| 585669                                     |BIDEWELL'S FLIP
                               | RED/WHITE        |CHIN-PEEK GOLDEN TAFFIE 521797
                               | 04-24-63         | RED/WHITE               |CHIN-PEEK LASSY

 HARBOURLIGHTS SCOTIA BOY                                                   |BOBO
 {M} JL125335                                     |DIGGER-------------
 RED/WHITE                                        |                         |QUINNIE
 06-16-77                     |MAJOUR OF SCHUBENDORF
                              | 540281                                      |BUTCH
===============================| RED/WHITE        |LASSIE (A)---------
                              | 12-19-57                                    |SASSIE
              |GREEN MEADOWS LAC-A-PAC PAL
              | 563858                                                      |FLASH
              | RED/WHITE                         |GEM OF GREEN MEADOWS 527800
              | 03-04-63                          | BROWN/WHITE             |DILLY
              |                |GREEN MEADOWS TAWNEE WAKON
              |                | 535824                                     |TEDDY
 Dam >        |                | RED/WHITE        |AUTUMN'S CINDERELLA 527799
 -----        |                | 08-08-61         | RED/WHITE               |BUFFY
 HARBOUR LIGHTS FOXY NISKU
 907807                                                                     |BIDEWELL'S FLIP
 RED/WHITE                                        |CHIN-PEEK SHEP 442958
 03-21-71                                         | RED/WHITE               |BIDEWELL'S LADY
                              |CHIN-PEEK LIM-BO----
                              | 684483                                      |BIDEWELL'S FLIP
                              | GOLDEN/WHITE      |CHIN-PEEK LASSY 442956
                              | 03-04-65                                    |BIDEWELL'S LADY
              |CHIN-PEEK STAR'S LADY
              | 722663                                                      |BIDEWELL'S FLIP
              | GOLDEN RED/WHITE                  |CHIN-PEEK GOLDEN KIM 442960
              | 08-06-66                          | RED/WHITE               |BIDEWELL'S LADY
                               |CHIN-PEEK GOLDEN STAR
                               | 548609                                     |BIDEWELL'S FLIP
                               | RED/WHITE        |CHIN-PEEK GOLDEN BELLE 442959
                               | 04-16-62         | RED/WHITE               |BIDEWELL'S LADY
```

```
                                                                           |DIGGER
                                                       |MAJOUR OF SCHUBENDORF 540281
                                                       | RED/WHITE            |LASSIE (A)
                                  |SCHUBENDORF'S SANDY-
                                  | 584077                                    |GEM OF GREEN MEADOWS
                                  | RED/WHITE          |GOLDIE OF SCHUBENDORF 529755
                                  | 05-07-63           | DARK FAWN/WHITE      |AUTUMN'S CINDERELLA
              |PAT OF SCHUBENDORF--
              | 627514                                                        |DIGGER
              | RED/WHITE                              |MAJOUR OF SCHUBENDORF 540281
              | 03-07-65                               | RED/WHITE            |LASSIE (A)
              |                   |SCHUBENDORF'S LADY--
              |                   | 584075                                    |GEM OF GREEN MEADOWS
              |                   | RED/WHITE          |GOLDIE OF SCHUBENDORF 529755
Sire>         |                   | 05-07-63           | DARK FAWN/WHITE      |AUTUMN'S CINDERELLA
-----         |
CHIN-PEEK KITTS' PAT                                                          |DIGGER
 926555                                                |MAJOUR OF SCHUBENDORF 540281
 GOLDEN RED/WHITE                                      | RED/WHITE            |LASSIE (A)
 03-24-70                         |SCHUBENDORF'S SANDY-
                                  | 584077                                    |GEM OF GREEN MEADOWS
                                  | RED/WHITE          |GOLDIE OF SCHUBENDORF 529755
                                  | 05-07-63           | DARK FAWN/WHITE      |AUTUMN'S CINDERELLA
              |SCHUBENDORF'S KITTY-
              | 776246                                                        |CHIN-PEEK SHEP
              | RED/WHITE                              |CHIN-PEEK LIM-BO 684483
              | 07-09-68                               | GOLDEN/WHITE         |CHIN-PEEK LASSY
                                  |CHIN-PEEK STAR'S LADY
                                  | 722663                                    |CHIN-PEEK GOLDEN KIM
                                  | GOLDEN RED/WHITE   |CHIN-PEEK GOLDEN STAR 548609
=========================================| 08-06-66    | RED/WHITE            |CHIN-PEEK GOLDEN BELLE

CAN CH COLTRIEV DRUMMER BOY, CD                                               |DIGGER
 {M} DYD86                                             |MAJOUR OF SCHUBENDORF 540281
 GOLDEN RED/WHITE                                      | RED/WHITE            |LASSIE (A)
 12-22-72                         |SCHUBENDORF'S SANDY-
                                  | 584077                                    |GEM OF GREEN MEADOWS
=========================================| RED/WHITE   |GOLDIE OF SCHUBENDORF 529755
                                  | 05-07-63           | DARK FAWN/WHITE      |AUTUMN'S CINDERELLA
              |SCHUBENDORF'S KELLIE
              | 776242                                                        |CHIN-PEEK SHEP
              | RED/WHITE                              |CHIN-PEEK LIM-BO 684483
              | 07-09-68                               | GOLDEN/WHITE         |CHIN-PEEK LASSY
              |                   |CHIN-PEEK STAR'S LADY
              |                   | 722663                                    |CHIN-PEEK GOLDEN KIM
              |                   | GOLDEN RED/WHITE   |CHIN-PEEK GOLDEN STAR 548609
Dam >         |                   | 08-06-66           | RED/WHITE            |CHIN-PEEK GOLDEN BELLE
-----         |
CAN CH CHIN-PEEK LADY DE-LAINE                                                |MAJOUR OF SCHUBENDORF
 892856                                                |SCHUBENDORF'S SANDY 584077
 GOLDEN RED/WHITE                                      | RED/WHITE            |GOLDIE OF SCHUBENDORF
 09-09-70                         |PAT OF SCHUBENDORF--
                                  | 627514                                    |MAJOUR OF SCHUBENDORF
                                  | RED/WHITE          |SCHUBENDORF'S LADY 584075
                                  | 03-07-65           | RED/WHITE            |GOLDIE OF SCHUBENDORF
              |CHIN-PEEK SUE BUFF--
              | 736386                                                        |CHIN-PEEK SHEP
              | RED/WHITE                              |CHIN-PEEK LIM-BO 684483
              | 09-10-67                               | GOLDEN/WHITE         |CHIN-PEEK LASSY
                                  |CHIN-PEEK SANDY-----
                                  | 722664                                    |CHIN-PEEK GOLDEN KIM
                                  | GOLDEN/WHITE       |CHIN-PEEK GOLDEN STAR 548609
                                  | 08-06-66           | RED/WHITE            |CHIN-PEEK GOLDEN BELLE
```

```
Sire>
-----
CAN CH SANDY MACGREGOR OF SPROUL
EJE72
RED/WHITE
05-25-73
                                                                              |DIGGER
                                                      |MAJOUR OF SCHUBENDORF 540281
                                                      | RED/WHITE             |LASSIE (A)
                          |SCHUBENDORF'S SANDY-
                          | 584077                    |                       |GEM OF GREEN MEADOWS
                          | RED/WHITE                 |GOLDIE OF SCHUBENDORF 529755
                          | 05-07-63                  | DARK FAWN/WHITE       |AUTUMN'S CINDERELLA
       |CAN CH RED ROCK STAR, CD
       | 831303                                                               |CHIN-PEEK SHEP
       | RED/WHITE                                    |CHIN-PEEK LIM-BO 684483
       | 08-14-69                                     | GOLDEN/WHITE          |CHIN-PEEK LASSY
                          |CHIN-PEEK STAR'S LADY
                          | 722663                    |                       |CHIN-PEEK GOLDEN KIM
                          | GOLDEN RED/WHITE          |CHIN-PEEK GOLDEN STAR 548609
                          | 08-06-66                  | RED/WHITE             |CHIN-PEEK GOLDEN BELLE

                                                                              |DIGGER
                                                      |MAJOUR OF SCHUBENDORF 540281
                                                      | RED/WHITE             |LASSIE (A)
                          |GREEN MEADOWS LAC-A-PAC PAL
                          | 563858                    |                       |GEM OF GREEN MEADOWS
                          | RED/WHITE                 |GREEN MEADOWS TAWNEE WAKON 535824
                          | 03-04-63                  | RED/WHITE             |AUTUMN'S CINDERELLA
       |CAN CH HARBOUR LIGHTS AUTUMN FANCY
       | 894180                                                               |MAJOUR OF SCHUBENDORF
       | RED/WHITE                                    |SCHUBENDORF'S SANDY 584077
       | 11-22-70                                     | RED/WHITE             |GOLDIE OF SCHUBENDORF
                          |BETTY OF SCHUBENDORF
==========================| 697785                    |                       |GEM OF GREEN MEADOWS
                          | RED/WHITE                 |GOLDIE OF SCHUBENDORF 529755
                          | 11-13-66                  | DARK FAWN/WHITE       |AUTUMN'S CINDERELLA

CAN CH SPROUL'S MAC-A-DOO                                                     |MAJOUR OF SCHUBENDORF
{M} KB61900                                           |GREEN MEADOWS LAC-A-PAC PAL 563858
RED/WHITE                                             | RED/WHITE             |GREEN MEADOWS TAWNEE WAKON
01-13-78                  |CAN CH DANNY BOY OF HARBOUR LIGHTS
                          | 918750                    |                       |SCHUBENDORF'S SANDY
==========================| RED/WHITE                 |BETTY OF SCHUBENDORF 697785
                          | 06-29-71                  | RED/WHITE             |GOLDIE OF SCHUBENDORF
       |MAJOR RUFUS OF GREEN MEADOWS
       | DUB733                                                               |MAJOUR OF SCHUBENDORF
       | RED/WHITE                                    |GREEN MEADOWS LAC-A-PAC PAL 563858
       | 10-04-72                                     | RED/WHITE             |GREEN MEADOWS TAWNEE WAKON
                          |MARY ANNE OF HARBOUR LIGHTS
                          | 926725                    |                       |CHIN-PEEK LIM-BO
Dam >                     | RED/WHITE                 |CHIN-PEEK STAR'S LADY 722663
-----                     | 03-21-71                  | GOLDEN RED/WHITE      |CHIN-PEEK GOLDEN STAR
MISS ACADIA OF SPROUL
ENC622                                                                        |GEM OF GREEN MEADOWS
RED/WHITE                                             |JOGGINS FOXY DUKE 592798
07-15-73                                              | RED/WHITE             |AUTUMN'S CINDERELLA
                          |ROBIE SURF OF GLENCOE
                          | 701886                    |                       |GREEN MEADOWS LAC-A-PAC PAL
                          | RED/WHITE                 |BLOND WOKWIS OF GOLDEN TESSY 676121
                          | 10-31-66                  | RED/WHITE             |GREEN MEADOWS GOLDEN TESSY
       |HAPPY HOLLY OF HARBOUR LIGHTS
       | DNA247                                                               |PAT OF SCHUBENDORF
       | RED/WHITE                                    |CHIN-PEEK GOLDEN LUCKY KIM 736025
       | 07-02-72                                     | GOLDEN RED/WHITE      |CHIN-PEEK LUCKY
                          |NICK'S FOXY SNOOPER-
                          | 866131                    |                       |SCHUBENDORF'S SANDY
                          | RED/WHITE                 |BETTY OF SCHUBENDORF 697785
                          | 12-19-68                  | RED/WHITE             |GOLDIE OF SCHUBENDORF
```

```
                                                                    |FLASH
                                          GEM OF GREEN MEADOWS 527800
                                            BROWN/WHITE             |DILLY
                      JOGGINS FOXY DUKE---
                        592798                                      |TEDDY
                        RED/WHITE         AUTUMN'S CINDERELLA 527799
                        08-02-63            RED/WHITE               |BUFFY
        ROBIE SURF OF GLENCOE
          701886                                                    |MAJOUR OF SCHUBENDORF
          RED/WHITE                       GREEN MEADOWS LAC-A-PAC PAL 563858
          10-31-66                          RED/WHITE               |GREEN MEADOWS TAWNEE WAKON
                      BLOND WOKWIS OF GOLDEN TESSY
                        676121                                      |GEM OF GREEN MEADOWS
                        RED/WHITE         GREEN MEADOWS GOLDEN TESSY 556404
                        01-20-65            RED/WHITE               |AUTUMN'S CINDERELLA
Sire>
-----
CAN CH ALEXANDER MACTAVISH                                          |SCHUBENDORF'S SANDY
  ESB904                                  PAT OF SCHUBENDORF 627514
  RED/WHITE                                 RED/WHITE               |SCHUBENDORF'S LADY
  09-15-73            CHIN-PEEK GOLDEN LUCKY KIM
                        736025                                      |CHIN-PEEK SHEP
                        GOLDEN RED/WHITE  CHIN-PEEK LUCKY 684481
                        11-10-66            RED/WHITE               |CHIN-PEEK GINGER JULIE
        NICK'S FOXY SNOOPER-
          866131                                                    |MAJOUR OF SCHUBENDORF
          RED/WHITE                       SCHUBENDORF'S SANDY 584077
          12-19-68                          RED/WHITE               |GOLDIE OF SCHUBENDORF
                      BETTY OF SCHUBENDORF
========================================  697785                    |GEM OF GREEN MEADOWS
                        RED/WHITE         GOLDIE OF SCHUBENDORF 529755
                        11-13-66            DARK FAWN/WHITE         |AUTUMN'S CINDERELLA
CAN CH SPROUL'S HIGHLAND PLAYBOY, CD                                |DIGGER
  {M} KY108963                            MAJOUR OF SCHUBENDORF 540281
  RED/WHITE                                 RED/WHITE               |LASSIE (A)
  12-13-78            GREEN MEADOWS LAC-A-PAC PAL
                        563858                                      |GEM OF GREEN MEADOWS
========================================  RED/WHITE         GREEN MEADOWS TAWNEE WAKON 535824
                        03-04-63            RED/WHITE               |AUTUMN'S CINDERELLA
        CAN CH DANNY BOY OF HARBOUR LIGHTS
          918750                                                    |MAJOUR OF SCHUBENDORF
          RED/WHITE                       SCHUBENDORF'S SANDY 584077
          06-29-71                          RED/WHITE               |GOLDIE OF SCHUBENDORF
                      BETTY OF SCHUBENDORF
                        697785                                      |GEM OF GREEN MEADOWS
Dam >                   RED/WHITE         GOLDIE OF SCHUBENDORF 529755
-----                   11-13-66            DARK FAWN/WHITE         |AUTUMN'S CINDERELLA
SPROUL'S TAWNEE PRINCESS
  DUD735                                                            |DIGGER
  RED/WHITE                               MAJOUR OF SCHUBENDORF 540281
  10-04-72                                  RED/WHITE               |LASSIE (A)
                      GREEN MEADOWS LAC-A-PAC PAL
                        563858                                      |GEM OF GREEN MEADOWS
                        RED/WHITE         GREEN MEADOWS TAWNEE WAKON 535824
                        03-04-63            RED/WHITE               |AUTUMN'S CINDERELLA
        MARY ANNE OF HARBOUR LIGHTS
          926725                                                    |CHIN-PEEK SHEP
          RED/WHITE                       CHIN-PEEK LIM-BO 684483
          03-21-71                          GOLDEN/WHITE            |CHIN-PEEK LASSY
                      CHIN-PEEK STAR'S LADY
                        722663                                      |CHIN-PEEK GOLDEN KIM
                        GOLDEN RED/WHITE  CHIN-PEEK GOLDEN STAR 548609
                        08-06-66            RED/WHITE               |CHIN-PEEK GOLDEN BELLE
```

```
                                                                                |PAT OF SCHUBENDORF
                                                         CHIN-PEEK GOLDEN LUCKY KIM 736025
                                                         | GOLDEN RED/WHITE    |CHIN-PEEK LUCKY
                                    |CAN CH RED RUSSEL OF JEFFERY
                                    | 812411                                   |SCHUBENDORF'S SANDY
                                    | RED/WHITE          |BETTY OF SCHUBENDORF 697785
                                    | 12-19-68           | RED/WHITE           |GOLDIE OF SCHUBENDORF
              |CAN CH CRUSADER OF JEFFERY COLDWELL, CD
              | GC33784                                                        |CAN CH RED RUSSEL OF JEFFERY
              | RED/WHITE          |JEFFERY OF PORT WILLIAMS DUD222
              | 02-17-75           | RED/WHITE           |CAN CH FLORETTE JEFFERY OF OVERTON
              |                    |RAPUNZEL OF JEFFERY COLDWELL
              |                    | FGC889                                    |PAT OF SCHUBENDORF
Sire>         |                    | RED/WHITE          |CHIN-PEEK WEE LADY SUSAN 843108
-----         |                    | 04-13-74           | RED/WHITE           |SCHUBENDORF'S KITTY
CAN CH WESTERLEA'S WHITE ENSIGN
JT34480       |                                                                |CHIN-PEEK GOLDEN LUCKY KIM
RED/WHITE     |                                         |CAN CH RED RUSSEL OF JEFFERY 812411
09-08-77      |                                         | RED/WHITE           |BETTY OF SCHUBENDORF
              |                    |JEFFERY OF PORT WILLIAMS
              |                    | DUD222                                    |CHIN-PEEK CHIP BAR-MAR CAR, CDX
              |                    | RED/WHITE          |CAN CH FLORETTE JEFFERY OF OVERTON 877394
              |                    | 10-23-72           | RED/WHITE           |CN OT CH CHIN-PEEK LADY SUSAN
              |CAN CH SHELBURNE OF JEFFERY COLDWELL
              | GC14690                                                        |GREEN MEADOWS LAC-A-PAC PAL
              | RED/WHITE                               |CAN CH RUSTY JEFFERY OF KEMPTVILLE 943282
              | 02-22-75                                | RED/WHITE           |TUSKET ISLE HEATHERTON
                                   |BO DIDDLEY OF JEFFERY COLDWELL
===================================| EGF679                                    |GREEN MEADOWS LAC-A-PAC PAL
                                   | GOLDEN RED/WHITE   |BUFF COLDWELL OF JEFFERY 943283
                                   | 04-29-73           | FAWN/WHITE          |TUSKET ISLE HEATHERTON
CAN CH WESTERLEA'S TRU RAY REBEL, CDX WC                                       |SCHUBENDORF'S SANDY
 {M} ME170282                                            |CAN CH RED ROCK STAR, CD 831303
RED/WHITE                                                | RED/WHITE           |CHIN-PEEK STAR'S LADY
03-05-80                            |CAN CH SANDY MACGREGOR OF SPROUL
===================================| EJE72                                     |GREEN MEADOWS LAC-A-PAC PAL
                                   | RED/WHITE          |CAN CH HARBOUR LIGHTS AUTUMN FANCY 894180
                                   | 05-25-73           | RED/WHITE           |BETTY OF SCHUBENDORF
              |CAN CH SPROUL'S HIGHLAND COMMANDER
              | HL82172                                                        |MAJOUR OF SCHUBENDORF
              | RED/WHITE                               |GREEN MEADOWS LAC-A-PAC PAL 563858
              | 06-08-76                                | RED/WHITE           |GREEN MEADOWS TAWNEE WAKON
              |                    |CAN CH HARBOUR LIGHTS AUTUMN FANCY
              |                    | 894180                                    |SCHUBENDORF'S SANDY
Dam >         |                    | RED/WHITE          |BETTY OF SCHUBENDORF 697785
-----         |                    | 11-22-70           | RED/WHITE           |GOLDIE OF SCHUBENDORF
CAN CH SUNDRUMMERS SEAWITCH
KJ101708      |                                                                |MAJOUR OF SCHUBENDORF
RED/WHITE     |                                         |GREEN MEADOWS LAC-A-PAC PAL 563858
05-29-78      |                                         | RED/WHITE           |GREEN MEADOWS TAWNEE WAKON
              |                    |CAN CH DANNY BOY OF HARBOUR LIGHTS
              |                    | 918750                                    |SCHUBENDORF'S SANDY
              |                    | RED/WHITE          |BETTY OF SCHUBENDORF 697785
              |                    | 06-29-71           | RED/WHITE           |GOLDIE OF SCHUBENDORF
              |CAN CH SPROUL'S HIGHLAND LASSIE
              | FCB490                                                         |JOGGINS FOXY DUKE
              | RED/WHITE                               |ROBIE SURF OF GLENCOE 701886
              | 02-20-74                                | RED/WHITE           |BLOND WOKWIS OF GOLDEN TESSY
                                   |HAPPY HOLLY OF HARBOUR LIGHTS
                                   | DNA247                                    |CHIN-PEEK GOLDEN LUCKY KIM
                                   | RED/WHITE          |NICK'S FOXY SNOOPER 866131
                                   | 07-02-72           | RED/WHITE           |BETTY OF SCHUBENDORF
```

```
                                                                                    |MAJOUR OF SCHUBENDORF
                                                        |GREEN MEADOWS LAC-A-PAC PAL 563858
                                                        | RED/WHITE                 |GREEN MEADOWS TAWNEE WAKON
                                    |CAN CH DANNY BOY OF HARBOUR LIGHTS
                                    | 918750                                        |SCHUBENDORF'S SANDY
                                    | RED/WHITE          |BETTY OF SCHUBENDORF 697785
                                    | 06-29-71           | RED/WHITE                |GOLDIE OF SCHUBENDORF
                |CAN CH WESTERLEA'S COAST TO COAST, CD
                | QG359380                                                   |CAN CH CRUSADER OF JEFFERY COLDWELL, CD
                | RED/WHITE                             |CAN CH WESTERLEA'S WHITE ENSIGN (BIS BISS) JT34480
                | 04-28-83                              | RED/WHITE                |CAN CH SHELBURNE OF JEFFERY COLDWELL
                |                    |CAN CH WESTERLEA'S COPPER VIXEN
                |                    | ME170285                                     |CAN CH SPROUL'S HIGHLAND COMMANDER
                |                    | ORANGE/WHITE       |CAN CH SUNDRUMMERS SEAWITCH KJ101708
  Sire>         |                    | 03-05-80           | RED/WHITE               |CAN CH SPROUL'S HIGHLAND LASSIE
  -----         |
CAN CH SANDYCOVE AT WESTERLEA, WC CD                                          |CAN CH RED RUSSEL OF JEFFERY
  SL488277      |                                        |CAN CH CRUSADER OF JEFFERY COLDWELL, CD GC33784
  RED/WHITE     |                                        | RED/WHITE                |RAPUNZEL OF JEFFERY COLDWELL
  06-14-85      |                    |CAN CH WESTERLEA'S WHITE ENSIGN (BIS BISS)
                |                    | JT34480                                      |JEFFERY OF PORT WILLIAMS
                |                    | RED/WHITE          |CAN CH SHELBURNE OF JEFFERY COLDWELL GC14690
                |                    | 09-08-77           | RED/WHITE               |BO DIDDLEY OF JEFFERY COLDWELL
                |CAN CH WESTERLEA'S SUMMER SUNSET
                  NN254684                                                    |CAN CH SANDY MACGREGOR OF SPROUL
                  RED/WHITE                              |CAN CH SPROUL'S HIGHLAND COMMANDER HL82172
                  07-23-81                               | RED/WHITE                |CAN CH HARBOUR LIGHTS AUTUMN FANCY
                                    |CAN CH SUNDRUMMERS SEAWITCH
===================================== KJ101708                                      |CAN CH DANNY BOY OF HARBOUR LIGHTS
                                      RED/WHITE          |CAN CH SPROUL'S HIGHLAND LASSIE FCB490
                                      05-29-78           | RED/WHITE                |HAPPY HOLLY OF HARBOUR LIGHTS

CAN CH WESTERLEA'S ILO AT THE WELL, CD |                                      |CAN CH CRUSADER OF JEFFERY COLDWELL, CD
  {M} TS575543                         |                 |CAN CH WESTERLEA'S WHITE ENSIGN (BIS BISS) JT34480
  RED/WHITE                            |                 | RED/WHITE               |CAN CH SHELBURNE OF JEFFERY COLDWELL
  09-10-86                             |WESTERLEA'S WINDSOR LAD
                                       | MS209318                                   |CAN CH ALEXANDER MACTAVISH
===================================== | RED/WHITE        |CAN CH SPROUL'S KINSMAN'S CEDAR FOX JV61896
                                       | 09-23-80        | RED/WHITE               |SPROUL'S TAWNEE PRINCESS
                |CAN CH WESTERLEA'S FIRST LIEUTENANT CD
                | NS262206                                                    |CAN CH SANDY MACGREGOR OF SPROUL
                | RED/WHITE                              |CAN CH SPROUL'S HIGHLAND COMMANDER HL82172
                | 09-24-81                               | RED/WHITE                |CAN CH HARBOUR LIGHTS AUTUMN FANCY
                |                    |CAN CH WESTERLEA'S SPRING MELODY
                |                    | KK69032                                      |CAN CH BELLBOY OF JEFFERY COLDWELL
  Dam >         |                    | RED/WHITE          |CAN CH WESTERLEA'S SCOTIAN GOLD HN78280
  -----         |                    | 05-26-78           | GOLDEN RED/WHITE        |CAN CH SHELBURNE OF JEFFERY COLDWELL
CAN CH WESTERLEA'S BONNY BLUENOSE (BISS)
  PU332648      |                                                             |CAN CH RED ROCK STAR, CD
  RED/WHITE     |                                        |CAN CH SANDY MACGREGOR OF SPROUL EJE72
  10-17-82      |                                        | RED/WHITE                |CAN CH HARBOUR LIGHTS AUTUMN FANCY
                |                    |CAN CH SPROUL'S HIGHLAND COMMANDER
                |                    | HL82172                                      |GREEN MEADOWS LAC-A-PAC PAL
                |                    | RED/WHITE          |CAN CH HARBOUR LIGHTS AUTUMN FANCY 894180
                |                    | 06-08-76           | RED/WHITE               |BETTY OF SCHUBENDORF
                |CAN CH SUNDRUMMERS SEAWITCH
                  KJ101708                                                    |GREEN MEADOWS LAC-A-PAC PAL
                  RED/WHITE                              |CAN CH DANNY BOY OF HARBOUR LIGHTS 918750
                  05-29-78                               | RED/WHITE                |BETTY OF SCHUBENDORF
                                    |CAN CH SPROUL'S HIGHLAND LASSIE
                                      FCB490                                         |ROBIE SURF OF GLENCOE
                                      RED/WHITE          |HAPPY HOLLY OF HARBOUR LIGHTS DNA247
                                      02-20-74           | RED/WHITE                |NICK'S FOXY SNOOPER
```

```
                                                                        |PAT OF SCHUBENDORF
                                                       |CHIN-PEEK GOLDEN LUCKY KIM 736025
                                                       | GOLDEN RED/WHITE    |CHIN-PEEK LUCKY
                                  |CAN CH RED RUSSEL OF JEFFERY
                                  | 812411                              |SCHUBENDORF'S SANDY
                                  | RED/WHITE           |BETTY OF SCHUBENDORF 697785
                                  | 12-19-68            | RED/WHITE           |GOLDIE OF SCHUBENDORF
             |CAN CH CRUSADER OF JEFFERY COLDWELL, CD
             | GC33784             |                                    |CAN CH RED RUSSEL OF JEFFERY
             | RED/WHITE           |JEFFERY OF PORT WILLIAMS DUD222
             | 02-17-75            | RED/WHITE           |CAN CH FLORETTE JEFFERY OF OVERTON
             |                    |RAPUNZEL OF JEFFERY COLDWELL
             |                     FGC889                              |PAT OF SCHUBENDORF
 Sire>       |                     RED/WHITE           |CHIN-PEEK WEE LADY SUSAN 843108
 -----       |                     04-13-74            | RED/WHITE           |SCHUBENDORF'S KITTY
 CAN CH JALNA'S RED EMPEROR
 HJ75877     |                                                         |PAT OF SCHUBENDORF
 RED/WHITE   |                                        |CHIN-PEEK GOLDEN LUCKY KIM 736025
 05-03-76    |                                        | GOLDEN RED/WHITE    |CHIN-PEEK LUCKY
             |                    |CAN CH RED RUSSEL OF JEFFERY
             |                    | 812411                              |SCHUBENDORF'S SANDY
             |                    | RED/WHITE           |BETTY OF SCHUBENDORF 697785
             |                    | 12-19-68            | RED/WHITE           |GOLDIE OF SCHUBENDORF
             |CAN CH CONTESSA OF JEFFERY COLDWELL
              DUD221               |                                    |PAT OF SCHUBENDORF
              GOLDEN RED/WHITE     |CHIN-PEEK CHIP BAR-MAR CAR, CDX 739740
              10-23-72             | RED GOLDEN & WHITE  |CN OT CH CHIN-PEEK LADY SUSAN
                                  |CAN CH FLORETTE JEFFERY OF OVERTON
=====================================  877394                          |PAT OF SCHUBENDORF
                                       RED/WHITE           |CN OT CH CHIN-PEEK LADY SUSAN 722659
                                       05-02-70            GOLDEN RED/WHITE    |CHIN-PEEK GINGER JULIE

 CAN CH JALNA'S OUR ONLY ONE, CD   |                                    |JOGGINS FOXY DUKE
 {M} RL437470                      |                    |ROBIE SURF OF GLENCOE 701886
 RED/WHITE                         |                    | RED/WHITE           |BLOND WOKWIS OF GOLDEN TESSY
 06-14-84                          |CAN CH ALEXANDER MACTAVISH
                                   | ESB904                              |CHIN-PEEK GOLDEN LUCKY KIM
=====================================  RED/WHITE           |NICK'S FOXY SNOOPER 866131
                                   | 09-15-73            | RED/WHITE           |BETTY OF SCHUBENDORF
             |CAN CH SPROUL'S TANTRAMAR TOBY, CD
             | GE26843             |                                    |SCHUBENDORF'S SANDY
             | RED                 |CAN CH RED ROCK STAR, CD 831303
             | 03-26-75            | RED/WHITE           |CHIN-PEEK STAR'S LADY
             |                    |CAN CH SPROUL'S MERRY DANCER
             |                     EJD74                              |GREEN MEADOWS LAC-A-PAC PAL
 Dam >       |                     RED/WHITE           |CAN CH HARBOUR LIGHTS AUTUMN FANCY 894180
 -----       |                     05-25-73            | RED/WHITE           |BETTY OF SCHUBENDORF
 SPROUL'S JENNIFER JALNA
 JH25020     |                                                         |SCHUBENDORF'S SANDY
 RED/WHITE   |                                        |CAN CH RED ROCK STAR, CD 831303
 04-10-77    |                                        | RED/WHITE           |CHIN-PEEK STAR'S LADY
             |                    |CAN CH SANDY MACGREGOR OF SPROUL
             |                    | EJE72                              |GREEN MEADOWS LAC-A-PAC PAL
             |                    | RED/WHITE           |CAN CH HARBOUR LIGHTS AUTUMN FANCY 894180
             |                    | 05-25-73            | RED/WHITE           |BETTY OF SCHUBENDORF
             |CAN CH SPROUL'S LADY MACGREGOR
              GE26835               |                                    |GREEN MEADOWS LAC-A-PAC PAL
              RED/WHITE             |CAN CH DANNY BOY OF HARBOUR LIGHTS 918750
              03-22-75              | RED/WHITE           |BETTY OF SCHUBENDORF
                                  |SPROUL'S TAWNEE PRINCESS
                                    DUD735                              |GREEN MEADOWS LAC-A-PAC PAL
                                    RED/WHITE           |MARY ANNE OF HARBOUR LIGHTS 926725
                                    10-04-72            | RED/WHITE           |CHIN-PEEK STAR'S LADY
```

```
                                                                                  |GEM OF GREEN MEADOWS
                                                       |JOGGINS FOXY DUKE 592798
                                                       | RED/WHITE               |AUTUMN'S CINDERELLA
                                    |ROBIE SURF OF GLENCOE
                                    | 701886                                      |GREEN MEADOWS LAC-A-PAC PAL
                                    | RED/WHITE        |BLOND WOKWIS OF GOLDEN TESSY 676121
                                    | 10-31-66         | RED/WHITE               |GREEN MEADOWS GOLDEN TESSY
                |CAN CH ALEXANDER MACTAVISH
                | ESB904                                                          |PAT OF SCHUBENDORF
                | RED/WHITE                            |CHIN-PEEK GOLDEN LUCKY KIM 736025
                | 09-15-73                             | GOLDEN RED/WHITE        |CHIN-PEEK LUCKY
                                    |NICK'S FOXY SNOOPER-
                                    | 866131                                      |SCHUBENDORF'S SANDY
                                    | RED/WHITE        |BETTY OF SCHUBENDORF 697785
Sire>                               | 12-19-68         | RED/WHITE               |GOLDIE OF SCHUBENDORF
-----
CNCHOTCH SPROUL'S ANGUS MACBETH, WC
JV61894                                                                           |MAJOUR OF SCHUBENDORF
RED/WHITE                                              |GREEN MEADOWS LAC-A-PAC PAL 563858
10-22-77                                               | RED/WHITE               |GREEN MEADOWS TAWNEE WAKON
                                    |CAN CH DANNY BOY OF HARBOUR LIGHTS
                                    | 918750                                      |SCHUBENDORF'S SANDY
                                    | RED/WHITE        |BETTY OF SCHUBENDORF 697785
                                    | 06-29-71         | RED/WHITE               |GOLDIE OF SCHUBENDORF
                |SPROUL'S TAWNEE PRINCESS
                | DUD735                                                          |MAJOUR OF SCHUBENDORF
                | RED/WHITE                            |GREEN MEADOWS LAC-A-PAC PAL 563858
                | 10-04-72                             | RED/WHITE               |GREEN MEADOWS TAWNEE WAKON
                                    |MARY ANNE OF HARBOUR LIGHTS
                                    | 926725                                      |CHIN-PEEK LIM-BO
                                    | RED/WHITE        |CHIN-PEEK STAR'S LADY 722663
==========================================| 03-21-71  | GOLDEN RED/WHITE        |CHIN-PEEK GOLDEN STAR

CAN CH ROSEWOOD AIR MARSHALL, CDX WC                                              |PAT OF SCHUBENDORF
{M} RN445391                                           |CHIN-PEEK GOLDEN LUCKY KIM 736025
RED/WHITE                                              | GOLDEN RED/WHITE        |CHIN-PEEK LUCKY
07-02-84                            |CAN CH RED RUSSEL OF JEFFERY
                                    | 812411                                      |SCHUBENDORF'S SANDY
==========================================| RED/WHITE |BETTY OF SCHUBENDORF 697785
                                    | 12-19-68         | RED/WHITE               |GOLDIE OF SCHUBENDORF
                |CAN CH CRUSADER OF JEFFERY COLDWELL, CD
                | GC33784                                                         |CAN CH RED RUSSEL OF JEFFERY
                | RED/WHITE                            |JEFFERY OF PORT WILLIAMS DUD222
                | 02-17-75                             | RED/WHITE               |CAN CH FLORETTE JEFFERY OF OVERTON
                                    |RAPUNZEL OF JEFFERY COLDWELL
                                    | FGC889                                      |PAT OF SCHUBENDORF
Dam >                               | RED/WHITE        |CHIN-PEEK WEE LADY SUSAN 843108
-----                               | 04-13-74         | RED/WHITE               |SCHUBENDORF'S KITTY
CAN CH JALNA'S EAGER BOOTS, CDX
HJ75874                                                                           |PAT OF SCHUBENDORF
FAWN/WHITE                                             |CHIN-PEEK GOLDEN LUCKY KIM 736025
05-03-76                                               | GOLDEN RED/WHITE        |CHIN-PEEK LUCKY
                                    |CAN CH RED RUSSEL OF JEFFERY
                                    | 812411                                      |SCHUBENDORF'S SANDY
                                    | RED/WHITE        |BETTY OF SCHUBENDORF 697785
                                    | 12-19-68         | RED/WHITE               |GOLDIE OF SCHUBENDORF
                |CAN CH CONTESSA OF JEFFERY COLDWELL
                | DUD221                                                          |PAT OF SCHUBENDORF
                | GOLDEN RED/WHITE                     |CHIN-PEEK CHIP BAR-MAR CAR, CDX 739740
                | 10-23-72                             | RED GOLDEN & WHITE      |CN OT CH CHIN-PEEK LADY SUSAN
                                    |CAN CH FLORETTE JEFFERY OF OVERTON
                                    | 877394                                      |PAT OF SCHUBENDORF
                                    | RED/WHITE        |CN OT CH CHIN-PEEK LADY SUSAN 722659
                                    | 05-02-70         | GOLDEN RED/WHITE        |CHIN-PEEK GINGER JULIE
```

```
                                                                                |PAT OF SCHUBENDORF
                                                     |CHIN-PEEK GOLDEN LUCKY KIM 736025
                                                     | GOLDEN RED/WHITE        |CHIN-PEEK LUCKY
                            |CAN CH RED RÜSSEL OF JEFFERY
                            | 812411                 |                          |SCHUBENDORF'S SANDY
                            | RED/WHITE              |BETTY OF SCHUBENDORF 697785
                            | 12-19-68                 RED/WHITE                |GOLDIE OF SCHUBENDORF
        |CAN CH CRUSADER OF JEFFERY COLDWELL, CD
        | GC33784           |                                                   |CAN CH RED RUSSEL OF JEFFERY
        | RED/WHITE         |                        |JEFFERY OF PORT WILLIAMS DUD222
        | 02-17-75          |                        | RED/WHITE                |CAN CH FLORETTE JEFFERY OF OVERTON
        |                   |RAPUNZEL OF JEFFERY COLDWELL
        |                    FGC889                  |                          |PAT OF SCHUBENDORF
Sire>   |                    RED/WHITE               |CHIN-PEEK WEE LADY SUSAN 843108
-----   |                    04-13-74                  RED/WHITE                |SCHUBENDORF'S KITTY
SOLIDAIRE OF JEFFERY COLDWELL, CD
JH60654 |                                                                       |PAT OF SCHUBENDORF
RED WHITE|                                           |CHIN-PEEK CHIP BAR-MAR CAR, CDX 739740
04-23-77|                                            | RED GOLDEN & WHITE       |CN OT CH CHIN-PEEK LADY SUSAN
        |                   |MARLYNBAR CHUKIE, CD
        |                   | DSB545                 |                          |CHIN-PEEK MAJOUR TYROL, CD
        |                   | RED/WHITE              |MARLYNBAR CHICK, CD 918505
        |                   | 09-21-72                 RED/WHITE                |CHIN-PEEK FANCY RED, CD
        |TAHGAHJUTE OF JEFFERY COLDWELL
         FNC480             |                                                   |GREEN MEADOWS LAC-A-PAC PAL
         RED/WHITE          |                        |CAN CH RUSTY JEFFERY OF KEMPTVILLE 943282
         07-23-74           |                        | RED/WHITE                |TUSKET ISLE HEATHERTON
                            |BO DIDDLEY OF JEFFERY COLDWELL
========================================= EGF679                               |GREEN MEADOWS LAC-A-PAC PAL
                             GOLDEN RED/WHITE       |BUFF COLDWELL OF JEFFERY 943283
                             04-29-73                 FAWN/WHITE                |TUSKET ISLE HEATHERTON

CAN CH CINNSTAR'S IAN OF LITTLE RIVER, CD WC                                    |CHIN-PEEK GOLDEN LUCKY KIM
 {M} 0081      1021648                               |CAN CH RED RUSSEL OF JEFFERY 812411
 RED/WHITE                                           | RED/WHITE                |BETTY OF SCHUBENDORF
 01-22-87                   |CAN CH CRUSADER OF JEFFERY COLDWELL, CD
                            | GC33784                |                          |JEFFERY OF PORT WILLIAMS
========================================= RED/WHITE |RAPUNZEL OF JEFFERY COLDWELL FGC889
                            | 02-17-75                 RED/WHITE                |CHIN-PEEK WEE LADY SUSAN
        |CAN CH WESTERLEA'S WHITE ENSIGN (BIS BISS)
        | JT34480           |                                                   |CAN CH RED RUSSEL OF JEFFERY
        | RED/WHITE         |                        |JEFFERY OF PORT WILLIAMS DUD222
        | 09-08-77          |                        | RED/WHITE                |CAN CH FLORETTE JEFFERY OF OVERTON
        |                   |CAN CH SHELBURNE OF JEFFERY COLDWELL
        |                    GC14690                 |                          |CAN CH RUSTY JEFFERY OF KEMPTVILLE
Dam >   |                    RED/WHITE               |BO DIDDLEY OF JEFFERY COLDWELL EGF679
-----   |                    02-22-75                  GOLDEN RED/WHITE         |BUFF COLDWELL OF JEFFERY
CAN CH WESTERLEA'S CINNAMON TEAL, CD
 1045      ME170277|                                                            |CAN CH RED ROCK STAR, CD
 RED/WHITE         |                                 |CAN CH SANDY MACGREGOR OF SPROUL EJE72
 03-05-80          |                                 | RED/WHITE                |CAN CH HARBOUR LIGHTS AUTUMN FANCY
                   |                   |CAN CH SPROUL'S HIGHLAND COMMANDER
                   |                   | HL82172                                |GREEN MEADOWS LAC-A-PAC PAL
                   |                   | RED/WHITE              |CAN CH HARBOUR LIGHTS AUTUMN FANCY 894180
                   |                   | 06-08-76                 RED/WHITE     |BETTY OF SCHUBENDORF
                   |CAN CH SUNDRUMMERS SEAWITCH
                    KJ101708           |                                        |GREEN MEADOWS LAC-A-PAC PAL
                    RED/WHITE          |                        |CAN CH DANNY BOY OF HARBOUR LIGHTS 918750
                    05-29-78           |                        | RED/WHITE     |BETTY OF SCHUBENDORF
                                       |CAN CH SPROUL'S HIGHLAND LASSIE
                                        FCB490                  |               |ROBIE SURF OF GLENCOE
                                        RED/WHITE               |HAPPY HOLLY OF HARBOUR LIGHTS DNA247
                                        02-20-74                  RED/WHITE     |NICK'S FOXY SNOOPER
```

TOLLER PEDIGREES

```
                                                                                    |JOGGINS FOXY DUKE
                                                        |ROBIE SURF OF GLENCOE 701886
                                                        |  RED/WHITE              |BLOND WOKWIS OF GOLDEN TESSY
                                    |CAN CH ALEXANDER MACTAVISH
                                    |  ESB904                                     |CHIN-PEEK GOLDEN LUCKY KIM
                                    |  RED/WHITE          |NICK'S FOXY SNOOPER 866131
                                    |  09-15-73           |  RED/WHITE            |BETTY OF SCHUBENDORF
                |CHALK BLUFF'S DOC HOLIDAY
                |  KQ125212                                                       |CAN CH RED ROCK STAR, CD
                |  FAWN/WHITE                             |CAN CH SANDY MACGREGOR OF SPROUL EJE72
                |  08-01-78           |                   |  RED/WHITE            |CAN CH HARBOUR LIGHTS AUTUMN FANCY
                |                    |CAN CH SPROUL'S LADY MACGREGOR
                |                    |  GE26835                                   |CAN CH DANNY BOY OF HARBOUR LIGHTS
                |                    |  RED/WHITE         |SPROUL'S TAWNEE PRINCESS DUD735
Sire>           |                    |  03-22-75          |  RED/WHITE            |MARY ANNE OF HARBOUR LIGHTS
-----           |
CHALK BLUFF'S REDWOOD JACK                                                        |MAJOUR OF SCHUBENDORF
0001            |                                        |GREEN MEADOWS LAC-A-PAC PAL 563858
RED             |                                        |  RED/WHITE            |GREEN MEADOWS TAWNEE WAKON
12-20-80        |                    |HARBOURLIGHTS VILLAGE SIRE
                |                    |  923529                                    |SCHUBENDORF'S SANDY
                |                    |  RED/WHITE         |BETTY OF SCHUBENDORF 697785
                |                    |  12-26-71          |  RED/WHITE            |GOLDIE OF SCHUBENDORF
                |HARBOURLIGHTS MIC MAC MARNIE
                   LN163291                                                       |JOGGINS FOXY DUKE
                   RED/WHITE                             |ROBIE SURF OF GLENCOE 701886
                   07-17-79                              |  RED/WHITE            |BLOND WOKWIS OF GOLDEN TESSY
                                     |HARBOURLIGHTS FUNDY BELL
                                     |  DNA694                                    |CHIN-PEEK GOLDEN LUCKY KIM
===========================================             |NICK'S FOXY SNOOPER 866131
                                        RED/WHITE       |  RED/WHITE            |BETTY OF SCHUBENDORF
                                        07-02-72
CAN/USCH SYLVAN'S RUSTY JONES WCX UD                                              |SCHUBENDORF'S SANDY
 {M} 0005       1014655                                  |CAN CH RED ROCK STAR, CD 831303
RED/WHITE                                                |  RED/WHITE            |CHIN-PEEK STAR'S LADY
07-10-82                             |CAN CH SANDY MACGREGOR OF SPROUL
                                     |  EJE72                                     |GREEN MEADOWS LAC-A-PAC PAL
===========================================                RED/WHITE         |CAN CH HARBOUR LIGHTS AUTUMN FANCY 894180
                                        05-25-73         |  RED/WHITE            |BETTY OF SCHUBENDORF
                |CAN CH SPROUL'S MAC-A-DOO
                |  KB61900                                                        |CAN CH DANNY BOY OF HARBOUR LIGHTS
                |  RED/WHITE                             |MAJOR RUFUS OF GREEN MEADOWS DUB733
                |  01-13-78                              |  RED/WHITE            |MARY ANNE OF HARBOUR LIGHTS
                |                    |MISS ACADIA OF SPROUL
                |                    |  ENC622                                    |ROBIE SURF OF GLENCOE
Dam >           |                    |  RED/WHITE         |HAPPY HOLLY OF HARBOUR LIGHTS DNA247
-----           |                    |  07-15-73          |  RED/WHITE            |NICK'S FOXY SNOOPER
CAN CH SPROUL'S FOXII NANA, CD
 I002    ML227496|                                                                |DIGGER
LT STRAW        |                                        |MAJOUR OF SCHUBENDORF 540281
06-08-80        |                                        |  RED/WHITE            |LASSIE (A)
                |                    |GREEN MEADOWS LAC-A-PAC PAL
                |                    |  563858                                    |GEM OF GREEN MEADOWS
                |                    |  RED/WHITE         |GREEN MEADOWS TAWNEE WAKON 535824
                |                    |  03-04-63          |  RED/WHITE            |AUTUMN'S CINDERELLA
                |MARY ANNE OF HARBOUR LIGHTS
                   926725                                                         |CHIN-PEEK SHEP
                   RED/WHITE                             |CHIN-PEEK LIM-BO 684483
                   03-21-71                              |  GOLDEN/WHITE         |CHIN-PEEK LASSY
                                     |CHIN-PEEK STAR'S LADY
                                     |  722663                                    |CHIN-PEEK GOLDEN KIM
                                        GOLDEN RED/WHITE |CHIN-PEEK GOLDEN STAR 548609
                                        08-06-66         |  RED/WHITE            |CHIN-PEEK GOLDEN BELLE
```

```
                                                                    |PAT OF SCHUBENDORF
                                                |CHIN-PEEK GOLDEN LUCKY KIM 736025
                                                |   GOLDEN RED/WHITE   |CHIN-PEEK LUCKY
                                |HARBOURLIGHTS SCOTIA BOY
                                | JL125335                             |GREEN MEADOWS LAC-A-PAC PAL
                                | RED/WHITE       |HARBOUR LIGHTS FOXY NISKU 907807
                                | 06-16-77        RED/WHITE            |CHIN-PEEK STAR'S LADY
                |HARBOURLIGHTS ALA GATTER
                | SN489403                                             |GREEN MEADOWS LAC-A-PAC PAL
                | RED/WHITE                      |HARBOURLIGHTS VILLAGE SIRE 923529
                | 07-07-85                       | RED/WHITE           |BETTY OF SCHUBENDORF
                | HARBOURLIGHTS RED KALI
                | KQ120175                                             |ROBIE SURF OF GLENCOE
Sire>           | RED/WHITE                      |HARBOURLIGHT'S FOREVER AMBER EGB327
-----           | 08-29-78                       RED/WHITE             |GREEN MEADOWS CANDY KISSES
CAN/USCH HARBOURLIGHTS RIP TIDE CDX WC
 I185      UN639631|                                                   |SCHUBENDORF'S SANDY
RED/WHITE          |                             |CAN CH RED ROCK STAR, CD 831303
07-22-87           |                             | RED/WHITE           |CHIN-PEEK STAR'S LADY
                   |CAN CH SANDY MACGREGOR OF SPROUL
                   | EJE72                                             |GREEN MEADOWS LAC-A-PAC PAL
                   | RED/WHITE                   |CAN CH HARBOUR LIGHTS AUTUMN FANCY 894180
                   | 05-25-73                    RED/WHITE             |BETTY OF SCHUBENDORF
                |WABANAKI'S VILLAGE VIXEN
                  PS335490                                             |GREEN MEADOWS LAC-A-PAC PAL
                  RED/WHITE                      |HARBOURLIGHTS VILLAGE SIRE 923529
                  09-15-82                       | RED/WHITE           |BETTY OF SCHUBENDORF
                                |HARBOURLIGHTS MISS MOLLY
======================================= ML222811                      |ROBIE SURF OF GLENCOE
                                  RED/WHITE     |HARBOURLIGHTS FUNDY BELL DNA694
                                  06-01-80       RED/WHITE             |NICK'S FOXY SNOOPER
|
CAN/USCH LONETREE'S BARNSTORMN JAKE CDX WCI HR                         |GREEN MEADOWS LAC-A-PAC PAL
 {M} 0241      1045525                           |CAN CH DANNY BOY OF HARBOUR LIGHTS 918750
RED/WHITE                                        | RED/WHITE           |BETTY OF SCHUBENDORF
02-05-91                        |CAN CH WESTERLEA'S COAST TO COAST, CD
                                | QG359380                             |CAN CH WESTERLEA'S WHITE ENSIGN (BIS BISS
======================================= RED/WHITE   |CAN CH WESTERLEA'S COPPER VIXEN ME170285
                                | 04-28-83        ORANGE/WHITE         |CAN CH SUNDRUMMERS SEAWITCH
                |CAN CH SANDYCOVE AT WESTERLEA, WC CD
                | SL488277                                             |CAN CH CRUSADER OF JEFFERY COLDWELL, CD
                | RED/WHITE                      |CAN CH WESTERLEA'S WHITE ENSIGN (BIS BISS) JT34480
                | 06-14-85                       | RED/WHITE           |CAN CH SHELBURNE OF JEFFERY COLDWELL
                | |CAN CH WESTERLEA'S SUMMER SUNSET
                |  NN254684                                            |CAN CH SPROUL'S HIGHLAND COMMANDER
Dam >           |  RED/WHITE                     |CAN CH SUNDRUMMERS SEAWITCH KJ101708
-----           |  07-23-81                      RED/WHITE             |CAN CH SPROUL'S HIGHLAND LASSIE
TRADEWINDS DUSTY JAMOCA UD
 0134       1037068|                                                   |CAN CH WESTERLEA'S WHITE ENSIGN (BIS BISS
RED/WHITE          |                             |CAN CH WESTERLEA'S FLYING FOX ME170284
11-20-88           |                             | RED/WHITE           |CAN CH SUNDRUMMERS SEAWITCH
                   |                             |CAN CH CASTLEKEEPS' MAGIC OF MERLIN
                   |                             | PW339660            |CAN CH SPROUL'S HIGHLAND COMMANDER
                   |                             | RED/WHITE           |CAN CH WESTERLEA'S SPRING MELODY KK69032
                   |                             | 11-23-82            RED/WHITE   |CAN CH WESTERLEA'S SCOTIAN GOLD
                   |CINNSTAR'S CAROLINA WREN
                   | 1050      SS505235                                |CAN CH CRUSADER OF JEFFERY COLDWELL, CD
                   | RED/WHITE                   |CAN CH WESTERLEA'S WHITE ENSIGN (BIS BISS) JT34480
                   | 09-03-85                    | RED/WHITE           |CAN CH SHELBURNE OF JEFFERY COLDWELL
                   |CAN CH WESTERLEA'S CINNAMON TEAL, CD
                     I045     ME170277                                 |CAN CH SPROUL'S HIGHLAND COMMANDER
                     RED/WHITE                   |CAN CH SUNDRUMMERS SEAWITCH KJ101708
                     03-05-80                    RED/WHITE             |CAN CH SPROUL'S HIGHLAND LASSIE
```

```
                                                                          |CAN CH CRUSADER OF JEFFERY COLDWELL, CD
                                                         |CAN CH WESTERLEA'S WHITE ENSIGN (BIS BISS) JT34480
                                                         | RED/WHITE               |CAN CH SHELBURNE OF JEFFERY COLDWELL
                                       |CHIN-PEEK KEL'S HAPPY TOBY
                                       | NN285865                         |SCHUBENDORF'S KELLIE
                                       | GOLDEN/WHITE    |CHIN-PEEK KEL'S KITTY GL23396
                                       | 07-24-81           GOLDEN RED/WHITE      |CHIN-PEEK TAMIE
                  |CHIN-PEEK KITT'S BARNEY
                  | RN626144            |                                  |SCHUBENDORF'S SANDY
                  | GOLDEN RED/WHITE    |SCHUBENDORF'S KELLIE 776242
                  | 07-03-84            | RED/WHITE                        |CHIN-PEEK STAR'S LADY
                  |                    |CHIN-PEEK KEL'S KITTY
                  |                      GL23396                           |SCHUBENDORF'S KELLIE
Sire>             |                      GOLDEN RED/WHITE |CHIN-PEEK TAMIE 846352
-----             |                      06-19-75           RED/WHITE     |CHIN-PEEK SUE BUFF
CAN CH WESTERLEA'S CHANCE FOR KYLADOR
 F297    XG841599|                                                        |CAN CH WESTERLEA'S WHITE ENSIGN (BIS BISS
 GOLDEN RED/WHITE|                                       |WESTERLEA'S WINDSOR LAD MS209318
 04-16-90        |                                       | RED/WHITE               |CAN CH SPROUL'S KINSMAN'S CEDAR FOX
                  |                    |CAN CH WESTERLEA'S FIRST LIEUTENANT CD
                  |                    | NS262206                         |CAN CH SPROUL'S HIGHLAND COMMANDER
                  |                    | RED/WHITE       |CAN CH WESTERLEA'S SPRING MELODY KK69032
                  |                    | 09-24-81          RED/WHITE      |CAN CH WESTERLEA'S SCOTIAN GOLD
                  |CAN CH WESTERLEA'S BONNY BLUENOSE (BISS)
                    PU332648                                               |CAN CH SANDY MACGREGOR OF SPROUL
                    RED/WHITE          |CAN CH SPROUL'S HIGHLAND COMMANDER HL82172
                    10-17-82           | RED/WHITE                        |CAN CH HARBOUR LIGHTS AUTUMN FANCY
                                       |CAN CH SUNDRUMMERS SEAWITCH
========================================= KJ101708                        |CAN CH DANNY BOY OF HARBOUR LIGHTS
                                         RED/WHITE       |CAN CH SPROUL'S HIGHLAND LASSIE FCB490
                                         05-29-78          RED/WHITE      |HAPPY HOLLY OF HARBOUR LIGHTS
                  |
CAN CH KYLADOR'S DEBONAIR ROB ROY (BISS)                                   |CAN CH CRUSADER OF JEFFERY COLDWELL, CD
 {M} BL084184     |                                      |CAN CH WESTERLEA'S WHITE ENSIGN (BIS BISS) JT34480
 RED/WHITE        |                                      | RED/WHITE               |CAN CH SHELBURNE OF JEFFERY COLDWELL
 06-16-93         |                    |CAN CH WESTERLEA'S TRU RAY REBEL, CDX WC
                  |                    | ME170282                         |CAN CH SPROUL'S HIGHLAND COMMANDER
========================================= RED/WHITE     |CAN CH SUNDRUMMERS SEAWITCH KJ101708
                  |                    | 03-05-80         RED/WHITE       |CAN CH SPROUL'S HIGHLAND LASSIE
                  |CAN CH FANCYSRUN FORMULA ONE
                  | F262   UQ658991    |                                  |SPORT OF JEFFERY COLDWELL
                  | GOLDEN RED/WHITE   |AMAGKUK OF JEFFERY COLDWELL HK16770
                  | 08-22-87           | GOLD/WHITE                       |TUSKET ISLE HEATHERTON
                  |                    |CANDICE-------------|
                  |                      RW523577                         |BOOTES OF JEFFERY COLDWELL
Dam >             |                      GOLDEN RED/WHITE |NOVASEQUIA OF JEFFERY-COLDWELL NQ278521
-----             |                      11-10-84           RED/WHITE     |CAN CH HONEY OF JEFFERY COLDWELL
CAN CH KYLADOR'S ALDEBARAN DESTINY
 YC898979         |                                                        |CAN CH DANNY BOY OF HARBOUR LIGHTS
 RED/WHITE        |                                      |CAN CH WESTERLEA'S COAST TO COAST, CD QG359380
 02-19-91         |                                      | RED/WHITE               |CAN CH WESTERLEA'S COPPER VIXEN
                  |                    |CAN CH SANDYCOVE AT WESTERLEA, WC CD
                  |                    | SL488277                         |CAN CH WESTERLEA'S WHITE ENSIGN (BIS BISS
                  |                    | RED/WHITE       |CAN CH WESTERLEA'S SUMMER SUNSET NN254684
                  |                    | 06-14-85          RED/WHITE      |CAN CH SUNDRUMMERS SEAWITCH
                  |CAN CH WESTERLEA KYLADOR'S SEA GYPSY, CD
                    VY737297                                               |WESTERLEA'S WINDSOR LAD
                    RED/WHITE          |CAN CH WESTERLEA'S FIRST LIEUTENANT CD NS262206
                    12-01-88           | RED/WHITE                        |CAN CH WESTERLEA'S SPRING MELODY
                                       |CAN CH WESTERLEA'S BONNY BLUENOSE (BISS)
                                         PU332648                          |CAN CH SPROUL'S HIGHLAND COMMANDER
                                         RED/WHITE       |CAN CH SUNDRUMMERS SEAWITCH KJ101708
                                         10-17-82          RED/WHITE      |CAN CH SPROUL'S HIGHLAND LASSIE
```

```
                                                                            |CAN CH DANNY BOY OF HARBOUR LIGHTS
                                                |SPROUL'S PRINCE OF BARRACHOIS EJE16
                                                | RED/WHITE              |MARY ANNE OF HARBOUR LIGHTS
                            |CAN CH SPROUL'S HIGHLAND REGGIE
                            | PL349972                                    |CAN CH SPROUL'S MAC-A-DOO
                            | RED/WHITE         |CAN CH SPROUL'S LADY MACDUFF LQ263991
                            | 06-24-82          | RED/WHITE              |CAN CH SCARLET GEM OF SPROUL
        |SPROUL'S APACHE SUNDOG
        | QQ399275                                                        |ROBIE SURF OF GLENCOE
        | RED/WHITE         |                   |CAN CH ALEXANDER MACTAVISH ESB904
        | 08-04-83          |                   | RED/WHITE              |NICK'S FOXY SNOOPER
        |                   |CAN CH SPROUL'S APACHE PRINCESS
        |                   | KY108952                                    |CAN CH DANNY BOY OF HARBOUR LIGHTS
Sire>   |                   | RED/WHITE         |SPROUL'S TAWNEE PRINCESS DUD735
-----   |                   | 12-13-78          | RED/WHITE              |MARY ANNE OF HARBOUR LIGHTS
CAN CH SPROUL'S HAPPY HIGGINS (BIS)
XW903349|                                                                 |CAN CH RED ROCK STAR, CD
RED/WHITE                                       |CAN CH SANDY MACGREGOR OF SPROUL EJE72
11-17-90|                                       | RED/WHITE              |CAN CH HARBOUR LIGHTS AUTUMN FANCY
        |                   |CAN CH SPROUL'S MAC-A-DOO
        |                   | KB61900                                     |MAJOR RUFUS OF GREEN MEADOWS
        |                   | RED/WHITE         |MISS ACADIA OF SPROUL ENC622
        |                   | 01-13-78          | RED/WHITE              |HAPPY HOLLY OF HARBOUR LIGHTS
        |SPROUL'S STACEY LEE-
        | UY693590                                                        |CAN CH ALEXANDER MACTAVISH
        | RED/WHITE         |                   |CAN CH SPROUL'S TANTRAMAR TOBY, CD GE26843
        | 12-19-87          |                   | RED                    |CAN CH SPROUL'S MERRY DANCER
                            |CAN CH SPROUL'S CELTIC KATE
========================================  PN325432                        |CAN CH DANNY BOY OF HARBOUR LIGHTS
                            | RED/WHITE         |SPROUL'S TAWNEE PRINCESS DUD735
                            | 07-01-82          | RED/WHITE              |MARY ANNE OF HARBOUR LIGHTS
CAN CH SEHIS LITTLE BRETON (DUAL BIS)|                                    |HARBOURLIGHT FUNDY STAR
{M} BL122719                |                   |SPIKE OF HARBOURLIGHTS JG108565
GOLDEN RED/WHITE            |                   | RED                    |HARBOURLIGHT'S GOLDEN TAMMIE
06-09-93                    |BOO-EVIL OF HARBOURLIGHTS
========================================| MY222810                        |HARBOURLIGHTS VILLAGE SIRE
                            | RED/WHITE         |HARBOURLIGHTS MISTY BLUE LG120176
                            | 12-28-80          | RED/WHITE              |HARBOURLIGHTS FUNDY GAL
        |HARBOURLIGHTS BIG SPLASH
        | VC683449                                                        |GREEN MEADOWS LAC-A-PAC PAL
        | RED/WHITE         |                   |HARBOURLIGHTS VILLAGE SIRE 923529
        | 02-16-88          |                   | RED/WHITE              |BETTY OF SCHUBENDORF
        |                   |HARBOURLIGHTS FOXY TAWNY
        |                   | ML190746                                    |ROBIE SURF OF GLENCOE
Dam >   |                   | RED/WHITE         |HARBOURLIGHTS FUNDY BELL DNA694
-----   |                   | 06-01-80          | RED/WHITE              |NICK'S FOXY SNOOPER
HARBOURLIGHTS HIGHLAN BELLE
YG917911|                                                                 |PAT OF SCHUBENDORF
RED/WHITE                                       |CHIN-PEEK GOLDEN LUCKY KIM 736025
04-29-91|                                       | GOLDEN RED/WHITE       |CHIN-PEEK LUCKY
        |                   |HARBOURLIGHTS SCOTIA BOY
        |                   | JL125335                                    |GREEN MEADOWS LAC-A-PAC PAL
        |                   | RED/WHITE         |HARBOUR LIGHTS FOXY NISKU 907807
        |                   | 06-16-77          | RED/WHITE              |CHIN-PEEK STAR'S LADY
        |HARBOURLIGHTS SCOTIA BELLE
        | PW320415                                                        |GREEN MEADOWS LAC-A-PAC PAL
        | RED/WHITE         |                   |HARBOURLIGHTS VILLAGE SIRE 923529
        | 11-12-82          |                   | RED/WHITE              |BETTY OF SCHUBENDORF
                            |HARBOURLIGHTS RED KALI
                            | KQ120175                                    |ROBIE SURF OF GLENCOE
                            | RED/WHITE         |HARBOURLIGHT'S FOREVER AMBER EGB327
                            | 08-29-78          | RED/WHITE              |GREEN MEADOWS CANDY KISSES
```

```
                                                                              |SCHUBENDORF'S SANDY
                                                        |PAT OF SCHUBENDORF 627514
                                                        |  RED/WHITE          |SCHUBENDORF'S LADY
                                     |CHIN-PEEK GOLDEN LUCKY KIM
                                     | 736025                                 |CHIN-PEEK SHEP
                                     | GOLDEN RED/WHITE |CHIN-PEEK LUCKY 684481
                                     | 11-10-66         |  RED/WHITE          |CHIN-PEEK GINGER JULIE
                  |HARBOURLIGHTS SCOTIA BOY
                  | JL125335                                                  |MAJOUR OF SCHUBENDORF
                  | RED/WHITE        |GREEN MEADOWS LAC-A-PAC PAL 563858
                  | 06-16-77         |  RED/WHITE                             |GREEN MEADOWS TAWNEE WAKON
                  |                  |HARBOUR LIGHTS FOXY NISKU
                  |                  | 907807                                 |CHIN-PEEK LIM-BO
Sire>             |                  | RED/WHITE        |CHIN-PEEK STAR'S LADY 722663
-----             |                  | 03-21-71         |  GOLDEN RED/WHITE   |CHIN-PEEK GOLDEN STAR
RIVERDUCK OF DROGSTA (SWED CH)
WL772605          |                                                           |CHIN-PEEK GOLDEN LUCKY KIM
RED/WHITE         |                  |HARBOURLIGHTS SCOTIA BOY JL125335
06-09-89          |                  |  RED/WHITE                             |HARBOUR LIGHTS FOXY NISKU
                  |                  |HARBOURLIGHTS MIGHTY MIKE
                  |                  | QL384100                               |ROBIE SURF OF GLENCOE
                  |                  | RED/WHITE        |HARBOURLIGHT'S HAPPY HOOKER EGB328
                  |                  | 06-19-83         |  RED/WHITE          |GREEN MEADOWS CANDY KISSES
                  |HARBOURLIGHTS FOXY AMBER
                  | SG474210                                                  |GREEN MEADOWS LAC-A-PAC PAL
                  | RED/WHITE        |HARBOURLIGHTS VILLAGE SIRE 923529
                  | 04-09-85         |  RED/WHITE                             |BETTY OF SCHUBENDORF
                                     |HARBOURLIGHTS FOXY TAWNY
=====================================  ML190746                               |ROBIE SURF OF GLENCOE
                                     | RED/WHITE        |HARBOURLIGHTS FUNDY BELL DNA694
                                     | 06-01-80         |  RED/WHITE          |NICK'S FOXY SNOOPER

DROGSTAS CAT-RI-ONA (SWED CH)                                                 |CAN CH SANDY MACGREGOR OF SPROUL
{F} S66722/90                                           |CAN CH SPROUL'S EARL OF JALNA, CD JB10193
RED/WHITE                                               |  RED/WHITE          |MARY ANNE OF HARBOUR LIGHTS
10-09-90                             |CAN CH JALNA'S PERSONALITY PLUS
                                     | LW152583                               |CAN CH CRUSADER OF JEFFERY COLDWELL, CD
=====================================| RED/WHITE        |CAN CH JALNA'S EAGER BOOTS, CDX HJ75874
                                     | 11-04-79         |  FAWN/WHITE         |CAN CH CONTESSA OF JEFFERY COLDWELL
                  |JALNA'S ZEALOUS ZEPHYR
                  | TQ582371                                                  |CAN CH CRUSADER OF JEFFERY COLDWELL, CD
                  | RED/WHITE        |CAN CH JALNA'S RED EMPEROR HJ75877
                  | 08-27-86         |  RED/WHITE                             |CAN CH CONTESSA OF JEFFERY COLDWELL
                  |                  |CAN CH JALNA'S BRAZEN BRAT
                  |                  | NU265820                               |CAN CH SPROUL'S TANTRAMAR TOBY, CD
Dam >             |                  | RED/WHITE        |SPROUL'S JENNIFER JALNA JH25020
-----             |                  | 10-03-81         |  RED/WHITE          |CAN CH SPROUL'S LADY MACGREGOR
FOBI TOLLERS VILHELMINA
S55695            |                                                           |CAN CH SPROUL'S EARL OF JALNA, CD
RED/WHITE         |                  |CAN CH JALNA'S QUEST FOR GLORY, CDX LW152590
08-11-88          |                  |  GOLD/WHITE                            |JALNA'S ELEGANCE IN RED
                  |                  |CAN CH ARDUNACRES COUNTRY QUINCE
                  |                  | PL304896                               |CAN CH SPROUL'S HIGHLAND COMMANDER
                  |                  | RED/WHITE        |CAN CH SUNDRUMMERS ARDUN ELLA MN258832
                  |                  | 06-17-82         |  RED/WHITE          |CAN CH SPROUL'S HIGHLAND LASSIE
                  |ARDUNACRES SANDY WONDERFUL
                  | RG416650                                                  |CAN CH WESTERLEA'S WHITE ENSIGN
                  | RED/WHITE        |CAN CH WESTERLEA'S FLYING FOX ME170284
                  | 04-18-84         |  RED/WHITE                             |CAN CH SUNDRUMMERS SEAWITCH
                                     |CASTLEKEEP'S SUNSET FIREDANCE
                                       PW339661                               |CAN CH SPROUL'S HIGHLAND COMMANDER
                                       RED/WHITE        |CAN CH WESTERLEA'S SPRING MELODY KK69032
                                       11-23-82         |  RED/WHITE          |CAN CH WESTERLEA'S SCOTIAN GOLD
```

```
                                                                            |WESTERLEA'S WINDSOR LAD
                                                    |CAN CH WESTERLEA'S FIRST LIEUTENANT CD NS262206
                                                    | RED/WHITE                     |CAN CH WESTERLEA'S SPRING MELODY
                                |WESTERLEA'S BRASS TOLLER (DKCH)
                                | PU332649                                  |CAN CH SPROUL'S HIGHLAND COMMANDER
                                | GOLDEN RED/WHITE   |CAN CH SUNDRUMMERS SEAWITCH KJ101708
                                | 10-17-82           | RED/WHITE            |CAN CH SPROUL'S HIGHLAND LASSIE
                |TUEHOLT RED WHAT A SURPRISE (DKCH)
                |                                                           |CAN CH CRUSADER OF JEFFERY COLDWELL, CD
                | RED/WHITE                         |CAN CH WESTERLEA'S WHITE ENSIGN (BIS BISS) JT34480
                |                                   | RED/WHITE             |CAN CH SHELBURNE OF JEFFERY COLDWELL
                                |WESTERLEA'S RED TILLY (DKCH)
                                | PE298399                                  |CAN CH SPROUL'S EARL OF JALNA, CD
                                | RED/WHITE         |JALNA'S QUILLO QUEST LW152588
Sire>                           | 03-27-82           | RED/WHITE            |JALNA'S ELEGANCE IN RED
-----
TUEHOLT RED BUFFALO BILL
                                                                            |CAN CH RED RUSSEL OF JEFFERY
RED/WHITE                                           |CAN CH CRUSADER OF JEFFERY COLDWELL, CD GC33784
                                                    | RED/WHITE             |RAPUNZEL OF JEFFERY COLDWELL
                                |CAN CH WESTERLEA'S WHITE ENSIGN (BIS BISS)
                                | JT34480                                   |JEFFERY OF PORT WILLIAMS
                                | RED/WHITE         |CAN CH SHELBURNE OF JEFFERY COLDWELL GC14690
                                | 09-08-77          | RED/WHITE             |BO DIDDLEY OF JEFFERY COLDWELL
                |WESTERLEA'S RED TILLY (DKCH)
                | PE298399                                                  |CAN CH SANDY MACGREGOR OF SPROUL
                | RED/WHITE                         |CAN CH SPROUL'S EARL OF JALNA, CD JB10193
                | 03-27-82                          | RED/WHITE             |MARY ANNE OF HARBOUR LIGHTS
                                |JALNA'S QUILLO QUEST
========================================  LW152588                          |CAN CH CRUSADER OF JEFFERY COLDWELL, CD
                                  RED/WHITE        |JALNA'S ELEGANCE IN RED HJ75875
                                  11-05-79          | RED/WHITE            |CAN CH CONTESSA OF JEFFERY COLDWELL

GOLDEN FOX JAMBOREE (FINN CH)                                               |CAN CH CRUSADER OF JEFFERY COLDWELL, CD
{M} SF18766/87                                      |CAN CH WESTERLEA'S WHITE ENSIGN (BIS BISS) JT34480
RED/WHITE                                           | RED/WHITE             |CAN CH SHELBURNE OF JEFFERY COLDWELL
05-06-87                        |WESTERLEA'S VOYAGEUR OF JALNA
                                | NN258247                                  |CAN CH SPROUL'S HIGHLAND COMMANDER
========================================  GOLDEN RED/WHITE  |CAN CH SUNDRUMMERS SEAWITCH KJ101708
                                  07-23-81          | RED/WHITE            |CAN CH SPROUL'S HIGHLAND LASSIE
                |JALNA'S GENTLE GIANT
                | QA360449                                                  |CAN CH SANDY MACGREGOR OF SPROUL
                | GOLDEN RED/WHITE                  |CAN CH SPROUL'S EARL OF JALNA, CD JB10193
                | 01-19-83                          | RED/WHITE             |MARY ANNE OF HARBOUR LIGHTS
                                |CAN CH JALNA'S LEGENDARY LOVE
                                | KE135934                                  |CAN CH CRUSADER OF JEFFERY COLDWELL, CD
Dam >                           | GOLDEN RED/WHITE  |CAN CH JALNA'S ENCHANTED RED EMBER HJ75876
-----                           | 03-29-78          | RED/WHITE             |CAN CH CONTESSA OF JEFFERY COLDWELL
JALNA'S NATIONAL NEWSWOMAN
RJ425725                                                                    |CAN CH RED RUSSEL OF JEFFERY
RED/WHITE MARKINGS                                  |CAN CH CRUSADER OF JEFFERY COLDWELL, CD GC33784
05-26-84                                            | RED/WHITE             |RAPUNZEL OF JEFFERY COLDWELL
                                |CAN CH JALNA'S RED EMPEROR
                                | HJ75877                                   |CAN CH RED RUSSEL OF JEFFERY
                                | RED/WHITE         |CAN CH CONTESSA OF JEFFERY COLDWELL DUD221
                                | 05-03-76          | GOLDEN RED/WHITE      |CAN CH FLORETTE JEFFERY OF OVERTON
                |CAN CH JALNA'S BRAZEN BRAT
                | NU265820                                                  |CAN CH ALEXANDER MACTAVISH
                | RED/WHITE                         |CAN CH SPROUL'S TANTRAMAR TOBY, CD GE26843
                | 10-03-81                          | RED                   |CAN CH SPROUL'S MERRY DANCER
                                |SPROUL'S JENNIFER JALNA
                                | JH25020                                   |CAN CH SANDY MACGREGOR OF SPROUL
                                | RED/WHITE         |CAN CH SPROUL'S LADY MACGREGOR GE26835
                                | 04-10-77          | RED/WHITE             |SPROUL'S TAWNEE PRINCESS
```

```
                                                                          |JOGGINS FOXY DUKE
                                                     |ROBIE SURF OF GLENCOE 701886
                                                     | RED/WHITE          |BLOND WOKWIS OF GOLDEN TESSY
                                  |HARBOURLIGHT FUNDY STAR
                                  | ESB902                                 |CHIN-PEEK GOLDEN LUCKY KIM
                                  | RED/WHITE         |NICK'S FOXY SNOOPER 866131
                                  | 09-15-73          | RED/WHITE         |BETTY OF SCHUBENDORF
                 |HILAN LAD OF HARBOURLIGHTS
                 | RS444081                                                |CHIN-PEEK GOLDEN LUCKY KIM
                 | RED/WHITE                          |HARBOURLIGHTS SCOTIA BOY JL125335
                 | 09-15-84                           | RED/WHITE         |HARBOUR LIGHTS FOXY NISKU
                 | |HARBOURLIGHTS TILLY THE TOLLER
                 | | QL360469                                              |ROBIE SURF OF GLENCOE
                 | | RED/WHITE                        |HARBOURLIGHT'S HAPPY HOOKER EGB328
Sire>            | | 06-19-83                         | RED/WHITE         |GREEN MEADOWS CANDY KISSES
-----            |
HARBOURLIGHTS SCOTIA DUKE                                                  |JOGGINS FOXY DUKE
TJ721105                                             |ROBIE SURF OF GLENCOE 701886
RED/WHITE                                            | RED/WHITE          |BLOND WOKWIS OF GOLDEN TESSY
05-27-86                          |CAN CH ALEXANDER MACTAVISH
                                  | ESB904                                 |CHIN-PEEK GOLDEN LUCKY KIM
                                  | RED/WHITE         |NICK'S FOXY SNOOPER 866131
                                  | 09-15-73          | RED/WHITE         |BETTY OF SCHUBENDORF
                 |HARBOURLIGHTS NOVA NIPPER
                   PG294549                                                |JOGGINS FOXY DUKE
                   RED/WHITE                         |ROBIE SURF OF GLENCOE 701886
                   04-15-82                          | RED/WHITE          |BLOND WOKWIS OF GOLDEN TESSY
                                  |HARBOURLIGHT'S GOLDEN TAMMIE
                                  | DLC797                                 |GREEN MEADOWS LAC-A-PAC PAL
====================================== RED/WHITE     |GREEN MEADOWS BUTTONS AND BOWS 878976
                                    06-24-72          RED/WHITE           |BETTY OF SCHUBENDORF
                                                                          |CHIN-PEEK KITTS' PAT
LYONHOUSE COLIN (UK)                                 |CAN CH COLTRIEV DRUMMER BOY, CD DYD86
{M} KCQ0008404Q01                                    | GOLDEN RED/WHITE  |CAN CH CHIN-PEEK LADY DE-LAINE
RED/WHITE                         |CAN CH SUNDRUMMERS HARBOUR MASTER, CD
12-15-89                          | LN157661                              |CAN CH SANDY MACGREGOR OF SPROUL
====================================== RED/WHITE     |CAN CH SPROUL'S HIGHLAND BELLE GL26851
                                    07-14-79          RED/WHITE           |CAN CH SCARLET GEM OF SPROUL
                 |CAN CH TAYANN TEDDY BEAR
                 | MQ205825                                                |CAN CH RED RUSSEL OF JEFFERY
                 | RED/WHITE                         |CAN CH BELLBOY OF JEFFERY COLDWELL FUE193
                 | 08-07-80                          | RED/WHITE         |CHIN-PEEK WEE LADY SUSAN
                 | |CAN CH LITTLERIVER TROUBLE
                 | | KP95104                                               |CAN CH CRUSADER OF JEFFERY COLDWELL, CD
Dam >            | | RED/WHITE                       |PRISELLA OF JEFFERY COLDWELL JB60996
-----            | | 07-26-78                        | RED/WHITE         |CAN CH FLORETTE JEFFERY OF OVERTON
JEM'S HAMISH'S GIRL OF LYONHOUSE
UW656405                                                                  |GREEN MEADOWS LAC-A-PAC PAL
RED/WHITE                                            |CAN CH DANNY BOY OF HARBOUR LIGHTS 918750
11-19-87                                             | RED/WHITE          |BETTY OF SCHUBENDORF
                                  |CAN CH WESTERLEA'S COAST TO COAST, CD
                                  | QG359380                               |CAN CH WESTERLEA'S WHITE ENSIGN (BIS BISS
                                  | RED/WHITE         |CAN CH WESTERLEA'S COPPER VIXEN ME170285
                                  | 04-28-83           ORANGE/WHITE       |CAN CH SUNDRUMMERS SEAWITCH
                 |WESTERLEA'S GLITTERING JEM, CD
                   RG422867                                                |CAN CH CRUSADER OF JEFFERY COLDWELL, CD
                   GOLDEN RED/WHITE                  |CAN CH WESTERLEA'S WHITE ENSIGN (BIS BISS) JT34480
                   04-19-84                          | RED/WHITE         |CAN CH SHELBURNE OF JEFFERY COLDWELL
                                  |CAN CH WESTERLEA'S SUMMER SUNSET
                                    NN254684                               |CAN CH SPROUL'S HIGHLAND COMMANDER
                                    RED/WHITE        |CAN CH SUNDRUMMERS SEAWITCH KJ101708
                                    07-23-81          RED/WHITE           |CAN CH SPROUL'S HIGHLAND LASSIE
```

MARTHA COVINGTON THORNE

Martha Covington Thorne was one of THE most respected handlers and field trainers of her era. This lady had forgotten more about dogs than most of us will ever know! She was working on a revision of her book **Handling Your Own Dog for Show, Obedience and Field Trials** (Doubleday, 1979) when she died, and the revision was neither completed nor published.

I had written to Martha, whom I knew in Ottawa, after I read her book, asking if she had ever worked with Tollers. Her reply came to me in two forms — one a column in a monthly dog magazine for which she wrote regularly, and the other piece included below. I have treasured this ever since Martha's untimely death in 1981 and have waited for the right opportunity to publish it. I can think of no better place than this book. I thank Martha, posthumously, for her warmth and good humor, her generosity in sharing her wealth of knowledge, and her unfailing dedication to dogs.

* * *

Let's not overlook the Nova Scotia Duck Tolling Retriever, recognized only in Canada, and even in that country it is a rarity to see one. When one does, most people don't recognize it.

Fortunately, in 1980, not one but two Tollers proudly took home Best in Show honors — which, for such an unknown, seldom-shown breed, is an accomplishment tantamount to successfully making love while standing up in a hammock! It was a distinct shock to the Toller fancy, believe me, so much so that when the second one hit this pinnacle, the trick eye-catching caption on the photograph advertising the win read: "A WHAT went Best in Show?"

On the plus side for this smallish, reddish-gold breed are these facts: He is equally at home beside the hearth or in the corner of a duck blind, easily handled in and out of boats, and small enough to be economically maintained and transported. He is, nonetheless, large enough to handle any bird from dove to goose and, unlike many of the rarer breeds used as retrievers, the Toller was admitted to licensed field trials in the late 1970s. Talk about a challenge! What a thrill it would be to train and handle the world's first Field Champion Nova Scotia Duck Tolling Retriever. Were it I, I should probably expire from the sheer pride of it all!

There is not much on the minus side of this breed except that, because it is a rare breed and has been largely maintained and evaluated on the basis of the way it does the work for which it was intended, there is a wide variety in type. Some are quite high on the leg, slabby, and narrow-headed — almost ugly to my personal eye. I much prefer the type most nearly personifying a Golden Retriever which has shrunk when washed (be sure to read the label!).

Tolling is the oldest method in the world to attract waterfowl. In the wild a fox and vixen will pair up to hunt their supper, one hiding in the reeds to pounce and finish off the curious waterfowl, the other rolling and playing and dashing hither and thither on the bank to draw the goose or duck ever closer. When I first started out with Mr. Fisher on the Eastern Shore of Maryland, we would often train young dogs along the shore of the Chesapeake Bay and in the early spring and late fall, great rafts of wild geese, swans, and ducks would float further and further inshore as we worked, fascinated by the movements of the retrievers. So tolling, which used to be the way thousands of waterfowl at a time were killed during the days of market hunting, when explosive charges were set, is not an exclusive Canadian pastime.

The birds were lured close enough by dogs which tolled to attract the wild fowl — that is, they ran up and down along the shore after stones skipped in the water by men hidden in the bushes. But the only place anyone ever bred a dog specifically for this purpose, a dog as nearly as possible to the conformation and color of the wily fox, was in southwestern Nova Scotia. For over 100 years breeders in this area jealously guarded their dogs and few were ever seen outside that area, much as was the case with the Boykin Spaniel.

A jaunty-gaited little guy weighing between 50 and 55 pounds maximum (I personally have never seen one that large), the Toller is rarely more than 20 inches at the withers. His intense love of retrieving more than makes up for his size. Remember what the mouse hiding under the mushroom said to the tomcat in the fairy tale? "I'm just as big for me," said he, "as you are big for you."

APPENDIX
Original Canadian Standard

Here is the original Canadian Kennel Club Standard for the Retriever (Nova Scotia Duck Tolling), as adopted by the CKC in 1945 when the breed was first given CKC recognition.

This Standard was drawn up by one man, Colonel Cyril Colwell of Halifax, Nova Scotia, who was most responsible for bringing the Toller to CKC recognition. It was supplanted by the present Standard, which came into effect January 1, 1982.

1. APPEARANCE:

The Nova Scotia Duck Tolling Retriever should be very muscular and heavy in bone, the head and neck should be carried slightly above a straight line with the back. When the dog is in action, the tail should be carried curled up over hind quarters. Size is absolutely necessary. There is a half sad expression, until the dog is put to work, when that sad expression springs to inquisitiveness and the dog trembles with excitement, alertness and determination.

2. CHARACTERISTICS:

Docile, non-roamer, exceptionally easy to train, born retriever on land or from water, cleanliness, timid, good guard dog, will fight as last resort, great swimmer, endurance, playful. The moment the slightest indication is given that retrieving is required, he sets himself for springy action.

3. HEIGHT:

The minimum height of an adult dog over eighteen months must be 20½ ins, that of a bitch 18½ ins.

4. WEIGHT:

The minimum weight of an adult dog over eighteen months should be 50 lbs., that of a bitch 35 lbs.

5. COLOUR:

Red or fawn, slightly lighter than that of an Irish Setter. Belly and underside of tail slightly lighter. No objection to white blaze on forehead, chest, toes and tip of tail. Most Tollers show white patch on chest and belly, and while this is not entirely objected to, it is more desirable to eliminate all white. White on shoulders and around ears or across back or flanks not permitted. Colour throughout should be that of a red fox.

6. COAT:

The hair is long, sleek and soft or silky, with a still softer undercoat. Coat at throat and ears extremely soft. These dogs retrieve from fresh and salt water during the coldest seasons, and therefore require the undercoat. Hair on face, legs and tips of ears is short. The coat is straight except down centre of back where it is wavy. The coat does not curl. There is, however, a tendency sometimes in winter coats for the hair at the throat to have a long loose curl.

7. HEAD:

Generally the head should resemble that of the Golden Retriever. The muzzle or foreface more desirable if broad. The size of head varies but not necessarily depending upon the size of the dog. For the entire length from the tip of the nose to the back of the occiput, 9 ins. is a good measurement. The length from the end of the nose to the point between the eyes should be about equal or preferably of greater length than from this point to the back of the occiput. The occiput peak is not prominent. The stop is concave and gradual.

a.) Lips. The lips should hang rather curved in front. Flesh colour preferable.

b.) Underline. The underline of the head, i.e. profile, should run almost in a straight line from the corner of the lip to the corner of the jawbone. The underline of muzzle from tip of nose to back end of lip is a clean convex curve.

c.) Jaw. Lower jaw thin. Lower side teeth fit inside upper side teeth. Soft in mouth.

d.) Nose and nostrils. The bridge of the nose should be fairly wide, about 1-1½ ins., and taper somewhat at tip. Nostrils are well open. Flesh colour preferred, no objection to black.

e.) Ears. The ears are medium size set high and well back on the skull and carried very slightly erect with tips falling forward. They are well feathered at back of the fold. The tips are nicely rounded to conform to round muzzle, the hair at the tips is short.

f.) Eyes. Golden brown to match coat. Flesh around eye flesh colour. Eyes should be set well apart.

8. FORELEGS AND FEET:

The forelegs should be perfectly straight, and big in bone. The feet should be well hardened for rough work, toes well arched, strong curved nails, and most important, feet to have strong web. Deep chest, belly fairly well drawn up.

9. NECK:

The neck should be of medium length, the junction between head and neck is not well defined, owing to long hair on the neck and at throat.

10. SHOULDERS:

The shoulders should be muscular and well sloped back, elbows well under the body.

11. BACK AND LOINS:

The back and loins should be strong.

12. HINDQUARTERS:

The hindquarters should be muscular and good in appearance, square across top. The hock is not set too low turning neither out nor in.

13. TAIL:

The tail should be about 12½ to 13 ins. long and well feathered Normally it is carried below the level of the back until the dog goes into action when it should be arched up above the line of the back but not touching hindquarters.

14. MOVEMENT:

Quick speedy action, a headlong rush, regardless of obstacles. The dog is docile, very playful. In action, the head is carried almost straight out on a level with the back, and the tail is always in motion.

This exhuberant trio is owned by Cheryl Tomayer.

Glossary of Titles

Tollers are multi-talented and attract the sort of people who like to compete with their dogs — hence the multitude of different letters before and after many of the names found in this book. Here is a brief listing of some of the titles:

Country Abbreviation
Am. – American
Can. – Canadian
UKC – United Kennel Club

CONFORMATION TITLES (before the name)
Canadian Kennel Clubs
CH – Champion:
GCH – Grand Champion
BIS – Best In Show
BISS(N) – Best in National Specialty Show
BISS(R) – Best in Regional Specialty Show
BPIS- Best Puppy in Show
American Kennel Clubs
CH – Champion:
DC – Dual Champion
GCH – Grand Champion
BIS – Best In Show
BISS – Best in Specialty Show
MBIS – Multiple Best in Show
United Kennel Club
GRCH – Grand Champion
CH – Champion

OBEDIENCE TITLES
Canadian Kennel Club
(Prefix – before the name):
OTCH – Obedience Trial Champion
OTCHX – Obedience Trial Champion Excellent
MOTCH – Master Obedience Trial Champion
GMOTCh – Grand Master Obedience Trial Champion
(Suffix – after the name):
CD – Companion Dog
CDI – Companion Dog Intermediate
CDX – Companion Dog Excellent
HIT – High in Trial
UD – Utility Dog
UDX – Utility Dog Excellent

American Kennel Club –
(Prefix – before the name)
NOC – National Obedience Champion -
OTCH – Obedience Trial Champion
VCCH – Versatile Companion Champion
(Suffix – after the name)
CD – Companion Dog
CDX – Companion Dog Excellent
UD – Utility Dog
UDX – Utility Dog Excellent
OGM – Obedience Grand Master
OM – Obedience Master
VCD1 – Versatile Companion Dog 1
VCD2 – Versatile Companion Dog 2
VCD3 – Versatile Companion Dog 3
VCD4 – Versatile Companion Dog 4
VER – Versatility Dog
United Kennel Club
GOCH – United Grand Obedience Champion
UOCH – United Obedience Champion
UUD – United Utility Dog
UCDX – United Companion Dog Excellent

HUNTING TEST
JH – Junior Hunter
SH – Senior Hunter
MH – Master Hunter
GMH –(Canadian) Grand Master Hunter
NMH – (Canadian) National Master Hunter

NAHRA–North American Hunting Retriever Association
SR – Started Hunting Retriever
HR – Hunting Retriever
WR – Working Retriever
MHR – Master Hunting Retriever
GMHR – Grand Master Hunting Retriever

NSDTRC (USA)
WC – Working Certificate
WCI – Working Certificate Intermediate
WCX – Working Certificate Excellent
For additional titles and titles for other activities, please consult the organization's pages on the internet.

Johnny, Dolly, Willy, Reba at 5 weeks. Owner Jamie Klein, Readyfor Nova Scotia Duck Tolling Retrievers.

BIBLIOGRAPHY

BOOKS

Browne, Montagu. *Practical Taxidermy*. London: Upcott Gill, c. 1875.

Collier, Eric. *Three Against the Wilderness*. Toronto, Ont.: Irwin & Co. Ltd. (paper), 1959.

Ganong, William J. F. *Description and Natural History of the Coasts of North America (Acadia)*. Tr. from works of Nicholas Denys. n.d.

Hancock, David. *Old Working Dogs*. Aylesbury, Bucks: Shire Publications, Ltd., 1984.

Heilen, Van Campen. *A Book on Duck Shooting*. Philadelphia, 1939.

Jameson, E. W. Jr. *The Hawking of Japan*. Davis, Cal.: Private, 1962.

Lanting, Fred L. *Canine Hip Dysplasia and Other Orthopedic Problems*. Loveland, Colo.: Alpine Publications, Inc., 1980.

Payne-Galloway, Sir Ralph. *The Book of Duck Decoys*. London: 1886.

Skinner, J. S. *The Dog and the Sportsman*. 1845.

Spencer, James B. *Hunting Retrievers: Hindsights, Foresights and Insights*. Loveland, Colo.: Alpine Publications, Inc., 1989.

Spencer, James B. *Training Retrievers for Marshes and Meadows*. Loveland, Colo.: Alpine Publications, 1990.

Walsh, John Henry. *The Dogs of Great Britain, America, and Other Countries*, 1879.

Walsh, John Henry. *The Dogs of Great Britain*. New York: Howell Book House, 1989.

Willis, Malcolm B. *Genetics of the Dog*. New York: Howell Book House, 1989.

ARTICLES

Aiello, Susan E. "Understanding Canine Seizures." *Dog Fancy*, April 1987, pp. 32-35.

Barnett, Keith C. "Eye Disease in the Dog." Gaines Dog Research Center: *Gaines Progress*, Fall 1976.

Botner, Gretchen. "Here's the Nova Scotia Duck Tolling Retriever." *Dog World*, April 1992, pp. 10-14.

Carter, Cynthia. "The Nova Scotia Duck Tolling Retriever." *Dogs*, July 1977.

Gleason, Lee Ann. "Cancer in Dogs: An Overview." NSDTRC (U.S.A.): *Quackers*, Spring 1993, p. 12.

Hemeon, R. P. "Toll and Retrieve." *Canadian Dogs*, October 1943.

Howard, Jeff. "The Truth about the Tolling Dog." *Illinois Game & Fish*, September 1991, pp. 44-47, 66-67.

Howard, Jeff. "Tale of the Tolling Dog." *Ducks Unlimited*, November/December 1992, pp. 75-80.

Huff, David G. "Orthopedic Diseases in Young Dogs of Large Breeds: Part IV, Hip Dysplasia." *Dogs in Canada*, February 1981, pp. 19-20.

Karas, Nicholas. "Dogs that Decoy Ducks." *Field & Stream*, September 1966, pp. 80-86.

Keller, Charlotte B. "Progressive Retinal Atrophy in the Nova Scotia Duck Tolling Retriever." NSDTRC (Can.): *Toller Talk*, Vol. 19, No. 3, Fall 1992, pp. 1-2.

Madjanovich, Janice. "Canine Hypothyroidism and Thyroid Testing." *Toller Talk*, Vol. 20, No. 1, Spring 1993, pp. 8-9.

Madjanovich, Janice. Ont. Vet. Coll., Univ. Guelph, Ontario. Personal communication, n.d.: Autoimmune disease; Flea allergy diermatitis; Immune mediated diseases; Immune system; Immunological disorders.

Nickerson, W. Avery. "A Very Special Duck Hunt." *Toller Talk*, Vol. 13, No. 3, Fall 1986, p. 23.

Norfolk, Jim. "National Gundog Show." *Our Dogs*, August 6, 1981.

Perdix. "Duck Dupers." *Shooting Times & Country Magazine*, August 24-31, 1994.

Rand, Vicki. "Dog Breeds of the World: The Nova Scotia Duck Tolling Retriever." United Kennel Club: *Bloodlines*, September/October 1990, pp. 28-33.

Robinson, Jerome B. "Decoy Dogs." *Sports Afield*, August 1981, pp. 64-65, 106-109.

Schmidt, Ben. "Working Retrievers: A Veterinarian's Viewpoint." Paper presented at seminar: Working Retrievers, Labrador Retriever Club of British Columbia, Langley, British Columbia, 1987.

Shea, Harold. "Tolling Ducks." *Time Magazine*, December 3, 1951.

Shea, Harold. "Little River Duck Dogs." *Winnipeg Free Press*, May 6, 1953.

Smith, H.A.P. Untitled. In *Ontario Out of Doors*, June 1983, pp. 56-61.

Spencer, James B. "The Nova Scotia Duck Tolling Retriever." *Wildfowl*, December/January 1986/87.

Stott, N. W., and Lamoreux, Lynn. "The Nova Scotia Duck Tollers." *Dog Fancy*, January/February 1973.

Taylor, Wilf. "Life in the Outdoors: The Nova Scotia Duck Tolling Retriever." *The Moncton Times*, June 6, 1972.

Thorne, Ward. "Little River Tolling Dogs." *Canadian Dogs*, April 1943.

VIDEO

Nickerson, W. Avery and Erna. "The Nova Scotia Duck Tolling Retriever Story." Yarmouth, Nova Scotia: produced by W. Avery and Erna Nickerson, © 1990.

Eddy drinking Stout.

Suggested Reading

BREED BOOKS

MacMillan, Gail. *A Breed Apart*. Halifax, NS: Nimbus Publishing, 1998.

BREEDING AND CARE

Carlson, Delbert G., and Giffin, James M. *Dog Owner's Home Veterinary Handbook*. New York: Howell Book House, 2nd Ed. 1992.

Eldredge, Debra M., DVM, Carlson, Liisa D., DVM, Carlson, Delbert G., DVM, and Griffin, James M., MD. *Dog Owner's Home Veterinary Handbook*, Edited by Beth Adelman. Hobocken, NJ: Howell Book House, 4th Ed. 2007.

Holst, Phyllis A., MS, DVM. *Canine Reproduction: The Breeder's Guide*. Crawford, CO.: Alpine Publications, 3rd Ed. 2011.

Monks of New Skete. *Art of Raising a Puppy*. New York: Little, Brown & Co., Rev. Ed. 2011.

Pitcairn, Richard H., and Pitcairn, Susan Hubble. *Dr. Pitcairns's Complete Guide to Natural Health for Dogs and Cats*. Emmaus, PA: Rodale Press, 3rd Ed. 2005.

Rutherford, Clarice, and Neil, David H. *How to Raise a Puppy You Can Live With*. Loveland, CO: Alpine Publications, 4th Ed. 2005.

Walcowicz, Chris, and Wilcox, Bonnie. *Successful Dog Breeding*. New York: Howell Book House, 2nd ed. 1994.

Williams, Mary Roslin. Reaching for the Stars: Formerly Advanced Labrador Breeding. Irvine, CA: Doral Publishing, 2000.

CHILDREN

Archer, Colleen Rutherford. *Foxy and the Missing Mask*. Moonbeam, ON: Penumbra Press, 1986.

Cohen, Susan, and Cohen, Daniel. *What Kind of Dog Is That?* New York: E.P. Dutton, 1989.

Lowell, Michelle. *Your Purebred Puppy*. New York: Henry Holt, 1991.

Unkelbach, Kurt. *Best of Breeds Guide for Young Dog Lovers*. New York: G.P. Putnam's Sons, 1978.

DVDS

Spencer, James B. *Duck Dog: Training Your Retriever*. Starkville, MS: Gun Dog.

Elliott, Rachel Page. *Dogsteps*. Wenatchee, WA: Dogwise Publishing, 2005

EBOOKS

Coldwell, Douglas. *The Love of Tollers*. http://www.toller1.com

GENERAL

Canadian Kennel Club. *Canadian Kennel Club Book of Dogs*. Rev. ed. Toronto: Stoddart, 1988. First published Toronto: General Publishing. 1982.

Fox, Michael W. *Understanding Your Dog*. New York: Coward, McCann & Geoghegan, 1974. New York: Bantam Books, 1977. St. Martin's Griffin; rev ed. 1992.

Hancock, Judith M. *Friendship: You and Your Dog*. New York: E.P. Dutton, Inc., 1986.

Monks of New Skete. *How to Be Your Dog's Best Friend*. New York: Little, Brown & Co., 1978. Rev. ed. 2002.

Siegal, Mordecai. *Good Dog, Bad Dog, New and Revised: Dog Training Made Easy*. New York: Henry Holt, 1991.

GENETICS

Hutt, Frederick B. *Genetics for Dog Breeders*. San Francisco: W. H. Freeman and Co., 1979.

Willis, Malcolm B. *Genetics of the Dog*. New York: Howell Book House, 1989.

MISCELLANEOUS

Gregory, Kay. *A Perfect Beast*. New York: Harlequin Books, 1989.

MacMillan, Gail. *Ceilidh's Quest*. Scenery Hill, PA: Double Edge Press, 2007.

PERIODICALS

American Kennel Club Gazette. New York: American Kennel Club: on-line issue. www.akc.org/pubs/gazette/digital_edition.cfm.

Dogs in Canada. Toronto, ON: Canadian Kennel Club. http://www.dogsincanada.com.

Gun Dog. Coral Gables, FL: Intermedia Outdoors Network: http://www.gundogmag.com.

Toller Talk. Information on NSDTR Club of Canada website. http:// www.toller.ca

Quackers. NSDTRC (U.S.A.): http://www.nsdtrc-usa.org.

STRUCTURE –MOVEMENT-BREED TYPE

Beauchamp, Richard G. *Solving the Mysteries of Breed Type*. 2nd ed. Freehold, NJ: Kennel Club Books, 2008.

Elliott, Rachel Page. *New Dogsteps*. Irvine, CA: Fancy Publications, 2009.

Lyon, McDowell. *Dog in Action: A Study of Anatomy and Locomotion as Applying to all Breeds*. Wenatchee, WA: Direct Book Service, 2002.

TRAINING

Bailey, Joan. *How to Help Gun Dogs Train Themselves*. Hillsboro, OR: Swan Valley Press, 2008.

Johnson, Glen R. *Tracking Dog: Theory and Methods*. Mechanicsburg, PA: Barkleigh Productions, Inc., 2003.

Johnson, Nancy E. *Everyday Dog: Training Your Dog to Be the Companion You Want*. New York: Howell Book House, 1990.

Roebuck, Kenneth C. *Gun-dog Training Spaniels and Retrievers*. Mechanicsburg, PA: Stackpole Books, 2011.

Rutherford et al. *Retriever Working Certificate Training*. Loveland, CO: Alpine Publications, Inc., 1986.

Spencer, James B. *Training Retrievers: Hindsights, Foresights and Insights*. Loveland, CO: Alpine Publications, Inc. 1989.

Spencer, James B. *Training Retrievers for Marshes and Meadows*. Loveland, CO: Alpine Publications, Inc., 1990.

Tarrant, Bill. *Problem Gun Dogs: How to Identify and Correct Their Faults*. Mechanicsburg, PA: Stackpole Books, 2002.

Tarrant, Bill. *Training the Hunting Retriever: The New Program*. New York: Howell Book House, 1991.

Thorne, Martha Covington. *Handling Your Own Dog for Show, Obedience and Field Trials*. New York: Doubleday & Co., 1979.

Wolters, Richard A. *Game Dog: The Hunter's Retriever for Upland Birds and Waterfowl*. New York: E.P. Dutton, Inc., 1995.

Ripper, owned by Terry Simons. Photo © PrincePrince Studios

Clubs

TOLLER CLUBS

CANADA
Nova Scotia Duck Tolling Retriever Club of Canada
http://www.toller.ca/

UNITED STATES
Nova Scotia Duck Tolling Retriever Club (U.S.A)
http://www.nsdtrc-usa.org/

UNITED KINGDOM
Nova Scotia Duck Tolling Retriever Club of UK
http://www.toller-club.co.uk/

AUSTRIA
http://www.retrieverclub.at

AUSTRALIA
http://au.groups.yahoo.com/group/tollersaustralia

BELGIUM
http://www.ducktollingretriever.be

DENMARK
Nova Scotia Duck Tolling Retriever Klub
http://www.tollerklubben.dk/

FINLAND
Novascotiannoutajat r.y.
http://www.tollerit.fi/

GERMANY
http://www.drc.de
Tollers are in the DRC governing all retrievers.

NORWAY
http://www.retrieverklubben.no

SWEDEN
Nova Scotia Duck Tolling Retriever Klubben
http://www.tollarklubben.se/

SWITZERLAND
http://tollerinfo.ch

THE NETHERLANDS
http://www.tollertales.nl

OTHER CLUBS

The Canadian Kennel Club
200 Ronson Drive, Suite 400
Etobicoke, ON M9W 5Z9
Canada
http://www.ckc.ca

The American Kennel Club
51 Madison Ave.
New York, NY 10010
www.akc.org

North American Hunting Retriever Association
PO Box 5159
Fredericksburg, VA 22403
http://www.nahra.org

United Kennel Club
100 East Kilgore Road
Kalamazoo, MI 49001-5598
http://www.ukcdogs.com

The Kennel Club
1-5 Clarges Street
Piccadilly, London W1J 8AB
UK
http://www.the-kennel-club.org.uk

FCI (Federation Cynologique Internationale)
Place Albert 1er, 13
B-6530 Thuin Belgium
http://www.fci.be

Australian National Kennel Council
P.O. Box 309
Carina, Queensland 4152
Australia
http://www.ankc.org.au

Time for a nap. Photo courtesy of Dan Rode.

About the Authors

Alison Strang, with her husband Roy, has had a Toller as part of the household since 1975. At that time, Alison had plans to breed Newfoundlands and had registered her kennel name, Westerlea, with the Canadian Kennel Club in 1974. (Westerlea was the name of the house of a very dear uncle and aunt in Scotland.)

Although born in Montreal, Alison grew up in Britain and was educated mainly at Dollar Academy in Scotland. Alison's mother was Canadian by birth and was determined to return to Canada after World War II. Following a short spell in Ottawa, the family trekked to the Pacific Northwest, and Alison finished high school in Yakima, Washington. Following junior college, she worked for three years for the Yakima Republic/Herald as a reporter.

After her marriage to Roy, also a former pupil of Dollar Academy, Alison spent the next twelve years in Africa, where Roy worked in forestry research. Four children were born, two girls in Tanzania and two boys in what is now Zimbabwe. The family dogs were mainly crossed Ridgebacks, common in eastern and southern Africa. After Roy received his Ph.D. in forest ecology from the University of London, the Strang family moved to Fredericton, New Brunswick, in 1966, where Roy worked for the Forestry Service of the Canadian Federal Government, and where the fifth Strang child, Catriona, was born. It was during summers spent in Nova Scotia that the Strangs first heard about the Little River Duck Dog, as Tollers are known Down East, and bought their first Toller, Shelley, for Catriona in 1975. It was not long before the Tollers took over!

The first Westerlea Toller litter was whelped in 1976, and Alison bred these wonderful little red dogs until health issues forced her to close Westerlea in 2009. She has done much promotion of the breed over the years and has written many articles for dog publications in Canada, the United States, Scandinavia, the United Kingdom, Italy, and Australia. She has been an active member of the NSDTR Club of Canada since 1975 and has held various offices, including editor of *Toller Talk* for several years. In 1988, Alison was invited to speak about Tollers to the World Congress of Kennel Clubs at its Toronto meeting. She was also invited to Scandinavia in 1993 and judged Toller shows in Sweden, Finland, and Denmark. In 1995, the Norwegian Retriever Club brought Alison to participate in a weekend seminar on the lesser-known retriever breeds and she also was keynote speaker at one of Switzerland's annual Toller weekends, in addition to giving a seminar in England.

Now retired, Alison helps to mentor some newcomers and still gives the occasional breed seminar.

Gail MacMillan says that her love of writing and dogs is much like the riddle of the chicken and the egg. She's not really sure which came first or when, since both date beyond definite remembrance. She does know that she was, for the first thirteen years of her life, the only child of an avid outdoorsman and devoted hunter. While her mother was busy buying her organdy dresses and the complete works of *Anne of Green Gables* by author L. M. Montgomery, her father was just as occupied teaching her to hunt and fish and drive a retired World War II army jeep through the bush. For her twelfth birthday, her father gave her a shotgun and a crisp, new twenty-dollar bill with which she immediately purchased her first puppy.

Later she graduated from business school. Although her father believed that she had attended with the goal of becoming a secretary, Gail had really only wanted to learn to type to be able to prepare the manuscripts of stories that she had been writing clandestinely for years.

In 1963, she married Ron MacMillan, a high-school teacher and devoted waterfowler and dog man. He encouraged both her interest in dogs and writing. They moved to Tabusintac, New Brunswick, an area noted for its waterfowl hunting and salmon fishing, and became avid Labrador Retriever fanciers.

In 1986, with her own children about to graduate from college, Gail received her degree in literature and history from prestigious Queen's University in Kingston, Ontario.

Over the years, dogs continued to be an integral part of the MacMillan family. Gail continued her writing career writing for various magazines both in the United States and Canada, had three novels for young adults published in New York, and a history book in Canada. Then she saw an article on Nova Scotia Duck Tolling Retrievers in a regional outdoor publication. It was a love at first sight that started an interesting chain of events in her life.

Several years later, when she actually had an opportunity to acquire a Harbourlights Nova Scotia Duck Tolling Retriever from W. Avery and Erna Nickerson of Yarmouth, Nova Scotia, she mentioned the fact to Bob Wilbanks, editor of *Gun Dog Magazine*, and he suggested that she write an article on her first year's experience with the pup. The resulting story appeared in the August/September 1992 issue of *Gun Dog* and resulted in Gail's winning a Maxwell Medal for the best article in a multi-breed/hunting magazine for 1992 from The Dog Writers' Association of America.

While in New York for the awards banquet, Gail met Betty McKinney, publisher of Alpine Publications, Inc. Two months later, McKinney offered Gail a contract for a book on Nova Scotia Duck Tolling Retrievers, provided she could work closely with a breeder-trainer.

Again fate stepped in. Alison Strang of Westerlea Perm. Reg. Kennel in Surrey, British Columbia, called to congratulate Gail on the article and mentioned that she, too, had aspirations of writing a book on Tollers. Immediately a partnership was born. And the rest became history.

"Ceilidh's Quest" her book about her Toller, Harbourlights Scotia Ceilidh, received the Maxwell Medal in 2007 as Best Book in the Fiction category (although it is a true) making Gail a a three time Maxwell Medal winner.

These days, Ron and Gail spend every spare moment at their camp in Tabusintac, New Brunswick, where their Toller, Fancy, can toll and retrieve to her heart's content with Pug Bruiser as a fascinated spectator.

INDEX

Abbott, Steve and Diane (Castlekeep Kennel) 43
Acadia, *see* Nova Scotia
Acadians, deportation of 5
advertising and marketing 221
agility 135-6
All-Breed Best in Show 23, 40, 42, 49, 54, 57, 63, 66
Allen, James 6
American interest
    Beran, Paul and Patty (Sagewood Kennel) 63-4
    Botner, George and Gretchen (Tradewinds Kennel) 65, 68
    Dorscheid, Sue and Mike Elmergreen (Springvale Kennel) 67
    Gleason, Joe and Lee Ann (Cayuga Kennel) 67
    Grossman White, Laura (Cinnstar Kennel) 60-1
    Hamilton, John and Marile Saterstraat (Lennoxlove Kennel) 62-3
    Norton, Kirk and Anne (Cabot Trail Kennel) 63
    United States registrations and the American Toller Club 58-9
    Van Sloun, Neil and Sue (Sylvan Kennel) 59
    Williams, Nelson and Evelyn (Lonetree Kennel) 66
American Kennel Club (AKC) 58-9, 95, 131-2, 134, 137
    See also Canine Good Citizen Test
American National Specialty (1994) 59, 67
American Rare Breed Association (ARBA) 59, 63, 67
American Toller Club 58-9, 61, 118
ancestry
    European 1-3
    North American 3-9
appearance 95-97
Australian influence 84
Austria 84
Autoimmune disease 178-9
    adrenalitis 178
    autoimmune skin disease 178
    hemolytic anemia 178
    polyarthritis 178
    systemic lupus erythematosus 178
    thyroiditis 178

Babine, Eddie 23
baiting 161
Basic Retrieving and Tolling Test (BRT) 66
behavior shaping 119
Beran, Paul and Patty (Sagewood Kennels) 63-4, 193
Bernache (Wilfred and Dianne Drouin) 55
Bidewill, Hettie (Chin-Peek Kennel) 33-5, 37
Bidewell (inbreeding) method 35

birds, *see* game birds
blinds 112, 115-6
"bluebird" days 115
boats, introducing Tollers to 126
body 104, 215
Border Collie 85
Botner, George and Gretchen (Tradewinds Kennel) 65, 68, 193
Boutilier, Frank and Roberta (Tollerbreton) 47
Breed, Best of 59, 75
Breed Standard 9, 58-9, 95-110
breeders
    Abbott, Steve and Diane (Castlekeep Kennel) 43
    Beran, Paul and Patty (Sagewood Kennel) 63-4, 193
    Bidewill, Hettie (Chin-Peek Kennel) 33-5, 37
    Botner, George and Gretchen (Tradewind Kennel) 65, 68, 193
    Boutilier, Frank and Roberta (Tollerbreton) 47
    Cap, Rena (Jalna Kennel) 37-9, 50, 58, 75, 193
    Collier, Irvin and Paula (Colliers' Kennel) 51
    Doberstein, John and Joyce 43, 193
    Dorscheid, Sue and Mike Elmergreen (Springvale Kennel) 67
    Drouin, Wilfred and Dianne (Bernache) 55
    Dunn, Derek and Pam (Kare Kennel) 29-31
    Dunphy, Vic and Heather (Marangai Kennel) 29
    Gleason, Joe and Lee Ann (Cayuga Kennel) 67
    Greensides, Lillian and Karen Wright (Kylador Kennel) 51-3, 193
    Grossman White, Laura (Cinnstar Kennel) 60-1, 65, 194
    Hamilton, John and Marile Waterstraat (Lennoxlove Kennel) 62-3
    Jeffery, Jim and Doug Coldwell (Jeffery Coldwell Kennel) 26-8, 49, 60-2
    Kish, Paul and Susan (Foxgrove Kennel) 53-5, 67, 118-29, 194
    MacDonald, Duncan and Arline (Ardunacres Kennel) 42-3, 72
    MacKenzie, Keith and Roberta (Tollerbrook Kennel) 25-6, 194
    Mann, Wileen, (Sundrummer Kennel) 36-7, 42, 57-8
    Martin, Lynda and Richard (Colony Kennel) 47
    McNamee, Terry (Rosewood Kennel) 50-1, 155, 194-5
    Nickerson, W. Avery and Erna (Harbourlights Kennel) 5, 15-21, 23, 25-6, 29, 33, 57, 74-5, 82, 91, 111, 115-7
    Norton, Kirk and Anne (Cabot Trail Kennel) 63, 85, 87, 195

Noullett, Mac and Joan (Sandycove Kennel) 46, 195
Pace, Eldon 16, 23, 25, 31, 33, 35, 115
Penner, Ann (Liscot Kennel) 50, 74
Riley, Colin and Jacquie (Rideau Kennel) 53
Roscher, Gerhard and Marjetta 84
Sproul, John and Mary (Sproul Kennel) 23-5, 37, 50-1, 57-8, 195
Stephens, Ken and Brenda (Jem Kennel) 49-50, 82
Strang, Roy and Alison (Westerlea Kennel) 26, 28, 39-42, 69, 80
Van Sloun, Neil and Sue (Sylvan Kennel) 59, 62, 65, 195
Williams, Nelson and Evelyn (Lonetree Kennel) 66
Wittwer, Elsbeth (Objibway Kennel) 84
Wong, Gerry and Doris (Starway Kennel) 46
breeders' opinions
    Beran, Patty 193
    Botner, Gretchen 193
    Cap, Rena 193
    Dobirstein, Joyce 193
    Greensides, Lillian and Karen Wright 193
    Grossman White, Laura 194
    Johnson, Eric 194
    Kish, Susan 194
    Mackenzie, Roberta 194
    McNamee, Terry 194-5
    Norton, Anne 195
    Noullet, Joan 195
    Sproul, Mary 195
    Van Sloun, Sue 195
breeding, art of
    breeding all-around Toller 189-90
    breeding systems 188-89
    brood bitches 191
    sale of good Tollers 189
    stud dogs 191-2
    Swedish method 190
    See also Breeder's opinions
breeding, expanding areas for 58
breeding stock, combining 16
British Toller Club 59, 83
Brittany Spaniel 6-7
brood bitch 191, 197
Brood Bitch Class 31
Browne, Montagu (author, *Practical Taxidermy*) 6
bumpers and wings 120
buyer education 219-21
buyers, interviewing prospective 219

Canada, hunting tests in
    Working Certificate (WC) 133
    Working Certificate Excellent (WCX) 134-5
    Working Certificate Intermediate (WCI) 133
    See also United States, hunting tests in
Canada, Upper
    Bernache 55
    Collier, Irvin and Paula (Colliers Kennel) 51
    Greensides, Lillian and Karen Wright (Kylador Kennel) 51-3
    Kish, Paul and Susan (Foxgrove Kennel) 53-5
    McNamee, Terry (Rosewood Kennel) 50-1
    Penner, Ann (Liscot Kennel) 50
    Riley, Colin and Jacquie (Rideau Kennel) 53
    Stephens, Ken and Brenda (Jem Kennel) 49-50
Canadian agility 135-6
    See also United States agility
Canadian Avalanche Rescue Dog Association (CARDA) 157
Canadian Kennel Club (CKC) 1, 7, 9, 25, 33, 35, 58, 69, 95, 118, 156
    Working Certificate Program 49, 54, 118
Canadian National Sportsmen's Shows 49
Canadian Pedigree Livestock Association 33
Canadian Toller Club 57
cancer 179
Canine Good Citizen Test 155-7
Canine Hip Dysplasia (CHD) 182-3
Cap, Rena (Jalna Kennel) 37-9, 50, 58, 75, 193
cataracts 181-2
Centennial Toller Specialty (Toronto, 1988) 31, 51, 74, 84
    See also Toller Specialty (Halifax, 1995)
Chesapeake Bay Retriever 6, 116
children, relationship with 86-8, 117
Chin-Peek Tollers and offshoots 33-6
coat and color 98-9, 215-7
Collier, Eric (author of *Three Against the Wilderness*) 7
Collier, Irvin and Paula (Colliers' Kennel) 51, 58, 63
coloring, breeding purpose 16, 35
    See also coat and color
Colwell Family, Colonel Cyril 5-9, 12-3, 91
commands, teaching basic 119
Companion Dog (CD) title 85, 131, 243
Companion Dog Excellent (CDX) title 85, 131, 243
Conformation, Top. See Top Conformation Toller
cover 123-5
"coy dog" 3
coyote dog cross 7-9
Crowell, Dick 23

Danish Toller Club 71
Dansk Kennel Club (DKK) 69
decoy pipe 3-4
decoys 2-3, 112, 115, 125-6
Delta Society see Pet Partners
Denmark 69-71, 83
Denys, Nicholas 3, 5
dermatitis. See flea allergy dermatitis (FAD)
development and socialization 118-9, 197
Digby County, Nova Scotia 5-6, 9
disqualifications 108, 197
distemper epidemic 9
Dobirstein Award 43, 46
Dobirstein, John and Joyce 43, 193

Dogs Magazine 57
Dorscheid, Sue and Mike Elmergreen (Springvale Kennel) 67
Drouin, Wilfred and Dianne (Bernache Kennel) 55
ducks. *See* game birds
Dunn, Derek and Pam (Kare Kennel) 29-31
Dunphy, Vic and Heather (Marangai Kennel) 29
England 2-3, 80-3
Europe 1-3, 17, 144
European influence
  Countries, other European 83-4
  Denmark 69-71
  Finland 75-78
  Norway 79-80
  Sweden 71-75
  United Kingdom 80-3
  See also Australian influence
eye checking. *See* hip and eye checking

faults, general 108
fearlessness 91-2
Federation Cynologique Internationale (FCI) 59, 69-70, 95, 133
fetching, force 123
field puppy 217-8
field tests 31, 39, 49, 58, 61, 73, 78
  See also Top Field Toller
field training
  behavior shaping 119
  boats, introducing Toller to 126
  bumpers and wings 120
  commands, teaching basic 119
  cover 123-4
  cover in the water 125
  decoys 125-6
  development and socialization 118-9
  force fetching 123
  gunfire, introducing puppy to 123
  line, getting puppy off of the 123-4
  mistakes 126, 128
  personality 119-120
  puppies, taking home 118
  retrieves, lengthening 122-4
  retrieves, water 124-5
  retrieving training, beginning 120
  terrain, introducing puppy to 121
  wing-clipped pigeons 121
Finland 75-8
Finnish Toller Club 77-8
first-aid kit 177
Fitzgerald, Adolphe 23
flea allergy dermatitis (FAD) 179-80
flyball 136
Flyball Dog (FbD) title 51, 53
Folkhard, H.C. (author, *The Wildfowler*) 3, 6, 111
forequarters 103-4
fowling pieces 3

fox-dog cross 7, 9
foxtail precautions 176
"French shore, the" 5
front (of dog) 214-5

gait 106-7, 112
game birds 1-3, 112, 115-6
geese. *See* game birds
genetic problems 9
Gleason, Joe and Lee Ann (Cayuga Kennel) 67
Greensides, Lillian and Karen Wright (Kylador Kennel) 51-3, 193
grooming 163-72
Grossman White, Laura (Cinnstar Kennel) 60-1, 65, 194
guard dogs. *See* watchdogs versus guard dogs
Gun Dog Magazine 63
gunfire, introducing puppy to 123

Hamilton, John and Marile Waterstraat (Lennoxlove Kennel) 62-3
Hancock, Colonel David (author, *Old Working Dogs*) 3
Hardenbroek, Baroness van 9
head (skull) 100-2, 213-4
health concerns
  cancer 179
  canine hip dysplasia (CHD) 182-3
  cataracts 181-2
  epilepsy 182
  first-aid kit 177
  flea allergy dermatitis (FAD) 179-80
  foxtail precautions 176
  general care 175-6
  hypothyroidism 180-1
  progressive retinal atrophy (PRA) 183-4
  seizures 181
  See also autoimmune diseases
hindquarters 105-6
hip and eye checking 31, 75, 187, 197
  See also canine hip dysplasia (CHD)
  see also progressive retinal atrophy (PRA)
Holland 2, 83, 89
hospital patients 91
Human Animal Bond Association of Canada (HABAC) 153
hunting abilities, growing recognition for 17
hunting companions, sold as 17
Hunting Retriever Club (HRC), United Kennel Club 66
hypothyrodism 180-1

instinct, breeding purposes 16
intelligence 85, 119-20

Jeffery, Jim and Doug Coldwell (Jeffery Coldwell Kennel) 26-8, 49, 60-2
Johnson, Eric 194

Karas, Nicholas 1

Kinney, Eddie 5-6, 9
Kish, Paul and Susan (Foxgrove Kennel) 53-5, 67, 118-29, 194

Latham Foundation for the Promotion of Humane Education 153
leash training 163
Little River Duck Dogs 1, 9, 25, 39
Littleriver Kennel 53

MacDonald, Duncan and Arline (Ardunacres Kennel) 42-3, 72
Mackenzie, Keith and Roberta (Tollerbrook Kennel) 25-6, 194
Mann, Wileen (Sundrummer Kennel) 36-7, 42, 57-8
marketing. *See* advertising and marketing
markings 3, 98
Martin, Lynda and Richard (Colony Kennel) 47
McNamee, Terry (Rosewood Kennel) 50-1, 155, 194-5
Micmac Indians 6, 8
mistakes. *See* training mistakes
modern era, beginning of 9
mongrels 3

Nacton decoy 4, 82
National Gundog Championship Show (1981) 80
National Specialty Show 35, 52-3, 66
neck 102-3
New Brunswick 3,5
Nickerson, Erna (Harbourlights Kennel) 5, 15-21, 25, 91
Nickerson, W. Avery 5, 15-21, 23, 25-6, 29, 57, 74-5, 82, 111, 115-7
North American Hunting Retriever Association (NAHRA) 59, 62, 66, 118, 133
North American Hunting Retriever Association (NAHRA) Tests 133
Norton, Kirk and Anne (Cabot Trail Kennel) 63, 85, 87, 195
Norway 79-80
Noullett, Mac and Joan (Sandycove Kennel) 46, 195
Nova Scotia 3-9, 15, 35, 63, 95, 117, 187
Nova Scotia Duck Tolling Retriever Club (NSDTRC) (Canada) 28-9, 40, 95
Nova Scotia Duck Tolling Retriever Club (NSDTRC) (U.S.A.) 58-9, 62-3, 95, 134
Nova Scotia Duck Tolling Retriever (NSDTR) Klubben of Sweden 75
Nova Scotia Guides' Association 9
Nova Scotia Provincial Archives 9

obedience 131, 218
Obedience Trial Champion (OTCh.) 131
Obedience Trial Championships 25, 35, 57, 59-63, 66
See also Top Obedience Toller
Opposite Sex, Best 59, 67, 75, 79
owner suitability 218-9

Pace, Eldon 16, 23, 25, 31, 33, 35, 115
Payne-Gallwey, Sir Ralph (author, *The Book of Duck Decoys*) 3-4
Pedigree Livestock Act 33
Pedigree Puppy of the Year Awards 53
Penner, Ann (Liscot Kennel) 50, 74
personality, Tollers'
    children, relationship with 86-8
    fearlessness 91-2
    field training 119-20
    protectiveness 85-6
    sensitivity 91
    toughness 88-91
Pet Partners 153
photographic records 9
pigeons, wing-clipped 121
pipe. *See* decoy pipe
"playing the dog" 112
Pottier, Judge Vincent J. 7-9, 57
Prince Edward Island 5
progressive retinal atrophy (PRA) 74-5, 183-4
protectiveness 85-6
punishment 112, 128
puppies, diary of 197-211
puppies
    advertising and marketing 221
    body 215
    buyer education 219-21
    coat 215-7
    field puppy 217-8
    front 214-5
    head 213-4
    health record 208
    idea pet 218
    interview with prospective buyers 219
    obedience 218
    owner suitability 218-9
    rear 215
    recipes for newborn puppies 204
    show-ring win potential 213-7
    taking home 118
Puppy in Group, Best 25, 31, 40, 53, 138
Puppy in Show, Best 25, 40, 53, 55, 66, 80, 138
purebred status 1

Quacker newsletter 63
quarantine laws 80, 82

Ralston-Purina Show of Shows 40
rear (of dog) 215
"red decoy dog" *See* "Coy dog"
registration requirements, CKC 9
retrieves, lengthening 122-4
retrieves, water 124-5
retrieving, beginning 120
Riley, Colin and Jacquie (Rideau Kennel) 53

Saskatchewan 9
Schubendorf Kennels (Eldon Pace) 16
seizures 181
senior citizen homes 91
service dogs 157
show dogs 16, 213-7
show handling classes 163
show training 159
showing
 baiting 161
 fun in showing 163
 grooming 163-72
 leash training for show 163
 show handling classes 163
 show training 159
 stacking 161-3
 step-by-step instructions 165-72
 whiskers 172
 See also Supplies for showing
size 98
Skinner, J.S. (author, *The Dog and the Sportsman*) 6
Smith, Henry Albert Patterson (H.A.P.) 9-11
socialization. *See* development and socialization
Spencer, James (author, *Training Retrievers for Marshes and Meadows*) 123
sporting demonstrations 57
Sproul, John and Mary (Sproul Kennel) 23-5, 37, 50-1, 57-8, 195
stacking 161-3
stamps, commemorative issues 14
standard, analysis of
 appearance 95-7
 body 104
 coat and color 98-9
 disqualifications 108
 faults, general 108
 forequarters 103-4
 gait 106-7
 head (skull) 100-2
 hindquarters 105-6
 neck 102-3
 origin and purpose of Toller breed 95
 size 98
 tail 106
 temperament 97
standard, 1980 revision of the 25
 See also Toller Standard
States Kennel Club (SKC) 59, 66
Stephens, Ken and Brenda (Jem Kennel) 49-50, 82
Strachan, J.D. 9
Strang, Roy and Alison (Westerlea Kennel) 26, 28, 39-42, 69, 80
Stud Book, requirements 58
stud dog 191-2, 197
Stud Dog, Best in Show 31, 74
supplies for showing
 brushes 164

scissors 164
 steel combs 164
Svenska Kennelklubben (SKK) 75
Sweden 17, 71-5
Swedish method, breeding 190
Swedish Toller Club Specialty Show (1992) 75, 79-80
Switzerland 84

tail 106
temperament 97
Temperament Test (TT) 51, 157
terrain, introducing puppy to 121
therapy dogs 155-7
Time magazine 33
Toller Club 25
Toller Specialty (Halifax, 1995) 31, 59, 63
Toller Standard 28, 58-9, 95-110
 See also Breed Standard
Toller Talk newsletter 28, 35, 115
Tolling 1, 6, 111-6
Top Conformation Toller 26, 29, 35, 40, 42, 78, 139-144
Top Field Toller 54, 134-5
Top Obedience Toller 35-6, 39-40, 42-3, 49, 51
Top Show Toller 40, 141-4
toughness 88-91
tracking 138
training 2-3
 See also Field training; leash training; show training
training mistakes 126, 128-9

United Kennel Club (UKC) 63, 133
United Kennel Club (UKC) Hunting Retriever Tests 133
United Kingdom 17, 80-3
United States agility 135-6
 See also Canadian agility
United States, hunting tests in 133-4
Utility Dog (UD) title 131

vaccinations 121
Van Sloun, Neil and Sue (Sylvan Kennel) 59, 62, 65, 195
versatility
 agility 135-6
 American interest 66
 Canadian agility 135-6
 Canadian Best in Show winners 139-41
 CD title 131
 CDX title 131
 dock diving 137
 Conformation shows 138-9
 Europe 144
 flyball 136
 Master Hunters 134-5
 obedience 131-2
 Rally obedience 137
 Specialty shows in Canada 141-2
 Specialty shows in the United States 142-3
 tracking 138

UD title 131
United States agility 135-6
United States, Conformation showing 142-3
United States, obedience for Tollers in 131-2
United States Best in Show winners 143
See also Canada, hunting tests in; Canadian agility; United States agility; United States, hunting tests in

watchdogs versus guard dogs 86
waterfowl *See* game birds
Westerlea Kennel 28, 39-42, 49, 52-3, 55, 60, 63-4, 67, 69-70, 74, 82, 90-1
Western (Canada) influence
    Cap, Rena (Jalna Kennel) 37-9
    Chin-Peek and offshoots 33-6
    MacDonald, Duncan and Arline (Ardunacres Kennel) 42-3
    Mann, Wileen (Sundrummer Kennel) 36-7, 42
    Strang, Roy and Alison (Westerlea Kennel) 39-42
whiskers 172

Williams, Nelson and Evelyn (Lonetree Kennel) 66
Wittwer, Elsbeth (Objibway Kennel) 84
wings *See* bumper and wings
Wood, David 2
wool trade 3
Working Certificate (WC) 133
    See also Canadian Kennel Club (CKC) Working Certificate Program
Working Certificate Excellent (WCE) 133
Working Certificate Intermediate (WCI) 133

Yarmouth County, Nova Scotia 5-6, 8-9, 14-5, 17, 26, 28, 33, 95, 112